Conrad & Lady Black

By the same author

Blind Eye to Murder: The Pledge Betrayed
Klaus Barbie: Butcher of Lyon
The Paperclip Conspiracy
Maxwell: The Outsider
Red Web
Tiny Rowland: A Rebel Tycoon
Heroes of World War II
The Perfect English Spy: Sir Dick White
Maxwell: The Final Verdict
Blood Money: The Swiss, the Nazis and the Looted Billions
Nazi Gold
Branson
The Paymaster: Geoffrey Robinson, Maxwell and New Labour
Fayed: The Unauthorized Biography
Broken Dreams: Vanity, Greed and the Souring of British Football
Gordon Brown

Conrad & Lady Black

DANCING ON THE EDGE

TOM BOWER

Harper*Press*
An Imprint of HarperCollins*Publishers*

Harper*Press*
An imprint of HarperCollins*Publishers*
77–85 Fulham Palace Road,
Hammersmith, London W6 8JB
www.harpercollins.co.uk

Published by HarperCollins*Publishers* 2006

2

The author asserts the moral right to
be identified as the author of this work

A catalogue record for this book
is available from the British Library

ISBN-13 978-0-00-723234-5
ISBN-10 0-00-723234-9

Set in Janson with Photina and Castella MT Display

Printed and bound in Great Britain by Clays Ltd, St Ives plc

This book is proudly printed on paper which contains wood
from well managed forests, certified in accordance with
the rules of the Forest Stewardship Council.
For more information about FSC,
please visit www.fsc-uk.org

For Ruth

CONTENTS

ILLUSTRATIONS

Launching the *National Post* in Canada in 1998 had won Black unusual popularity and applause. But his dream quickly lost over $100 million, propelling his empire and his personal fortunes towards the abyss. © *Reuters.*

At Christmas 2002, Black unexpectedly arrived at the annual party held by Lord Rothermere, the chairman of Associated Newspapers. © *Alan Davidson/The Picture Library Ltd.*

In New York, Laura Jereski, an analyst at investment fund Tweedy Browne, was digging up embarrassing revelations about the running of Black's commercial empire. © *Adam Friedberg.*

Paul Healy, Black's corporate relations manager. © *Robert Maass.*

Hollinger director Richard Perle, a former member of President Reagan's administration. © *AP/Empics.*

Black and David Radler. © *Tibor Kolley/The Globe and Mail.*

Richard Breeden and Gordon Paris. © *AP/Empics.*

Breeden's damnation of Black's 'kleptocracy' led to a Delaware judge describing Black as 'evasive and unreliable'. © *EPA.*

During October 2003 Conrad Black ignored the criticism and investigation of his conduct, and toured bookshops promoting his massive biography of Franklin D. Roosevelt. © *Tibor Kolley/The Globe and Mail.*

On 15 November 2005 Black and Amiel made a deliberately sparkling appearance at a Toronto party. Later that week, Black would be indicted to face charges in Chicago. © *UPPA/Photoshot.*

ACKNOWLEDGEMENTS

This book was inspired by three people in contrasting circumstances. For months, Frank Johnson urged me to consider writing Black's life. I resisted until, at 1.30 a.m. during a splendid party in Venice in October 2005, Simon Heffer declared, 'Tom's the only man who can really write about Conrad's life. I wish he would do it.' Since Simon's many qualities do not include instinctive generosity to myself, I was instantly impressed. Finally, over lunch with Ruth Jackson at Zucca, a lost eatery in Notting Hill, I was persuaded. To all three I am grateful, because writing this book has been an unmitigated pleasure which I hope the reader will share.

Writing unauthorised biographies has become an unintended speciality. Discovering the truth while being denied access to the subject of the book depends upon the trust of reliable eyewitnesses. Fortunately, well over two hundred people agreed to be interviewed while I was researching this book. Their generosity is a principal source of information, for which I am grateful. While Conrad Black and Barbara Amiel declined to be interviewed, I was only aware on a few occasions of the influence of their request that people not speak to me. At one stage Conrad Black offered to cooperate, on the condition, it seemed, that the book not be published until after his trial. I did not accept the offer. Barbara Amiel did not reply to my letter.

I do want to thank many journalists and writers who have helped. Some wish to remain anonymous, but among the remainder I must first acknowledge my three predecessors. Peter C. Newman, Conrad Black's first biographer, wrote *The Establishment Man* in 1982. Everyone who has written about Black since owes Newman a great debt. His exhaustive research and astute judgement at a critical moment in Conrad Black's career were invaluable. Richard Siklos, the biographer in 1995, was granted access to Black himself, his family and friends. Siklos's account, *Shades of Black*, is valuable, and I am grateful for the help he personally gave me in New York. The third book, *Wrong Way: The Fall of Conrad Black* by Jacquie McNish and Sinclair Stewart, is a robust account of Black's deeds, published in 2004, within months of his fall from grace. I relied on that book for many contemporaneous reactions, and I am enormously grateful for Jacquie McNish's generous guidance and insight.

In Canada, I was given remarkable help by Debbie Melnyk, the producer and director of a fine television biography of Black. I am also grateful to David Olive, Linda McQuaig, Eric Reguly, Rick Cash and Larry Zolf. I was well cared for in Toronto by the excellent staff at the Soho Metropolitan Hotel.

In London, I owe a great debt to Mark Hollingsworth and Mary Ann Nicholas, especially for their research in Palm Beach. Olly Figg and Barrie Penrose, old friends in my cause, were also very helpful. Robert Barrett was invaluable in tracing the family histories. My thanks to Rob Evans of the *Guardian* for guidance on how to use the Freedom of Information Act. A long conversation with David Cornwell was valuable inspiration at a critical moment.

The legal chores were undertaken with humour by David Hooper. Jonathan Lloyd of Curtis Brown provided as always rocklike support. I owe both of them unquantifiable thanks. Richard Johnson and Robert Lacey at HarperCollins were efficient and very supportive. As always, my thanks to my family, especially my mother Sylvia Bower, whose passion and encouragement inspired me in childhood. She has never stopped urging me on.

Finally, acknowledgement is due to Conrad Black himself. *A Life in Progress*, his engaging autobiography, is the authentic voice of Black in 1993. In his present circumstances, that book is probably excessively revealing.

Tom Bower, London, September 2006

PREFACE

Conrad Black's email arrived at 1.15 a.m. on 1 April 2006, April Fool's Day in London. Black, whom I had known since the mid-1980s, was well aware of this book's progress, and said he had been contacted by many of his and his wife's acquaintances, seeking his advice as to whether they should talk to me. His response was nothing if not graphic:

> *Dear Tom,*
> *Many people have contacted Barbara and me asking if they should talk with you. Our usual response is that you have made it clear that you consider this whole matter a heart-warming story of two sleazy, spivvy, contemptible people, who enjoyed a fraudulent and unjust elevation; were exposed, and ground to powder in a just system, have been ostracised; and largely impoverished, and that I am on my way to the prison cell where I belong. It is the false rise and well-deserved downfall of crooked charlatans; a variant on your treatments of Maxwell, Fayed, and Rowland. You have expressed essentially this view many times that have been reported to me.*

He asked me to prove that I was not writing 'a pompous, defamatory celebration of the supposed demise of people you personally dislike'. In justification of his indignation, and keen that I should understand his innocence, he continued:

> *The rough facts are that I am an honest businessman; the chances of my committing an illegality are less than zero, this will be clear when my accusers have to prove beyond a reasonable doubt the guilt of innocent people and not just manipulate the agencies of the US and*

Canadian governments to act on the pre-emptive presumption of guilt and conduct a prolonged assassination of careers and reputations.

Conrad Black believes that he is the victim of political and personal prejudice. He has damned those seeking 'a big scalp (mine)', and believes his persecutors first sought his social ostracism and bankruptcy, and later destroyed his 'fine company'. Under his ownership, he commented with some reason in his second email during the night, the two *Telegraph* newspapers in London were better 'compared to what preceded and followed us'. In his opinion, the only victims of his personal and corporate downfall were the creators of a successful enterprise. Other than himself, he argued, no one lost money – shareholders, traders or pensioners. His critics and his American prosecutor contest that claim.

Convinced of his acquittal, Black pledged himself to 'turn the tables on our oppressors'. He would wreak vengeance upon those responsible for his demise: 'We will bring this entire, gigantic, malicious persecution down around the ears of its authors.' He was, he wrote later that night, proud of his robustness. Three years after the news of his predicament emerged, and one year before his trial, he observed that no one could deny that 'despite my wildly applauded setback I am completely undaunted, and that I am not a tight-lipped source of "no comment"'. Indeed, his high-profile appearances around Toronto had become the stuff of gossip.

In another email during that night, Conrad Black keenly anticipated the stardom that he would achieve at his trial, which was due to start in Chicago in March 2007:

My trial will be timely; Thermidor will have dawned, and legally responsible capitalism will survive, like Talleyrand and Fouché.

He concluded:

I promise a spectacular trial . . .
Regards, CONRAD BLACK.

Conrad Black's life story is not the familiar tale of a tycoon's 'rise and fall', or the tragedy of a self-delusional fantasist. Rather, it is the drama of a plutocrat and aristocrat who stands accused as a kleptocrat. He will arrive in Chicago preceded by two damning findings: the first by a court in Delaware, the second by a special committee of investigators appointed with his approval. The investigators' withering 513-page condemnation of Black's business methods would have destroyed most men, and his vigorous protestations of innocence have won him some sympathy. The riddle is just how he has found himself in this position. In the search for an answer it is important to understand his marriage to Barbara Amiel, and her own behaviour.

Beautiful, intelligent and vivacious, Barbara Amiel appeared over the years to follow her husband in promoting herself and her opinions. In Toronto, London and New York she became famous for aggressively advancing her libertarian, conservative and politically incorrect philosophy. Exceptionally, she based much of her distinctive and lauded journalism upon her own remarkable life, provocatively describing her personal experiences, especially in relation to drugs, sex, personal relationships and cash. Her 1986 article 'Why Women Marry Up' is one of her many prophetic, self-fulfilling accounts of seeking fame and millions which would climax sixteen years later in her immortal admission, 'I have an extravagence that knows no bounds.' Quite consciously, she invited the public to examine every aspect of her private life, and in turn wrote revelatory accounts of others' lives. In many respects she is a unique woman, which was precisely her attraction to Conrad Black.

However, to blame Barbara Amiel for Conrad Black's apparent downfall would be simplistic. Black is responsible for his own fate, although Amiel undoubtedly influenced the circumstances which have led to him facing his destiny in a Chicago courtroom. She is, of course, not accused of any crime; nevertheless, she did closely accompany him during his meteoric rise after 1992 in London, New York and Toronto. She not only shared his desire for the spotlight, but assumed serious responsibilities in the management of his six hundred newspapers. As a well-paid director of his corporation, she influenced the choice of the papers' editors, their policies and their appearance. Barbara Amiel is not known ever to have cautioned the staff of those papers to restrain their invasion of other people's privacy. Her power was never in doubt, not least because she allowed no one to forget her status. In recognition of her contribution, the corporation paid over $1 million of her salary to Black-Amiel Management, an offshore account in Barbados. She also earned substantial sums from stock options, and charged the corporation millions of dollars in expenses for the use of jets, homes, staff and much more. Her conduct made her an important factor in the series of events which has led Lord Black to what for him will be a unique experience – judgement by a jury of twelve common men and women.

Conrad Black's story is emphatically not a Shakespearian tragedy or the struggle of a flawed hero. In every respect, Black was consciously responsible for his conduct. In the course of the last twenty years, there is no evidence of him confronting dilemmas or crises of conscience about right and wrong. On the contrary, he is proud to have followed his principles. Both Lord and Lady Black are convinced of his inevitable acquittal. But that judgement depends upon an anonymous jury, and there is more than irony in the fact that a man who isolated himself amid privilege throughout his life should now have to rely on the common people to decide his fate. Considering his disdain for the mass censure he has received over the past months, Conrad Black's certainty that he will be acquitted by a jury is remarkable. The well-educated subject of this book has not taken to heart the lines of John Dryden, the seventeenth-century poet:

> *Nor is people's judgment always true:*
> *The most may err as grossly as the few.*

INTRODUCTION

The Wedding,

26 January 1985

'Six months at most. I give this marriage just six months.'

'Come off it, Posy. How do you know?'

'Because I lived with David Graham in London. Every night he came home with a different girl.'

Posy Chisholm Feick, a sixtyish Canadian travel writer and socialite, had grabbed the attention of every guest around the table: 'They came in every shape and size. Even a black girl with a shaved head.' The band struck a high note in the crowded 'Stop 33' room at the summit of Toronto's Sutton Place Hotel, but, encouraged by her audience, Posy continued uninterrupted. 'I saw them every morning. He'd rush off to work, leaving the girls to struggle by themselves.'

'So what?' asked Allan Fotheringham, the veteran political columnist.

'Well,' smiled Posy, with the confidence of an expert in sex and marriage, 'one of them said he's a lousy lay. Barbara won't like that.' Eyes narrowed and mouths pursed.

'Just hold on for the ride,' smiled Peter Worthington, the editor-in-chief of the *Toronto Sun*.

'Barbara wants what's best for Barbara,' added one man, recalling painful rejection. 'She's too restless,' sighed another failed suitor. 'And David's so boring,' chimed a new voice.

'Let's take bets,' said Posy, spotting the bride swaying in her white, backless Chanel dress. Posy's wager was certainly high, but the loud Latin American music and the alcoholic haze prevented anyone hearing the size of Allan Fotheringham's risk. 'It won't last long,' shouted Posy, throwing back another glass. 'She's a wild and crazy girl,' said Fotheringham, speaking with the benefit of carnal experience of the bride. 'She's got an eye for the big chance. This is it. She won't let it go.'

The forty-four-year-old bride now interrupted the jousting at the large round table. After fluttering around a room filled with sober politicians, famous millionaires, rich professionals and Canada's media moguls, including Conrad Black and his wife Shirley, Barbara Amiel appeared to welcome the sight of the group of rowdy journalists. For twenty years that crowd had represented her social and professional background, but her marriage indicated her removal from them. Famous throughout Canada as an opinionated columnist, Amiel had just resigned as comment editor of the *Toronto Sun* to join her third husband, David Graham, in London. The rollercoaster years of drugs, adultery and emotional mayhem were over. She was, she had admitted, 'ashamed of my personal life'.[1] She had shared beds with too many 'beach boys and wildly unreliable bohemians'. They were good for 'steamy novels but short unions'.[2] Years of notoriety would be replaced by domesticity, motherhood and fidelity.

For the uncynical at the wedding party, Barbara Amiel's choice was understandable. David Graham was handsome and seriously rich. Shrewd investments in the fledgling cable network business had produced a company worth US$200 million,* and homes in Toronto, New York, Palm Beach, St Tropez and London worth another $100 million. For the former middle-class north London girl known to plead, 'My father was very poor and unemployed,'

* Unless the context indicates otherwise, throughout the book monetary values are given in American rather than Canadian dollars.

the prospect of returning home in style was irresistible. Graham's motives also appeared unimpeachable.

Barbara Amiel was renowned not only for her beauty, wit and intelligence, but also, among the favoured, as a remarkable sexual companion. 'Sex is great with Barbara,' confirmed one of her wedding guests. 'A great body, and her breasts are big and beautiful. Like lovely fried eggs.' 'Yeah,' agreed another connoisseur. 'She wants to be admired for her brains, but she keeps pushing her breasts into men's faces.' Amiel would be the first to admit that sex, 'the key to our entire being', was her trusted weapon.[3]

During the evening, for most men gazing at a seemingly tough, unemotional personality, Amiel's thin waist, long dark hair and Sephardic looks were alluring but unobtainable. Only David Graham and her former lovers realised that her harshness was a masquerade, honed during a tough battle for survival, to gain protection from rejection. Behind the façade the bride was a vulnerable woman, desperate to fulfil her lovers' fantasies. Like cosmetics applied every morning, she relied on her chosen man's image to project herself. After dallying in the past with left-wing politics, a hippie lifestyle and impoverished men, she had chosen to be reincarnated by marrying class, wealth and looks. 'You can't believe how good David is in bed,' she had said to a girlfriend just days before her wedding, with seeming conviction. 'I couldn't do without this man. I had to have him.'

Few believed that Graham, a quiet, unexciting man, matched Amiel's description. Rather, many assumed, her head had been turned after researching an article for *Maclean's* magazine entitled 'Who's Who in Canada's Jet Set'. Gushingly, she had written that the rich, with their private planes and pampered lifestyles, 'live our fantasies in a world which has no borders, just locations'.[4] To join that world, she had decided to 'marry up', a phrase she would use in the headline of a subsequent confessional article.[5] The 'trade-off', she admitted, was crude: 'her looks for his money – his power as her meal ticket'. Together, Barbara Amiel and David Graham could present themselves around the globe as a 'power couple', rich and influential.[6]

Established 'power couples' were scattered across the Sutton Place's party room. Sitting with Ted Rogers, head of the Rogers Communications empire, was Conrad Black, the owner of an expanding newspaper group. Like many of Canada's establishment, Rogers praised Black's intellect, but voiced suspicions about the pompous businessman's eagerness to make money. Branded as a 'bad boy' or a 'bad joke', Black had not won admirers since saying in the early 1980s, 'Greed has been severely underestimated and denigrated, unfairly in my opinion . . . It is a motive that has not failed to move me from time to time.' Strangely, he seemed impervious to the impression his admission had created. Bad publicity was nothing new to the ambitious Black. Over the previous two decades, while seeking the spotlight as a supporter of right-wing causes, the aspiring media baron had placed himself in many firestorms. His outspokenness was a characteristic which he shared with Barbara Amiel.

Black's admiration for the bride was curious. Professionally, she represented much that he despised. Rather than writing on the basis of careful, measured research, she was famous for spewing out gut prejudices. Years earlier, her left-wing sentiments had been interpreted by Black as envy of the rich and powerful, but after changing boyfriends, her politics had somersaulted. The former Marxist had changed colours, and now chanted her praise for capitalism. Meeting Amiel for the first time at a dinner party in Toronto in 1979 had converted Black into a fan. How could he resist a woman who professed her admiration for his blockbuster biography of the right-wing former Premier of Quebec, Maurice Duplessis? Like so many men in 'Stop 33' that evening, he had become enamoured of her star qualities. There were also similarities between them.

Conrad Black and Barbara Amiel had both been afflicted by depression, insecurity and exposure to suicide. Both their fathers had killed themselves, and both Black and Amiel had had moments of the deepest despair at certain points in their lives. Neither imagined that the wedding reception was a mere interlude before the consummation of their own explosive relationship, but with hindsight their eventual union seems almost inevitable.

Fate determined a strange climax for both of them at the end of the reception. Sharing a limousine, Conrad Black and Allan Fotheringham argued violently, and parted on bad terms. Across town, lying in bed after her wedding celebrations, Barbara Amiel was presented by her new husband with a pre-nuptial agreement that had been drawn up earlier. 'Sign here,' said Graham. Amiel did as she was ordered. She was in love.

1

A Timely Death

Flopped in his armchair, regularly refilling his glass with neat vodka, George Black sermonised to his thirty-one-year-old younger son Conrad throughout the night of 29 June 1976. Despite the appearance of civility presented by the chintz and the solid furniture in the grand house in the Bridle Path, Toronto's most prestigious neighbourhood, the resentful sixty-seven-year-old regularly vented his bitterness on the subject of wealth and power. Frustrated by isolation and depression, the ailing recluse had astutely accumulated substantial capital from his business activities, but his withdrawn personality and habits had deprived him of any influence, with one exception: his son Conrad.

Over the years, his father's lectures on history, power and finance had inculcated in Conrad similar feelings about supremacy and manipulation. Systematically, George had dragooned the youthful Conrad to utilise his photographic memory by giving boastful theatrical performances at social occasions. With little prompting, the precocious boy had paraded his expertise on Napoleon, Franklin D. Roosevelt, Abraham Lincoln, Charles de Gaulle and other political giants. Similarly, if the opportunity arose, audiences were amazed by his encyclopaedic recitations of battleships, armies and warfare stretching back to the eighteenth century. Without hesitation, as a party piece the teenager could recite the names of all the ships, armies and generals engaged in the most obscure European battles, or of successive prime ministers and monarchs over two centuries, or, if allowed, repeat keynote speeches of statesmen long dead. 'Reel off the fifteen leading ships in the Spanish Armada,' George Black would order, 'and the names of all the admirals in the First World War.' His son's memory was infallible. Late into the night, amid a mist of tobacco smoke, those tutorials and memory games about world history infected the loner's mind with the importance of defying the vulnerability of human weakness.

Stifled by depression, George Black failed to appreciate the burden he was inflicting upon his son. The father offered his children no physical affection, and his wife Jean, always known as 'Betty', was similarly cold and remote. In that loveless atmosphere, Conrad compensated for his emotional insecurity by revelling in the lives of historic heroes. At eight, he had been smitten by the memoirs of General de Gaulle, the underdog who rebelled against unpopularity and overcame adversity to become a national hero. Defiance was a trait Conrad Black was encouraged to admire by his father, an outsider cruelly spurned by lesser men.

Ever since George Black had been unceremoniously dismissed in 1958 from the Argus Corporation, a sprawling Canadian conglomerate, his resentment had festered. During their all-night sessions, Conrad Black was imbued with a mission to exact revenge upon those responsible for humiliating his father. He knew them well, because, despite his reclusiveness, George Black had introduced his son to a remarkably privileged lifestyle.

Few could have imagined the transformation of George Black over the previous thirty-six years. In 1940 the tall, articulate, aggressive twenty-nine-year-old accountant was managing a factory in Montreal producing propellers for Allied war planes. With pride, he recounted how his company was the only Canadian government-owned manufacturer during the war to earn a profit. But there was also frustration. The graduate from Winnipeg, a provincial outpost, damned his work as unglamorous and his colleagues as 'a hopeless bunch'.[1] In July 1944 his future appeared lacklustre, until the banker Edward P. Taylor, also from the Canadian provinces, offered an escape. Unlike George Black, Taylor had identified a recipe for great personal wealth.

Ten years older than Black, Taylor enjoyed the expensive lifestyle of a clever but unpopular speculator who paraded as a prominent racehorse owner at the Jockey Club of Canada. In 1944 he was convinced that the end of the war would unleash huge prosperity. To exploit that opportunity, he established Argus with a group of like-minded Toronto investors, including Eric Phillips and John 'Bud' McDougald. Based at 10 Toronto Street, an elegant, two-storey, neo-classical building not far from Bay Street, the city's financial area, the partners pooled their assets invested in Canadian companies. Among those investments was Canadian Breweries, which George Black was invited to manage on the company's behalf.

During those all-night sessions, which started in Conrad's childhood, George Black regaled his son with stories of his struggle to transform Canadian Breweries into an international success. Promoted as the company's president in 1950, he had savagely cut costs, dismissed staff and created success from disaster. The prize was phenomenal growth – sales and profits had tripled – delivering Taylor's ambition to control the world's biggest brewery, embracing Canada, the USA and Britain. The downside was the effect on Black's health. Insomniac and increasingly intoxicated, he would arrive in his office at midday, boasting that because he delegated authority his presence was not required. Management of the empire, he insisted, could be achieved by telephone, without the need for him to visit the factories. The essence of business, George emphasised to his son, was strategy rather than micro-management. In reality, 'delegation' had become George Black's excuse to recover from hangovers and the morning's vodka.

High among Black's priorities was the need to confront the trade unions, which he despised. In 1958, by forging an alliance with other brewers, he challenged the unions to remove their restrictive practices, provoking an acrimonious strike. As his profits evaporated, Taylor lost confidence in Black. He wanted to avoid strikes and reverse the decentralisation. 'You're out of your skull,' Black told Taylor. In October 1958 George Black was fired. He damned Taylor, cleared his desk and went home. At forty-seven, he was unemployed, and had received no thanks for his achievements. From the sidelines he watched as Canadian Breweries declined. No longer the world's biggest brewer, the company was sold in 1968 to a competitor.

Bitter but realistic, George Black noted how greed, arrogance and dishonesty had become the hallmark of Argus's directors. While some in Bay Street embodied the best of Presbyterian honesty, Taylor and Bud McDougald, the company's president, were financial cowboys enjoying a reckless lifestyle, avoiding taxes and cheating the minority shareholders. At the hub of that intrigue, McDougald used intimidation and flattery to disguise rampant dishonesty, known in Toronto Street as 'pushing the envelope'. As George Black understood so well, McDougald was using Argus, a company floated on the Canadian stock exchange, as his private piggybank, spending shareholders' money to fund a tycoon's way of life.

Well-dressed and shamelessly ostentatious, McDougald played the mogul to perfection – serving dinner on gold-plated china, hanging chandeliers in his garage, travelling in custom-built cars and private planes, and walking with an undisguised swagger to impress his audience. Teetotal, uneducated but shrewd, the former bond salesman posed as Canada's pre-eminent social and commercial aristocrat, suavely speaking way above his financial weight, and accustomed to fawning treatment. Unlike other Canadians, McDougald drove around London like royalty in a Rolls-Royce

Silver Wraith, mixing with nobles like the Duke of Wellington, the Marquess of Abergavenny and Lord Crathorne, and standing near the Queen when she inspected her racehorses being trained in his stables at Kingsclere in Hampshire.[2] In Palm Beach, McDougald was the President of the Everglades Club, the social centre for the local super-rich, where Jews were not admitted as members, or even for lunch. In future years this did not diminish Conrad Black's apparent awe for McDougald's technique of buying people off with presents and perks.

Argus's operations were fundamentally dishonest. In their private capacity the company's directors bought shares in companies involved in the media, catering, retail, chemicals, forestry and agriculture, including Massey-Ferguson, one of the world's biggest farm equipment manufacturers. They then resold those same shares to Argus, at a profit. The casualties of this insider dealing were Argus's public shareholders. The directors' dishonesty, as George Black had impressed upon his son, was compounded by another ruse.

Argus controlled assets worth $4 billion, but that control did not reside with the shareholders. Instead, the company was run by the six principal shareholders of a private company called Ravelston, named after a Scottish estate owned by McDougald's ancestors. Before his dismissal, George Black had bought 22.4 per cent of Ravelston's shares; McDougald and Phillips each held 23.6 per cent. Aware of George Black's astute investment and his acute understanding of the Argus directors' subterfuge, McDougald had, from an early stage, understood the benefits of flattering Conrad Black.

In 1965, on Conrad's twenty-first birthday, Bud McDougald gave the precocious young man a painting of Napoleon and, unprecedentedly, membership of the Toronto Club, the meeting place for the city's elite, entry to which was zealously controlled by McDougald himself. The advantages for Conrad Black were remarkable. Toronto's commercial life was fixed by the club's members as they ate, drank and played within the protected building. Finance for their deals was supplied by Canada's leading financial institution, the Canadian Imperial Bank of Commerce (CIBC), substantially influenced by McDougald, who was a director. To help his protégé's career McDougald arranged for Black to become, at thirty-two, the youngest director in the bank's history. That generosity split Conrad's loyalties. Despite his father's anger, he practically worshipped McDougald's mystique and power. While puffing a cigar in the Toronto Club, Black would enjoy repeating McDougald's homily, 'If these bankers had any brains, we'd be lending them money and they'd be getting rich, instead of the other way round.'

Although George Black resented McDougald's success, he retained his stake in Ravelston. At some stage, he calculated, there would be an opportunity for revenge and profit. That ambition was inculcated into Conrad Black. Steeped in the minutiae of Argus's personality conflicts and financial dubieties, Conrad emerged with a sophisticated understanding of the inherent deception of the way in which the company was run. Argus rarely held more than a 25 per cent stake in a company, yet McDougald and Taylor behaved like the proprietors, as if they were the owners of the whole lot. Similarly, by assertion and performance, they intimidated Argus's minority shareholders into believing that they were entitled to behave as the proprietors of the whole company. Their successful intimidation of the little people was a seminal inspiration to Conrad Black.

Besides his father and Bud McDougald, there was a third formative influence on Conrad Black: the lessons of history. Even before his teens, Conrad admired from his copious reading the rise from obscurity to immortal fame of giants who irreversibly changed mankind's fate. Egoistic self-righteousness, he realised, could overcome adversity, and popular acclaim bestowed permanent glory. The mere appearance of Napoleon or Abraham Lincoln among soldiers and supporters had raised hopes and entrenched loyalty to the leader. History's heroes, Black learned, exploited their opponents' weaknesses, outwitted their deceptions, manipulated their ambitions and assembled a coalition of allies to secure victory. Nurturing his own fantasies of eventually standing in the limelight and enjoying similar grandeur, he awaited his chance for revenge. Patience, planning and perfidy would be required to destroy his father's tormentors.

On most days George Black would awake in a melancholic daze at lunchtime, spend the afternoon speculating on the markets, and after dinner would watch television while drinking himself into a stupor before his long night-time conversation with Conrad. Just before daybreak he would climb the stairs to his bedroom. His wife Betty, a sports enthusiast from the Riley family, whose wealth came from insurance and finance, had little in common with her husband. In recent years, barely tolerating a man who rarely emerged from his house or met visitors, she had condemned her husband as a self-righteous snob and disappeared into her own rooms. Their unpleasant co-existence was interrupted in September 1975, when Jean Black was diagnosed with terminal liver cancer.

Eight months later, Conrad, Monte, his elder brother by four years, and their father, accompanied by a nurse, flew with the dying woman in a private plane loaned by Argus to Bermuda, which Jean had always dreamt of visiting. Shortly after their return, on 19 June 1976, she died. George Black declared himself too ill to stand by her grave. After the funeral the mourners returned to the family house, to be told that George was too sick to appear at the wake. Only his closest friends remained when he finally emerged, depressed and showing little will to live. 'Are you planning a trip during the summer?' asked one, Douglas Bassett. 'Yes,' replied Black. 'To the dentist in late July.'

Ten days later, after another night-time discussion with Conrad, George Black slowly climbed the stairs. As he reached the top, his son heard cracking wood, and saw his father fall over the banister onto the ground floor.[3] Carried by Conrad into the library, George Black said that he no longer had the will to live. 'Life is hell,' he told his son as they awaited the doctor. 'Most people are bastards, and everything is bullshit.' The doctor's diagnosis was bleak. His father, Conrad was told, was unlikely to survive. Despite the prognosis, Conrad returned to his own home and watched a Charlie Chan film. His viewing was interrupted by a telephone call. George Black, the doctor announced, was dead. Many, occasionally including his son, believed that he had committed suicide. At thirty-two, Conrad Black was an orphan with a purpose.

Toronto's financial leaders gathered for George Black's funeral. The pall bearers, who included all Ravelston's directors, were led by Bud McDougald and E.P. Taylor. Conrad watched McDougald with particular interest. While he admired 'the ultimate Canadian tycoon',[4] he recognised that he represented Canada's 'corporate rot', and that his fortune had been earned in a uniquely dishonest manner called 'tollgating'.[5] Conrad's later pious denunciation of the legend's 'venality and self-delusion' at his father's graveside did not undermine his endorsement of McDougald's crushing piety: 'Some are chosen, some are not.' In the jungle, Conrad Black was committed to stand among the chosen.

Bud McDougald, like Ravelston's other major shareholders, Black noted, had no children. Their wives were uninterested in business. Those circumstances would be his opportunity. Ingratiating himself with the older directors was not a chore, but rather an investment. Among Conrad Black's skills was flattering old, lonely, rich people.

After their father's funeral, Conrad and Monte Black called on Bud McDougald, who controlled the fate of the two young men's assets. To Conrad's relief they were 'welcomed most graciously'. Whereas Conrad had condemned McDougald as a 'snob, bigot ... and an unlearned reactionary' who had succumbed to 'jet-addicted decadence', on that particular day he encountered 'an elegant and considerable figure'.[6] After a brief discussion the brothers emerged with a satisfactory deal. Conrad was given a directorship of Argus and Ravelston, while Monte was given directorships of other companies. As if to confirm his younger brother's intellectual superiority, Monte agreed that Conrad should inherit their parents' grand house amid seven acres in Bridle Path's Park Lane Circle. The house matched Conrad's ambitions. Unlike Monte, an unthreatening *bon vivant* with a fondness for big cigars, fast cars and good food, Conrad's dream was to join the establishment and to control an empire matching those of Canada's principal families, including the Eatons, the owners of the country's dominant department store chain; the Westons, who owned a food and retail business; the Bronfmans, whose fortune was built on alcohol during the Prohibition; the Thomsons, the media family whose assets included the *Times* newspapers in Britain; and the investors Paul Desmarais of Power Corporation and Hal Jackman, the inheritor of a large investment fund.[7] Stuck on the periphery, Conrad Black hoped to use his inheritance to become a power on Bay Street and a member of Toronto's financial mafia. His life over the previous thirty-two years had been a preparation for that struggle.

Privilege and prejudice had been Conrad Black's roots since his birth in Montreal on 25 August 1944. By the age of five, when the family moved to Toronto, he was cosseted by cooks, butlers, nannies and chauffeurs. In the winter holidays he escaped Toronto's freeze in the Bahamas. At Nassau's Porcupine Club he gazed with his father at the Mellons, du Ponts and other American magnates. Although George Black did not rank among the super-rich, he was a successful businessman with an astute intellect.

Well-read, and always irritated by those who misused the English language, he noted his son's exceptional gifts and became preoccupied with creating an extraordinary individual out of him.

Obsessively he ordered Conrad to recall facts, both relevant and irrelevant. After intensive games of chess, his son was encouraged to read encyclopaedias and, like himself, recall what he read. Conrad's bedrooms were filled with books about the military, wars and politics. He learned not only the names of the world's ships, both commercial and naval, but their weight, armour thickness and guns. In the midst of the Korean War Conrad Black sat transfixed listening to David Brinkley's news broadcasts, and watched the television reports of the McCarthy hearings in Washington targeted at unearthing Communist sympathisers. Influenced by his father in favour of capitalism, he grew up with a hatred of those on the left, whom he later damned as 'phoney, envious and mediocre bleeding hearts whining and snivelling about meritocratic Darwinism'. Nowhere in Black's education or experience was there any sympathy for the anonymous, simple, honest masses born underprivileged and without special talents. On the contrary, there was boastfulness when in 1952 his father arranged his purchase of a single General Motors share costing $59. The eight-year-old Black had dollar bills spilling from his pockets. When one fell into the mud, he carefully washed it. His journey across the Atlantic on the *Queen Elizabeth* the following year to watch the coronation in London enhanced the image of a spoilt child taking luxury for granted.

From the age of eleven the unsporting, overweight Black was driven every day to Toronto's Upper Canada College, one of the country's elite private schools, in a chauffeur-driven Cadillac. Awkward and isolated, he was not a natural enthusiast for a society focused on conformity and obedience. During his school day he could be certain that his family's servants were cleaning his room, washing his clothes and preparing his dinner. Occasionally the chauffeur returned to serve lunch in the limousine. Voices, books and images conjured up for the young Black a romantic fantasy of enjoying the same unlimited power as history's titans, assured that whatever he willed would be carried out. Entitlement bred defiance and insolence, fashioning a personality which enjoyed a fight and savoured inflicting defeat. Black's childhood, remarked John Fraser, a school friend, was like prison for a pre-teenager convinced that he was smarter than the system.[8]

The scoffs directed at the tubby outsider, Conrad believed, were driven by 'spite and envy', one of the oft-repeated phrases that encapsulated his life's credo. His encyclopaedic knowledge, he assumed, was resented, reinforcing his sense of superiority and hatred of regimentation. He construed his teachers as remote from reality, and their authority as a misuse of power. History, he believed, showed how those exercising authority were flawed. Success was won by those who were unwilling to obey laws. Those who failed to admire him were dismissed as despicable. Teachers whom he judged to be inferior excited his contempt. Defiance, in Black's interpretation, showed courage. His insolence did not pass unpunished. Regularly he received corporal punishment on his backside or hands with rulers, slippers and even a riding crop. The 'official terror', he later recalled, imposed by flagellators, homosexuals and failures transformed him from a 'sceptic to a rebel, an insurrectionist and an anarchist'.[9]

There was equal hatred of his fellow pupils who succumbed to the teachers' tyranny. Black promoted himself as the spokesman against the sadism of his inferiors. 'This school is like a concentration camp,' he told John Fraser in the midst of a typical fury. 'E.P. Taylor could buy this silly place fifty times over. He'd subdivide and make some money off it.' Fraser and others were baffled by Black's anger. Life at Upper Canada was little different from that at other schools. The school's summer camp motto: 'In the boy is seen the man' – would prove to be remarkably pertinent.

In May 1959 the school was being rebuilt, and the fourteen-year-old Black spotted lax security in the administrative offices. One night, with little consideration of the consequences, he returned to the building and picked the lock of a room containing the records of the cadet corps. In the hope of avoiding military duty and sport, he removed his own records. On a subsequent night he broke into the room of a teacher whom he particularly disliked and altered the records of some pupils, and in another break-in he copied out the academic records of many pupils. His success bred an outrageous plot to steal and sell the school's final examination papers.

With two other pupils, he broke into the school's main office, pocketed the examination papers and used his knowledge of other students' weaknesses to offer them the relevant papers for an appropriate price. Those in greatest need paid the most. With an exaggerated sense of his own skills, the trademark of any buccaneer, he was excited by the risks he was running. He staked everything on an attempt to demonstrate his bravado and his uniqueness. Thirty-four years later, he would proudly admit to having 'completely undermined the system' and to have caused 'utter chaos'.[10] Blinded by contempt to the possibility of any flaws in his genius, his last throw was calculated to extract revenge for his injured innocence. He gambled that either the authorities were too stupid to discover his deeds, or that his expulsion would be a painless pleasure.

The extraordinary examination results that followed provoked questions, and Black's role was discovered. Expulsion was inevitable. He felt no shame, and resisted accepting any blame. He dismissed the school's principal as an 'insufferable poltroon', and derided his wife, whose parting words were that his 'life was over', as a 'desiccated old sorceress'.[11] He consoled himself that he had received 'much moral authority by my failure', and even John Fraser felt that he was 'the hero of the hour'. Later, Black described his crime as 'a fundamental subversive' plot intended to undermine and overthrow a regime which he compared to that of Nazi Germany. His contempt for those pupils who had exposed his dishonesty matched his scorn for those who were outraged by it. The boys who had bought the stolen papers had wasted their money, but the honest students were also forced to retake the examinations. Black's condescension towards the innocents, combined with a genuine grievance against those who burnt his effigy on the lawn outside his home, reflected his cavalier arrogance. 'As I walked out of the gates,' he wrote self-servingly thirty-four years later, 'a number of students who literally twenty-four hours before had been begging for assistance – one of them on his knees – were now shaking their fists and shouting words of moralistic execration after me. I've never forgotten how cowardly and ungrateful people can be.'[12] He blamed the teachers, the school and the system, denying any personal responsibility for his wrongdoing. On the Day of Judgement, Black expected those vilifying him to have to answer for their lack of faith in himself. He was entitled to their praise, not their scorn.

There was a distinctive aspect to Black's crime. His home environment – the vengeful father, the ineffectual mother and his solitary adoration of history's heroes – had created an individual who worshipped bronze effigies. Steeped in the blood and glory of history's heroes, Black's self-glorification justified trampling on the weak. In his philosophy, society's masters were permitted to break laws. Veering off the beaten track was imbued in his character. With that notion implanted in his mind, he had lost the only impediment to committing a major crime – a conscience. Black the schoolboy imagined himself to be an unacknowledged genius entitled to break the law. 'I am neither proud nor ashamed of what happened,' he wrote. 'It was an awful system whose odiousness was compounded by banality and pretension.'[13]

George Black excused his son as a 'compulsive insubordinate' eager to prove his credentials as a capitalist.[14] The school rejected that explanation, believing that the father was blind to his son's reckless disregard for rules and morality. Spared any proper parental reprimand, Conrad waited for his mother and father to find a new school. Lonely, he remained in his bedroom listening to long-playing gramophone records of Franklin D. Roosevelt winning the wild applause of a crowd in Madison Square Garden for denouncing American capitalism, the rich and politicians' deviousness, on his way to becoming President. Roosevelt, he would say admiringly, was a misunderstood hero, defiantly ignoring his physical paralysis to shape the world's future.

Over the next four years Black passed through two more schools – leaving each because of misbehaviour – before being coached in a crammer to scrape a pass in his final school exams in 1962. His mediocrity reflected his laziness. His reliance on his father's indulgence and finances was reflected in his unwillingness to focus on his study of journalism and then history at Carleton University in Ottawa, an inferior college. Lodging at the expensive Savoy Hotel in Ottawa rather than in student accommodation, he spent his days sleeping or listening to parliamentary debates, and sharing the hotel restaurant in the evening with senators. The consequence was inevitable. During the summer holidays in 1963, while he was visiting historic and literary sites in France with his elder brother Monte, the college warned that he risked expulsion. His schoolboy notions of genius had been shattered. Laziness had bred failure. Instead of returning to study he remained in France as a tour guide, and later travelled to Spain to meet Brian Stewart, a Canadian friend.

Black arrived in Spain depressed, admitting his inability to cope with life's normal challenges. His initial escape from despair was to read a biography of the American newspaper tycoon William Randolph Hearst, the model for Orson Welles's Citizen Kane.

The combination of politics, history and power appealed to a dilettante seeking a purpose. In his fantasy, the ostracised upstart dreamt about basking in public adoration. Whatever he said would be believed because he uttered the last, irrefutable word. Undecided whether he should become a historian or try to earn some money, he resolved at least to overcome his laziness and improve his performance at college.

Back in Ottawa, Black had the good fortune to meet Peter White, the ambitious assistant of a minister in the federal government. Through White, six years older than himself, he was introduced to Canadian politics and politicians. At parties, political meetings and in committees, he became immersed in the country's political system. In the era of ruptured dreams after President Kennedy's assassination, White, Black and Brian Stewart drove to Atlantic City to witness the beginning of Lyndon Johnson's 1964 presidential election campaign. Standing among 23,000 people stirred by Bobby Kennedy's speech urging support for the civil rights campaign, Black sensed that he was present at a moment of history, adoring the image of a towering politician, serene among the excited masses. The theatre of leadership transformed Johnson into Black's latest hero.

The daydreams barely changed after his graduation from Carleton University with a poor degree in 1965, and the completion of his first year of a law degree. Financed by some profits earned on the stock exchange, an inheritance of over $200,000 from his grandparents and regular income from his parents, Black spent part of his summer in Ireland with Galen Weston, the future head of the retailing family, and later drove to Eastern Europe. The news from Ottawa was bad. After failing his law exams, he had been expelled from the university. At twenty-two, he was categorised as a flop. 'It was time,' he decided, 'to outgrow mischief and debauchery.'[15]

Peter White offered Black salvation – a half interest in two small weekly papers, the *Knowlton Advertiser* and a French-language paper, serving townships near Montreal. The investment would cost Black $500. He settled in Knowlton, a small lakeside community, and single-mindedly began editing the small-circulation newspapers. Living in a poorly heated boathouse, he spent the day struggling to find news and advertisements, and trying to master the finances of printing and distribution. At night he read Joseph Conrad and other classic authors in the hope of furthering his quest to understand life, and after midnight spoke for hours on the telephone with his father about politics, history and the stock markets. At dawn, George Black looked across the lawns to the willow trees and swimming pool, and decided to go to bed. In Knowlton, his son also went to sleep, establishing a lifelong habit of rarely rising before noon.

The escape from 'mischief and debauchery' was consolidated the following year, when Montreal hosted the world fair Expo 67, and General de Gaulle visited Canada. The combination of parties and witnessing de Gaulle's provocative remark that Quebec should declare its independence from Canada taught Black, he would later claim, that he had been 'a rather silly and undiscriminating rebel'. He enrolled for a law degree at Laval University in Quebec City, an additional challenge because he was one of few English students among the French, although this was a test he endured in comfort. He rented a superb penthouse overlooking the St Lawrence river in the fashionable Port Royal Building close to the entertainment quarter, and drove a Cadillac. Since Peter White had become an assistant to Daniel Johnson, the Premier of Quebec, Conrad Black could combine studying, social life and involvement at the heart of Canada's political life.

As a conservative in a leftish-liberal country divided by the French and English languages, Black suffered a double frustration. The Conservatives had repeatedly failed to offer any solution to Canada's permanent problem of containing the separatist demands of the French in Quebec; and secondly, as he was told by a Liberal politician, 'We're the party of government here. The Conservatives are like mumps. You get them once a lifetime.' Nevertheless, Black engaged self-confidently in politics, supporting the English-speaking Conservatives, and to his delight people took seriously his self-conscious party pieces, cultivated since childhood. Using unusually complex vocabulary, he effortlessly recited endless historical details from memory in performances which, he persuaded himself, convinced audiences of his genius and his political acumen.

In 1969, Peter White once again offered the next step. The *Sherbrooke Record*, a daily newspaper with a circulation of 8,000 published near Montreal, was offered for sale. John Bassett, the owner, was distressed. His marriage had disintegrated and his investment in a new office building and new printing presses had plunged the business to the verge of bankruptcy.[16] On the eve of completing the purchase, White introduced a twenty-six-year-old business-school graduate, David Radler, into the deal. Radler, described by some as mischievous and with few pretensions, was a rough, ambitious fortune-hunter who had learned trading from his father, a restaurateur, and who had recently been selling native handicrafts from a shop at Expo 67. His ratty, sharp manner and his spartan lifestyle emphasised his preoccupation with money. In background and manner Black and Radler had little in common, but they complemented each other's ambitions. Black wanted influence and wealth, while Radler enjoyed mastering the mechanics of creating that wealth. Black brought the vision of a strategy, while Radler was keen to sweat their assets. The chores at the *Sherbrooke Record* could be easily divided. Radler would be responsible for the financial management, including advertising and printing, while Black and White filled the space between the advertisements with editorial reports. They borrowed C$18,000 from a bank, and inherited thirty-two employees and a business which had lost $180,000 over the previous twenty-two months.

'Rape and kill' was the journalists' metaphorical judgement about the impact of Black's arrival. Archives were dumped, photographs were destroyed, wages were frozen, expenses were slashed and half the employees were fired. The remainder were squeezed into a smaller building. Under Radler's merciless penny-pinching, employees were fined for wasting paper, pencils and their own time. Radler and Black scrutinised any expenditure over $5, and the staff's written complaints resulted in two-cent fines for wasting paper. Any other conduct deemed to be unacceptable was punished by a $2 levy. Stories of Black and Radler's nastiness became legion. Helen Evans, the newspaper's social diarist, was docked three days' pay for taking time off to bury her husband.[17] Black was proud of his 'oppression', claiming that his employees departed qualified for better jobs.[18] Suppliers discovered that their bills would only be paid after repeated threats. 'A good newspaper,' Black would be heard later to say, 'is one that makes money.' After just two months, the new owners were delighted by their results. In Radler, Black had discovered his ideal partner. While he enjoyed journalism and pontificating about the world, Radler focused on maximising advertising revenue and restraining the journalists. 'I just screwed that bunch of journos,' Radler loved to joke. He inflicted similar parsimony upon himself, taking packets of sugar from restaurants for his personal use. His frugality was mirrored in his pride at discovering a newspaper's ideal manpower: 'a three-man newsroom – one journalist and two advertising salesmen'. Despite a declining circulation because it ignored local stories and reported politics prejudicially, the *Sherbrooke Record*, with vastly reduced costs, earned a profit. Instead of losing $10,000 a month, it made $15,000. A further loan for Black and Radler to acquire their next newspaper was agreed by their bank, based on them applying a similar formula.

Ownership of newspapers, combining money, politics and the opportunity to win influence, was a natural sanctuary for Black. Posing as a putative press baron he appeared at political conventions in Canada, and contacts among the staff of LBJ, by then retired from politics, arranged remarkable access for Black during a trip to South Vietnam in 1969. With the help of the American ambassador he interviewed President Nguyen Van Thieu, and to his glee his account in the *Sherbrooke Record* was republished across the USA. Soon after, he travelled through South America, his journey culminating in a stopover in Cuba to witness a marathon five-hour speech by Fidel Castro to his poverty-stricken admirers. Next stop was a visit to Bud McDougald in Palm Beach.

Ever since the sixteen-mile island became colonised in the late 1800s as a winter refuge by the Rockefellers, Vanderbilts, Morgans and Carnegies – America's oligarchs and robber barons – Palm Beach had been a haven for celebrities and the world's richest players. Their mansions were imposing, their manicured lawns dazzling and their undisguised wealth awesome. Some would carp that Palm Beach, populated by 'up and down folk', was 'a sunny place for shady people' enjoying an extravagant social life of dinners, dances and parties – and that was precisely the attraction for Conrad Black. The principal qualification for newcomers to mix with the old dynastic fortunes was money. 'Some people are offended by extreme opulence,' Black would later tell Peter C. Newman, his first biographer, 'but I find it sort of entertaining.' McDougald was Black's mentor in his quest to achieve that affluence. McDougald had the nerve to travel unashamedly to London for private visits at Argus's expense, and generally to pilfer the company's assets. Among his prizes was the Rolls-Royce Silver Wraith which he 'purchased' from Massey-Ferguson at a dishonestly low price. McDougald's traits, described later by Black as 'lassitude, greed and vanity', encouraged Black's own ambition to possess $100 million and to have the means to escape Canada's winters.[19] The handicap in 1970 was his psychological turmoil.

Throughout the 1960s Black had revealed a lack of sympathy with the era. Buttoned up in suits, and rarely seen without a tie, he arrived at raucous Friday-night parties stiff and solemn. Rather than enjoying the sexual and cultural revolution, he castigated youthful rebels as 'banal' and 'superannuated poltroons', and showed disdain for men wearing frilly shirts and pink bell-bottom trousers.[20] Some interpreted his reticence as shyness, an inferiority complex or a sense of inadequacy concealed by his remarkable vocabulary. Others, like the journalist Hubert Bauch, were unsympathetic. 'Black's the most arrogant, obnoxious man I ever met,' said Bauch.

In March 1970, Black awoke to a massive anxiety attack. Sweating profusely, hyperventilating and racked by apprehension about his fate, he was on the verge, some believed, of committing suicide. The accumulation of his loveless childhood, his academic failure and his social insecurity had become an intolerable burden. He sought help in psychoanalysis. Over the next two years he consulted W. Clifford M. Scott and Vivian Rackoff in his efforts to examine what he called 'my altruism and the dark side'. Subsequently, he also attended the Clarke Institute of Psychiatry in Toronto for help to cope with his demons. One diagnosis suggested a narcissistic personality disorder – defined as an exaggerated sense of one's own self-importance and uniqueness. The sufferer, according to experts, has a propensity to take advantage of others in the interest of self-aggrandisement. Others diagnosed Black's problems as arising from his loveless, dysfunctional home. Intense psychiatry cured Black of his immediate self-destructive urge, but several personality traits remained, including a sense of his entitlement and a lack of conscience. He frivolously described that combination as the 'Nietzschean philosophy' that 'all that does not kill me makes me stronger'. The mention of Nietzsche, the German philosopher whose anti-Christian arguments in favour of the '*Übermensch*' or 'superhuman' made him attractive to the Nazis, revealed the essence of Conrad Black as a self-important hunter for celebrity.

By 1972, Black felt that all his 'guiding principles were in place'. He believed in God, and in human and economic freedom, and condemned those who prospered from the high taxes paid by others.[21] Echoing his father, he regarded trade unionists as 'self-seeking frauds who cared little for the workers and often were gangsters or Communists'. Union leaders he characterised as 'corrupt Luddites' and 'advocates of feather-bedding'. Pertinently, he was silent about honesty, respect for the law and help for the disadvantaged.[22] Fixed firmly on the right wing, he was on the losing side of the Conservatives' defeat in Canada's 1972 general election by Pierre Trudeau, a popular Liberal who, as Black saw it, campaigned against America and capitalism and in favour of the East European Communist states. In Black's opinion, Trudeau, 'more than anyone, turned Canada into a people of whining, politically conformist welfare addicts'.[23] Cut off from Canada's mainstream politics, Black felt surrounded by Quebec's aggressive nationalists and anti-Vietnam war deserters from America, whom he scorned as 'insolent and contemptible'.[24] Conventional and right-wing, Black focused his support on the conservative rich. Supporting minority causes appealed to a man who identified his own plight with underdogs. In a reflection of his own unpopularity at school, he sought to discover the goodness in other disliked personalities. That quest presented a contradiction. While venerating Roosevelt, Lincoln and Napoleon, he also pleaded for the understanding of charlatans, especially those symbolising the tradition of Huey Long, the notoriously corrupt but populist Governor of Louisiana in the 1920s and thirties.

Searching for other lost causes, Black alighted on the life and career of Maurice Duplessis, the dominating political leader of

Quebec from 1936 to 1959. In popular opinion, the former Attorney General and Premier was condemned as a rude, drunken, corrupt dictator who ruled the province as a quasi-fascist in alliance with the Catholic Church. To resurrect Duplessis's reputation, and in the process to rescue his own appalling academic record, Black registered at McGill University to produce a thesis for an MA degree about the rogue's life.

Diligently, Black obtained exclusive access to Duplessis's private papers, and fleshed out the background of the era by interviewing Duplessis's contemporaries. In pursuit of the truth he travelled to Cameroon to meet one of them, Cardinal Paul-Émile Léger, an eloquent French Canadian missionary. For days they sat in the African bush discussing religion, poverty, life and the fight against disease. Entranced by Léger's intellect, self-denial and altruism, Black could have been influenced by his understanding of morality, the poor and society. Instead, while he found a new hero, whom he would nominate for the 1973 Nobel Peace Prize (it was won by Henry Kissinger), he rejected the purity of Léger's philosophy. The encounter in Africa was nevertheless a turning point. Inspired by Léger, and with the help of Bishop Carter of London, Ontario, he witnessed the power of the pulpit. Rather than being the enemy of authority, Black was transformed into a man of authority himself. The confirmation of his conversion was the conversation he began with God. In this continuing dialogue, Black would consult the Almighty and be reassured that whatever course of life he decided upon – any plan, ruse or conspiracy – would improve mankind. How far, he would ask, could he go without becoming unstuck? 'If I go so far, will you still love me?' His Maker's approval was crucial if Black was to face down those who vilified him. And God always gave His approval. The integrity of Black's credo was the life of Duplessis, who had also suffered personal abuse. Through that corrupt leader's life, Black sought the answers to his own purgatory, and he was rewarded. His vilifiers, God assured him, would have to answer for their lack of faith in Himself.

On his return to Quebec from Africa in 1971, Black began his attempt to restore Duplessis's reputation. 'Much of what his critics decried as dictatorship and corruption was really a puckish love of farce,' wrote Black, who credited Duplessis's authoritarianism with building new roads and power plants. 'Maurice Duplessis had too great a sense of the farcical to be arrogant,' he added admiringly about a politician who accumulated an estimated C$100 million from corrupt payments. In an exhaustive seven-hundred-page text, Black suffocated the reader with endless quotations intended to support every argument in Duplessis's favour. Unable to focus on the essential facts and crystallise both sides of the argument, the reader was exposed to a tidal wave of prejudice.

After reading Black's thesis, Ramsay Cook, McGill University's external examiner, criticised the apparent rehabilitation of Duplessis. He brushed aside the smokescreen of Black's elephantine effort, and identified the flaws in his scholarship and the fallacy of his conclusions. Black's belief that history was determined by leaders, not by mass movements or a battle of ideologies, was, Cook declared, as unconvincing as his undisguised admiration of dishonest power-brokers. In particular, Cook was unsettled by Black's excusing of Duplessis's criminal character, and he was minded to block the award of the MA. In order to secure his degree, Black had no alternative but to make the necessary alterations, although his anger about Cook's 'offensive' opinions and 'fairy-land view of Quebec' reflected his intolerance of criticism. In 1976 the thesis would be published as a 684-page book.[25] Inevitably, Cook was asked by a newspaper, the Toronto *Globe and Mail*, to write a review. Unhesitatingly, he expressed his dislike of the book's unstructured length and verbosity. 'Anyone,' he wrote, 'who can endure this ramshackle volume to the end will likely conclude that though ... Duplessis triumphed rather easily over most of his enemies, he has finally come a cropper in the hands of an admiring biographer.' Black was incensed. 'A slanted, supercilious little twit', he called Ramsay, after personally confronting the newspaper's publisher. Black's modest manner hid violence towards anyone questioning his work; he damned anyone who questioned his sympathy as a 'quasi-fascist Jesuit myth-maker' or an 'illiterate bootlicker'.[26] His self-esteem led him to neglect compromise in his arguments. To prove his superiority he even bought substantial quantities of his book in order to conceal its sluggish sales.

Similar aggression was directed against the Quebec nationalists after the Liberal Robert Bourassa won the 1970 election to become the province's Premier. Contrary to his election pledges, Bourassa abolished English as an official language, discriminating against English Canadians. There was no future for Black in a state intent on separation from the country. Damning the 'hypocrisy, narcissism and obfuscation' of the French Canadians and mocking the placid English-speaking community as 'gin-swilling grumblers of no consequence',[27] he resolved, after eight years in Montreal, to return to Toronto. The notoriety he had gained after his expulsion from three schools had, he assumed, been forgotten. He arrived in the English-speaking city in July 1974 as a comparative stranger.

Conrad Black's homecoming was opportune. Argus's finances were deteriorating, and relations among the company's ageing directors had become fraught. Bud McDougald and E.P. Taylor, while still enriching themselves at Argus's expense, had become bitter rivals. Much to McDougald's dissatisfaction, Taylor had been encouraging Paul Desmarais, the controller of the multi-billion-dollar Power Corporation, to make a bid for Argus. Desmarais's failure, and the antics of Bay Street's cowboys, were a foretaste of the turmoil once Argus's old directors began to die. In anticipation of that future battle, Black resumed his relations with old friends including Fred Eaton of the department-store chain dynasty which he identified as 'Canada's ultimate establishment family'.[28] Their affection was mutual. 'Jesus Christ,' gushed Eaton, 'Conrad's got a spectacular mind working there.' Invited to roast-beef lunches with Eaton were Galen Weston, Hal Jackman, and George Black's old friend Douglas Bassett. Black spoke lengthily over wine and whisky about history and politics, and explained how he intended to extend his influence in politics by purchasing newspapers considered too small by Roy Thomson, the country's dominant publisher and owner of *The Times* and *Sunday Times* in London. Systematically, Black and Radler telephoned owners with offers which, over the next three years, harvested twenty titles, including such local papers as the *Alaska Highway News* and the *Daily News* of Prince Rupert, all financed by loans secured against the *Sherbrooke Record*. Proudly, Black would assert that besides his original $500 investment, all his expansion consolidated in Sterling Newspapers, a new company, was financed by loans and profits. The *Sherbrooke Record* would be sold in 1977 for C$865,000, forty-eight times its purchase price eight years earlier, which did not account for $1 million profit used to buy other newspapers. During those years, the partners rarely met. 'I know exactly what he's going to do without going near what he's doing,' said Radler about Black. Their shared ambition for money – and Black's for fame – cemented their relationship.

Black was seeking the celebrity of an influential politician. Exaggerating the importance of his twenty tiny newspapers, and concealing his dependence upon his inheritance, Black's cultivated manner – relaxed, self-indulgent and opinionated – suggested a man of influence and independent wealth. His articulate advocacy of raw capitalism in an increasingly socialistic society attracted television producers eager to stage debates. Frequently he appeared on TV to support Claude Wagner, a politician renowned for accepting bribes and acknowledged by Black as suffering from petulance, superficiality and indecisiveness. The eccentricity of his opinions, and the charade of his eminence, obscured Black's insecurity. In 1977, to satisfy his need for companionship, he asked Shirley Walters, a secretary in his office, to marry him.

The daughter of an accountant, Walters possessed an incomplete education, little ambition and no interest in politics or history. A decent, solid woman, following the breakdown of her marriage she was vulnerable to her employer, who had limited sexual experience. Although Black would claim to have been the surprised target of predatory women when he was young, eyewitnesses suggest few carefree relationships before he met Walters.[29] His proposal of marriage was hastened by the discovery of Walters's pregnancy. There was, however, a complication: Walters's divorce could not be completed before the child's birth. Black was fearful of the criticism of Toronto's social leaders, especially Bud McDougald, if the existence of his illegitimate child was discovered.[30] After he had overcome Walters's prevarication, they resolved to keep the pregnancy a secret and to withhold Black's name from the birth certificate.

Jonathan Black's birth in November 1977 was followed by the news on 15 March 1978 of Bud McDougald's death in Florida. The chatter around Bay Street was deafening. Few of those gazing at McDougald's face in his open coffin were filled with sadness. Only McDougald's widow wept; others were preoccupied by the succession. Skilfully, Conrad Black moved closer to the grieving woman, reminding her of his affection for her husband, whom he later described as 'a very elegant kind of con man', a judgement possibly of admiration rather than condemnation.[31] McDougald, championed as Canada's supreme business leader, epitomised so many of Black's ambitions. 'Bud was very skilful at presenting the carrot and making sure it wasn't within anyone's grasp,' Black noted.

For more than twenty-five years, George Black's son had been nurtured for the moment of vengeance. 'I appear,' Conrad Black said in self-congratulation, 'to have been the only person who took note of the fact that Mr McDougald had died on the Ides of March. He always had a Caesarean bearing, and his succession was not much better organised.'[32] The lesson of his father's dismissal was to foresee deception and to marshal sufficient force to out-manoeuvre any rivals.

The empire's immediate fate was to be decided at Argus's first board meeting after McDougald's death. As usual, Conrad Black arrived late, and was surprised to find that the three elderly directors had taken advantage of his unpunctuality, voting to deny the Black brothers executive directorships. 'Don't rush your fences,' Black was told. Youth would need to wait its turn. 'It was an utterly disgraceful performance,' Black publicly proclaimed. Yet quietly he welcomed the rebuff.[33] By demonstrating his true status, the other directors had compelled him to focus on the only worthwhile outcome – seizing the whole empire for himself; and, he puffed, they underestimated his abilities.

Argus, although valued at C$4 billion, was financially troubled. The controlling stakes in the various companies had produced good dividends for the shareholders, but bad management had wrecked the businesses. Dominion Stores Ltd was an old-fashioned chain of supermarkets; Hollinger Mines was managed by a lazy director who undertook no activities other than collecting $40 million a year in dividends from iron-ore mining; while Massey-Ferguson, with 45,000 employees, would lose C$257 million in 1978.[34] Argus's directors were certainly incapable of reviving the group. Black's quandary was how to organise the old guard's removal.

The ownership of Ravelston and Argus was diffuse. To obtain a majority vote depended upon a matrix of complicated relationships and trusts. In that quagmire there were potential allies, enemies and neutrals. To win control, Black would require dexterity and genius, seducing some and flattening others. Events, Black reminisced, needed to be treated 'with a certain rhythm, maintaining a kind of symmetry as if you were conducting a symphony orchestra'.[35] Since his relations with most of the directors were bad, there was nothing to lose from a gamble.

From his study of history, Black had learned how simple gestures could lead to critical alliances, especially a show of concern for the beleaguered. In preparation for the struggle Black had targeted Dixon Chant, a chartered accountant employed by the late Eric Phillips, one of the key shareholders. Chant had suffered a heart attack, and Black visited him in hospital. Sympathising with the distressed came naturally to the unhurried, verbose aspirant. Chant would prove to be Black's critical ally as the dust dispersed after McDougald's funeral.

Black's objective was two widows – Maude 'Jim' McDougald and her sister Doris, the widow of Eric Phillips. Together with the Blacks', their shareholdings in Ravelston would amount to a controlling interest in Argus. Living together in Palm Beach, neither woman was blessed with intelligence or an understanding of business. McDougald, believing in his own infallibility, had never bothered to appoint a reliable, trustworthy lawyer or to explain to his wife how to cope after his death. Isolated in Florida's sunshine, neither woman guessed that Black felt no pity for their weaknesses when he arrived to offer his assistance. Nor could they imagine the seducer's thrill he must have felt.

Conrad Black was dressed conservatively, his animal cunning concealed behind a warm embrace of gentle assuredness. Some would carp at his cultivated condescension, but that would be a mistaken view. Rather, Black had perfected an approach towards the distressed that would serve him well over the coming years. Now he won the widows' trust by obsequiously trimming his manner to put them at ease. He too appeared to be 'grieving'. The tone of his voice and his gestures persuaded his prey that the three of them shared a common cause. The other major shareholders, explained Black, were crudely manoeuvring against the widows' interests. 'You're being marginalised,' he warned them. 'We must do something about this.' After uttering reassurances about his desire to protect their interests, he urged them to pool their shareholding with his. The two women believed his colourful reports about their husbands' former colleagues, and were gradually persuaded to trust their gracious, wise visitor. Black's next step determined the remainder of his life.

He asked the widows to sign a contract which empowered his use of their Ravelston shares in any vote against the other factions. Combined, their 70 per cent stake could compel the remaining shareholders to sell out to himself. That extraordinary power had originally been crafted by the widows' late husbands to control the empire in their own interests. Puzzled and ignorant, the widows hesitated on the brink, uncertain about the financial advantage of Black's proposition. He suggested they consult Doris Phillips's adviser Dixon Chant, who Black knew had become irritated by the behaviour of Argus's executives. Unlike Black, who had visited Chant in hospital, the other executives were disdainful of him. Just as Black had planned, Chant encouraged the widows to trust him.[36] In the conversation which followed, Black performed the role encapsulated by Dostoevsky in *Crime and Punishment*: 'An honest and sensitive man opens his heart, and the man of business listens and goes on eating – and then eats you up.' Black listened and spoke, and eventually the women signed the agreements without extracting any payment in return. He had achieved power for nothing except the cost of a flight to Florida and the emission of a lot of hot air. Events now assumed a momentum which his adversaries would struggle to halt. 'My brother and I,' chortled Black, 'were in a position to blow the . . . factions away when we wished.'[37] He laughed about those arrogant old Bay Street habitués who underestimated young men, and about the 'grieving disinterested widows'. His coup was a masterstroke.

As the news seeped out, Ravelston's other directors were flummoxed. Tasting his first blood, Black enjoyed comparing himself to those heroic military geniuses whose biographies he devoured. 'Never interfere with an enemy when he is in the process of destroying himself,' he liked to quote from Napoleon.[38] Adopting military stratagems against weak foes like the widows and Ravelston's other directors satisfied Black's fondness for self-congratulation.

News of his victory at the widows' expense prompted calls from Canadian journalists to Florida. Their questions were the widows' first inkling of their mistake. 'I have a bird brain about business,' admitted Maude McDougald, 'and I don't know anything about it.' Doris Phillips was equally disarming. 'You know more about it than I do,' she confessed after admitting ignorance about the 'hundreds of documents' she had signed since her husband's death.[39] As the interviews increased, the widows began denouncing Black as a trickster, claiming incomprehension. 'Like absolute idiots and birdbrains,' said Maude McDougald, 'we signed and signed and signed without reading at all.' In Toronto, Black dismissed their pleas of innocence as 'an utter fraud'.[40] He was not prepared to accept any blame. He was always in the right.

Inside 10 Toronto Street, Black confronted the director who had told him, 'Don't rush your fences.' Empowered with the widows' shares, the young rebel announced that he had not appreciated the snub. That director and all the others were ousted forthwith. In Black's imagery, his rivals were 'trussed up like a partridge to their guillotine. I would not fidget and fumble with the blade levers . . . Off with his head.'[41] News of their resignations sparked uproar. Bay Street had never in living memory witnessed such a coup. As the owner of newspapers, Black assumed that he had the expertise to orchestrate sympathy from the media. To win over Patrick Watson, who was producing a CBC (Canadian Broadcasting Corporation) television documentary about him, he posed in Hal Jackman's basement in front of a gigantic model army to illustrate his prowess as a strategist, spawning the false illusion that he regularly engaged in war games. 'I was asked by the widows,' said the hero, 'to pull the trigger and decapitate the enemy because the ladies would not hear of moderation.' As the criticism of his actions increased, newspaper journalists were introduced to another Blackian tactic – his unusual eloquence in conjuring up images which could only be contradicted by accusing him of lying. Black insisted that he had acted 'neutrally' in dismissing the old guard, and that it was the 'rapacious' widows who had taken the initiative by asking for the transfer of authority to himself. Experts, he claimed, had 'explained laboriously to them in monosyllables and with examples adapted to the mind of a child of ten, and they understood and approved every letter of every word of the agreement'.[42] To those who remained doubters, he exclaimed, 'Any suggestion that I would hoodwink two bereaved septuagenarian widows is patently ridiculous.'[43] Those newspapers which still stubbornly dared to repeat the widows' assertions received the threat of a writ for defamation. Several newspapers surrendered, but Black was powerless to prevent CBC TV transmitting its documentary, which featured the widows expressly denouncing him. Their appearance created an unfortunate legacy as he approached his next hurdle.

The document signed by the widows gave Black the power to vote on their behalf, but did not give him the right to buy their shares. While he could remove rival directors, he could not ultimately control the company's governance. To resolve the confused situation Black sought total control and complete ownership. In the summer of 1978 the fate of Canada's biggest conglomerate was a cliffhanger, dependent upon Black's strategy.

All the players, including Black, were minority shareholders.

Black's fate depended upon the decision of two of these. Moving between Winston's, Toronto's best restaurant, the Toronto Club and 10 Toronto Street, he sought to break the deadlock in a manner which was previously unseen in Bay Street. Black's ace was his unique grasp of the complexity of the Argus and Ravelston empire. In the daisy chain of companies, few understood the flows of cash and power. Only Black's photographic memory could make use of the intricate jigsaw of different people with minority interests in all the companies in order to outwit other shareholders. He understood that by seizing control of Ravelston, he would automatically control Argus.

Throughout the exhausting battle, the widows were buffeted by suitors, professional advisers and the other besieged shareholders. In Black's subsequent description, 'the fate of some of Canada's most famous companies now unfolded in an atmosphere of almost unrelenting buffoonery'.[44] The reality was intimidation, stormy meetings, and vicious threats of dismissal and lawsuits. Around the clock Black cajoled shareholders, directors and employees to support him, or at best not to sell their shares to his opponents. Black's survival depended partly on the success of two friends, Fred Eaton and Hal Jackman, in gathering support for himself. On 2 July 1978 the battle reached its climax when the widows agreed to sell their Ravelston shares to Black for C$20 million. Black offered $18 million, and the deal was settled at $18.4 million. Winning total control thereafter was purely mechanical, and cost just $12 million. For a total of $30 million, Black now owned a corporation controlling assets worth $4 billion. He compared the defeated old guard to 'generals fighting a war by methods of the last one. They could not conceive of any corporate alternative to trench warfare, attrition and promotion by seniority. They were completely over-confident.'[45] Black's final hurdle was to find the money, and the entire $30 million was borrowed from two banks.[46] To reduce his debt he sold off parcels of Ravelston shares to trustworthy friends, especially Fred Eaton, Doug Bassett and Hal Jackman.

With victory came the spoils. Number 10 Toronto Street, constructed as a post office in 1853, became the Black brothers' headquarters. A huge bronze eagle in full flight was hung over the fireplace to reflect Conrad's ambitions. To fulfil his Hearstian fantasy, other rooms were furnished with historic symbols and mementos, especially of battles and generals. At the age of thirty-four, Black embellished his performance as a Bay Street player by holding court in Winston's, at the Toronto Club or in his own dining room. Comparisons with Orson Welles in *Citizen Kane* were not resented by a prototype tycoon eager to pull the levers of power. 'If my father knew what I've done,' he confided with pleasure, 'he'd roll in his grave.'

Propelled into the spotlight in that prestigious building, Black enjoyed the controversy he had invited. Some 'old money' families recalled his theft of the school's examination papers. Others, including members of the Toronto Club, suspicious of the speed of his rise to wealth and celebrity, dubbed the new star 'Conrad the Barbarian'. His coup may not have been dishonest, they carped, but Black was certainly 'cruel'. Any such judgements, in Black's mind, were buried by his nomination as 'Man of the Year' and 'Boy Wonder'. The *Globe and Mail*, Toronto's leading newspaper, anointed him 'Businessman of the Year'. Having outfoxed the establishment, Black felt himself assured of victory in every future battle. Compared to other businessmen in Canada's small pond, he ranked himself as a star. Convinced that he could manipulate journalists, a breed he disdained, he portrayed himself in interviews as a historian lamenting society's 'moral torpor' and the 'decline of civilisation'.[47] With pleasure he pontificated, 'I suspected I was starting ticking a public and press-relations time bomb.'[48] To his glee, his clever asides were published uncritically. He would, he smiled, continue the traditional Argus dinners, inviting the country's 150 most important men. No one, he guessed, would refuse the invitation of a man with unique style, so superbly erudite among bankers, politicians and intellectuals, able to articulate the advantages of capitalism over the creeping socialisation of their country.

Reflecting on his victory, Black suggested that he drew pertinent lessons from the criticism he had received then for the remainder of his career. 'The lesson of June is to be wary of setting out in the most cynical way to use people you have underestimated. The pickpocket whose pocket is picked receives, and deserves, little sympathy... In finance, only proprietors can consistently act like proprietors.'[49] That statement exposed a confusion in Black's attitude towards business. He was suggesting that only a 'proprietor' – someone who owned 100 per cent of a company – could behave selfishly, regardless of others. 'My natural sympathies are with the proprietors whose own money is at stake,' he said, admiring the personal control of companies enjoyed by Galen Weston, Fred Eaton, Ken Thomson, Hal Jackman and the American moguls. With their substantial control of their businesses, they shone in Black's eyes compared to mere professional managers. Black's misfortune was that he was not a proprietor. He lacked the money to buy out Argus's other shareholders. Yet, as a raw capitalist, he was emphatic that proprietors and investors were bound to live by the laws of the jungle. 'There is not,' he emphasised at this critical moment in his career, 'and should not be, any safety net for the rich.'

Amid the excitement, on 14 July 1978 Conrad Black married Shirley Walters. Considering his aspirations, Black did not arrange the society wedding some had expected. His old friends understood the socially insecure groom's desire to be certain of a loyal, unstrident wife who would provide him with a domestic refuge. After the small ceremony, witnessed by a handful of friends, twenty people gathered at Black's house for dinner. At 10 p.m., exhausted by the takeover battle, he left his guests and bride and went to bed. On the wedding certificate he listed his profession as 'historian'. That was a critical claim for what would follow.[50]

2

The Stain

ON 15 JULY 1978, the day after his wedding, Conrad Black sat with David Radler and Peter White by his swimming pool to discuss the future. Becoming a billionaire was a possibility. With hard work and astute management, Argus could evolve into a global business. Serious hurdles, Black knew, needed to be overcome. After years of exploitation, Argus was short of cash and the companies had been bled dry. Transforming the lame ducks would be exhausting. Living off dividends and expenses in Bud McDougald's fashion was no longer possible. Black was faced with a choice: either hard work and the possibility of creating enormous wealth, or limited work and a good life. Sitting in the sunshine in the midst of his seven-acre garden, Black did not welcome the prospect of devoting mind-numbing attention to the intricate details of production, finance and markets. His ambition was to become a man of influence, enjoying the luxury of a cash machine. Getting money, not least to repay his debts, was a priority. His candid confession about 'not gambling more than my original $500 in 1966 on the Argus project' was largely accurate.[1] Other than his inheritance, his wealth depended upon drawing cash from the companies he controlled.

Black's entry into the huge chairman's office at Massey-Ferguson headquarters in Toronto was a symbolic moment. Over 131 years the corporation had symbolised Canada's virility, although the image had become flawed. With over C$1 billion of debt, the company was on the verge of self-destruction. Poor products, strikes and a recession among American farmers jeopardised its prospects. Conrad Black had placed himself in the spotlight with the aim of saving the jobs of 48,000 employees. Although Argus owned just 16 per cent of the company, Black was empowered by the shareholders to act as the sole owner.[2] Within hours of his welcome, delegations of bankers, politicians, trade union representatives and journalists arrived to hear about his intentions. He compared his plans with the tactics of his military heroes. Alternately he summoned the image of Napoleon transforming a rabble into a victorious army in Italy in 1795, or he cited the British tactician Captain Basil Liddell Hart, the inventor of tank warfare after 1917. The military analogies suited his temperament. Succumbing to the vision of himself as the genius executing a brilliant victory, he spoke to the media about rescuing Canada's jewels. All his visitors departed reporting the chairman's optimism and his pledge to rescue Massey-Ferguson from the brink of collapse, if necessary by investing his own fortune.[3] They agreed that having fought hard to take over Argus, Black was accountable for saving Massey, possibly with government help.

Simultaneously, Monte Black became responsible for Dominion Stores Ltd, which employed 25,000 employees in 376 supermarkets. Dominion was a substantial business with annual sales of C$2.4 billion, but bad management had reduced its annual profits to just $24 million. Monte Black was not the natural choice to revive a decrepit supermarket chain's fortunes. Decent and genial, he preferred not to have to rise early in order to undertake the grinding routine of visiting each shop to improve its profit margins, ensure regular supplies of fresh food and supervise its refurbishment. Rather, he enjoyed playing around in planes and big cars, and hosting uproarious parties. 'Monte's idea of management,' said a fellow director, 'was saying, "Let's have a good lunch," stepping into his chauffeured car and afterwards enjoying a long snort of whiskey in the Toronto Club.' Since Conrad rarely got out of bed before noon and was congenitally unpunctual, there was little pressure on Monte to change his own habits. Within weeks he was floundering. The pressure fell on Conrad, and he spontaneously announced his discovery of a cancer in Dominion. The company, he declared, was plagued by employees who were 'notorious crooks', stealing about $30 million every year and thus destroying the business. But instead of quietly recruiting good staff and improving controls, Black publicly denigrated the company's executives.[4] He pinpointed chief executive John Toma, describing him, without supporting evidence, as the architect of 'murky relationships' with suppliers and accusing him of overseeing staff whom he damned as 'trained reptiles' whose 'financial ethics' were similar to 'the profligate corruption of looters'.[5] Few understood how humiliating the staff could save Dominion Stores, but Black regarded 'shock' and the consequent 'conspiracy of embarrassed liberal silence' as an effective management tool.

When that failed he fired Toma, who disputed the allegation, and appointed David Radler as the chief executive. Among the bewildered observers was Galen Weston, the head of a rival retail chain. Neither Weston nor others, however, noted Black's unannounced agenda. Unnoticed, Ravelston began levying management fees on Dominion which would total $40 million over the next seven years, denuding the company of cash. Commercially, Black's strategy was folly, but any criticism would be a misunderstanding of Black's purpose. He was unwilling to undertake the necessary work – he wanted cash – and in his conversations with the Almighty, his Maker agreed that as the victim of ungrateful and dishonest employees, he was entitled to reward himself with substantial fees.

By January 1980 Black was also struggling to save Massey-Ferguson from bankruptcy. He resisted undertaking fact-finding tours of the company's plants across America and Europe to discover the cure for its inability to match its competitors. Out of his depth, he remained in Toronto, dismissing the cynics and reassuring those concerned about the future of the remaining 30,000 employees, despite the growing recession. By early May, as the company's plight deteriorated further, Black publicly insisted that he could save it if he received help from the government and his bankers. In fact, however, he was calculating the tax advantages of abandoning Massey-Ferguson.

Black's friend Hal Jackman, the manager of a major fund and a substantial investor in Ravelston, had become alarmed. Black's intentions and promises to invest in Massey-Ferguson were puzzling, not least because Jackman knew Black had no real money. He was a man, Jackman realised, prone to overestimating his worth. During a 'boozy night's drinking', Jackman was candid. 'Your hubris and ego,' he said, 'are getting in the way of running this business.' Black nodded. 'Conrad,' continued Jackman, 'there's nothing in this for me. I want out. Buy my Ravelston shares.' 'Right,' replied Black.

In September 1980 Black executed a dramatic stunt to avoid a costly disaster. After blaming the government for refusing to offer adequate help, he simply gave Argus's shares in Massey-Ferguson to the employees' pension companies and announced that he was walking away. Such acts would be characteristic of a career notable for dramatic entries and exits. Just before leaving the chairman's office, Black removed from the wall a painting showing a gun carriage moving through a battle-scarred street in Arras, France, past a Massey dealer in 1918. Conrad Black appreciated trophies.

Canada was shocked by Black's conduct. He was no longer a whizz kid but another Bay Street cowboy abandoning his responsibilities to thousands of families and the nation. In the media, Parliament and even among members of the Toronto Club, he was criticised as a profiteer without a social conscience, exploiting legal loopholes and manipulating companies' assets for his personal profit. 'I gave them no comfort at all,' was all Black would say in his contradictory accounts of his negotiations with the government about the future of Massey-Ferguson.[6] Arousing suspicions did not trouble Black, but he was intolerant of the consequences. In the *Toronto Sun*, Peter Worthington, the editor, accused 'Conrad Tricky' for incurring Massey-Ferguson's horrendous debts. The criticism stung Black. His vilifiers deserved punishment for not recognising his glory. The *Toronto Sun* received a writ for defamation – the first of dozens which he would issue over the next twenty-five years – and a carefully crafted letter written in his unique style: 'For the record (not that the *Sun* is a newspaper of record to anyone who does not suffer from severe lip-strain after half a minute of silent reading), the *Sun*'s theory that we should mortgage all the assets . . . to bail Massey out of a mess that none of us had any hand in creating, is too asinine to merit further reply'.

Reading his published letter in the *Toronto Sun* and contemplating the legal battle pleased Black. He had uttered, he imagined, the last word on the subject, and his critics were forever silenced. He could not imagine that his would-be peers – the Bronfmans, Westons and Thomsons – were embarrassed by his retreat at the expense of his employees and his refusal to rebuild the business. Observers noted that Victor Rice, Black's successor at Massey, was fighting to save the company: he would succeed in increasing the share price from $1 in 1980 to $78 in 1999. They carefully considered Rice's judgement of Black – 'His perception of what he was doing and reality were two different things' – and concluded that Black was 'a flash-in-the-pan'.[7] Conrad Black resented any disparagement. Others, he believed, were always to blame for his misfortunes. Spoilt as a child, he protected himself by accusing his critics of jealousy. 'All those pent-up forces of envy and disbelief,' he sneered, 'finally showed their true colours.'[8] To bolster his sense of his own infallibility and innocence he damned his critics for resenting his 'unbroken string of successes'. Verbal flourishes, he believed, would cover his escape. 'The only charge that anyone can level against us,' he would say, 'is one of insufficient generosity to ourselves.'[9] Attracting envy to himself, he reasoned, confirmed his success.

Conrad Black was thirty-six-years old. His morality was as rigidly fixed as his ambition. He wanted wealth and influence. Preoccupied with manipulating his debts, his developing plan appeared to critics to transfer Argus's real wealth from the public shareholders into Ravelston, the private company which he controlled. In his self-proclaimed 'campaign of manoeuvre' he initiated a bewildering succession of loans, dividends and special payments, shifting the ownership of companies and debts between Argus and Ravelston. In the process, Ravelston got richer while the price of Argus shares fell.[10] 'This policy,' he would boast, 'led over that time to what was probably the greatest compression of corporate dealing in Canadian history.'[11] Outsiders, confused and suspicious, sold their Argus shares. As the price of the shares fell, Black used the cash which Argus earned from selling its assets to finance his own purchase of the company's shares, so increasing his personal stake in the company.[12] Pushing up prices and selling at the peak, the Bay Street cowboys were infamous for 'pumping and dumping' shares. Black did the opposite. As one of his managers quipped, 'Conrad went to the dentist and ordered him to drill. When the dentist said that he could see no cavities, Conrad told him, "Drill anyway. I feel lucky today . . . ".'[13] Peter Newman, Black's first biographer, credited him with 'taking rabbits out of apparently empty hats'.[14] Others saw a magician waving an empty hat, treating employees as 'toy soldiers' and, for his own self-enrichment, ignoring the interests of minority shareholders. 'We originally created wealth out of thin air,' he boasted, 'but in a way that was perfectly licit.'[15] Legality had assumed a special meaning for Black. The repercussions were immediate.

The public debate about his conduct fed Black's ambition to buy more newspapers and to become a broker of influence. His targets were publications whose owners, he asserted, were alcoholics and incompetents who had either succumbed to damaging strikes or had failed to fund the necessary investment in new plants and buildings. Included in his wish-list for purchase were Toronto's *Globe and Mail*, the *Ottawa Journal*, and the *Montreal Star*. Repeatedly, the vendors rejected his offers and preferred to deal with Roy Thomson.[16] Frustrated and needing money, Black lurched in the opposite direction and agreed to sell Sterling Newspapers for $14 million. But after scrutinising the figures, the prospective purchaser withdrew, pronouncing his dissatisfaction with the accounts.[17] Black's consolation was a conference organised by the Economist Intelligence Unit in Toronto. 'Massey-Ferguson's former chairman has agreed to sponsor the conference,' Andrew Knight, the *Economist*'s editor, told Peter Jay, the recently-retired British ambassador to Washington. 'Can you arrange for Henry Kissinger to make a keynote speech?' Jay succeeded, and was talking to Kissinger in the conference hall's ante-room before his appearance. Black seized his chance. As Jay began to escort Kissinger onto the platform, he was powerfully pushed from behind. Reeling to the side, he noticed Conrad Black striding up to Kissinger. 'This way,' smiled Black, engineering his introduction to a relationship which would bless his career. Before he returned to Washington, Kissinger had been seduced by Black's profound knowledge and charm. Making use of this new relationship depended upon Black increasing his wealth.

With the option of buying more newspapers closed to him, Black identified mining as a certain profit-maker, and resolved to expand Argus's investments in that field. Argus owned Labrador, an iron-ore extractor. For tax reasons, Labrador could benefit by involvement in oil exploration. After careful research, Black targeted Norcen Energy Resources, an undervalued oil and gas explorer. In December 1979 he had bought 10 per cent of the company's shares from an investment group. The following day he telephoned Ed Bovey, the company's chairman, to discuss his investment. Black would insist that, with Bovey's agreement, he raised his stake to 40 per cent by February 1980.[18] The investment was financed by bank loans, but essentially, in a complicated, tax-efficient procedure, Black used Norcen's own money to finance his purchase. Next, using Norcen as his vehicle, he searched for another mining company in the United States. His motives were partly financial, but they were also social. Ever since he had visited London in 1953 and Palm Beach in the 1960s, and had left Montreal in disgust with Quebec's separatist politics, Black had been dissatisfied with Canada. The country, in his opinion, was a narrow-minded backwater, and its politics were boring. America, by contrast, was exciting. For a social adventurer, Palm Beach was a natural stage on which to launch his presence in America.

In 1980 Conrad Black took his first step towards joining America's rich set. He bought an unimposing colonial house at 150 Canterbury Lane, on the north end of Palm Beach island. The comfortable 8,700-square-foot house did not enjoy a sea view, but it was located near the resort's nobility. Shirley Black employed an interior designer to decorate the house in Colefax & Fowler style, and although there were grumbles among local tradesmen about Black's 'ungentlemanly' quibbles over their bills – like any shrewd businessman, he carefully examined the accounts – the social rewards were gratifying. Assiduously, Black cultivated Jayne Wrightsman, a former manicurist who had married an oil billionaire. After her husband's death Wrightsman had used her inheritance to become Palm Beach's patrician hostess. Invited for cocktails and dinner parties, Black worked hard to establish himself as a guest guaranteed to amuse others by reciting from his encyclopaedic memory of history and politics. 'Come for dinner in Palm Beach,' Wrightsman said to the London merchant banker Rupert Hambro. 'I've met this hugely intelligent man who is so wonderful. He's called Conrad Black.' Hambro knew Black from summer weekends staying at the businessman Bob Dale-Harris's farm north-east of Toronto. Meeting him again in Florida, he noticed how Black had changed. Touched by the glamour of big money, Black was flattered that Wrightsman, a kind, generous person, was attracted to him, and that by turn he had become a subject of conversation.

The proof of Black's social acceptance was his proposal for membership of the Everglades Club, the meeting place of Palm Beach's elite. The obstacles were Maude McDougald and Doris Phillips, the two Argus widows. Both still resented their humiliation, and campaigned to blackball their tormentor. Their tactics were in vain. Imperceptibly, Black organised his nomination and election without any formal notification. 'Clubs are not democratic,' the widows were told.

Shirley Black was uninterested in the Everglades Club and her husband's social ambitions. Politics and business provoked indifference in the modest woman who appeared to some in Palm Beach as shy and 'childlike', relying on her husband to book babysitters and make other domestic arrangements. While he excelled at the formal dinners, lecturing on the refinements of French furniture or the career of an obscure general, she sat awkwardly, unappreciative even of his sense of humour, which occasionally, with the help of a few glasses of wine, reduced him to tears while he hilariously mimicked characters and accents. Regardless of Shirley's disenchantment, with Wrightsman's patronage Black was introduced into the society he yearned to emulate.

Cultivating the right image, Black knew, was essential to acceptance. Walking into a room, he took care that his large, physical presence captured the space around himself. Gracious but also aloof, his self-assured manner left onlookers in no doubt of his attitude: 'I'm Conrad Black, take it or leave it.' His quiet voice and gentle movements suggested that he was neither bombastic nor nasty. With studied stateliness suggesting coiled energy, he intimidated some, but never succumbed to an intemperate outburst. Speaking quietly, his big, intelligent, slightly oriental grey eyes fixed in an immobile face, he aroused curiosity whether his fluent, verbose language was expressing anger or pleasure, never using a short word if a longer one was appropriate. His new friends were impressed by his seamless prose and his prodigious memory.

Black's next step was to accumulate the level of wealth so abundantly evident on the island. During his first holiday in Palm Beach he attended a rousing election speech by the Republican presidential candidate Ronald Reagan, whom he supported against President Jimmy Carter, a politician he loathed. Black's enduring memory, besides Reagan's appearance, was of the limousines parked outside the Breakers Hotel. As far as the eye could see were the biggest Mercedes and the most expensive Rolls-Royces, some lengthened, Black noted, 'in proof of their owners' ingenuity at devising methods of spending an additional $100,000 on a $200,000 automobile'.[19] He himself had begun indulging his appetite to join the high-spending class. As well as his small yacht he had already accumulated several cars, including a Cadillac, a Mercedes and McDougald's Rolls-Royce in London. On some of the bonnets he mounted a gold-plated eagle killing a snake. The symbol matched his goal.

Houses reflect their owners' characters, and Black's plans for the demolition and reconstruction of his parents' home in Toronto confirmed his taste for grandeur. The Bridle Path had become the city's 'Millionaires' Row'. Black's architect produced plans to match his client's aspirations. The mansion's new entrance hall would be two storeys high, and a distinctive, high-domed rotunda modelled on the roof of St Peter's Cathedral in the Vatican was to be erected over a library that would house at least 20,000 books. The story was spread that Black intended to repose on an eighteenth-century cardinal's chair while reading about Napoleon in the midst of a palace that could host Toronto's biggest parties. Others suggested that the chair was the one Napoleon sat on when signing treaties. Black's illustriousness was confirmed when he persuaded Archbishop Carter of Toronto and Bishop Aloysius Ambrozic, both future cardinals, to formally bless the new library. Black was not a Catholic, and since he was not noticeably religious, outsiders believed that the prelates were invited as props in his developing plan to present himself as a serious player. Those cynics did not appreciate his dependence on conversations with God to justify the realisation of his entitlement. The priests' presence validated his relationship with his Creator.

Black's growing self-confidence of his ranking among the elect was enhanced in 1981 when he accepted an invitation to attend the Bilderberg Conference, an annual gathering of over a hundred of the world's rich, famous and influential personalities. Dubbed by critics as the 'Burnt-Outs club', the conference was created in the mid-1950s by Prince Bernhard of the Netherlands to improve relations among members of NATO. As a representative of Canada, Black flew to Holland, where he began a series of special intellectual and personal relationships. Among those with whom he eventually bonded were Gianni Agnelli of Fiat, the newly appointed US Assistant Defense Secretary Richard Perle, the conservative American columnist George Will and Andrew Knight, the British editor of the *Economist*. He also renewed his acquaintance with Henry Kissinger. The participants at the conference were impressed by the studiously casual Canadian businessman, sauntering into meetings to regale his audience with his remarkable memory. 'I'm a fatalist,' he explained in one conversation. 'I believe that people's destinies are always more fascinating than their day-to-day reactions.' His heroes, he continued, were common men whose dreams of greatness materialised after they had overcome huge adversity – Napoleon, de Gaulle, Abraham Lincoln, Marshal Foch, Lyndon Johnson and Franklin Delano Roosevelt. Whatever their personal faults, they were vindicated by their success. Historic acclaim, he argued, excused treachery. Eventual vindication after widespread hatred was the qualification for his worship. He preferred to forget that the rest of mankind lived by other rules – namely contemporaneous judgement.

Mixing with multi-millionaires and power-brokers fed Black's fantasies. Bilderberg was a magnet for romantics, social climbers and conservatives, and like his new associates Black was aghast that America had surrendered in Vietnam rather than staying on to secure total victory. Their common Saviour was Ronald Reagan, the restorer of conviction to political life. As Black spoke, endlessly reciting juicy historic details, he visualised the prospect of becoming celebrated himself, providing quotations for later generations to savour. That surely was his destiny.

The following year Black invited Kissinger to address a group of Canada's elite in Toronto. The former US Secretary of State, attracted to expensive meal tickets, was easily flattered by Black's material generosity and scholarly praise. That Christmas Fred Eaton would give a copy of Kissinger's memoirs to Black, and thereafter he would often hear from his friend, 'I've just had lunch/dinner with Henry, and he says . . . ' Having gained an entrée to both the Bilderberg cast and Palm Beach's aristocrats, Black sensed his opportunity to join the American establishment. Stepping up would require his own fortune.

Expanding into American mining seemed the perfect way to realise his financial and social ambitions. In January 1979 he had identified Hanna Mining, the world's second-largest iron-ore producer, based in Cleveland, Ohio, as an ideal target. After secret discussions with Fred Eaton and Edward Battle, another director of Norcen, they agreed to accumulate enough shares covertly to buy Hanna at a bargain price.

Hanna was owned and managed by the Humphreys, a long-established family which was embroiled in numerous feuds. Argus and Hanna both owned an interest in the Iron Ore Company of Canada, which was run by Hanna with a 26.5 per cent stake, compared to Argus's 10.5 per cent. That connection provided Black with the opportunity in June 1980 to initiate a conversation with George Humphrey, Hanna's vice president. Humphrey, Black knew, was disgruntled by the Hanna board's refusal to appoint him as chief executive. Instead, the family had selected Bob Anderson, a professional mining expert. Humphrey's mother, a widow, shared her son's anger. As a master of exploiting dissatisfaction, Black called on George Humphrey, offering his condolences and help. Seducing dissatisfied shareholders, Black knew from the capture of Argus, was an ideal tactic in take-over battles. With that chore completed, Black made use of repeated opportunities to meet other vulnerable members of the Humphrey family across America – in country clubs, boardrooms, restaurants and at a society ball. In August 1981, believing that his credentials were established, he sought the family's approval to buy shares in Hanna. He would claim that both George Humphrey and Bob Anderson had offered no objections to his purchase of 'some shares',[20] but the family and the company's directors would insist that his proposal was firmly rejected.[21] Events would bear out the family's version.

During August 1981 Black's company Norcen secretly bought 4.9 per cent of Hanna's shares. The purchase was entirely financed by a C$20 million loan from CIBC. In securing that loan, Black, a director of the bank, demanded special treatment, stipulating that 'secrecy was paramount'. No statements regarding the loan and the purchase were to be delivered by the bank to Norcen's office; and Hanna's shares were to be bought by the bank, using an undisclosed numbered account. On 9 September, after the shares had been bought, Black summoned a board meeting of Norcen directors in Toronto. Fred Eaton, Edward Battle and others were in no doubt about his intention. 'We want a friendly take-over,' Black agreed with his directors. Bill Kilbourne, the company's secretary, accurately recorded in the minutes of the meeting that the purchase of shares in 'the target company' was completed, 'with the ultimate purpose of acquiring a 51 per cent interest at a later date'.[22] Black signed those minutes.

Having secretly agreed his company's objective, Black took a decision which could have increased his personal wealth. If the take-over of Hanna was successful, the value of Norcen's shares would rise. To benefit personally from that increase, Black offered to buy back Norcen shares from his own shareholders. By law, he and his directors were required to tell their shareholders the full truth about their intentions regarding Hanna. Yet their letter, sent on 16 October 1981, did not reveal their secret purchase of Hanna's shares or their resolution on 9 September to mount a take-over bid.

During October, again in secrecy, Black increased his stake in Hanna to 8.8 per cent. As soon as the second purchase was detected, Bob Anderson telephoned Black and accused him of breaking the rules. Black was prepared for the onslaught. Conjuring a performance as a helpful, innocent and sincere intellectual, he sought to smooth-talk the American into believing that his intention was simply cooperation. Only Black could have feigned surprise that Anderson's response was, in Black's own description, 'an antagonistic, hostile and even frenetic reaction'.[23] A meeting was summoned in Cleveland. Black flew south, to be told by Anderson to retreat and to sell off his shares. He ignored the warning. To enhance the impression of his virtue, he expressed his 'hurt' and 'outrage' that Anderson, a 'rather underwhelming' person, treated him with disdain and condescension.[24] Undeterred and eager to raise his interest to 20 per cent, Black approached other Hanna shareholders, including old female members of the Humphrey family. He offered them all 'an alliance' against Hanna's directors. War had been declared.

In Black's opinion, his secrecy was consistent with normal trading in Toronto. Bud McDougald and the other Bay Street players had never considered behaving in any other fashion. In the heat of battle, he said, companies often misrepresented their intentions. Such tactics were aided by Canada's weak regulators. Toronto's stock market was supervised by the Ontario Securities Commission (OSC), which had never, in Black's experience, so much as slapped a reprobate's wrist in punishment for a crime. Reared in that wild-west monoculture, the aspiring tycoon did not understand that the stakes and rules for playing in the United States were different from those in his own crude backwater.

The investment by Norcen required Black to disclose his intentions to America's all-powerful Securities and Exchange Commission, the SEC. In his submission, he described the purchase of nearly 13 per cent of Hanna's shares as 'an investment position', concealing his intention to mount a take-over bid. Convinced that his cultivated performance, combining his eloquent vocabulary, benign demeanour and forceful personality, would steamroll the opposition, he flew on 2 April 1982 to Palm Beach with Rupert Hambro on Black's Challenger, the private plane he had inherited after the Argus coup. At the same time, Monte Black was dispatched to Cleveland to deliver a threat. Unless, said Monte, Bob Anderson and the Humphreys agreed to Norcen owning 30 per cent of the company and acquiring an influential position on the board of directors, Norcen intended to launch a take-over bid for 51 per cent of Hanna on 5 April.

This was the Blacks playing hardball. Anderson's response to the ultimatum was emphatic. Amid raised voices and papers flung on the table, Monte's offer was rejected. Twisting the screw, Anderson applied to the Cleveland court for an order preventing the bid. Black was so exposed, Anderson reasoned, that any shot was guaranteed a hit. In his claim, Black was accused of 'fraud and racketeering' because he and Norcen had submitted false information to the SEC.

The counterattack surprised Black. Lawyers representing Hanna unexpectedly invaded Norcen's headquarters. Their trawl of documents produced the board minutes of 9 September 1981, describing Black's 'ultimate purpose' to take over Hanna. Anderson's lawyers were thrilled. It was 'like a grenade with the pin pulled', admitted Black.[25] Black's deception broke the US Securities Act and exposed him to prosecution. Hanna's share price plummeted from $74 to $26.

Black's cabal had been caught red-handed. 'Bill, you dumb idiot,' Black screamed at Kilbourne, Norcen's company secretary, at an emergency meeting of his fellow directors. 'Why did you put that in the minutes?' 'Horseshit,' replied Kilbourne. 'That's what you said at the meeting. You signed it. You should have read it.' Black calmed down. The thrill for his partners was watching 'such a bright guy at work'. After some thought, Black fashioned his response: 'I'll say, "I'm innocent. This is ridiculous. This is a misunderstanding, a technicality."' His audience were impressed by his apparent calm under fire. Black the performer always conjured up a mask of sublime assurance of success.

The threat from America coincided with mixed fortunes in Canada. The shuffling of assets at Argus had not ceased. To avoid tax and to marginalise the minority shareholders, Black was constantly reorganising his companies. The complexity of the changes provoked fears among shareholders that Argus's money was disappearing into other companies in which the group had an interest, including Hollinger, a mining company, or that Argus was heading for bankruptcy.[26] Those fears were compounded by Black's self-aggrandisement. In 1982 Argus earned profits of C$7.6 million, but nearly C$2 million was spent on the directors and their expenses. The generosity to himself and his associates was part of Black's calculated plan to ensure that everyone would 'remain friends'.[27] Protestors found their voices drowned out. The company's annual general meeting on 26 May 1982 lasted fourteen minutes – one minute longer, Black was disappointed to note, than Bud McDougald's record.

Inspired by Napoleon, Black's doctrine – kill or be killed – was deployed in self-justification and self-defence. Contemptuous of his critics, he had been flattered by featuring in a television series as a member of the Canadian establishment; and by Andy Warhol's visit to Toronto, where Black had commissioned him to paint his portrait. The decisive accolade was his coronation as Canada's 'Establishment Man' by Peter Newman, the editor of the weekly *Maclean's* magazine, who promoted 'Canada's leading capitalist' as the personification of the Conservatives' rebirth, with brains. Others reflected that Newman could more accurately have pronounced Black as the anti-establishment man.

Emboldened by his glorification in Toronto, Black repelled the questions hurled by American lawyers and SEC officials with stubborn denials of any blame. 'I relied,' he told his questioners, 'on Norcen's overworked company secretary to record accurate minutes of the board meeting, and he made a complete mistake because he had wrongly surmised that a take-over was intended.' The directors' discussion, he continued, was 'hypothetical'. Challenged that he signed the board minutes as accurate, Black replied, 'I signed the minutes without reading that part of it.'[28] To outwit his accusers he relied on his confident mastery of English, a parade of the power of his memory and a loquacious reinterpretation of the facts. To friends, however, he expressed terror. 'They're out to get me,' he railed to Peter White. Black was humiliated by what he conceded was 'a mess'.[29] To his good fortune, the Americans did not interview Fred Eaton. 'I was at the meeting,' he told Black, 'and the minutes were accurate.' 'Well,' replied Black, 'we'd better watch ourselves in the future.'

In the weeks before the trial was due to begin in Cleveland, Bob Anderson's lawyers were publicly vilifying Black, with wild allegations – which he robustly denied – that he was a criminal, a racketeer and more besides. Over four days of cross-examination in a packed court in early May 1982, he defiantly denied his accusers' explanation of all the events. At the end of his testimony he returned to Toronto convinced that Judge John Manos would accept his interpretation. Denying the truth and rewriting history had been a tool of the world's greatest leaders – dictators and democrats alike. To survive and succeed, Black adopted their doctrine.

On 13 May Black was entertaining Toronto's establishment at Hollinger's annual dinner. Judge Manos's judgement was still awaited. In the middle of the evening a messenger whispered to Black that Canadian police had started a criminal investigation of himself and his lawyers for conspiring to defraud Argus's shareholders. Black knew precisely what had aroused police suspicion: Norcen's inaccurate offer on 16 October 1980 to buy back its own shares. The circular to shareholders, signed by Black, stated that he could not envisage any new circumstances which could influence the share price. At that precise moment, he had been planning his bid for Hanna. Issuing misinformation could be a criminal offence. By the end of the dinner Black had formulated his defence. He had become, he would claim, the target of a conspiracy between his rivals, Canadian politicians and the police. He would denigrate the investigation as an 'Orwellian drama' and 'a charade', because the legal case was 'too fatuous and preposterous' to merit any discussion.[30] Finally, he would castigate the familiar motives of his critics: the police investigation, he would say, reflected 'the destructive complex of envy at its most ignorant and visceral'; his enemies were 'manipulating' the system by 'a smear job'. Creating an aura of aloofness, he walked from the dinner telling those enquiring about his fate, 'There is no evidence. There is absolutely nothing.' His forceful indignation was intended to suffocate doubters and to confirm his admirers in their belief of his innocence. His last word, he persuaded himself, had silenced his questioners.

Unlike in America, Black personally knew those involved in the investigations in Toronto, and understood the regulators' frailties. 'I'll talk to the Attorney General,' he announced. Just hours after the dinner he was sitting in the office of Roy McMurtry, Ontario's Attorney General. The politician met Black without any officials, even those directing the investigation. In his quiet, mellifluous manner, Black cast blame on a range of people, including even the future Prime Minister Brian Mulroney, at that time a rising politician in Ottawa and a director of Hanna. 'The powder trail from this trumped-up charade of an investigation leads straight to Brian's door,' Black told the Attorney General.[31] 'He was far enough along in the chain that generated the Norcen investigation that his fingerprints wouldn't be on the knife.'[32] In his quiet tirade, Black made a series of allegations against politicians, law officers and the police – which they in turn would describe as figments of his fertile imagination. Over the next days, McMurtry and the police resisted Black's pressure to stop the investigation.

The reality check was Judge Manos's decision. On 11 June 1982 he found against Black, declaring that Norcen had committed 'manipulative violations'. '[Black's] construction of the record,' declared the judge, 'is strained and unpersuasive.' The evidence, he continued, 'established conclusively' that the take-over had been contemplated at the board meeting on 9 September 1981, 'if not earlier'. Black was tarred as unreliable. Inevitably, he was terrified. There could be severe repercussions in Canada, including a photograph of him being arrested in handcuffs. He regularly called his lawyer Peter Atkinson to ask for reassurance. Hal Jackman had no doubt that Black was the architect of his own misfortune. 'Conrad's a *poseur*,' he sighed. 'He's always pushing the envelope to get away with it. Pushing beyond reasonable bounds.'[33] Black's terror was concealed from public view. To journalists he coolly returned Jackman's criticism, characteristically describing him as drunkenly playing war games in his library. 'Not an easy partner,' said Black, with the air of reluctant wisdom. While Jackman posed as a great businessman, continued Black, he had sold his Ravelston shares 'risibly cheap'.[34]

The civil judgement in Cleveland threatened to spiral into a criminal prosecution. The SEC charged Black with having 'made untrue statements of material facts' to both Hanna and the SEC, and to having 'engaged in fraudulent, deceptive and manipulative acts and practices'. Black was on the edge. To prevent a prosecution he agreed with the SEC to formally sign a 'consent decree', promising to abide by American laws in the future. The process required no admission of wrongdoing by Black, but there was a sting: if he broke American laws again, the SEC could reactivate the criminal prosecution.[35]

Once it was agreed and signed, Black had no intention of allowing the verdict to remain unchallenged. Those who asked Black about the saga were regaled by tales of his victory as a witness against Anderson's lawyers. Later, going further into fantasy, he described in his autobiography how, at the end of his testimony, Judge Manos had invited him into his chambers and gushed, 'In twenty years as a judge, you are the finest witness I've ever had in my court. Whatever my verdict, from what I've seen this week, it won't reflect unfavourably on you as a witness.'[36] Not surprisingly, Manos had no recollection of such a bizarre encounter, but seeing the story in print convinced Black that his critics had been silenced.

The settlement in America was a relief. In Canada, however, the process continued. The investigators, Black knew, were considering charges, and were determined to send him to prison.[37] Assiduously, he began working among Toronto's establishment to terminate the embarrassment. He prided himself on smooth-talking the regulators into accepting that he was blameless, and shoving newspaper critics aside with the brash, self-confident quip: 'These people are demagogues of the marketplace without a stake in anything.'[38] But his oratory was unexpectedly ineffective.

Black had become a target of hate among a section of Toronto society. The 'Black Factor' mentioned by a critical analyst was cited as evidence that Black was merely a manipulator of shares, rather than a master of management.[39] Bankers distrusted his restructuring of the share ownership of his companies, which gave him control without a majority of shares; some institutions questioned whether he had any motives other than self-enrichment, which he barely denied; antagonistic politicians were suspicious of his assumption of special influence among power-brokers; some journalists suspected his assertion of his own special position; others criticised his complete lack of managerial experience, including at the *Sherbrooke Record*, which was actually run by Radler; and journalists repeated the government's announcement that the police investigation was 'ongoing'. In reply, Black categorised some of his critics as the hard, political left, and others as the 'grumbling detritus of the Establishment Old Guard in the billiard room of the Toronto Club', due for an early appointment with the undertaker.

Fighting for his reputation, he hired Eddie Greenspan, a criminal lawyer, and accused his critics of waging a vendetta against him. He conjured up conspiracies between the American regulators, the prosecutors, the police and all his critics. Convinced that his telephones were being illegally bugged, he approached Paul Godfrey, a senior member of Toronto's Police Commission, and demanded that the investigators should be investigated, rather than himself. No bugs were discovered. He then told Roy McMurtry, the Attorney General, to stop the feud against him, but to his surprise he was ignored.

The investigation, Black decided, could only be defeated by using the media. Summoning journalists, he explained that he was fighting not for himself but for the poor underdogs who lacked the money to defend themselves against similar 'injustice'. His refusal to cower and hide, he repeated, was provoking the investigators' conviction of his guilt. 'It's the fascistic mentality of an element of the police,' he opined. The police, he continued, were behaving like 'Kafkaesque, Orwellian, Koestlerian thugs'.[40] The imagery of 'Conrad Black – The People's Champion' attracted some publicity: and then came the stunt.

In the midst of the investigation Black invited John Fraser, his old school friend, for lunch at Winston's, Toronto's best restaurant. As the two men entered, Black saw a slew of the city's power-brokers – politicians, newspaper publishers and bankers – scattered across the room. 'Half this restaurant already imagines me wearing a prison suit,' he growled to Fraser. Sitting with his back to the crowd, he spotted a cockroach above Fraser's head. 'Ariana!' he bellowed, calling the manager. 'Look at that cockroach! I told you that if you let McMurtry in here I wouldn't give you my business.' The whole restaurant burst out laughing.[41] Black was a master of theatrics. As the laughter died away, he quietly confessed to Fraser, 'The whole trauma sometimes stops me getting out of bed.'

The police were unimpressed. Nine criminal charges were drawn up against Black, endorsed by the Attorney General. Until the last moment it seemed that Black would be indicted and tried. He was perilously balanced on the brink. But, literally at the last minute, during a midnight meeting on 9 July 1982, the charges were dropped. The reasons were never explained. Black was ecstatic. 'I have been absolutely exonerated,' he exclaimed the following morning, adding, 'There's not one shred of evidence of any kind.' Overnight, he resumed his stance as the master of cool. 'The jackals and piranhas smelled blood,' he quipped. 'They thought they had me, that I was about to go up the chimney in a puff of smoke. [But] I never had any fears how it was going to end up. It's all atmospherics in the United States. They never believed a goddamn word of all that bunk about racketeering.'[42] Behind the reasonableness was real anger towards those who refused to accept his distortions. In particular, he accused Roy McMurtry of being 'malicious as well as pusillanimous and incompetent',[43] and he damned Linda McQuaig, a Canadian journalist who had revealed details of the police investigation. 'I thought McQuaig should have been horsewhipped,' he commented, 'but I don't do those things myself and the statutes don't provide for it.'[44] Losing the battle in Cleveland had furnished him with a lesson. 'For years,' he later told a Canadian, 'I wondered what the difference between Canada and the United States really was – apart from the French Canadians and the monarchy. Now I know. This is a gentle place, and that's a real hardball league down there.'[45] As the heat diminished, his self-confidence returned. 'Tittle tattle,' he told questioners dismissively. 'It's all unimportant.'

Black's poise was vindicated by Bob Anderson's agreement in late July 1982 to a settlement. Wiping away the blood, Black thought that he emerged the victor. He paid a further $90 million to become Hanna's dominant shareholder, bringing the total price to $130 million.* Anderson became a director of Norcen and Black became a director of Hanna. Pertinently, the investment would prove to be disastrous. Hanna did not fulfil Black's expectations, and the company's share price tumbled. The Humphreys

* In an agreed swap of shares, Norcen bought 20 per cent of Hanna shares while Hanna sold its shares in Labrador.

had the last laugh. By then, Black's bandwagon had moved on.

Conrad Black emerged having perfected an infallible method for removing the stains on his reputation. As a prolific student of biography, he knew that general impressions were more important than unfavourable details. The trick was to offer reasonable explanations, persuasively interpreting the worst in a more positive light. Over dinner with old friends, he spoke of rewriting his father's failings, boasted about his theft of the school exam papers as 'my first true act of capitalism, but no big deal', and praised Radler's ruthlessness in sacking newspaper employees. 'The lobsters don't get up and walk out of the tank,' he laughed, enjoying a quip he would use many times thereafter. To propel his self-promotion he had given regular access over the previous years to Peter Newman, the editor of *Maclean's*. Every Dr Johnson, thought Black, requires a Boswell. Newman, he recognised, was intelligent but awestruck. The resulting biography, called *The Establishment Man*, published in October 1982, suited Black's purpose, not least because it was well written and favourably reviewed. 'The biggest blow job in Canadian history,' commented Larry Zolf, a television presenter.

Newman had been encouraged to cast his subject as an intellectual and a philosopher. 'Every act must have its consequences,' Black told Newman, posing as the profound historian who did not believe in redemption or atonement.[46] 'Hal Jackman and I agree,' he continued, 'that we're basically more Nietzschean than Hegelian.' Black 'revealed' his sympathy with the 'exquisitely sad comment by the seventeenth-century French satiric moralist Jean de la Bruyère that "Life is a tragedy for those who feel, and a comedy for those who think."'[47] Newman was encouraged to conclude, 'He has trouble working out any form of understandable motivation for himself.' Blessed with that smokescreen, Black's disarming confession, 'I may make mistakes, but at the moment I can't think of any,' was recorded without comment.[48] Despite

Newman's talent, several of Black's fundamental flaws remained concealed. The cosmetics were impenetrable.

Initially, Black was delighted by the book. Reading his own interpretation of himself fed the conviction that journalists were easily beguiled. Self-interest, however, dictated that he maintain a chasm between himself and potential critics. The publication in Newman's own *Maclean's* of articles describing his Norcen troubles justified that caution. In 1983, fearing further allegations of dishonesty, he issued a writ for defamation against Newman and the magazine. His prosperity depended upon suppressing any objective examination of his fortune-hunting and perpetuating the myth of his being self-made, unblessed by any inheritance: 'I'm rich and I'm not ashamed of being wealthy. Why should I be? I made all my money fairly.'[49]

In 1983 Black was, by the scale of his own ambitions, neither rich nor powerful. His gross wealth was about C$200 million, but most of that was used as collateral against loans. His debt was increasing, and he decided that he would sell Argcen's (Argus's successor) stake in Standard Broadcasting and Dominion Stores Ltd. Just as he had failed in mining and oil, so he had proved ineffectual at Standard Broadcasting, the owner of several radio stations, and Radler's attempts to save Dominion had proved dismal. Newspapers, he agreed with Radler, were their best option. By slashing costs they could make profits, and newspaper ownership would satisfy his craving for political influence. His passion was to own the *Washington Post*, but more realistically he wanted Southam, Canada's biggest newspaper chain. The owners, Radler spotted, had borrowed large sums to modernise and expand, but the business remained unprofitable. Only by making massive cuts would the group earn satisfactory profits. Black and Radler bought a small stake in the company, and made an offer wrapped around an uncongenial pronouncement. Southam, Black sneered outrageously, was run by long-haired, dope-smoking freaks left over from the 1970s. His offer to buy the company was rejected. Black was stuck. Frustrated by Canada's politics and concerned about his image, he was aware of his shortcomings. 'I'm a great believer,' he had told Peter Newman, 'in not becoming hypnotised by the rhythm of one's own advancement. I have always felt it was the compulsive element in Napoleon that drew him into greater and greater undertakings, until he was bound to fail.'[50]

The 'compulsive element' was a characteristic Conrad Black shared with Barbara Amiel. Another common quality was living behind a mask. A third similarity was incompatibility with their spouses. After seven years of marriage the Blacks were irreconcilable, but were in mutual denial about their inevitable fate. Similarly, on 26 January 1985, Barbara Amiel also denied the obvious. Like Conrad Black, she had hoped that happiness would follow her marriage vows to the multi-millionaire David Graham. The expensive wedding party on the thirty-third floor of the Sutton Place Hotel, with a spectacular panoramic view of Toronto, was intended to seal her bliss. Instead, her itinerant search for permanence was doomed. Fate determined that Conrad Black should witness the beginning of her predicted disappointment.

3

The Survivor

The origins of a woman later renowned as a 'drama queen' were remarkably ordinary.

In summer 1940, Barbara Amiel's parents, middle-class Jews, moved from central London to Chorley Wood near Watford, north of the capital, to escape the Luftwaffe's remorseless bombardment. On 4 December 1940, the day of her birth, the area around her grandparents' homes in the East End was blazing. Among the subsequent victims of the incendiary bombs would be Isaac Amiel, her paternal grandfather, the owner of a sweet shop and an air raid warden.

Harold and Vera Amiel greeted their daughter's birth with joy but understandable fear. The Blitz was the prelude to an anticipated German invasion, and if Britain was defeated, the fate of the country's Jews was uncertain. Harold Amiel, a twenty-five-year-old solicitor, had joined the Buffs, the Royal East Kent Regiment, and was due to be posted to the 8th Army in North Africa. In his absence his wife Vera, a strikingly good-looking woman of twenty-four, could rely on her family: her sister Katherine, a doctor, and Harold's three younger brothers and older sister Irene, had also left London. Several of them, including Harold and Vera, had settled in Chorley Wood.

In common with all their relations, Harold and Vera had been born in London's squalid East End, but long before the outbreak of the war most of the Amiels and the Barnetts (Vera's family) had escaped from the Jewish ghetto. The new generation, including a midwife, a doctor, a school teacher, an actuary, lawyers and businessmen, had abandoned regular attendance at synagogue and had consciously assimilated into British society. Although the Amiels stemmed from a well-known family of Sephardic Jews from Spain, and the Barnetts were descended from Vladimir Isserlis, an Ashkenazi scholar in Russia, Barbara and her cousins growing up in Chorley Wood were only vaguely aware that their family's arrival in Britain had followed the discovery of great-grandfather Isserlis floating in the River Dnieper with a knife in his back. To escape the pogroms his widow had sold valuables to buy tickets on a boat sailing to Britain. Sixty years later, the fate of Europe's Jews was rarely discussed in Chorley Wood. Rather, some families were preoccupied with persuading Britons to support the socialist or Communist parties in the next elections. Irene Amiel's husband Bernard Buckman, the owner of department stores, was particularly close to two rich Jewish families, the Sedleys and the Seiferts. Together they championed and financed the British Communist Party. Barry Amiel, Harold's younger brother, was also a member of the Communist Party. Among that group, Harold and Vera Amiel were known to be markedly uninterested in politics.

Vera was also noted as a neurotic, which caused tension during Harold's return on leave in late 1942. Since their marriage in June 1939 the articulate and intelligent lawyer, now newly promoted as a major, had become disturbed by his wife's emotions. That concern appeared to be brushed aside as he regaled his nephews and nieces with stories about the war and handed out epaulettes taken from captured Italian generals. The prizes from the battlefront would remain an indelible memory among the boys after they had bade Harold farewell on his return to Africa. In Harold's absence his second daughter Ruth was born in 1943. One year later, Lieutenant Colonel Amiel's war ended. Shot in the shoulder by a sniper while riding in a Jeep in Italy, he was repatriated as an invalid. Dressed in his colonel's uniform, he spent time playing with his four-year-old daughter Barbara, who had struck up a close friendship with Peter Buckman, her older cousin. 'Will you marry me?' Peter asked Barbara. 'We can't,' she replied. 'We've both got dandruff, and that means that our children will be bald. I learned that in biology.'

During the last months of the war, Harold arranged to establish a solicitors' partnership with his younger brother Barry. At the same time, he fell in love with a woman called Eileen Ford. Some would blame the tensions of the war for the breakdown of Harold and Vera's marriage in 1945; others said that Vera was an uneducated neurotic and an unsuitable wife for a cultured lawyer. Divorce was common in the immediate post-war period, but Vera was unusually incandescent about Harold's infidelity, not least because she had partly financed his new law partnership.

Despite the Amiels' ugly arguments about money, Barbara Amiel was more fortunate than the many children who had lost their fathers in combat. Nevertheless, her early childhood was insecure. 'I've suffered from insomnia all my life,' she would write. 'My earliest memory as a child of four was being sedated to sleep.'[1] There was, however, support from Mary Vangrovsky, Harold's mother. After the divorce in 1946 and Harold's marriage to Eileen in 1948, she gave her son money to set up a new home, and cared for her two granddaughters. By then Vera and her daughters were living in Hendon, in north-west London.

Barbara Amiel's early school years were comfortable. Although affected by the general post-war austerity and the rationing of food and clothes, she attended North London Collegiate, one of England's best state schools for girls, and enjoyed the privileges of a middle-class upbringing. There were ballet lessons, excursions to the theatre and cinema, visits to the new Festival Hall to hear Dame Myra Hess play Grieg, and regular meetings with her father at weekends.[2] Forbidden by Vera to entertain his two daughters in his new home, Harold would take the girls to visit their cousins – Anita Amiel in Swiss Cottage and the Buckmans in Hampstead – for lunch and tea before returning to Hendon. In the era of the nationalisation of major industries by the Labour government and the Cold War division of Europe, politics was passionately discussed in many homes, especially by Jews, a number of whom ranked among the leadership of the left-wing parties. Stimulated by the arguments, especially while visiting the Buckmans, Barbara Amiel would recall her growing understanding of their 'interest in creating a more just society . . . through socialism'.[3] At thirteen she was an intelligent, socially aware schoolgirl enjoying a stable life. Her mother was considering transferring her to Roedean, the expensive private boarding school on the south coast, but instead opted for a more dramatic change.

In the early 1950s Vera had begun a relationship with Leonard Somes, a non-Jewish draughtsman. Among the Barnetts and Amiels, Somes was regarded as decent and unassuming, but intellectually unimpressive. In 1953 Vera married him and declared that they would emigrate to Canada to find a new life. Amiel would later write that emigration was her mother's only option, because the British class system discriminated against working-class men like her new stepfather, but that was fanciful. Many ambitious working-class Britons earned fortunes in the post-war era. Leonard Somes's difficulties were his lack of talent and purpose, and his social unease. Canada, promised the advertisements, was a guaranteed escape from austerity and offered an idyllic future. Barbara's fate was decided. By then her father had two more children, the elder of whom, a boy, was mentally handicapped. There was no possibility of Harold Amiel caring for his elder daughters.

The emigrants arrived in Hamilton, near Toronto, at the end

of autumn 1953. There was disillusion rather than a honeymoon. The job Leonard Somes was expecting had disappeared, and after their savings were spent he was compelled following a long period of unemployment to work as a labourer at a local steel mill. Home life in Tragina Avenue, recalled Amiel, was a desperate 'rat race' to 'make ends meet'. The family's plight worsened when her mother went into premature labour. Although she and her son survived after weeks in hospital, Amiel was horrified that her mother's wedding ring had been 'wrenched from her finger' by a robber in the hospital's parking lot.[4]

At fifteen, Barbara Amiel was angry. In place of a comfortable home in London, an excellent school and endless cultural excursions, she found herself marooned in a grim wasteland surrounded by uneducated, insular provincials. Her mother, she screamed, was responsible for the calamity. Relations between Leonard and Vera deteriorated. They decided to move to St Catharines, a nearby town where there was the promise of a better job and a bigger home, a necessity since Vera had discovered that she was again pregnant. The only obstacle was Barbara, and there were furious arguments. Vera condemned her daughter's behaviour as unreasonable. For her part, Barbara judged her mother to be neurotic and unstable, and she was equally dissatisfied with her stepfather's lacklustre achievements. Although she would write twenty-five years later that her stepfather was 'a handsome, warm man of whom I was enormously proud', at the time she was infuriated by his responsibility for her plight.[5] In her mother's version of events, there was concern about Barbara's education. She was settled at the local school, and was ambitious to attend university. The best temporary solution, they agreed, was for Barbara to stay with neighbouring friends and to visit her family at weekends. Accordingly, her clothes were packed and carried to her temporary home.[6] Barbara's version is more apocalyptic. She describes arriving home from school one day at the age of fourteen to discover all her possessions 'packed in a cardboard box next to the front door. My mother was very apologetic. "Your stepfather and I can't cope with you any more, so you have to move out." They found me a room in a house on a council estate and paid my rent until the end of the school term.' The publication of Barbara's account in 1980 would cause great hurt to Vera and Leonard, and to many others in her family who disputed her recollection of events.

Growing up alone without a family became increasingly difficult. In Amiel's various descriptions, she lodged in a part-time brothel while revising for her high-school exams at St Catharines Collegiate, or was a tenant with an unpleasant Polish family. She kept her concentration by stuffing her ears with wax earplugs, but after the 'hurt had passed and I had cried a bit, after I got over the fright of sleeping in cellars underneath the furnace pipes, I came to cherish my freedom'. During her adolescence, she would also write, she found herself 'in the middle of a room, stranded, sitting in my own urine, sitting for hours, too frightened to cry and too frightened to move'.[7] Her occasional companions in sexual experimentation and drinking alcohol were the children of Polish émigrés and Canadian aboriginals. To accommodate that lifestyle she moved into a boarding house during the week, and stayed with a succession of girlfriends' families at the weekends. To finance herself, she worked in the evenings and holidays, in a drugstore, a fruit-canning factory and clothes shops. Illness forced her once to return temporarily to her parents' home, but she soon resumed life in Hamilton. Told she was entitled to a 'secure home' by a social worker, she later commented, 'I had never thought about what I was entitled to. Things were simply taken as they came.'[8] Her brave struggle was rewarded by her securing the grades to study philosophy and English at the University of Toronto. Amiel had become a toughened, streetwise survivor. Her 'wild' days, she would write thirty years later, left a legacy. 'Something decent died in me, or perhaps was stillborn: I would never be able to create a successful family life.' Incorrect reports suggested that she never saw her mother again.[9] Her anger at Vera was compounded by another surprise. In 1959, on the eve of going to university, she and her sister were invited by their family to return to England for their summer holidays.

Unknown to Amiel, in early 1956 her father had become severely troubled. Harold Amiel had been stealing money from clients and from his solicitors' partnership. Exposure was imminent. Fearing disgrace and the anger of his younger brother Barry, he went on 19 April to his mother's flat in Marylebone while she was on a winter cruise, and took an overdose of barbiturates. A verdict of suicide was declared by the coroner one week later. In their grief, the families decided not to tell Harold's two daughters in Canada, partly because he rarely talked about them, and also because he had not mentioned them in his last will, signed the day before his death. Barbara's cousins were told that Uncle Harold had died of his wartime wounds. Amiel's sole memento of her father was a photograph of him dressed in a colonel's uniform. Many years later she described her father swallowing the tablets while listening to Wagner's *Die Meistersinger von Nürnberg*.[10] In contrast, Barry Amiel recalled that his brother was reading a good book and eating an apple before his death.

Considering her hardships over the previous six years, Barbara Amiel's arrival at university had been achieved at a price. Emotionally she was unstable. To relieve her stress and tiredness she swallowed a dozen Codeine 222 tablets a day, and took antidepressants to help her sleep. The physical result was an undernourished, sultry young woman with deep black shadows under her eyes. Sprawled across the bed in her room in the students' hall of residence were panda bears and other soft toys. On a shelf was the solitary photograph of her father in uniform. 'Welcome to the Jewish Common Room,' laughed fellow-student Larry Zolf as the thin Barbara entered the Junior Common

Room. 'The most beautiful fellow-travelling Marxist I have ever seen,' was Zolf's conclusion after a few conversations revealed her fascination with Stalin, 'and certainly the most intelligent.' Curious about her past, Zolf asked the shy girl about her family. 'Oh, my father was very poor and unemployed,' replied Amiel, 'and we were kept afloat by a rich uncle.' Other family members do not recall those circumstances.

Sitting regularly in the JCR, the centre of her social life, with her new best friend Ellie Tesher, Amiel confessed her need for security. 'Who's that?' she asked when a handsome, dark-haired student walked in. 'That's Gary Smith,' replied Tesher. 'He lives in Forest Hill' (an affluent area of Toronto). 'I think I'll marry him,' said Amiel flatly.

Gary Smith, a gentle, quietly-spoken law student, was the son of Harry Smith, the owner of the once-famous Prince George Hotel in Toronto and a member of a well-known family. In 1958 Harry Smith had opened the luxurious Riviera Hotel in Havana, Cuba, in partnership with Meyer Lansky, the Mafia boss, who owned the hotel's casino. Fidel Castro's revolution one year later terminated their investment. In an attempt to recoup some of their money, Tony Bennett, Sammy Davis Jr and Sophie Tucker were booked to appear at the Prince George Hotel, and the income their performances generated was substantial. The downside was Harry Smith's chronic and unsuccessful gambling in casinos across the USA. Nevertheless, to Barbara Amiel, the Smiths appeared a wealthy, stable Jewish family who might offer her salvation.

Amiel enjoyed Gary Smith's adulation. Silently, he admired her skills in political argument – the legacy, she said, of those family debates in north London. As her self-confidence grew, she became the centre of attraction in student debates as a fiery supporter of neo-Marxism and Leon Trotsky. 'You don't know the difference between Trotsky and a hole in the ground,' laughed Zolf. Once their relationship had become established, Smith was untroubled by Amiel's frequent indifference towards him, even when she treated him like an imbecile. Gladly he satisfied her craving for cashmere sweaters, her enjoyment of expensive trips and, at the weekends, her desire to smoke pot and win at Monopoly. 'Sex is good with Barbara,' Smith confided, albeit that it invariably took place in the back of the car he borrowed from his parents – by no means an uncommon experience among their age group. Her thin waist and large, high breasts were breathtaking. 'If anything,' Smith murmured, 'Barbara needs breast reduction, they're so huge.' Many years later, Conrad Black was to make the same type of comment publicly. Smith had never met such a sexually experienced woman who frequently took the initiative. His placid temperament could easily cope with her dramatic, even histrionic moods, but while Amiel was vitriolic in criticising others, she was vulnerable to even friendly mocking of herself. In those helpless moments he provided the support she needed, especially during the weeks when she consulted the college psychiatrist about her hallucinations and her growing addiction to Codeine. A doctor prescribed Elavil, an antidepressant. 'The drug,' she wrote, 'was to be my undoing [and the cause of] my erratic emotional life . . . I never realised quite how drugged I was for those seven years.'[11]

Amiel's erratic life had started long before the summer of 1962, but that year was a landmark. Isaac Barnett, her grandfather, died and bequeathed her £400. She flew to London with Gary Smith to collect the money and see her family. In the new, exciting environment, Amiel's imagination let rip. Smith was under the mistaken impression that she had found her father's corpse after he committed suicide, and she suggested that she had been brought up as a Marxist, mixing with the Seiferts and Sedleys, the rich Jewish Communist families who lived in mansions in Hampstead, although neither family could recall her presence in their homes, or her being invited to their frequent parties. She would later recollect that she was met at Heathrow by 'my Maoist uncle's chauffeur', while Gary Smith recalls them taking a bus into the city and walking to a hotel.[12] The Amiels and the Buckmans recall trying their best to care for their niece whose innocence had, it seemed, been irretrievably lost. As a gesture of their consideration, her uncle Bernard Buckman suggested that she join the British delegation to that year's World Youth Festival in Helsinki, a Soviet-sponsored summer camp for Communist supporters. Amiel bade farewell to Gary Smith and set off, passing through the newly-built Berlin Wall, to compare the theory of Communism discussed at university in Toronto with the reality.

Eighteen years later, Amiel would assert that the Helsinki experience had immediately and fundamentally changed her political opinions, although the student who returned to Canada still spoke as a Marxist. The noticeable difference was her change of personality. The shy trepidation had been replaced by a flaunting of her sexual attractions. With her family's support, she did not need to work that summer. Instead she stayed with Florence Smith, Gary's aunt, while he continued to live with his parents.

Despite her growing dependence on the Smiths, Amiel's visit to Helsinki did bring about one basic change – she began to live a double life, which would continue until she married Conrad Black. She would travel to Montreal, moving in circles where people played with 'real drugs', and discovering that she got high on marijuana more quickly if she used a pipe. While apparently faithful to Gary Smith, she also enjoyed other sexual relations.[13] The Canadian idol of the era was Leonard Cohen, the brilliant, handsome poet and singer. Cohen's philosophy appealed to countless female admirers who flocked to the star in the hope of seducing him. Amiel suggests that she joined the queue. Cohen, she said, could offer women 'everything, except of course fidelity ... In his own terms he is not unfaithful to anyone because he cares for them all.' The poet's attitude towards free love and open relationships, while caring for all his lovers, appealed to Amiel's gypsy temperament.[14] 'The secret that Leonard shares with Casanova,' she would write, 'is the one that costs him dear: it is real desire.' Amiel showed the same unfaithfulness, but in her case it was to satisfy different requirements. She always needed a man, but hated relying on other people. Her dilemma was how to balance her dependence and her desire for independence. Unlike Cohen, she would not advertise her roaming, astutely compartmentalising her life.

Just after completing her final university examinations in 1963, Amiel opted for financial stability. 'I wrote a message under the seal of your degree,' she told Gary Smith, referring to a romantic gesture she had made while preparing the degree certificates in the university administrator's office. 'It's a love message,' she confided. Days later, at the end of a sexual session in Gary's father's car, she unexpectedly snapped, 'Let's get married.' Gary understood the reasons. Barbara was fed up with sex in the back of a car. She wanted a bed, security and, above all, money. Their first date for the ceremony was abandoned. 'We've got cold feet,' Gary told his parents. A few weeks later they were married in a rabbi's study in front of eight witnesses including her mother and Leonard Somes, Gary's parents and Larry Zolf. At the party afterwards in the Smiths' family apartment, Zolf pushed through gamblers, bookmakers and scam artists to ask a small man, 'Are you Meyer Lansky?' 'So what if I am?' he growled.

The newly married couple rented an apartment on Toronto's Spadina Road, and while Gary Smith began his career as a lawyer, Amiel was employed as a secretary and script assistant in the television section of CBC. Not long afterwards, there was a terrible shock. Harry Smith, having lost all his money gambling, was arrested with his brother and accused of fraud. Soon after, he was convicted and imprisoned. Instead of joining a stable Jewish family, Amiel had associated herself with criminals. It was not long before she realised that her decision to marry Gary Smith had been short-sighted. Domestic life with the modest lawyer was dull compared to the thrills at CBC, especially following her appearance on the cover of *Toronto Life* magazine. Increasingly, she returned home late and too tired for sex. Just nine months after their marriage she asked her husband, 'Do you know what I'm thinking?' 'I would not presume to know what's going on in your head,' replied Smith. 'This isn't working. I'm off.'

Late that night in summer 1964, George Jonas, a twenty-nine-year-old Hungarian émigré also employed by CBC, was driving along Spadina Road and spotted Amiel crossing the street, 'weighed down with more baggage than a ten-hand army mule'. 'Don't tell me,' said Jonas. 'You just robbed a dwelling and can't remember where you parked the getaway car.' 'Close,' she replied. 'I just split up with my husband.' 'Great,' said Jonas. 'Let's go have coffee.' 'Can't,' said Amiel. 'Have to unload all this stuff before seven. Call me tomorrow if you like.'[15]

Jonas, a right-wing intellectual, was an unusual character in Toronto. Alternately, he dressed in black leather and rode a motorcycle or assumed the mantle of a Central European, carrying a silver-headed cane as a prop to his hand-kissing and heel-clicking. In London or New York his act might have been ridiculed, but Amiel was attracted to the ambience of an East European intellectual's home filled with books, music and passionate arguments. Since her visit to Helsinki she had moved from the far left towards the political centre, and Jonas's fervent anti-Communism was appealing. For his part, Jonas said, 'I found her very attractive and thoroughly unpleasant.'[16] That was not a barrier to a relationship, and nor was Sylvie, Jonas's wife. Jonas and Amiel began an affair, although Amiel did not regard it as an exclusive attachment. She was now better fed and dressed, making her breasts appear larger. 'The bigger and more pronounced they are,' she would later write, 'the more attractive they are.'

Depending on her mood, she could appear flat-chested, while on other occasions the size of her breasts fuelled speculation about implants. 'I've got one thing you haven't got,' she boasted to male journalists vying for the same interview: 'cleavage.'[17] Shamelessly, she would ask a colleague for advice about something she had written, and while he read her pages, rest a breast on his shoulder. As she self-consciously walked through CBC's corridors like a queen with an entourage, her remarkable physique excited drooling and gossip. At parties, men were mesmerised by her sexuality. 'Holding her thin waist was so erotic, so powerful,' sighed one admirer. Some of her relationships ended with her 'seeing stars' after being hit by a boyfriend;[18] one ended in an abortion;[19] but almost invariably her men, including cameraman Ed Long, discovered that after one night, they were forgotten the following morning. Long's attempt to seek an explanation was spurned by Amiel, who turned her back as he approached. 'I could cope with three men a week at CBC,' she would later jokingly tell a boyfriend. 'Each man was satisfied with two nights, and that left me one night to wash my hair.'

'She's gorgeous,' announced Ross McLean, regarded as CBC's most brilliant producer. Moses Znaimer, another producer, agreed that Amiel, who was then employed as a secretary by Perry Roseman on *The Way It Is*, a current affairs programme, should be turned into a star. Glamour photographs were distributed to promote the new celebrity interviewer. Her debut was not a success. The autopsies of Amiel's on-screen abilities were merciless. 'She comes across as affected but not stylish,' said one producer. 'She's too guarded, not sharing her personality with the audience. She's not a natural.' Another senior producer agreed: 'Her fine-boned chiselled features make her attractive but you can't take her seriously.' 'Too nervous and lacks gravitas,' concluded a third, who carped that her prominence had been won by manipulating Ross McLean. Unexpectedly, Amiel's overt sexuality had undermined her professional ambitions. Producers were reluctant to use a woman whose appearance and manner were distracting. The struggle for success increased her insecurity, although initially she ignored her failure. 'All in all, I learned to be a reasonably smart-ass interviewer,' she would recall in self-praise.[20] Appearing in a 1966 TV satire as a bikini-clad temptress of Eddie Shack, a wild ice-hockey player, did not enhance her image as a serious journalist.[21] Her on-screen career was in jeopardy. In her search for blame she would admit that she had been 'too self-conscious', and she later conceded that her appearance as 'a lacquered apparition with bouffant hair, glazed smile and detachment bordering on the unconscious, often reinforced by the mandatory dosage of Elavil', was not a winner.[22] But the real cause of her misfortune, she decided, was a CBC 'syndrome' that excluded 'non-leftists' from appearing on the channel. Although it was not a full left-wing 'conspiracy', she said there was a prejudice against her anti-Communism. She also perceived another bias. 'I'm unhappy with my nose,' she told Claire Weisman, an artist who was temporarily answering telephones in the building, 'and I'm having it fixed.' Weisman was surprised. 'Why?' she asked. 'Haven't you noticed it?' said Amiel. 'Noticed what?' 'You're Jewish, aren't you?' 'Yes.' 'Haven't you noticed the anti-Semitism here?' 'No,' replied Weisman. 'Absolutely not.'

Amiel had long been unhappy about the shape of her nose. Variously described as 'Roman' or 'soft Jewish', it curved gently down, whereas she wanted the 'turned-up' nose prevalent among the gentile, white Anglo-Saxon community. She confided her dissatisfaction to George Bloomfield, a gregarious CBC producer whom she had 'spotted' a year earlier. Soon after introducing herself, she rented a flat in Bloomfield's block in Toronto's High Park, and a few weeks later she moved into his apartment. 'I don't like my nose,' she had repeated for a year. 'It's a perfect nose,' replied Bloomfield mechanically, but eventually he agreed to pay for the surgery. The doctor produced a nose described by Bloomfield as 'pug' and by Larry Zolf, now also employed at CBC, as a 'button nose' and 'an insult to the Jewish people. Amiel was ashamed of the perfectly good Jewish nose she had. Now she looks like a crazed Shirley Temple.'[23] Amiel's depression intensified. 'It'll improve,' the surgeon assured her. Frequently plunging into her handbag to take pills, Amiel set off to California as senior CBC producer Eric Koch's script assistant to film a documentary, *Culture Explosion*. 'She's a bright, moody Jewish girl cursed by her mental fragility,' concluded Koch, who became disenchanted with Amiel at a family dinner hosted by his brother. 'I'm not feeling well,' she announced, clearly bored. 'Take me home.' 'Out of the question,' Koch replied, outraged by her selfish behaviour towards his family. 'Sit down.' Refusing to obey, Amiel asked a member of the film crew to drive her to her hotel. Clearly she was prepared to live only on her terms. She had, Koch heard, walked out of concerts if a more exciting alternative sprang to mind.

Back in Toronto in 1968, George Bloomfield was preparing to move to New York and make feature films. One night he and Amiel were disturbed by the doorbell. Bloomfield stumbled out of bed. 'Who is it?' he asked. 'Telegram,' said the voice. Bloomfield opened the door, and was pushed aside by Gary Smith. Finding his way into the bedroom, Smith saw Amiel. He then left. Soon after, Amiel's mother and stepfather visited the flat for an unemotional but civilised reconciliation. The ghosts of her 'wild years' were being interred. To break from her past, she decided to abandon CBC and move with Bloomfield to New York. 'I'm a camp follower,' she admitted.[24] Soon after their arrival she found a nose surgeon used by Hollywood's stars. Bloomfield agreed to pay for the second operation. This time she declared the result 'great'.

Life in New York suited Amiel. Bloomfield was fun, and paid for all her needs. 'Ten seconds after waking up,' he recalled, 'we'd both be laughing.' She began to read voraciously, stretching her intellect. Unlike in Toronto, she was surrounded by the 'chic world' of film celebrities, and came eagerly close to anti-Vietnam war and pro-feminist agitators, notably Jane Fonda and Alan Alda, who were working with Bloomfield. Hovering around Fifth Avenue, she watched the rich buy furs and jewellery, envious of how they recognised each other and could 'trade fashion names and tips'.[25] At length, she justified to Bloomfield her considerable expenditure of his money on exclusive brands: 'You've got to have the right belt, purse, shoes and scarf. The dress doesn't matter.' Her easy-going manner, friendliness towards everyone, and willingness to engage in any fantasy Bloomfield suggested in their bedroom, suggested a happy woman. Unseen by others, however, there was another side.

The prescription of the antidepressant Elavil, described by Amiel as 'my undoing', had neutralised her sense of responsibility. 'Nothing was my fault,' she recalled, because 'everything is socially or chemically determined'.[26] Drugs, Bloomfield complained, had become a routine part of his girlfriend's life. Screaming in her face, he discovered, grabbed her attention. 'When you take drugs you look just like your mother,' he shouted at her. Amiel stood silently, pushing both wrists upwards. Like make-up, the image of the independent and tough woman evaporated, replaced by a vulnerable individual requiring direction to cope with her confused emotions.

Bloomfield would be editing his latest film with Alan Alda in London, where the producers were providing a luxury flat near Buckingham Palace for three months. Amiel was excited. Since her own career as a freelance writer had ground to a near halt, the change would be stimulating. Her relationship with Bloomfield was friendly but no longer passionate. She could use the trip to develop her skills as a hostess. In anticipation of dinner parties, she invested heavily in weighing scales, cooking dishes, recipe books and measuring spoons. To the surprise of Lazlo Kovacs, a guest at one of her London dinner parties, she wore a stopwatch around her neck. Anxiously she watched the seconds tick away. 'Quick, finish your plate,' she urged, 'the next course is coming.' Everyone, including Bloomfield, would recall the fuss rather than the meal.

Life in London offered a good chance for Amiel to renew her relations with the Buckmans, especially Irene, her father's older sister, and Peter, her cousin. 'Do you think it's too scandalous?' she asked, modelling a revealing bikini in front of Peter Buckman. Did her choice, she was anxious to know, defy the propriety expected of a Jewish princess? Buckman assured her that she looked beautiful. Meeting the Buckmans was fun, especially Uncle Bernard, the businessman and property developer. 'You're very proud of him, aren't you?' said Bloomfield. Amiel nodded. Her uncle's large house in Hampstead, the country home he had bought his son, his own houses on the Côte d'Azur and in St Moritz, his big car and a suspected Swiss bank account excited a woman who wanted wealth but also remained committed to some socialist ideals. In one respect, Bernard Buckman was a mini-idol for both George and Barbara. During his many business trips to China he had met Mao Tse-tung and Chou En-lai, the Communist leaders, whom they both venerated. Plaintively, Amiel urged Bernard Buckman to negotiate Mao's approval of a film which would feature Edgar Snow, the author of *Red Star Over China*, a eulogy of Mao's revolutionary war. Bloomfield would be the producer. Buckman agreed, but Snow's death terminated the plan. Amiel's disappointment revealed no suggestion of disapproval of her uncle's profitable combination of business and politics.

Amiel's return to Toronto in 1972 was auspicious. She started writing for local magazines, a divorce was arranged with Gary Smith, who cited her adultery with Bloomfield, and she began searching for a new life after what Bloomfield would later call 'five aimless years'. By then her sexual relations with Bloomfield were rare. He was focused on his work, and was unconcerned whether she was sleeping with other men. He had steadfastly ignored her desire for children. In need of a man, Amiel approached George Jonas to resume their relationship. Her politics were shifting sharply to the right, she needed intellectual stimulation and a totally different life. By living with Jonas, she could concentrate far more on her own work.

George Jonas had been living for several years with Beverley Slopen, a literary agent. Amiel's appearance in their apartment did not immediately alarm Slopen. She knew Amiel as 'a hypochondriac who George might take for a weekend to the Bahamas but could not afford to take shopping'. She did not anticipate that Amiel would provoke a very public split between her and Jonas, after which Amiel returned to her apartment in Chestnut Park Road. 'I've decided to leave,' she told Bloomfield calmly. Bloomfield was not surprised. 'Found someone else?' he asked. 'I'm going back to George,' said Amiel. That news did shock Bloomfield. How, he wondered, after five years living with supporters of the feminist and anti-war movements, could she live with such a right-wing man? He never received an answer. Soon after, Bloomfield was called by Jonas and invited to meet at the Coffee Mill, his favourite Hungarian restaurant. According to Bloomfield, while they spoke Jonas took out a gun and showed it under the table. 'I can't live without her,' said Jonas. 'Don't try to take her away.' Jonas describes Bloomfield's scenario as 'ludicrous, the invention of a film producer'. Whatever the truth of the matter, the emotions of twenty-five years previously are evidently undiminished.

In her new life Amiel worked frantically, laboriously writing acclaimed magazine articles on various social issues throughout the night, carefully choosing each word in her efforts to express original opinions in a cautious climate. Simultaneously, she re-emerged as a popular television pundit to disparage Marxism, feminism and Canada's dependency culture. Trading on the image of a sexy intellectual, she showed off bruises at a dinner party and declaimed, 'Sex is no good without pain.' Together with Jonas she posed as a star with brains and beauty, charm and attitude. Those unconvinced by her self-education during her years with Bloomfield credited Jonas as her Svengali, dubbing her 'the finest second-hand mind in Canada'. This further eroded her self-confidence, already undermined by the painful withdrawal symptoms after she had given up Elavil. She became fearful of cancer and other illnesses. Her critics spoke of borderline narcissism – which she interpreted as evidence of her growing importance.

Living with Jonas, a poet, journalist and political philosopher, was ideal for an aspiring writer. In October 1974, having discovered that Jonas was also Jewish, she announced, 'I've made an appointment with the local rabbi.' They were to marry later that month, in a synagogue, with only six guests. Over the following months Amiel's self-confidence soared. Although she voiced a fear of being disliked, and hesitantly dismissed her urge for children as premature, she asserted absolute certainty about her political convictions. Having shed her last vestige of sympathy for compassionate government, she placed herself in the vanguard of the cause of restoring red-blooded capitalism to socialistic Canada.

Peter Newman, the mercurial editor of *Maclean's*, Canada's only popular political magazine, was impressed by Amiel's right-wing, anti-authoritarian, iconoclastic criticism of modern fads. In 1966 she had written an astutely argued article, 'Let's Reinstate Debtors' Prisons', for the magazine, advocating that debtors who failed to pay their bills should be imprisoned.[27] Ten years later Marci McDonald, a star columnist, resigned, and there was a vacancy. 'Marci was a bitch,' said Newman admiringly, 'but we've got a bigger bitch to take her place.' Amiel's extreme conservatism, he calculated, would attract profitable controversy.

National prominence enhanced Amiel's visible self-confidence. 'She was the sort of woman,' Newman noted, 'who kept spilling out of her dresses, then blamed the dresses.'[28] Her response to those who whispered about implants was savvy. 'If I used silicone,' she told Newman, 'my breasts would be twice as big. I don't do things by halves.'[29] Fame and independence sparked her weariness with Jonas. Marrying a Jew, she discovered, was not such a good idea after all. His emotional needs were too similar to her own, and rather than partying, he preferred staying at home. Jonas was not the first man to discover the truth of her confession, 'I'm polyandrous.' One man could not satisfy her. She was constantly propositioned by men and women, married and single. The ferociously heterosexual Amiel wanted to experiment with most kinds of relationships and sexual antics.

Hanging around the *Maclean's* office late one evening towards the end of 1976, Amiel noticed Peter Brimelow, the magazine's handsome twenty-nine-year-old business editor, born in Lancashire, England. Drawing on her consummate experience, she made signals to encourage his approach. The long dark hair and green eyes of the seductress who had just been named 'Canada's most beautiful woman' by a magazine was irresistible to the younger journalist, unaware of the licentious world he was entering.

'I've got to go for an appointment,' Amiel often told Jonas, with whom she was writing *By Persons Unknown*, a prospective non-fiction bestseller about a Canadian businessman who hired killers to murder his wife, a fashion model. In great secrecy she visited Brimelow's flat. If she went away overnight, Jonas believed she was travelling on an assignment. Her infidelity evoked no crisis of conscience. As with her other relationships, Amiel's self-indulgence was to please her latest admirer. 'You're a luxury,' she told Brimelow in bed. 'You're of no use to me other than for sex and passion.' Bites and scratches were his badges of her eroticism.

'What makes people good lovers,' she later reflected, 'is not their sexual technique but their sexual being. Extremes of ineptitude aside, it is not how a man touches you, but who the man is that determines your sexual response.'[30] The rawness was her attraction: 'No matter how many times the act is performed, one is still in awe of its potential . . . whether it is done for love or for money, for spite of for kicks, the sexual act remains the key to our entire being.'[31] Whether fooling around with Brimelow, joking about another affair with a Hungarian bankrobber who 'stored gelignite under my bed', or mimicking mutual friends, Amiel blessed her eternal youth. 'I'll never get old,' she said. 'That's a battle I'll never lose.' The chilling implication was her preference for death rather than looking at a wrinkled face in the mirror. Inevitably, the relationship bore a cost. Brimelow was not the first to discover that losing one's heart to Amiel meant a loss of self-control, and she enjoyed witnessing helplessness in her men. Lying in bed with Brimelow early on New Year's Eve in 1976, she knew that later, while she was celebrating with her husband, Brimelow would be partying with a girlfriend. Seized by a mixture of insecurity and fury at her inability to control Brimelow, she dug the nails of both hands deeply into his chest, drawing blood. Brimelow's girlfriend, Amiel smiled, would get the message.

Hard work, stylish writing, deep thought, exceptional looks and unconventional opinions had transformed Barbara Amiel into the nation's conservative star. Describing herself with relish as a 'very merchandisable' right-wing pundit or 'the redneck in a Givenchy dress', she invited notoriety and a reputation for bitchiness as the Jew who criticised Israel, the advocate of personal responsibility and the critic of equal-opportunity politics.[32] Without loyalty or deference to the Canadian establishment, the outsider reproached the natives. While pouting about her need for privacy, revelations about her sentiments in *Maclean's* became the cornerstone of her journalistic shock. Like many celebrity pundits, she occasionally confused intelligence with wisdom. Her prominence transformed a spat with the Ontario Human Rights Commission after she described Germans during the First and Second World War as 'Huns' into a national debate. 'You'd have saved us a lot of trouble,' said Newman, 'if you'd called them "Sauer Krauts".' To Newman's surprise, Amiel burst into tears. 'She's a woman without a sense of humour about herself,' the editor concluded,[33] puzzled by her insistence that 'harsh words can't harm me'.[34] Her sensitivity did not always extend to thoughtfulness about others. Careless about the magazine's schedules, she delivered articles with trembling hands at the editorial office after the deadline, clutching her head to relieve the pain of giving birth to a masterpiece, and awaited the applause. 'A drama queen,' concluded Peter Newman, 'and a whining pest over each lost comma and adjective.' For sympathy, she constantly telephoned Peter Brimelow. Even in the middle of the night she required an audience to hear about her work, her upsets and the praise she had attracted.

The relationship between Amiel and Brimelow was intense, yet to Brimelow's despair she would not abandon Jonas. In revenge, Brimelow began an affair with Amiel's assistant Dia, an attractive Anglo-Indian. 'You're having her, aren't you?' screamed Amiel. 'How could you?' Brimelow was unapologetic. Amiel refused to leave Jonas, he retorted, so why could he not also have an affair? Walking a tightrope, Amiel justified her own infidelity while condemning her lover's.

In early 1979, Brimelow accepted a job in Washington, where his latest girlfriend, called Maggie, lived. In recent weeks he had described Maggie to Amiel as a potential wife. Amiel was given a choice. If their relationship was to survive, she would have to leave Toronto and her husband. Still undecided, she arrived at Brimelow's flat with her sister Ruth. After Ruth's departure, Amiel remained to say farewell. In bed, she announced a game of noughts and crosses on Brimelow's chest. Her scratch marks were deep, the blood oozed. She knew that Maggie would understand.

A transitional moment in Amiel's life had arrived. She was still married to Jonas, but she visited Brimelow three times in Washington, and at the same time started an affair with Sam Blyth, thirteen years younger than herself, and with similar looks to Brimelow's. After two months, her decision was final. 'It's time to see Sam,' she told a friend. She abandoned her husband and long-time lover, and moved into Blyth's dilapidated Toronto home. The dalliance, she reckoned, would extricate herself from her marriage. Handsome, charming and poor, Sam Blyth offered new excitement. 'A big adventure,' said Amiel. 'A lot of fun, like a journey in a big cookie jar.'[35] Brimelow took the news calmly, while Jonas was distressed about no longer meeting Amiel's requirements. 'She was not a housewife,' he said, 'and I am not a house-husband. We agreed what we should do is find a wife, for both of us.'[36] Jonas soon recovered. 'How would you like to go to Paris for breakfast?' he asked a Korean woman managing a restaurant. They eventually married.

Amid that hiatus Amiel began writing *Confessions*, her autobiography, a mixture of political polemic and attention-seeking striptease. 'I am a wandering Jew,' she wrote. 'I always have my toothbrush handy. My allegiance is not to any piece of earth or particular set of rock outcroppings. My allegiance is to ideas, and most especially to the extraordinary idea of individual liberty . . . My suitcase is packed. I do not feel bound to any country or any popular will more than to my own conscience.'[37] In an article published simultaneously in the magazine *Chatelaine* called 'Nothing Succeeds Like Excess', she confessed to being a shameless, self-promoting exhibitionist who enjoyed intellectual domination. Her critics unfairly classified such confessions as proof of the 'borderline personality disorder' suffered by attention-seeking addicts, or narcissism. Amiel's sophisticated political arguments, however, protected the book from ridicule when it was published in 1980.

Rescuing Canada from socialism and 'the spiritual and moral bankruptcy into which it has fallen' was the heart of Amiel's cause.[38] Like Conrad Black, she condemned the *Globe and Mail* and the Liberal government of Pierre Trudeau for distorting the policies of anti-Marxists and conservatives. The Liberal 'thought police', she wrote, were conducting a 'witch-hunt' against those championing the individual against the state. She railed against the bureaucrats promoting political correctness, multi-culturalism and the conditions of working women, and their fellow travellers who were championing sexual harassment prosecutions, denigrating prostitutes, inventing child abuse as a political weapon, lamenting men's abuse of the clitoris and generally suppressing opportunities. Her black cleaner in New York, she complained, had refused to move out of a poor neighbourhood and seek a better education for her children because she expected improvements to be brought to her at public expense.[39] The Canadian media and political establishment, she protested, were deliberately concealing the horrors in China and the Soviet Union. Forgetting her former support for the anti-Vietnam war movement, she confessed to having 'little sympathy or respect for draft-dodgers', and 'loathed the sight of pretend-moralists'.[40] She was, she wrote, thrilled that Jane Fonda had been arrested by US Customs for carrying drugs which turned out to be Codeine given to her by Amiel for a headache. 'I was filled with a warm glow,' she wrote. 'It was my contribution to the war effort.'[41]

Confessions also included a florid description of Amiel's English roots. After interviewing most of her family during her stay in London in 1971, she described herself as born into a family of British Marxists. The exaggeration justified what she admitted were 'snide remarks' about Bernard Buckman. In ungrateful language, she condemned her uncle as an unprincipled, rich hypocrite, living in his big, sunlit Hampstead home where 'the clichés bounced off the cut crystal' while indulging in 'wilful blindness' about China and the Soviet Union's repression and bloodshed.[42] One assertion which hurt the Buckmans was that the family was 'financed by mainland China'.[43] 'She's abused our hospitality and twisted the family history,' Bernard Buckman told his wife Irene. 'Forgive her,' urged Irene, uneasy about her niece's mistreatment by the Amiels. But even Irene was puzzled by Barbara's inaccurate reconstruction of her background in her attempt to prove her new values. In a book extolling the importance of a journalist's honesty, complained Irene, Barbara's inventions were surprising.

The contrast between Amiel writing her book in Sam Blyth's unkempt home, even wearing a coat when the electricity was cut off, and her personal credo was notable. 'I knew what I wanted,' she wrote about her time in London in 1971. 'To be dropped at Selfridges's or Harrods to pick up fresh salmon and search for quails' eggs,' besides taking lessons to be a hostess and sharing a masseur with Lady Weidenfeld.[44] She had become envious of the Canadian jet set's use of private planes, 'clubby travellers wafting across borders with sleek impunity', living 'our fantasies'. Her reality check was a conviction that those birds of paradise had no 'durability' and that few would survive.[45]

More revealing, considering her future conduct as Lady Black, was her attitude towards materialism. 'The true spirit of liberalism,' she wrote, 'simply judges everyone on his or her own merit . . . We are all responsible for ourselves. That is not callous. That is liberation.'[46] Transgressors, she warned, would be punished: 'Greed can be held in check by ordinary criminal laws.'[47] Her most pertinent comment, in the light of Conrad Black's problems twenty-three years later, was her reproach, in *Maclean's*, of John Dean, Richard Nixon's dishonest legal adviser in the White House during the Watergate scandal. Amiel was scathing about Dean's 'moral myopia' as a party to the President's cover-up. Instead of accepting personal responsibility for his conduct, she wrote, he 'still clings to the soothing thought that it was all somebody else's fault', blaming 'the environment [for his crimes] rather than a person's own morality'.[48]

In January 1981, soon after the book's publication, Amiel and Blyth visited Mozambique. She wanted to witness the damage wreaked by Western aid on native agriculture while sustaining Marxist regimes. The journey ended in embarrassment. Attempting to enter the country without visas, they were arrested and imprisoned for some days. She would later claim to have eaten her press pass to avoid recognition. 'That would have been difficult,' said Peter Newman. 'It's plastic.' Others quipped that the hardest bit to swallow would have been Newman's signature, or her own. Amiel's plight, and her melodramatic plea that her life was in danger, provoked anger from the Canadian ambassador, who was irritated by her behaviour, and from rival journalists. But Peter Worthington, the editor of the *Toronto Sun*, was surprised by the apparent jealousy. 'She's sailing through life like the Spanish Armada,' he said, apparently unaware that the Armada was destroyed by the English navy and a storm. Amiel's values and humour, he decided, were ideal for his newspaper. On her return she was appointed a columnist on the *Sun*, and her life became even more hectic.

Living in squalor with Blyth while renting a comfortable apartment in Forest Hill, she wrote regularly about her abortion, her drugs, her family feuds and her love life. Playing the Jewish card, the impoverished Jew became the aggrieved Jew championing prejudice. Her private life became as varied as her writing. 'I've got this penchant for young men,' she told a girlfriend. Blyth became just one of several young boyfriends, including twenty-four-year-old journalist Daniel Richler, whom she met during a radio debate. Their affair began soon afterwards. Arguing and laughing in restaurants, Amiel was carefree about her reputation. Just a month after starting the relationship with Richler, there was a silence followed by a sigh during a telephone conversation. 'This isn't going anywhere,' she declared. The relationship was over. Her 'penchant' was for other young men, including Eric Margolis, a freelance journalist specialising in the Middle East whom she met at a lunch hosted by one of her many admirers. The host's misfortune was that Amiel, impressed by Margolis's charm and expertise about Islam, decided to pursue him. 'I'm coming over,' she announced in a telephone call. 'I've got another date,' replied Margolis. But finally he succumbed, and discovered what he called 'an Act of God', Amiel's breasts. To her irritation, Margolis was too independent, frequently rejecting her suggestions that she visit his flat. 'Is there someone else there tonight?' she asked. If Margolis answered 'Yes,' she was sufficiently liberal to cope. But if he replied 'No, I'm working, babe,' she became incensed, repeatedly calling, seeking to change his mind. 'You're like one of the boys,' laughed Margolis.

At the age of forty-one, Amiel had reached a crossroads. Fearing loneliness, she was seeking marriage in order to have children and embed her social and professional ambitions. Margolis, she decided, was ideal to give her life that structure. He was intelligent, independent and good fun. Frustratingly, he did not show the obedience she liked in her men, and was patently weary that she always wanted to win her point. Amiel could not resist bickering that he should be rich and famous. A fraught ten-day trip to Hong Kong and China ended with her demand, 'Marry me!' 'No,' he replied, 'I'd end up in jail.' 'Why?' she asked. 'Because I'd wring your neck.' Amiel did not give up her marital ambitions despite an overture from a new admirer. In 1983 Peter Worthington offered her the editorship of the *Toronto Sun*'s comment section. She would, Worthington believed, succeed as the newspaper's ambassador for ideological conservatism, providing a public profile on

TV shows to attract the Thatcherites among Canada's East European migrants. To celebrate her appointment she was taken by Doug Creighton, the *Sun*'s publisher, to Winston's. There are two versions of what followed during the lunch.

In the first version, Creighton asked Amiel in a loud voice, 'Are you fucking Peter?' The restaurant fell silent to hear the answer. Amiel jumped up and ran to the lavatory. According to the second version, Creighton kept naming Worthington. 'Why do you keep mentioning Worthington?' Amiel asked. 'Well, he was your predecessor, he hired you, and he trained you as editor. I'm just trying to say he's gone.' Waiting for a moment of silence, Amiel screeched, 'You think I'm fucking him, don't you?' Creighton was nonplussed, but replied, 'Yes.' 'Well,' she said, 'I'm not.' Worthington's explanation of the exchange is benign: 'Doug was mesmerised by her. She dazzled him. He was persuaded that she was a bombshell.'

Worthington issued the invitations to Amiel's appointment party: 'The *Sun* has a new editor. It's a girl.' Transfixed by Amiel, Worthington became unhappy that Eric Margolis was asked by Amiel to edit the comment section in her absence. The triangle could lead to the farce of Worthington calling at Amiel's flat while she was at Margolis's. There was gossip that on one occasion Amiel was standing outside Margolis's flat, waiting for another woman to leave, while Worthington stood outside Amiel's flat, waiting for her to return. Amiel's eccentric personal life and odd hours spread into the editorial newsroom. Either she arrived dressed in a chocolate-brown velour tracksuit, looking harassed with unkempt hair and sunglasses, or she appeared as carefully groomed as a *Vogue* model. 'Either a bag lady or a $1 million outfit,' commented Worthington. On one occasion she strode purposefully past Christie Blatchford, one of Canada's notable columnists, wearing an 'open trenchcoat, under which could be clearly seen a black bustier, garter belt and fishnet stockings'.

Amiel's gyrating moods were experienced by Allan Fotheringham, another columnist and an occasional boyfriend, during a trip to Vancouver. After flying 3,000 miles to a gathering of theologians, Amiel felt inclined to shock. Ten minutes after arriving at the party, Fotheringham was surprised to hear her shrill 'Fuck!', followed minutes later by a loud 'Cocksuckers!' Soon after, the two were standing alone in the garden. The theologians had fled into the house.

By 1984 Amiel's limitations as an editor were causing even Worthington unease. While she was appreciated by some women journalists as an intellectual, fun, right-wing babe, Worthington marked her down as 'a dangerous writer'. She was, he decided, 'not an original thinker but a clear thinker. She marshals other people's ideas and then personalises them. She knows how to get under people's skin and find their Achilles heel.' That talent was inadequate when the news broke of Britain's response to Argentina's invasion of the Falklands in April 1982. Amiel needed guidance about 'our line'. Repeatedly she tried to call Worthington, who was out of reach climbing mountains in China. In desperation, she telephoned George Jonas. 'I'm against the British,' said Jonas. So that was the *Toronto Sun*'s line, and Jonas was given a column as a poet and later as a commentator. Amiel's attitude did not inspire loyalty. 'Her people skills are not great,' sighed Worthington. 'She's focusing on people she likes, and she's not happy working in the background instead of the spotlight.'

Amiel had reached yet another crossroads. Margolis, she decided, was a *bon vivant*, uninterested in commercial success. The relationship, she concluded, just like her other concurrent affairs, was pointless. In 1982 she had met David Graham, the good-looking, rich stepbrother of Ted Rogers, Canada's leading communications mogul. Four years older than Amiel, Graham represented upper-class wealth from the Ottawa Valley. Relationships with WASP businessmen, she decided, were less complicated than with men of mixed European backgrounds. 'A relatively simple person,' she would write, 'can be a very attractive quality in a lover.' By 'simple' she did not mean 'unintelligent', just not 'psychologically complex'. Complexity, she decided, 'is an awful pain in the neck in lovers. It can create mood swings, whining and sometimes meanness [because] good lovers paradoxically want to please no one but themselves.'[49] Graham was, she decided, uncomplicated, and therefore a good lover. To keep everyone on their toes, she introduced the new to the old. Margolis met Graham, and smiled his lack of concern. Amiel chose Graham, not suspecting that twenty years later Margolis would own a multi-million dollar vitamin company with over three hundred employees. 'I'm hankering for David,' she told a friend. Committing herself to Graham reflected her desperation for domesticity and a child.

Graham, renowned for his many relationships with glamorous women, wanted a home-maker in London, but was casually unspecific about his other requirements. A beautiful, intelligent woman was appealing, but marrying a forty-four-year old Jewish libertine who paraded her 'erratic emotional life', implying sexual promiscuity, was an untested experience. At least there was good reason to believe that Amiel had abandoned her pose as an opinionated, left-wing hippie. Recently she had praised the virtues of wealth and comfort. 'I so loathe the permissive, promiscuous society,' she had written, 'and so long for fidelity, stability and monogamy, but it is always just out of my reach. There is a thing called discipline. I have tried to inflict it on my work. I've tried to inflict it on me. But all that emerges is self-indulgence. Really, I won't talk about my personal life, because I am ashamed of it.'[50]

One minor forewarning for Graham of the perils of cohabiting with Amiel occurred at the wedding of Roy Faibish, a Canadian television producer and political adviser, at Chelsea Register Office in London. Amiel arrived with Graham, and met the CBC

TV producer Patrick Watson with his girlfriend Caroline. 'She's so cute,' said Amiel. 'You've been together for some years. I always marry the men I sleep with.' This carping comment to someone who was familiar with Amiel's career at CBC provoked a blistering argument in front of thirty guests. Graham noted his fiancée's independent spirit. Unlike other women, she had achieved fame on her own account, without depending on a rich husband's wealth. Marrying her would not expose him to a financial liability – in fact she could be generous – but harnessing her strong character would be a challenge .

On 2 July 1984, while visiting Nantucket, off the coast of Massachusetts, Barbara Amiel and Graham married. Soon after the ceremony, Graham was badly injured in a car crash in France. After his recovery Amiel decided to celebrate the marriage again in Toronto, and to host a party at the Sutton Place Hotel.

No man in '33 Stop', the hotel's summit banqueting room, could have appeared to be less attractive to Barbara Amiel than Conrad Black. The two had met in 1979, at a dinner party in Toronto hosted by Black's friend John Bassett, and had since discovered that they shared conservative opinions. The eventual union of two insecure Canadians dreaming of glamour, fame and fortune among the jet set could have been predicted by no one.

4

Salvation

Conrad Black drove away from Barbara Amiel's wedding party in a bad mood. Having agreed to give Allan Fotheringham a lift in his limousine, he discovered that his companion was drunk. He didn't like Fotheringham. The journalist had a habit of telling the truth about the aspiring press tycoon, and one truth was that Black's finances were not in good shape. He was determined that in the future he would have his revenge. 'As [Fotheringham] stepped out of the car,' Black would write years later, 'he fell flat in front of the doorman.' Although the story was denied by Fotheringham, Black ordered his editor to run it anyway: 'Let him sue.'[1]

Black disliked most journalists. Their 'sanctimonious and tendentious' assertion of independence while greedily grabbing his dollars was as irksome as their refusal to accept his own judgement of himself. In public testimony he had once damned journalists as 'a very degenerate group. There is a terrible incidence of alcoholism and drug abuse.' Since then, his contempt had increased as he and David Radler struggled to build a newspaper business.

The original $500 investment in the *Knowlton Advertiser* in 1966 had grown into the American Publishing Company. The slender profits depended upon Radler's constant criss-crossing of the country searching for savings and imposing cuts, and monitoring the financial results on a primitive central computer. Radler's gospel never changed: 'Count the chairs,' he habitually ordered. Halving the number of employees was his familiar recipe, regardless of the consequences for the newspaper's quality. Having exhausted the search in Canada, the two men began scouring America for small community newspapers with circulations as low as 5,000. In particular they wanted free shopping publications, weekly and community newspapers enjoying monopolies and a lot of advertising. By 1986 they owned eighty daily newspapers in thirty states, and fantasised about creating an empire to rival the two Goliaths, the *Washington Post* and the *New York Times*. In the meantime Black would have been satisfied with Toronto's *Globe and Mail*, but he had recently been outbid by Ken Thomson, not least because under Black's control the newspaper would have been made to reflect his conservative opinions. 'I hate its leftish, pompous tenor and the editor's smarmy pretensions,' he had said. Ever since, the *Globe*'s journalists, he believed, had been unfairly scrutinising his business. He heard that the newspaper's editors were planning an article describing 'a rapacious, right-wing Bay Street baron' who 'milked' his businesses, 'destroyed public companies' and oppressed minority shareholders 'in a series of complex corporate shuffles designed primarily to fill his own coffers'.

Throughout his life, Black had cared little for the working classes. Politicians, he believed, should encourage and protect the rich rather than mollycoddle the poor. His true colours had been shown at Massey-Ferguson, and in 1985 he expressed similar ire against the employees of Dominion Stores. Radler's attempt to revive the supermarket chain had failed. Selling the whole company to one buyer had proved impossible. The shabby supermarkets, Black knew, could only be sold piecemeal and the workers given compensation for losing their jobs. He blamed the staff for his predicament. Accusing them of gross larceny, he sniped in public, 'Lobsters are walking out of my stores.' The suggestion of theft was akin to throwing fuel on the fire, but Black enjoyed watching the effect of his provocation. 'I'll win,' he told a friend, 'because I say these things in such an erudite way.' His verbal assault disguised the true reasons for the sale. Ravelston's debts had risen to C$150 million, and the banks were pressing for repayment of loans worth C$40 million advanced to Dominion. Some whispered that Black was on the verge of bankruptcy.[2] His salvation, he decided, was the Dominion Stores pension fund. To profit from the company's sale, he anticipated using much of the fund's C$62 million surplus for redundancy payments and to repay the company's loans, a potentially permissible if controversial move. With skilful negotiation, he persuaded the Pensions Commission of Ontario to authorise his appropriation of those funds.[3] The commission's approval provoked outrage among trade unions. 'He's the representative of bloated capitalism at its worst,' complained one prominent politician. Thrilled to engage in verbal combat, Black accused his critics of being 'a symbol of swinish, socialist demagoguery'. The trade unions sued the Pensions Commission, claiming that legal requirements were unfulfilled. At the *Globe and Mail* journalists began investigating Black's handling of his employees' pension fund. The article would conclude, 'He has been wrong when found with his hand near the cookie jar.'[4]

Black was once again a hate figure, and the banks were alarmed. Under pressure to sell his assets, including his private plane, he became ill, damaging his relations with his brother Monte, who was in the midst of an acrimonious divorce. Unexpectedly, Monte agreed to sell his equal interest in the business for $22.4 million, some suspected because he had proven to be unhelpful to his brother's schemes. Conrad later justified the transfer as a scheme to help Monte avoid a more expensive divorce settlement. Black raised the purchase money by mortgaging his homes in Palm Beach and Toronto. The comparatively small amount exposed the limited value of the Blacks' business. Their inheritance and the opportunities after the Argus coup had been squandered. Instead of glorying in his status as a global billionaire, Black was slithering along Bay Street sucking a lifeline.

Monte's replacement as finance director was John 'Jack' Boultbee, an aggressive tax planner.[5] 'Jack will bring some imagination to our accounts,' Black told a friend. Physically, Boultbee was hardly attractive. His hair was dyed black, his suits fitted badly over a paunch, and there were ugly gaps between his teeth. For professional rather than aesthetic reasons, he remained hidden from public view, known as 'the man behind the curtain'. After his appointment, Black and Radler made no decisions without Boultbee's scrutiny and approval. He became the brains behind all their schemes, and expected to be rewarded accordingly.

Jack Boultbee had little time to settle into his new position. A Canadian court overruled the Pensions Commission and ordered Black to return C$37.9 million to Dominion's pension funds. Simultaneously, Don Fullerton, the head of the Canadian Imperial Bank of Commerce, told Black, his friend and a fellow director, to repay a C$40 million loan. After selling his 41 per cent stake in Norcen for C$300 million to repay his debts, Black once again reassessed his business. Eight years after the Argus grab, everything had been sold except the collection of small newspapers. Some of Argus's shareholders complained about the fate of the company's assets, although Black denied any wrongdoing. Posing as the great capitalist entrepreneur, he had accomplished a vanishing trick, and everyone appeared to have lost money.

During 1985, with Radler and Boultbee's help, Black again restructured his business. In discussions between them, Boultbee offered 'scenarios' to produce profits and avoid taxes. Each one was offered to lawyers and accountants with a request: 'Will it play?' If approved, there was a professional's letter – a 'good housekeeping certificate' – giving the trio approval to proceed to the edge of legality. In the succession of complicated transactions,

Black once again appeared to his critics to have legitimately profited from asset stripping and insider dealing.[6] Sterling, the company controlling his newspapers in Canada, was sold to Hollinger, also owned by Black, for $37 million, which he took in Hollinger shares. Most of the cash ended up as management fees in Ravelston, his private company.

Those events had spurred the *Globe and Mail* to finally publish their investigation, under the headline 'Citizen Black: Can a Right-Wing Tycoon Buy his Way into the Press?'. Black did not appreciate the criticism. He blamed the 'Canadian spirit of envy' for failing to glorify tycoons like himself. With delight, he announced that he would sue the *Globe* to 'painfully punish' his critics by forcing them to prove that his dealings were dishonest. That hurdle, as the newspaper's lawyers soon discovered, would be more than difficult to surmount.

Black drew strength for his battle from the like-minded supporters of raw capitalism gathering in May 1985 for the Bilderberg Conference at Arrowhead, near New York. He regarded his fellow guests as close friends, akin to his family. Among them was Andrew Knight, the editor of the *Economist*. Knight was more than an intelligent, genial, successful editor. As a global networker, he was entrusted with indiscretions and secrets. 'Let's have another fiery Armagnac,' Black suggested. Over several drinks after midnight, Black confided his frustration at having failed to buy a major Canadian newspaper. Naturally, he omitted mentioning the distrust of himself in his own country. 'Canada's a backwater,' he complained. 'I sometimes wish I was an American and could own the *Washington Post*.' 'If you're looking for a big newspaper, Conrad,' replied Knight, in what would undoubtedly be the most decisive sentence ever uttered in Black's career, 'the *Daily Telegraph* might be a possible target.' Too much Armagnac had flowed for Knight to notice Black's reaction.

The *Telegraph* was among the world's most successful broadsheets, selling 1.2 million copies daily, 750,000 more than the London *Times* and 300,000 less than the *New York Times*. But the headline success disguised dire problems. The *Telegraph*'s sales were 300,000 lower than five years earlier, and the company was losing about £1 million a month. The reasons were painful. Compared to its rivals, the *Telegraph*'s advertising revenues had fallen steeply, and the trade unions were effectively blackmailing the company. Every year the employees hired to compose, print and distribute the newspaper were illicitly pocketing millions of pounds, either by threatening to strike just before the paper was due to be printed, or by signing on under names like 'Mickey Mouse' and disappearing to work in another newspaper or as taxi drivers. Within its decrepit headquarters in Fleet Street, the *Telegraph*'s ageing executives appeared helpless, and refused to recruit younger experts to stem the haemorrhage of money.

Isolating himself in a sanctum on the top floor of the *Telegraph*'s building was Lord Hartwell, formerly Michael Berry, the newspaper's seventy-five-year-old chairman and editor-in-chief. Abstemious and shy, Hartwell cared passionately about journalism, reading every word he published. His solution to the trade unions' theft was radical. Two modern printing plants were under construction in London's Docklands area and in Manchester. By using computers rather than traditional printing craftsmen, he could expel his dishonest employees from the industry forever. Hartwell's experts had estimated the modernisation would cost £130 million.

One aspect of the *Telegraph*'s poor management was the inaccurate accounts prepared by Coopers Lybrand, the auditors. Consistently, the company's costs were underestimated. The *Telegraph*'s drift towards insolvency had remained unnoticed until, halfway into the Docklands plant's construction, Hartwell was told that the building costs had increased by £89 million. Unperturbed, he asked his old friend Evelyn de Rothschild, the chairman of the merchant bank N.M. Rothschild, to find lenders on the market. Trusting the famous bankers to care for his interests, Hartwell approved Rothschild's prospectus to raise the money. The result was disappointing. A group of banks agreed to lend £50 million only if Hartwell provided a further £30 million. To Hartwell's surprise, by May 1985 he had found only £20 million. A further £10 million was needed before the loan could be secured. Sketchy rumours about Hartwell's plight had reached Andrew Knight before he flew to America for the Bilderberg Conference. He returned to London with the news of Black's enthusiastic interest.

Travelling on the Tube from Heathrow airport to London, Knight was surprised to read a *Times* report of the *Telegraph*'s failure to find sufficient money. He immediately telephoned Evelyn de Rothschild. 'I think Michael Richardson must have leaked it,' said Rothschild. Richardson was the bank's director responsible for raising the loan. Greedy and sly, Richardson would in later years find it difficult to prove his integrity, but in 1985 he was still trusted. 'We need another £10 million,' continued Rothschild, 'and can't find anyone.' 'Would any money be welcome?' asked Knight. 'Even from a North American?' 'I would see no problem,' replied Rothschild. By the next day, Knight had received the prospectus and other reports. 'Horrendous,' he muttered. At the outset, Richardson had failed to warn Hartwell that £130 million would be insufficient to build the new printing plants, and had subsequently refused to seek out other reputable investors.

Excited by the news, Knight telephoned Black. The time in Toronto was 8 a.m. on Monday, 20 May, and it was Victoria Day, a public holiday. Black was asleep, and to Knight's surprise refused to take the call until lunchtime. Knight interpreted that rebuff as an amusing idiosyncrasy rather than the lazy arrogance he would later perceive. For a fleeting moment he considered telephoning Katharine Graham, the impeccable owner of the *Washington Post* who would make an ideal proprietor of the *Telegraph*. The thought soon evaporated.

Once awake, Black rapidly understood his latest chance of taking advantage of another's distress. 'I'll fax you Rothschild's papers,' said Knight. 'I don't have a fax machine here,' replied Black. Noting his casualness, Knight sped to meet Lord Hartwell. 'Would you be prepared to accept a Canadian investor?' asked Knight. Trusting the emissary, Hartwell agreed to meet Black in New York. Knight was doubly delighted: first by Hartwell's eagerness, and second by Rothschild's failure to undertake any enquiries about Conrad Black's reputation and probity. Unbriefed, Hartwell flew by Concorde to New York on 28 May, under the mistaken assumption that the money was being offered by Conrad Ritblat, a London property developer. Behind him in the aircraft sat his directors and Michael Richardson, uncertain of his loyalties.

Conrad Black had not yet arrived when the group entered a scruffy suite in the Hilton Hotel at Kennedy airport. Twenty minutes later, he appeared. He was struck by the Dickensian eccentricity of Hartwell and his entourage, seemingly carrying the dust and smells of olde London from which they had reluctantly taken a day's leave. Hartwell resembled the battered Ford Cortina car in which he daily drove himself to Fleet Street. The others looked like characters from *The Pickwick Papers*. Sitting next to Hartwell was Black's old friend Rupert Hambro, who had been in the plane from London. Frustratingly, Hartwell had spent the entire flight scrutinising every word of that day's *Telegraph*, which prevented the banker from initiating a probing conversation. His misfortune was rectified by Richardson's opening remarks: 'Lord Hartwell needs an investor offering £10 million,' said the banker, confirming the *Telegraph*'s plight.

Black required no advice about his tactics. His cultivated performance, concealing a burning ambition to become a media tycoon, suggested a gentle knight coming to the rescue. 'All I have to worry about is which pocket the money's coming from,' he told Hartwell as he described his achievements and his limitless cash flow.[7] There was no hint that his bankers in Toronto were demanding the repayment of loans, or that he was being publicly described in some quarters as dishonest. Nor did he reveal that he would need to borrow the £10 million he was offering Hartwell. Before committing himself, however, he wanted to tilt the odds in his favour. He and Hambro excused themselves and went for a walk, despite the heat and humidity, in the hotel garden. Hartwell, they agreed, was clearly on his last legs. The question was how to use the loan to capture ownership of the *Telegraph*. Knight had suggested that Black should only agree to invest £10 million in exchange for one strict condition: if Hartwell needed more money, he would be contractually bound to first ask Black, who would then become the *Telegraph*'s majority shareholder. 'It could take five years before he needs the money and you get the newspaper,' Hambro cautioned. There was, he explained, uncertainty about Britain's newspaper industry. Eddie Shah, a printer, had provoked a bitter battle outside his premises at Warrington in Lancashire by using non-union labour. If Shah won, the trade unions' grip over the *Telegraph* might be weakened, but nothing more. Neither Hambro nor Black knew that Rupert Murdoch, owner of *The Times* and the *Sun*, was building a new printing plant in Wapping, near Tower Bridge, and was secretly planning to destroy the print unions by printing all his newspapers with non-union labour. Better-informed than Hambro, Knight had estimated Hartwell's eventual downfall within two years. Either way, the two men agreed as they returned to the suite, the opportunity was astonishing. 'It's a wonderful entrée,' concluded Hambro. Black nodded. He scented blood.

Hiding his excitement in a performance that would have been worthy of an Oscar, Black formally made his offer of £10 million for 14 per cent of the *Telegraph*'s shares, on condition that if

Hartwell needed to raise more money, Black should have the right of first refusal, and that any investment would give Black a majority shareholding in the company. At that moment Michael Richardson ought to have intervened to warn his client about the possible consequences. Instead, he remained silent. Hartwell, he had decided, was beyond saving. 'My role,' he would later say, 'was to ensure the successful placement of the loan, not to care for the Berry family's interests.' Unprotected by Rothschild's, Hartwell replied without fully understanding the implications of Black's condition, 'I don't think, Mr Black, we can resist that.' Convinced that he would not need more money, Hartwell agreed to gamble his empire for just £10 million.

As Black watched Concorde take off for London carrying Hartwell and his entourage, he understood the astonishing opportunity organised by Andrew Knight. He had cast the bait, the reel was running, and once the pressure slackened he would jerk the rod and wind in the line. There was a risk, but it was limited. As he returned to his plane he could reflect that only six years after the turmoil and aggression following Bud McDougald's death, he might be about to become a legitimate media tycoon in London. The outstanding hurdle was whether Hartwell would honour his verbal agreement within a formal contract. Black entrusted the final negotiations and drafting to Dan Colson, a friend from McGill University who was now working as a lawyer in London. Colson was to ensure that the pre-emption clauses giving Black an irrefutable right to the company were watertight.

If anyone in the City or the British establishment had wanted to protect the *Telegraph* from a foreign predator, there was still time to do so. Black was not entirely unknown in London. In the early 1980s he had appeared at a dinner held by Charles Price III, the American ambassador, and was introduced to Tim Bell, the famous publicist who had been at the heart of organising Margaret

Thatcher's first election victory. Bell, well connected and liked, was among those needed by Black if he was to persuade the establishment in London of his wealth and honesty. Gratifyingly for Black, that was unnecessary in 1985. Although Knight was aware of Black's reputation, he remained silent, while others did not bother to attempt to discover the truth from contacts in Canada. Unlike the protests that had greeted Rupert Murdoch's purchase of *The Times* in 1981, no one in London understood or even cared about Hartwell's fate, least of all his financial advisers. 'Rothschild's,' the banker David Montagu would say, 'handed the Berry family's balls to Black on a silver platter.'

Hartwell's fate was inescapably sealed on 13 June 1985. After the agreement was signed, Black's behaviour was orchestrated by Knight. 'Don't say a word when the announcement is made,' he ordered, 'and stay in Toronto, out of sight.' Without protest, Black obeyed. If his reputation was discussed in London, he knew, there could still be problems once Hartwell's plight became terminal.

In anticipation of the crisis, Andrew Knight organised a group of advisers to represent Black on the *Telegraph*'s board. Besides Rupert Hambro and David Montagu, employed by Jacob Rothschild's small merchant bank after his family bank had been sold to Merrill Lynch, Knight selected Frank Rogers, an experienced newspaper executive, and Lord Rawlinson, a former Conservative MP and law officer. If anyone in London could have understood Black's pedigree it was Jacob Rothschild. Renowned for combining his serious patronage of the arts with partnerships alongside buccaneers like James Goldsmith and Lord Hanson, Rothschild had in 1969 advised Saul Steinberg, a rising New York tycoon, during the takeover of the Labour MP Robert Maxwell's publishing business. In the course of the negotiations Rothschild had publicly exposed Maxwell as a crook, causing his downfall and disgrace. Yet in 1985 neither Rothschild nor David Montagu appears to have considered asking about Black's reputation in Canada, or to have looked at old newspaper cuttings. Even among the City's most honest scions there was a *laissez-faire* response to the foreign incomers passing through the capital, even to someone who had landed a remarkable deal at the *Telegraph*.

At Knight's suggestion, David Montagu was appointed chairman of the *Telegraph*'s audit committee. Within weeks he unearthed Coopers Lybrand's negligence. The prospectus issued by Evelyn de Rothschild's bank to raise the original £80 million had stated that during the following six months the *Telegraph* would earn £5.5 million. Instead, it had lost £14.4 million. 'An unutterable shambles,' Montagu told Black, confirming that the *Telegraph*'s financial problems were worse than anyone imagined.

Black arrived quietly in London in early September 1985. Over the following days, with Knight as his guide, he was introduced to his new team. In an interlude, he telephoned the *Telegraph*'s classified sales department from his hotel room. 'I want to place an advertisement,' he told the saleswoman. Her reply was staggering. The newspaper, she announced, was full for several weeks. She advised him to try the *Guardian* or *The Times*. This was better than Black had imagined. On 24 September Black set out for dinner at Lord Hartwell's house in Westminster, where at Richardson's suggestion Hartwell was hosting a celebration to mark the completion of the financing arrangements. 'There's a need to tiptoe,' Knight warned Black, 'so the deal doesn't get busted.' Black was seated next to Nicholas Berry, Hartwell's forty-three-year-old younger son. He intended to present himself as a family man offering help to another family in unfortunate distress.

The dinner was Nicholas Berry's introduction to the fate of his inheritance. Until then, Lord Hartwell had excluded his two sons from the family business. During his conversation with Black, Berry concluded that the Canadian had 'taken advantage of an old man', and was untrustworthy. Looking across the table at

Richardson, he was equally shocked. Not only had Rothschild's issued a misleading prospectus and failed to protect his father in New York, but Richardson appeared to be courting Black as a potential new client. 'Anyone but Black,' he told his father. 'We've got to find an alternative source of money.' Reports of Berry's renewed hunt for money soon reached Black. Lord Hanson, the Australian tycoon Robert Holmes à Court and representatives of the Australian Fairfax group were regaled with disparaging comments about Black, and all announced their interest in financing the *Telegraph*. To their dismay, they all discovered that the contract was watertight. Berry was powerless, but was also angry about N.M. Rothschild's original failure to introduce these more suitable investors. 'Sour grapes,' said Richardson in reply to Berry's protests. Nicholas Berry, Black concluded, had become 'a pestilential irritation to us'.[8]

Two months later, Hartwell was sinking. By November the *Telegraph*'s costs were out of control, and the banks refused to advance more money. On the brink of insolvency, only one source of finance was available. From Toronto, Conrad Black offered to advance £20 million in return for 50.1 per cent of the shares and control of the company. At one stage during the tense negotiations conducted by Dan Colson, Hartwell agreed to Black's take-over, only to reverse his decision soon afterwards. At a critical meeting, the peer appeared first oblivious to his imminent downfall, and then helpless. He collapsed under the stress, and was carried comatose from the boardroom. 'If he dies, it will save time,' quipped David Radler from Toronto. While he was careful never to say anything cruel in public, Black did not shed any crocodile tears over his quarry. Gleefully he reported that 'Lord Fartwell', *Private Eye*'s caricature, was sinking. 'It had become surrealistic,' he concluded, 'as tenacious resistance to the inevitable eventually always does, the surest sign that the endgame was finally afoot.'[9] Conrad Black could not have anticipated how his scathing homily would become appropriate to himself eighteen years later.

As the hours ticked by, Black and Colson applied the pressure, humiliating Nicholas Berry and forcing his father's capitulation. On 11 December 1985, the decent amateur surrendered. For just £30 million, Black had won control. To appear magnanimous, he agreed to Knight's suggestion that Hartwell should remain as the company's chairman and editor-in-chief, and that it was he who should announce the transfer of ownership at a press conference. Among the journalists gathered was John Fraser, Black's old school friend, who was now working for the *Globe and Mail*. 'He does not want to be any sort of newspaper tycoon,' Fraser heard Hartwell say. 'We have not sold out.' Fraser's smile widened as Hartwell continued, 'I'm happy to report that Mr Black is an entirely passive investor with no known interests in the British newspaper business.' Fraser's smile grew broader. 'They're finished,' he thought. 'Everyone from Newfoundland to Victoria will be laughing and cheering Conrad on. They couldn't even be bothered to make just one phone call to Canada.'

In Toronto, Black would have agreed. Overnight he had been transformed from a small-time publisher into an international star. 'I've hit the jackpot,' he laughed to a friend in a telephone conversation. 'It's a once-in-a-lifetime chance.'[10] Black's critics wrongly assumed that he had 'pulled a fast one', while he himself portrayed the deal as the product of genius, 'maintaining a kind of symmetry as if you were conducting a symphony orchestra'. In reality, he had merely grasped an offer created by an old man's short-sightedness and a bank's incompetence. All that remained was to find £20 million. Despite his claim a few weeks later to have 'earned more than $100 million' over the years, he did not possess any meaningful sum of money.[11] At first he asked his closest friends, including Fred Eaton, 'Do you want a piece of the action?' Eaton prevaricated, while others, wary of Black since the Norcen scandal, refused outright. Finally, having sold his other assets,

Black scraped together £20 million, helped by his directorship of the Canadian Imperial Bank of Commerce.

In his hour of triumph, Black was elated but realistic. He knew his personal handicaps. He was unqualified to combat the British trade unions' regular blackmail, and his financial experience of small newspapers across North America was inadequate to resolve the *Telegraph*'s plight. 'Let Radler sort them out,' he suggested to Andrew Knight. 'Out of the question,' replied Knight. The appearance in Fleet Street for just one hour of the ratty, uncouth hypochondriac, obsessed by fetishes about germs, would raise destructive questions about Black himself. 'Radler is forbidden to come to London,' ordered Knight. 'He's not the sort of person I'd like to see inside the *Telegraph* building.' 'Yes,' agreed Black. 'I don't think the *Telegraph* is quite ready for David.' A few days earlier, Knight had been invited to attend the Hollinger board meeting in Toronto summoned to approve the *Telegraph* deal. The sight of Radler, Peter White and Monte Black plotting like cronies about 'a scheme to finesse this' and 'get control of that' had shocked him. 'They sniggered like bad schoolboys,' Knight later told David Montagu. The worst, reported Knight, was Monte acting like a buffoon. Before leaving Toronto, Knight heard about the details of the Dominion pensions and Norcen controversy. Black, he realised, would not survive in London without his help.

Knight agreed to become the *Telegraph*'s managing director, on condition that he was given the option to buy 5 per cent of the *Telegraph*'s stock for £1 a share. 'Outrageous greed,' snarled Colson. Knight's request, Black chorused, was a sign of 'avarice', and displayed 'impenetrable arrogance'. In his experience, journalists never had the upper hand. Knight's insistence was a novelty, but Black reluctantly acknowledged that without Knight the deal would not have occurred, and without Knight he risked losing his £30 million. Wherever he went in Washington and New York, the power-brokers always asked, 'How's Andrew?' Everyone praised

Knight, and he realised he was fortunate to have him as an ally. Reluctantly, he succumbed. 'If you're Canadian you start with one strike against you,' he conceded. The price of being a fish in the big pond was to obey. He accepted the contract submitted by Knight, and headed to Palm Beach for Christmas.

In the sunshine he could reflect that, after seventeen years, he now owned a substantial business. The formula for his partnership with Radler remained their complementary differences. Black liked networking and loathed pernickety chores, while his partner, alias 'The Refrigerator' because he was cold and hard, enjoyed sweating the profits by repeatedly probing each newspaper's finances. Their trusting relationship was cemented by distance: Radler moved to Vancouver, 2,000 miles from Toronto, where he could be with his family, while Black constantly commuted between cities, anticipating the public glory after he took control of the *Telegraph*. In Florida, mixing with Jayne Wrightsman and the other Palm Beach aristocrats, his fantasies expanded. Lord Beaverbrook and Lord Thomson, the two outstanding Canadian newspaper proprietors, had been treated with deference in Britain. Both had won access to Prime Ministers, and there was every reason, one day, to expect 'Lord Black' to follow in their footsteps. Status symbols meant a lot to Black, and although he acknowledged Knight's warning not to appear as a lusting social mountaineer or a foreign profiteer, he did not intend to emulate Roy Thomson, whose chauffeur would buy a Tube ticket for his employer at Uxbridge station on the Metropolitan Line so he could travel the eight miles to Fleet Street. Black intended to use the Rolls-Royce Silver Wraith which Bud McDougald had appropriated from Massey-Ferguson. Repeating over cocktails in Palm Beach, 'I'm the proprietor of the *Daily Telegraph*,' the image of his destiny unfolded. Not as a mere press baron, but as a world leader – like the power-brokers who featured in countless history books in his library. His youthful fascination for visiting the graves of the famous had not been forgotten. Only the name and the dates were carved on the tombstones of Churchill, de Gaulle, Bismarck and Napoleon. One day, in the long-distant future, his grave might be similarly stark and potent, reflecting his influence on mankind's fate.

The formal approval of the *Telegraph*'s shareholders was due on 20 February 1986. In anticipation, Andrew Knight was executing a revolution. At Knight's suggestion, Black approved two new editors. Max Hastings for the *Daily Telegraph*, Black agreed, was a brilliant albeit surprising choice. The military historian, writer and broadcaster was a maverick, but could prove to be inspired. Knight's selection of Peregrine Worsthorne for the *Sunday Telegraph* caused Black more concern. Unaware that his life's ambition to be a newspaper editor was about to be fulfilled, Worsthorne had just lamented in the *Spectator*, then not owned by the *Telegraph* group, about the nightmare of a Canadian ruffian and asset stripper buying the *Telegraph*. Knight overcame Black's reservations. 'To my amazement,' Worsthorne recalled, 'he offered me the opportunity of my lifetime.' Others had agreed with Worsthorne that Black's imminent arrival in London was not a blessing. Charles Moore, the editor of the *Spectator*, commissioned John Ralston Saul, the noted Canadian writer, to write a piece introducing the *Telegraph*'s new owner. 'While Mr Black personally grows ever richer,' Saul wrote witheringly, 'some of his companies grow ever poorer.' To prove his argument, Saul cited how, over the previous five years, Black's six publicly quoted companies had lost 21 per cent of their value. He observed that by posing as a historian, regurgitating huge amounts from his prolific reading and immersion among the famous at Bilderberg, Black assumed that he possessed unique insight. Black confused, suggested Saul, proximity and scholarship with understanding, and mistook bombastic proclamations for wisdom: 'The driving force of his personality and his brilliant sense of applied historical perspectives will impress all who meet him. Only with time may they feel that the driving force deforms the perspective so that the masterful conclusions are wrong.' Considering the fate of Conrad Black's shareholders, his brother and the Argus widows, Saul concluded: 'One searches for the spirit of sacrifice in Mr Black's career and finds self-help.'[12]

Black was outraged. There was too much truth in Saul's assessment for comfort. Personal denigration normally provoked an instant writ for defamation, but on this occasion Black was urged by Knight to be cautious. Media owners in Britain did not issue writs, he was told, and if, just days after his coup, his first reaction to criticism was nuclear, people would become suspicious. Accepting the advice, Black confined himself to a letter to the *Spectator* which, he preened himself, would alert London to his erudition. Saul was accused of being 'dishonest and malicious', and possessed of 'sniggering, puerile, defamatory and cruelly limited talents'. By contrast, in a sanitised version of his own past, Black presented himself as 'unaware of any minority shareholder discontent'. He continued, 'I have never had any difficulty with . . . any regulatory authority.' No one in London, he assumed, would know about the SEC's 'consent' terms linked to his bid for Hanna, or about the complaints from Argus shareholders. London tasted, for the first time, Black's 'truth'.

Charles Moore did not regard Saul's analysis as anything more than a provocative and forgettable point of view which entirely failed to prove Black's dishonesty. Those who did ask Knight about Black's 'sketchy reputation in Canada' were reassured, 'It's in the past and isn't relevant.' There seemed every reason to accept that endorsement. David Montagu was less sanguine. 'There are all sort of strains arising,' he told Black, 'not least the *Spectator* article. We must take care. Here's a list of how to stay clean.' Radler was to have nothing to do with the *Telegraph*; Black was to restrict himself to two visits a year to London until he was given the all-clear; and he was to limit himself to 60 per cent ownership of the *Telegraph*. In return, Montagu had negotiated blue-blooded seal of approval. Cazenove's, the London establishment's stockbrokers, would represent the *Telegraph*, and Sir Martin Jacomb, a respected City personality, had accepted a directorship. Altogether, said Montagu, the *Telegraph*'s new ownership was blessed with 'a clean bill of health'. Black congratulated him, relieved that Saul's warning had been ignored. 'Am I doing all right?' he asked Montagu, Jacomb and Hambro individually, reflecting his lack of self-confidence; and they, pleased by his civility, his care for Hartwell's feelings and their impression of Shirley as 'a perfectly nice, unambitious wife', agreed that Black could be trusted.

John Ralston Saul's warning also made no impression among the *Telegraph*'s staff. As Black walked for the first time through the rabbit warren of dusty, dimly lit offices, he was reassured by the blank faces that confirmed his anonymity. 'I've just seen a very sinister man in the corridor,' said a breathless journalist, diving into the cartoonist Nicholas Garland's office. 'He looks like a mass murderer. Do you think we should tell security?' 'Oh, no,' replied Garland. 'That's the new proprietor.'[13] The few who met Black, including Hastings and Worsthorne, were intrigued by a proprietor who enjoyed discussion, was intelligent and informed and, at Knight's insistence, promised to make them rich. The senior executives were given share options, chauffeurs and generous expense accounts. 'It's like the heavens opening,' proclaimed Worsthorne. Black could afford to be generous. During the night of 25 January 1986, Rupert Murdoch had moved his entire newspaper operation to Wapping. Confronted with barbed wire and an army of aggressive police, the trade unions' grip was shattered. Instead of 2,000 printers, Murdoch's newspapers would now be produced by 570 electricians. With government support, Murdoch was certain to succeed eventually, and Conrad Black would be one of the beneficiaries, although Murdoch's new strength as a competitor added urgency to Black's task.

The *Telegraph*'s circulation was sliding, and the finances were precarious. To attract new and younger readers, Max Hastings introduced features about rock music and fashion, and special pages for women readers. Dozens of older journalists were fired. 'Max is good at drowning kittens,' smiled Black, appreciative of his editor's ruthlessness in his quest to improve the newspaper and earn profits. One of Black's early contributions was a suggestion to consider employing a Canadian journalist who had recently arrived in London. 'I think you ought to take a look at her,' he told Andrew Knight. 'What's her name?' asked Knight. 'Barbara Amiel.' 'I'll see her,' Knight replied, but he discovered that Amiel was not interested, and the suggestion came to nothing.

More importantly, Black was concerned about Hastings's politics. 'Rupert Murdoch called,' he told Knight. 'He told me I was crazy to appoint Hastings as editor.' 'He told me the same,' replied Knight, 'but I'm ignoring him.' Hastings's unpopularity with Thatcherites like Murdoch and the *Spectator* columnist Paul Johnson justified his appointment, said Knight. Under Hastings, the newspaper would cease to be the Conservative Party's mouthpiece, and would become more combative and original. 'One more thing, Conrad,' said Knight. 'When you're unhappy about something in the papers, don't telephone the editor. Write a letter for publication.'

5

The Visit

'CAN YOU ARRANGE IT?' Conrad Black repeatedly asked Andrew Knight during March 1986. Impatient to reap the prizes due to the *Telegraph*'s proprietor, Black yearned to meet Margaret Thatcher, one of his idols.

During the few weeks since he had become recognised as the *Telegraph*'s owner, Black's lifestyle had changed markedly. Friends had begun introducing him to London society. Jennifer d'Abo, a successful businesswoman, hosted pizza dinners in her kitchen. Witty and light-hearted, Black amused d'Abo's guests with his endless insights and information apparently gleaned from many sources – either his newspaper editors or politicians. The word spread that the *Telegraph*'s new owner was a desirable social catch. David Metcalfe, an insurance broker, grandson of Lord Curzon, was another eager host. At a succession of cocktail receptions, dinners and weekend parties, Black's warmth and intelligence were noted and he was embraced. 'A loyal and good friend,' concluded Metcalfe and others who accepted Black at face value. 'Conrad believed,' Metcalfe would tell a friend, 'that the world was his oyster, and London society reassured him that his performance was acceptable.' Since the City establishment had been joined by Max Hastings, Peregrine Worsthorne and the veteran former *Telegraph* editor Bill Deedes in endorsing their employer, there seemed no reason to dig into his past.

When Black was in London countless invitations to parties, dinners and opening nights at the theatre and Covent Garden began arriving, flattering his self-esteem. His lust for more than 'a ringside seat at everything' grew, inflating his opinion of himself and validating his importance in Canada. The opportunities to meet British and foreign politicians in London fed his hunger to consort with the mega-rich and the powerful in the White House, Buckingham Palace and Downing Street. The *Telegraph* was not merely the means to earn an income and propagate his ideas, but had become his passport to social climbing. 'Who's that?' Black asked Paul Johnson's wife Marigold when they met at a party in the French Embassy. 'And who's that? And that person, is he important?' Marigold Johnson was shocked. 'I realise the allegation is about that I am somewhat of a seeker of celebrities,' Black later admitted, 'and in one sense I suppose that's true. But my purpose is that celebrities who are justly celebrated can be very useful to you.'[1] The casualties were the celebrities' wives, including those of Jacob Rothschild and the Duke of Marlborough. 'I won't again sit next to a man who lectures me throughout dinner,' said one wife, 'about the layout of the navies at the Battle of Jutland or reels off a list of all the kings of Sweden since the eighteenth century.' Black's new friends were undecided whether his amusing lectures reflected arrogance, insecurity or insensitivity. Like others, the Johnsons were puzzled by Black's parochialism. On his first visit to their house he looked shocked by a plate of mussels, especially when other guests ate them by hand. As a preliminary to meeting Margaret Thatcher, Andrew Knight arranged to call on Charles Powell, Thatcher's foreign policy adviser, in Downing Street. 'What do you think Powell thought of me,' Black repeatedly asked Knight afterwards. The judgement in Downing Street, Knight did not reveal, was that Black was 'a provincial hick'.

'Hello Margaret,' smiled Black as he entered Chequers with Andrew Knight on 2 April 1986. Thatcher's close staff, accustomed to calling her 'Prime Minister', were surprised by Black's assumption of equality. They were to be even more surprised by his conduct. After the pleasantries, Black embarked on a monologue, lecturing his hostess about her place in British history alongside Pitt and Disraeli. His fluent performance was honed as much to massage his own ego as to flatter his audience. He was too enraptured by his own verbal elegance to notice his hostess's astonishment. Propriety required that she mask her impatience and 'listen carefully'. The Conservative Party relied on the *Telegraph* group, and it was politic to humour its owner. Her concealment succeeded. Unknown to her visitor, Thatcher rarely listened to what she was told. Her only interest was what she would say in reply. Impervious to her true sentiments, Black was pleased, as they bade farewell, that Thatcher 'patted me most considerately on the shoulder and said, "That is very good, Mr Black. Do come back."' As his Rolls-Royce drove down the gravel driveway, Black asked Knight impatiently, 'How did it go? What do you think she thought of me? Do you think she respected me?' For several days he repeated the questions. 'I'm sure she thought you know more about the history of the Tory Party than she does,' replied Knight, protecting Black from the truth, 'but that only goes so far.'

Before their meeting, Thatcher had been aware of Black's opposition to hanging, not because he was against capital punishment, but because he felt hanging was 'too good for them'. She had wrongly assumed that that was said in jest. After their meeting, she told her aides that compared to Black, 'I'm a liberal wet.' An intimidating bore, she concluded of the new proprietor. Unlike Rupert Murdoch, whom she genuinely liked, she decided to tolerate Black because the *Telegraph* was important, but he would be classified as 'low profile'.

Over the following days Black regaled many about his successful visit. Among his listeners was Peter Munk, a self-made Canadian billionaire whose company, Barrick, would become the world's biggest gold extractor. Shortly after visiting Chequers, Black flew with Munk by helicopter to Highgrove to lunch with Prince Charles. Munk had skied with Charles at Klosters, and offered him an opportunity to persuade a friendly newspaper proprietor to treat the royal family with more consideration. 'You'll like Prince Charles,' Munk told Black. 'He's a good guy and you should help him.' Their encounter began with a tour of Highgrove's organic garden. At the beginning of lunch Charles explained his vegetarianism. Black seized the cue. Throughout the meal, a torrent of history poured from him, describing the British royal family's eating habits. Ignoring Charles's obvious distaste for the excruciating details of his grandfather George VI's tendencies, Black did not stop until minutes before he departed. 'Not a success,' Charles later told an aide. Gossip about Black's behaviour spread around London. 'He's such a heavy personality to escort around,' Knight told a friend. 'I have to keep him away from the paper to prevent revolt.' Black himself was sensitive to that danger. Without protest, he even obeyed Knight's instruction to stay away during the Queen's visit to the newspaper's new premises as part of her tour of London's Docklands. That was a worthwhile price to pay if he was to shed his tarnished reputation in Canada. With patience he could emerge as a cleansed, acceptable character in London, and become influential and rich.

Max Hastings, an excellent journalist, historian and analyst, was a valuable ally in that quest. Energetically, Hastings was transforming the *Telegraph* into a respectable mouthpiece for independent Conservatism. Black, however, was not wholly enamoured. There were, he noted, some unattractive aspects of Hastings's Toryism. The editor was critical of Margaret Thatcher's strident antagonism towards the public services; he bore an Englishman's mistrust of American politicians; and he was convinced that the *Telegraph*'s future depended on abandoning its blind support for the Conservative Party. As proprietor, Black was entitled to express his opinions and to seek to persuade his editor to reconsider his newspaper's position on any issue. His profound knowledge of history and his ability to recite tidal waves of obscure political facts strengthened the credibility of his opinions. The correlative was his myopic intolerance of contrary views and his distrust of those who wrote for his papers. 'I'm not a particularly great admirer of journalists,' he said. 'A great many of them are irresponsible. They have great power, and many of them are extremely reckless.'[2] Among those he most distrusted was the polemicist Christopher Hitchens, who had suggested in the *Spectator* in July 1985 that the announcement of President Reagan's cancer treatment deliberately concealed his more serious Alzheimer's. In a protest letter to the *Spectator*, Black criticised Hitchens as 'a disgrace to the profession [who] should not be employed'. Hitchens's article, Black continued, was motivated by 'nasty, macabre, vulgar and insolent claptrap' which revealed the 'lack of integrity and serious analysis in British and most foreign reporting of American affairs'. To silence Hitchens, Black threatened to buy every newspaper that offered him employment. Although Hitchens's article would prove to be accurate, Black showed no remorse. He espoused, as Max Hastings discovered, his own version of the truth.

Black's disagreement with Hastings's opinions remained restrained until the US Air Force bombed Libya on 14 April 1986 in retaliation for Colonel Gaddafi's support of a terrorist attack in Berlin. Black, preparing to fly to Britain to attend the Bilderberg Conference at Gleneagles in Scotland, was infuriated by the *Telegraph*'s condemnation of President Reagan's bombardment. His newspaper, he believed, should reflect his own unquestioning support of America. He admonished Hastings for his 'seriously fallacious analysis of what was really happening'. Colonel Gaddafi had after all, said Black, supplied the IRA with weapons. Black wanted a warmer embrace of Reagan and America. Hastings disagreed. Black's brand of American Republicanism, he said, was unsuitable for a British audience. On that issue, Black won. 'Since Conrad was the principal shareholder in the paper,' Hastings would concede, 'it would have appeared discourteous to trample gratuitously on his most cherished convictions.'[3] That exchange was a precursor to more intervention. Black would forbid the use of the word 'Irangate', referring to the secret and illegal supply of weapons by President Reagan to Iran, on the grounds that the Watergate affair was far more serious; and while tolerating Hastings's support for sanctions against South Africa to end apartheid and his opposition to capital punishment, he would criticise his 'incorrect thinking' about Northern Ireland. To Black's credit, he did not countermand Hastings's dismissal as a columnist of Margaret Thatcher's daughter Carol for working as a freelance without permission. The Prime Minister was livid, and pledged never to invite Hastings to Downing Street again.[4] Black was embarrassed, but tolerated his editor's authority, although increasingly Hastings received not only letters of complaint but midnight telephone calls from across the Atlantic, during which Black would nitpick at length, regardless of the time.[5] Black's intolerance towards journalists matched his fierce reaction to those in Canada who had questioned his honesty in business.

Black's political certainties concealed his personal insecurity. Despite the psychoanalysis thirteen years earlier, he continued to suffer 'bouts of miscellaneous obsessive fear' and depression. One cure was his growing interest in religion, especially the mystical teaching of Cardinal Newman, the nineteenth-century English theologian and philosopher.[6] In Newman's view, a man's personality cannot be called into question, because God reveals Himself in a man's conscience. Black's interest in Newman provoked intense conversations with God, drawing him closer to the hierarchical Catholic Church. His need for spiritual assurance from the font of undisputed authority was matched by his wife Shirley's own increasing attachment to the Catholic Church, but this only widened the schism in their marriage as they stumbled over their incompatibility.

At Knight's suggestion the Blacks had bought a house in Well Road in Hampstead, in north-west London, near Knight's home. The leafy district had been historically fashionable with writers and artists, but not among London's social elite. To the inhabitants of Knightsbridge and Belgravia, Black's choice of neighbourhood, a twenty-five-minute drive from Harrods, reflected his provincialism. Some assumed that he knew no better, while others correctly judged that Shirley felt more comfortable living a middle-class life beyond the carping gripes of London's socialites. In the interests of his marriage and Knight's stricture to remain out of sight, Black endorsed his wife's desire for modesty. Their principal home, they agreed, would remain in Toronto. Their divided lives intensified her misgivings and his turmoil. Her concerns were ignored while he sought to resolve his own confusion. His solution, after long conversations in England with the writer and scholar Malcolm Muggeridge, and in Toronto with Archbishop Carter, was to formally convert to Catholicism. 'I was resistless against the benign temptations of religious practice,' Black wrote, but he recognised the need for Catholicism's 'sane, rigorous and consoling' teaching to comfort his spirit. Catholicism's inflexibility about morality and conscience perfectly suited a man who enjoyed breaking the rules. Notionally, he accepted Cardinal Newman's opinion that a man's conscience was the 'powerful, peremptory, unargumentative, irrational, minatory and definitive [words of] God speaking in our minds'.[7] That was precisely the process of self-justification that preceded all his misdeeds. On 18 June 1986 Black was formally converted, and thereafter he wanted to be known as a passionate and uncompromising believer. Conrad Black had crossed another Rubicon.

Under the management of Andrew Knight and Max Hastings, the *Telegraph*'s losses of £15 million in 1986 were transformed in 1987 into a small profit. The paper's circulation began to increase, and Black bought the conservative weekly the *Spectator* from the Australian Fairfax Group, which had plunged into financial crisis. Hollinger's shares in Canada soared as the value of Black's coup and Rupert Murdoch's victory in Wapping became evident. 'I want to build a first-class newspaper company,' Black told a London newspaper, and added, 'I am not a seeker after status here,' denying his expectation of a peerage. No one cast doubt on his claim to possess assets worth C$650 million, and no one queried the huge loans against which he had used his assets as collateral.[8] Although Black was wealthy, he lived in a comparatively modest home in Hampstead, and while his journalists shared some of the profits, there were limits. Journalists who compared his income with their own when asking for a pay increase were lampooned. 'I earn a lot because I'm a capitalist,' he said gleefully, 'and you are a seeker after the truth.'

In the summer of 1987 the *Telegraph* moved from Fleet Street to South Quay in London's Docklands. Under Knight's plan, the company's 2,200 printers would be reduced to 507 men supervising automated machines and robots, while the 413 men currently employed to compose the hot metal plates would be replaced by twenty-seven technicians. If the plan succeeded, the *Telegraph*'s profits in 1988 were projected to rise to £29 million. At that moment, the first fissure in Black's hitherto unruffled performance opened. 'They're mad,' Dan Colson told him. 'Don't let them deman. There'll be strikes.' Colson had assumed a special role in Black's business, but Knight was appalled by his interference. 'You've got to back myself and the management,' Knight insisted during a telephone call to Canada. Without an alternative, Black agreed. The redundancies were achieved without strikes, and the *Telegraph*'s annual profits were projected to rise to £40 million.

This was the beginning of Conrad Black's halcyon era, and he was flying. His income from the *Telegraph*, and the prospect of selling his 5 per cent stake in the Southam newspaper group in Canada at a considerable profit, reinvigorated his appetite for deals and expansion. In that atmosphere, he decorated his new office in Docklands with the symbols of tyrants and inspirational leaders, including busts of Cardinal Newman and Napoleon. Few could understand his fascination for the ruthless French warmonger, but the media's attention to his passion for a despot tickled Black's self-importance. 'I've never found him an attractive personality,' Black said about Napoleon, while admitting his fascination for 'a great talent . . . a military commander and a mythmaker'.[9] Hero-worship fed Black's illusion of his own growing importance among the world's leaders.

At the 1987 Bilderberg conference by Lake Como in Italy, hosted by Gianni Agnelli, the chairman of Fiat, Black was treated like a head of state, speeding around the area with a police escort. For the next twelve months, in anticipation of the leaders of the Group of Seven countries' meeting in Toronto, Black assiduously cultivated Margaret Thatcher. 22 June 1988 was his red-letter day. In her speech to the Ottawa Parliament in the morning, Thatcher praised Black as the most important Canadian in London. That evening she appeared as guest of honour at the Hollinger annual dinner. Surrounded by Canada's elite, Black introduced the world-famous leader, and in reply Thatcher praised her host as a star who was continuing the tradition of Canadians in Fleet Street, mentioning Lord Beaverbrook and Lord Thomson. After great applause, Thatcher was in turn thanked by Henry Kissinger, who also referred to Black in glowing terms. No one could ignore that night's adulation of their host. Certainly, Black believed, his fellow countrymen would be persuaded to forget their earlier slurs. He anticipated a peerage and much more. He had already called at 10 Downing Street and asked Charles Powell, 'What does one have to do to get a peerage?' Unfortunately, Powell had not been helpful, so Black put out feelers among Thatcher's advisers. His peerage, he believed, would not take long. Like Roy Thomson, he too might be posthumously remembered in St Paul's Cathedral, although he was unsure whether Thomson's commemorative plaque in the crypt – 'He gave a new direction to the British newspaper industry. A strange and adventurous man from nowhere, ennobled by the great virtues of courage and integrity and faithfulness' – would do him sufficient justice. Only Hal Jackman, bemused by Hollinger paying a fortune to entertain politicians, offered a reality check. 'Why do you have all these people for dinner, Conrad?' he asked. 'Good for business,' replied Black. 'More like social climbing,' laughed Jackman.

Intoxicated by his new life, Black began planning to spend hundreds of millions of dollars to realise his fantasies of rivalling Rupert Murdoch. 'I'm not impecunious like Rupert,' he told his staff at an introductory dinner in Curzon Street. In 1988 Murdoch was buying television stations across Australia and America, and launching the Sky satellite television channel in Britain. If he planned to similarly embrace the new media and consolidate his business on a sound footing, Black should have recruited experts and examined future trends. Instead, he used his limited funds to buy newspapers, the only business he understood.

As 'a public relations gesture . . . to [reduce] the libel chill' he bought *Saturday Night*, a loss-making Canadian political and cultural magazine.[10] Robert Fulford, the magazine's respected editor, was invited for lunch at Black's house. Fulford had to wait for some time before Black finally appeared. In a tense atmosphere, he struggled with a tough steak until Black declaimed, 'I call up writers and tell them what I don't like.' Black's 'supercilious' manner, Fulford concluded, reminded him of 'Orson Welles's characterisation of Citizen Kane'. He lost his appetite for the new owner and, to Black's disappointment, resigned. Black's attempt to appease Toronto's journalists had failed. John Fraser, his old school friend, was appointed as editor instead.

Undeterred, Black began assiduously to create an alternative fan club, unconnected with journalism but material to his reputation. In 1988, at a dinner party at the French Embassy in London, he met Lord Carrington, the former British Foreign Secretary who had just retired as Secretary General of NATO. As his party piece, Black asked Carrington, 'Do you know who was a very bad Prime Minister? It was Harold Macmillan.' After a scorching debate, Carrington was furious about the Canadian's disparagement of an old friend. The next morning, Black telephoned Carrington and invited him for lunch. During the meal he asked the respected politician, 'Would you like to become a director of the *Telegraph*?' Carrington was amazed. 'I thought that was probably the most magnanimous thing you could possibly imagine,' he told a friend. 'He's a very generous man. I admire him more and more.' Carrington's endorsement overcame an important obstacle to Black's status in London. With David Metcalfe, Carrington proposed him for membership of White's, London's premier gentlemen's club in St James's. The eminence of his two proposers ensured Black's swift entry.

After Carrington's appointment, Black recruited the tycoon James Goldsmith, Hartwell's former banker Evelyn de Rothschild and Lord King, the chairman of British Airways, onto the *Telegraph* board. Even Black was surprised at how easily British personalities succumbed to his invitations. Since he was the majority shareholder, the directors would wield only limited influence. He did little to arouse their suspicions. During their discussions, none had the feeling that Black was 'on the make'. Money, it appeared, merely financed his interests rather than being his principal objective.

Among those interests was attracting more famous people into his orbit, in order to enhance his own reputation. His mechanism was an invitation to join either the *Telegraph* or Hollinger Inc.'s advisory board. The advisory directors' role was unusual. To Black, they were ornaments with titles, happy to be his companions over a well-cooked lunch, to look through his annual report and, following a presentation by the editors of the two *Telegraph* newspapers, discuss world affairs. For him they were well-paid cogs in the machinery of his career, shrewdly selected to enhance his self-esteem and protect him from recrimination. Legally, they were little more than the description bestowed by Tiny Rowland, the infamous chief executive of Lonrho, on his directors: 'They're Christmas tree decorations,' said Rowland, adding sinisterly, 'Any director voting against me is expected to resign.' Among those included in Black's dining club were Dwayne Andreas, the chairman of American agricultural giant ADM; the British businessman Lord Hanson; Jacob Rothschild; Richard Perle, the US Assistant Defense Secretary responsible for President Reagan's 'Star Wars' defence dream, who had resigned in 1987; Henry Kissinger; three journalists, David Brinkley, William Buckley and George Will; and Stephen Jarislowsky, a Canadian fund manager. 'Conrad walked into the board room like Napoleon Bonaparte,' Jarislowsky recalled, 'and then we looked through an annual report about Conrad doing things that we hadn't been consulted about.'[11] In common with his fellow directors, Jarislowsky was not suspicious. 'I don't think Conrad's basically unethical or immoral,' he reassured a concerned co-director. 'He just believes he can pit his own brilliance against anybody.'[12]

The order banning Black from London had evaporated, and he now felt himself to be at the centre of London's circles of influence and power. Nothing could prevent him imagining himself walking into the Grill Room at the Savoy and being greeted by Lord Rothermere and Sir David English of Associated Newspapers at one table, Bill Deedes and Peregrine Worsthorne entertaining Cabinet ministers at two other tables, and Lord Carrington at a fourth table. Among that company, he persuaded himself, he commanded widespread admiration. 'Let us be completely frank,' he admitted. 'The deferences and preferments that this culture bestows upon the owners of great newspapers are satisfying . . . As the beneficiary of that system, it would certainly be hypocrisy for me to complain about it.'[13] Those acknowledgements at the Savoy, his star-studded board of directors, and the cash flowing into his coffers encouraged Black's ambition to perform as an acquisitive international media player. 'We are friendly buyers,' he told Lord Stevens, the chairman of United Newspapers, which owned the *Daily Express* and a large network of regional newspapers, on 24 March 1988. The rival group was a target in Black's plan to expand his empire. Before Lord Beaverbrook's death in 1964 the *Express*'s circulation was four million copies, but twenty-four years later, daily sales had fallen to 1.6 million. To Stevens's surprise Hollinger, posing as the white knight, bought a 1 per cent stake in the company. By November 1989 Black would own 8.8 per cent of his rival. With limited understanding of the problems such a move would involve, he hoped to amalgamate the two newspaper groups.

In Canada, David Radler regarded Black's unfocused spending spree, which required huge loans to satisfy his social and political ambitions, irritating. In response, the number-cruncher resolved to raise his own status. An observant Jew, he decided to bid in an auction for the *Jerusalem Post*, Israel's only English-language newspaper. Although Black had shown little interest in Israeli politics, he supported Radler's $20 million purchase in 1989, despite the fact that ownership would provide no commercial advantage. An additional complication was that the staff and readers of the unprofitable newspaper were critical of Israel's provocative occupation of Palestinian territory, while Radler supported the aggressive Zionism of Ariel Sharon, shortly to become Minister for Housing Construction. Nevertheless, Radler paid double a rival's bid, and ravaged the newspaper's office. The editor and a large number of journalists resigned, and their replacements endorsed Israeli settlements of Palestinian land. The circulation and advertising revenue dipped. Over the next weeks Radler attempted to reduce the *Post*'s losses while Black sought to prove his importance by appointing Richard Perle, the publisher Lord Weidenfeld, and even Robert Maxwell as directors of the newspaper. None would wield any influence, but each was flattered to be associated with Conrad Black, a man of rising importance. Vanity had supplanted commercial sanity. The reward was international acknowledgement of Black as a media baron.

Black's increasing self-assurance encouraged his interference in the *Telegraph*'s editorial policies. Among his chosen intellectual journalists, including Simon Heffer and Dean Godson, there was delight that Black engaged in discussions about Richard Nixon's civil rights policies and the minutiae of Washington affairs, and his request to meet the maverick politician Enoch Powell. They welcomed his challenges to Hastings, especially after the editor condemned as an 'execution' the SAS's 'shoot-to-kill' of three unarmed IRA assassins in Gibraltar in March 1988. To those admirers, Black belied the caricature of rich, stupid North Americans. He was good company, well read, and espoused safe, conventional political convictions. His indifference towards health, education and social issues raised no doubts; similarly, his admirers did not question why their employer focused on supporting policies which protected the interests of the rich. But it was that prejudice that would end the honeymoon at the *Telegraph*.

In 1989, Andrew Knight sensed that his relationship with Black had deteriorated. He was being marginalised from commercial decisions by Dan Colson and Joe Cooke, a management consultant. Without any announcement, quite separately, Black and his Canadian cabal had reverted to familiar habits and decided – as they were legally entitled to do – to take more money out of the

Telegraph for their own benefit. Black and Radler were persuaded that they could run the company better than Knight. In 1989 Black and the other directors increased their interest-free loans from Hollinger Inc. – Black's from C$3.5 million to C$7.3 million – using money which had been transferred from the *Telegraph*'s profits. They used the loans to buy Hollinger Inc. shares, an unusual ploy by the directors of a public company.[14] To provide even more money for himself, Black also demanded a squeeze on the *Telegraph*'s costs. An army of consultants descended on the journalists. Their questions and conclusions were derided as varying between inane and lunatic. 'How long does it take to write a newspaper article?' asked one consultant, while another enquired, 'How long does it take to edit an article?' On their recommendation, the staff was to be cut by 25 per cent and the *Daily* and *Sunday Telegraph*s were to be merged into a seven-day operation under Max Hastings, with Peregrine Worsthorne responsible merely for the *Sunday*'s comment section. Newspaper professionals knew that this plan was foolish. Hastings would be unable to work seven days a week and also produce a distinctive Sunday newspaper that would satisfy readers seeking a completely fresh approach. Black's insistence, despite Hastings's opposition, provoked resignations and an ineffectual thirty-six-hour strike. 'One of the great myths of the industry,' scorned Black, 'is that you need journalists to produce a newspaper.'[15] Black's overt dislike of subordinates was encouraged by his success in imposing his plan. 'Come and meet the staff,' suggested Hastings, in an attempt to heal the wounds. Black refused, overtly disdainful towards those who produced his profits.

In June 1989 Andrew Knight told Black that he had decided to resign. Black refused to accept his departure. Although he wanted to manage the business himself, he felt more secure with Knight's presence. In August, Knight insisted on an announcement and his immediate resignation as chief executive. 'Stay as a non-executive director,' urged Black. Knight agreed. 'I bet you're going to Rupert,' said Black, conscious that his bitterest rival had been entertained by Knight at lunch in the *Telegraph*'s canteen on a boat moored in Docklands. 'Are you going to Rupert?' 'Absolutely not,' insisted Knight. Black repeated the question repeatedly throughout the autumn, always receiving Knight's denial. In December, three days after his latest assurance, Knight resigned, and his appointment to manage News International's British operations was announced. Black was furious. Not only was Knight deserting him for Murdoch, but he was entitled to cash in share options worth about £14 million, allowing him to pocket £7 million after tax. 'You gave Andrew his unbelievable opportunity,' raged Colson, 'and now he's been disloyal and enriches himself beyond his wildest dreams.' Like Black, Colson understood loyalty to be owed in one direction only.

'How shall we announce your departure?' Colson asked Knight irritably. 'Well,' replied an exasperated Knight, 'just say what a great time it has been and how wonderful I am, and that I'm the best thing since sliced bread.' Black took the last quip at face value, publishing Knight's words disparagingly. His sense of humour had disappeared. Knight's behaviour, he said publicly, had added 'new depth, warmth and colour to the meaning of the word "shit"'. He even released an exchange of private letters with Knight.[16] Among his accusations, Black blamed Knight for his 'pessimistic, divisive, erratic and joyless management style', which had reduced the *Telegraph* group to 'a squalid and demoralised level of constant internecine dispute'.[17] No one recognised that description, but some had a measure of sympathy for Black's lament: 'I never begrudged him his financial coup, only the relentlessly devious and unrepentant manner in which he stole away to our chief competitor, denying at every stage that he was doing so.'[18]

The *Telegraph*'s management was firmly under Black's control. Considering his record over the previous decade, the company's finances were endangered. Uninterested in the details of the price of newsprint, advertising contracts and the costs of distribution, which Knight had mastered, Black decided to rely on Joe Cooke, Dan Colson and Jeremy Deedes, the son of the *Daily Telegraph*'s former editor. Their first decision was to abandon the merger between the newspapers.

Having imposed himself upon the *Telegraph*'s management, Black decided to move his family permanently to London on 30 June 1989. Success in Britain had increased his disenchantment with Canada. Despite its natural resources and talented people, the sluggish economy was permanently burdened by a huge national debt and unemployment. The country's political life, Black believed, was moribund, and its politically-correct cultural life had prompted many gifted people to flee. He disliked the state-approved discrimination against English-speakers in Quebec, a province governed, he believed, by extremists and a 'corrupt' trade union movement, promoting 'mediocrity' and 'philistinism'. Equally, he opposed the 'Kafkaesque procedures' imposed on private businesses to employ minorities, regardless of their qualifications. He carefully choreographed his final reckoning.

On 29 June 1989, the Hollinger annual dinner in Toronto would be Conrad Black's farewell appearance in Canada. Ronald Reagan was his guest of honour. Knowing that the former President's accelerating Alzheimer's would protect him from any accusations of discourtesy, Black first compared the President's intelligence and knowledge to Roosevelt's and Disraeli's, and then lashed out at Canadians' 'spiteful envy' as the cause of his departure. The next morning, he knew, the *Globe and Mail* would humiliate itself in a grovelling apology for wrongly defaming 'Canada's most respected businessman'.[19] The declaration epitomised the success of about fifteen writs for libel he had issued over the previous four years. His efforts had effectively suppressed any reasoned criticism. Fear of further writs would, he must have hoped, protect him in the future. Too many journalists calculated that to annoy Canada's most prominent newspaper proprietor would harm their careers. Having the last word in the *Globe and Mail* convinced Black of future bliss.

Later that day, Shirley and two of the Blacks' three children* arrived at their new house in Robin Grove, Highgate, adjacent to Hampstead but even further from the capital's fashionable centre. Living in the suburb confirmed Black as a man of modest tastes living within his means. In appearance, the Blacks were renowned as 'one of the Canadian establishment's happiest marriages'.[20] In reality, Shirley was unenthusiastic about the move to London. She had agreed on condition that if she was unhappy there, she could return to Canada. Three months later, Black arrived late, alone and angry at Lord Weidenfeld's seventieth birthday party at the National Portrait Gallery. Some guests speculated that not all was well in his home, but it was not domestic turbulence that was hindering the Canadian's ambitions.

The departure of Andrew Knight had emboldened Black. For three years he had watched Max Hastings's growing social and journalistic success. Black shone thanks to Hastings's achievements, provoking some envy and a desire to share the tributes. In part, Black wanted to beat his rivals in Canada, particularly Galen Weston, the billionaire who regularly met the Queen and who rented Fort Belvedere, Edward VIII's home in Berkshire at the time of his abdication. He wanted to join the highest levels of the British establishment. Pomposity and pretensions associated with 'castle creeping' began to infect his personality. Those traits were encouraged by his increasing social success.

To prove his importance, in January 1989 Black invited Margaret Thatcher for lunch or dinner at the next Hollinger

* Jonathan, born in 1977, had been followed by a daughter, Alana (born 1982), and another son, James (1986).

board meeting that September. To lure the Prime Minister he mentioned that she would be among friends, including Henry Kissinger, Lord Carrington and the property developer Paul Reichmann. She rejected the invitation. Undeterred, Black suggested that the directors visit the Prime Minister for twenty minutes in Downing Street. The idea was supported by Charles Powell because, as he minuted Thatcher, 'We need to keep the management of the *Telegraph* on side (particularly now there are rumours that Conrad Black is thinking of buying the Express Group).' Thatcher agreed. At noon on 6 September 1989, Black arrived in Downing Street with a convoy of eight cars, containing seventeen men who had been summoned at Hollinger's expense to attend the company's board meeting in London and to witness Black's new status. Self-assuredly, he led Lord Carrington, Fred Eaton, Monte Black, David Radler, Dan Colson, Dixon Chant, Hal Jackman and the rest into the Cabinet Room. Kissinger had dropped out because of his mother's illness, and Paul Reichmann was absent because of financial difficulties. Black had been offered a thirty-minute slot in which to hear the Prime Minister's opinions about the international situation. Ninety minutes later the visitors departed. Black was ecstatic. Over lunch, he proposed that the directors' fee for attending board meetings should be raised from $500 to $1,500, and that their annual fee should be increased to $12,000. Amid much merriment, his proposals were approved unopposed. After a pause, the party reassembled at Brooks's Club in St James's for dinner with James Goldsmith, bankers Rupert Hambro and Sir David Scholey, and the journalist Auberon Waugh. At midnight the group travelled to Docklands for a tour of the *Telegraph*'s printing plant. By the early hours of the following day, no one doubted the invulnerability of Black's fame and fortune. The *Telegraph* was consistently producing profits of £40 million per year, and Black's 83 per cent stake in the company, after he had bought the Berry family's shares for a total of £130 million, was worth £420 million. In addition, he had sold some Reuters shares for over £40 million in cash, and he had made about £20 million by moving the *Telegraph*'s offices from South Quay into Paul Reichmann's new tower block at Canary Wharf. Increasingly he was mentioned in the same breath as Murdoch and Maxwell, both acknowledged as international media tycoons. Unspoken was Hollinger's dependence on the *Telegraph*. Eighty per cent of the company's operating profits and 60 per cent of its revenue came from the single asset. Despite this dependence, Black openly criticised *Telegraph* journalists as 'revenging, money-grubbing know-nothings'. Journalists in general, he said at that time, were 'temperamental, tiresome and nauseatingly eccentric and simply just obnoxious'.[21] His mastery of malevolent language was his badge of superiority.

Black's self-confidence in 1990 coincided with the beginning of a recession which was threatening to destroy many fortunes. Paul Reichmann was heading for bankruptcy, Rupert Murdoch was financially semi-paralysed, and Robert Maxwell's fortune was disappearing. Black was also in danger. In his bid to rival Murdoch, he was in the midst of spending $302.1 million to buy 288 newspapers and magazines across North America on behalf of American Publishing.[22] Although Hollinger Inc.'s accounts showed that the company enjoyed a surplus of over £30 million in its cash flow, and had £40 million on deposit, there was insufficient income to repay the interest on debts of C$685 million. Black needed new funds to sustain Hollinger's higher costs. His method was crude but effective. Without telling the company's minority shareholders as required by law, he began in December 1990 to borrow money from the *Telegraph*. By May 1992 he had quietly transferred £33 million to private companies which he controlled. Those withdrawals should have been mentioned at the regular Tuesday management meetings in London, but instead Black spoke at length about his recent conversations with famous politicians. Key issues about the *Telegraph*'s finances, the introduction of colour and the newspaper's labour problems were only patchily discussed.

With that sluicing perfected, Black added a new mechanism to divert extra money. Instead of receiving a salary from Hollinger Inc., a publicly owned company, he decided that Ravelston, his private company, which was owned 65 per cent by him and 14 per cent by Radler, should charge management fees for the services of himself, Radler, Colson and Boultbee. Without the details being revealed, Hollinger Inc.'s shareholders could no longer decide how much Black and the others should be paid, or check their expenses. Black's invention was simple. Once a year, Ravelston would present a bill to Hollinger Inc. for the services of the directors. Switching hats and posing as the chairman of Hollinger Inc., Black asked the directors to approve the payment of Ravelston's invoice. Without demur they agreed, and millions were transferred from the public company to Ravelston for Black and Radler to divide up. The losers were Hollinger Inc.'s minority shareholders and the public company itself, because it was denied cash to spend on improvements and expansion.

There was no mood either in London or in Toronto to scrutinise Black's new arrangements. In London, during late November 1990, he appeared as a kingmaker in the wake of the Conservative Party's surprise revolt against Margaret Thatcher. Appalled by the plots, he had initially pledged the *Telegraph*'s support for the Prime Minister.[23] Amid constant discussions and telephone calls with senior Tories, he found himself at a dinner party which included the maverick Tory MP Alan Clark, James Goldsmith and the gambler John Aspinall – three unreliable men. They persuaded Black to prevent Hastings supporting Michael Heseltine in the leadership contest against Thatcher, and the *Telegraph* remained neutral. Nevertheless, Thatcher fell after the first ballot on 20 November. Black was shocked by her downfall, confirming his peripheral grasp of Conservative sentiments. His ignorance was revealed by his public curse of 'spite and envy' as the reasons for her demise. Faced with having to make a rational choice about her successor, he again revealed his shallow understanding of British politics. Without anticipating the consequences, he told Heseltine, the favourite to be the next leader, that he could not expect the *Telegraph*'s support. The result was confusion. Hastings would have supported Heseltine, but because of Black's veto the *Telegraph* officially supported Douglas Hurd, a no-hoper, while Black, who opposed both Hurd and John Major, supported no one.[24] Black did not emerge with any credit for influencing by default the Conservative Party's surprise choice of John Major. Disdainful of the new Prime Minister, Black was tempted to plot with right-wing and anti-European Conservatives to mount an immediate challenge. He only hesitated so as to avoid endangering his peerage. 'It goes with the job,' he had told Fred Eaton years earlier. For four years he had anticipated that Thatcher would ennoble him. Her departure had denied him that prize. Expecting her successor to fulfil the obligation, Black suppressed open criticism of John Major, and in anticipation became concerned about his wife's name. 'Lady Shirley' lacked gravitas. 'People here don't invite Shirleys to dinner,' his wife agreed. 'With the greatest respect to all the Shirleys in the world,' explained Mrs Black, 'it was never a name I particularly liked.' At her husband's request, she chose to rename herself Joanna. 'How's Shirley?' Nigel Wade, the *Telegraph*'s foreign editor, asked Black soon afterwards. 'We're calling her Joanna now,' replied Black, deadpan.

The casualty of Black's posturing was his marriage. Even before they arrived in London, Joanna disliked his egoistic materialism. His opportunism, self-promotion and self-importance affronted her honest, simple values. While Black hated Canada's provincialism, she disliked London's celebrity culture. 'Ultimately,' she said, 'I no longer belonged in that country.'[25] She gained no pleasure from her husband's perpetual social pretensions. Compared to their quiet domestic home life in Highgate, characterised by Conrad saying, 'Let's order a pizza,' his showmanship among the rich celebrities was excruciating. With anguish, she performed her best at receptions and dinner parties, but she did not enjoy talking about politics and business with aggressive strangers, and she suffered sniggers at the Chelsea Flower Show when she arrived in a turquoise leather suit. Gradually, she realised that her marriage had been a mistake from the outset, prompted purely by her pregnancy. While Conrad thought the birth of their first child had brought them together, she knew that it had united incompatibles. Black, she would say, was 'better than 90 per cent of husbands', but he made her unhappy.[26] Like him she had converted to Catholicism, but her interest in religion was profound. Their homes, admitted Black, 'were virtually turned into seminaries, where I was not her *de facto* preferred male company'.[27] By 1991 their marriage had 'fallen apart'. She had fallen in love with a priest who, after his excommunication, she would marry. In June she told her husband that the marriage was over. In the most succinct damnation of Conrad Black, Joanna would explain, 'I didn't leave him for anybody. I left him for me.'[28] The blow to Black was considerable. Not so much the loss of Joanna as a friend and wife, but the stigma of rejection. Miserable and fearing embarrassment, he urged her to remain silent.

The divorce settlement was dictated by Black. He wanted to pay a lump-sum settlement to Joanna and pay maintenance to the children through their trusts, and sought Joanna's agreement that the children's surnames would not be changed. With her consent, they parted. For one week during the summer he flew with his two youngest children and a nanny to Inverness to spend time with Scottish landowner Simon Fraser in Beaufort Castle. He showed no emotion about his impending divorce. Paul Johnson, another guest, became tired by Black's lectures at each meal. 'One thing you mustn't do,' said Johnson, 'is accept a peerage.' Black smiled, 'Paul, don't wag that Jesuitical finger at me.' 'Oh, I see,' exclaimed Johnson. 'You do want a peerage.'

By the end of the summer, business rather than the break-up with Joanna dominated Conrad Black's life. From London, he was planning to bid for the Australian Fairfax newspaper group; in America, he and Radler continued to buy small newspapers, still hoping for a chance of a major title; and in Canada, he was once again damned as dishonest for the latest restructure of Hollinger Inc. He retaliated with writs. To protect himself from criticism, he had expanded his court of advisory directors to include Paul Volker, the former chairman of the US Federal Reserve, Alfred Taubman, the chairman of Sotheby's, and Zbigniew Brzezinski, the former Security Advisor to President Jimmy Carter. In addition, there were plans to recruit Margaret Thatcher, Giovanni Agnelli and Chaim Herzog, the former President of Israel, to his advisory board. These relationships, he claimed, warranted the payment to each advisory director of up to $25,000 plus expenses for attending two meals a year. To regale those directors and stage a gala coronation, Black had persuaded Jacob Rothschild to lend Spencer House, an eighteenth-century palace in St James's, for Hollinger's annual dinner in October 1991.

For the sake of appearances, Joanna Black agreed to return from Canada and jointly welcome Margaret Thatcher and two hundred others with her husband. Over £1 million was spent for all Hollinger's directors to fly to London on Concorde, be met by chauffeurs and accommodated in Park Lane hotels. Some directors would be paid an additional $25,000 to attend. On Black's insistence, Max Hastings was ordered to abandon his holiday and fly by helicopter to London to address his employer's guests. Eyewitnesses would swear that they spotted Joanna Black shudder at the sight of Conrad holding court, boasting of his latest conversations with a cast list of notables. None of those giants in dinner jackets, gleaming white shirts and polished shoes laughing with their host, she knew, understood his fatal flaws. Joanna herself understood the cause of her misery. For thirteen years she had lived with a showman. Even though she was standing near Monte Black and Cardinal Carter, who had both flown with her from Canada, she was isolated, and was relieved not to have become Lady Black. London society, she realised, had not only embraced Conrad at face value but had connived in a fictitious creation.

As part of her final gesture, Joanna had agreed to attend a dinner given by Malcolm Forbes Jr for Ronald and Nancy Reagan, and to host a dinner with her husband for a large group at Harry's Bar. If that hectic schedule did not persuade her to swiftly return to Toronto, then her husband's final command would have. 'Let's go to Annabel's,' he ordered at midnight, leading his guests to the Belgravia nightclub. At that time another Canadian in London, Barbara Amiel, frequently headed for the same fashionable basement.

6

Inevitable Union

Adultery, severe depression and its consequences, divorce, concurrent relationships and fame as a newspaper columnist had preoccupied Barbara Amiel since her marriage six years earlier, yet she showed no noticeable injuries. In October 1991 she was contemplating leaving London for America with William Goldman, the Hollywood scriptwriter who included *Butch Cassidy and the Sundance Kid* and *All the President's Men* among his credits. But Amiel was hesitating to pack her suitcase and abandon stardom in London. The familiar faces at Annabel's, smiling their greetings towards her, validated her self-description as 'a survivor'. Many, including Conrad Black, had generously offered help since the collapse of her marriage to David Graham. Fate, she thought, might deal another surprise card.

Her disillusion with her third husband was as swift as had been predicted at the wedding reception in Toronto. David Graham rented a flat in Eaton Place, but frequently travelled on business, and during his irregular residence in London he showed limited appreciation of his wife's appearance and domestic talents. She tried to cook, on one occasion proudly offering guests an Italian dish variously described as 'hideous' and 'awful', and, at the age of forty-four, she was hoping to conceive. The desire for motherhood had come late in life, and was a source of considerable anguish. 'I cry every time I have the curse,' she told a friend over coffee in Pimlico. There was bleeding, pain and visits to a fertility clinic. Eventually she had a miscarriage. Writing in *Maclean's* magazine, she described the reaction of a woman 'just like me' who was told by a nurse the sad news that she could not have children. 'The woman', continued Amiel, was aware that 'a large black crow is sitting on her shoulder . . . its beak hard and yellow, ready to gnaw out her insides. She hoped it would.' Six years previously she had written about her abortion at the age of twenty-four: 'I have no sentimental feelings about the child I killed. But I find my reasons morally reprehensible . . . At the time I had my own abortion I believed it to be morally wrong . . . I chose murder.'[1] Her misery was not helped by David Graham's affairs, especially with an actress, and the discovery that she was bored. One dinner-party conversation with Graham's friends had been dominated by a discussion about mortgages. In Canada, Graham was an important man – there had been much laughter during one trip to Toronto when he coincidentally sat at the Coffee Mill with George Jonas and Gary Smith – but in London he appeared dull, plainly uninterested in politics, culture and social gossip. His wealth barely compensated for Amiel's disappointment.

In despair, she sought work. She appealed to Conrad Black for help, and he asked Max Hastings to interview her. 'I think it is quite in order to proceed with Ms Amiel,' wrote Black. 'On the appointed day,' wrote Hastings, 'a vision of fine cheekbones and huge, deep, penetrating eyes surmounted by a mane of black hair swept into my office swathed in furs. I have seldom been so discomfited.' The encounter was not a success. 'I saw Barbara Amiel,' Hastings reported to his employer. 'I cannot say that I think it was one of my great performances in that after a forty-five-minute chat, she told me that she found me most frightening. I said that made two of us.'[2] Next she approached Peregrine Worsthorne, the editor of the *Sunday Telegraph*. Amiel arrived in her attacking armour, impeccably dressed, with pungent perfume wafting in her wake through the newsroom. Worsthorne recalled, 'This highly glamorous, sexy girl strode through on high heels into my office and closeted me behind closed doors.' Again she was unsuccessful. The editor was unimpressed by her attitude and her expectation of a high salary. There was better news at *The Times*. John O'Sullivan, an assistant editor whom she had known since 1980 and who was staying as a guest in her flat in Eaton Place, offered a contract for a weekly column.

Amiel's success in finding a job was tempered by the disintegration of her marriage. Her late-night calls to friends in London and Canada, including her sister Ruth, were alarming. 'I've taken Valium tablets,' she told Judith Steiner, a friend living in north London. 'What should I do?' 'Go straight to hospital,' Steiner recommended. At 10 a.m. the following day, Dick Nielson, a Canadian television producer, arrived to film an interview for 'Woman of the Year'. A maid opened the door. 'I don't know where Mrs Graham is,' she announced. 'She's not in her bedroom and a bottle of pills next to her bed is empty.' Nielson was alarmed, and rang the local hospital. The doctor, thinking he was David Graham, told him that Amiel was being treated for an overdose. 'I'm not her husband,' said Nielson. 'Well, would you call her husband,' said the doctor, 'and tell him what has happened.' Nielson immediately telephoned David Graham. 'Dick, where are you?' asked Graham. 'I'm in Barbara's flat.' 'Where?' 'On her bed.' A stunned Graham paused and then said, 'Would you lean forward and see if there's a white dinner jacket hanging on the door?' 'Yes, there is,' replied Nielson. 'Would you bring it back to Toronto?' asked Graham. After her recovery, Amiel was bewildered by her plight. 'You don't realise how the world is out there,' she told a friend. 'Everyone is out to get you.'

John O'Sullivan offered his help and friendship. He asked her to go with him to dinner with the well-known journalist Frank

Johnson, who at the time was living with the *Daily Telegraph*'s literary editor Miriam Gross. Johnson was particularly fond of German sausages and beer, a taste he shared with the publisher George Weidenfeld, who was also invited. Amiel's entrance into Johnson's kitchen provoked the sixty-seven-year-old Weidenfeld's eyes to pop out on stalks. This beautiful woman, he soon discovered, was fascinated by English society. 'I hear you know something about opera,' said Amiel, slicing a bratwurst. For the next hour Weidenfeld could not be restrained. Anecdotes were followed by famous names, and then by an account of his privileged access to every opera house in the world. Frank Johnson, another opera aficionado, was pummelled into silence. The following weekend Amiel was seated next to Lord Weidenfeld at La Scala in Milan.

There was no woman in London who understood men better than Barbara Amiel. 'My dears,' she told a group of women after an exercise class, 'apart from Anatole France and Albert Schweitzer, there is no man interested in anything but sex.' She categorised the men with whom she enjoyed sexual relations into three types: men of wealth, men of power and civilian non-combatants, namely men who were unthreatening, fun and trusted confidants. Weidenfeld represented both wealth and power. Through his publishing house Weidenfeld & Nicolson he had cultivated a wide range of relationships. Regularly he entertained in his beautiful flat overlooking the Thames an international cast of multi-millionaires, politicians and cultural giants. He offered to introduce Amiel into that charmed world. 'It's like a box of candy,' she admitted in smitten tones to a friend of Weidenfeld's. The publisher, she said excitedly, had invited her for dinner with Princess Margaret. With great seriousness, Amiel explained the protocol of behaviour in the Princess's presence. 'One is not allowed to leave before Her Majesty does,' she said. 'Well, Barbara,' replied her friend, 'most people in London would do anything to avoid eating with Margaret, but have fun.' Weidenfeld could do more than introduce Amiel to wealth, culture and intelligence. He was renowned for his sexual antics. Few young women in London publishing or journalism had not been propositioned by 'Lord Popeye', as he was lampooned by the satirical magazine *Private Eye*. 'Not so much a casting couch,' women laughed, 'more a casting Chesterfield.'

Just as Amiel was smitten by Weidenfeld's social life, so he was infatuated by her body and mind. He would happily pander to her reputation as a self-absorbed sex-kitten.[3] They had, he told friends, so much in common. Both were Jewish, fascinated by the same subjects and excited by sex. To conceal their affair, on one occasion Weidenfeld and Amiel asked Gina Thomas, a journalist, to invite and escort David Graham to the theatre. Thomas agreed, allowing Amiel to enjoy the best of all worlds. With her husband's wealth she could indulge in expensive clothes, while her lover provided a remarkable social life.

The magical blend prompted Amiel to write 'Why Women Marry Up' for *Chatelaine* magazine, a sermon, a confession and a description of the man she was seeking. 'It is about time,' she wrote, 'we dismissed those ugly words of criticism like "meal ticket" and "gold digger" that accompany a so-called "good marriage".' Nevertheless, she appreciated the attraction of 'trade-offs' in marriage: her looks for his money, his power as her meal ticket. Life in London, she explained, had ended her 'racing pulses'. Instead, with 'the survival instinct programmed into us', women like herself were searching for powerful men who would help them in pregnancy and after childbirth, and would provide sufficient money to maintain standards when the professional New Woman stopped work. Power, she wrote, is an aphrodisiac which 'protects and offers a shield from the world', satisfying a woman's 'most basic instinct of vulnerability'. Power is 'sexy, not simply in its own right, but because it inspires self-confidence in its owner and a shiver of subservience on the part of those who approach it'. A person with power has an 'indefinable mystique'. Her ideal, she declared, was 'the power couple'. She continued, 'the woman likes to select a man who has more financial power than she does'. Not just for security, but because wealthy men 'answer her common-sense realisation that they will be confident enough to cope with her prominence'.[4] Amiel's eloquent self-analysis portrayed a woman riven with materialistic ambition, which aroused suspicions of manipulation but left uncertainty, especially among those close to her, about the objectives in her undefined endgame. Clearly her marriage to David Graham had provided the wealth she desired, but not the power. He had not fulfilled her requirements. In summer 1986, soon after the article was published, Graham also appeared to be no longer interested in Amiel. He was seeing another woman, and Amiel agreed to move out of their home. Lord Weidenfeld was ecstatic. 'He's crazy about me,' Amiel told friends. Graham, however, soon reconsidered his decision.

Amiel had rented a mews house in Pimlico. A four-poster bed with a mirror in the ceiling had been installed in the upstairs bedroom, and a range of nightdresses were hanging around the room. Her friend Judith Steiner was delighted to spend time with 'a gossip fest, a box of endless merriment and fun', always the helpless soul unable to replace lightbulbs. One Sunday evening after a day's cycling in the Chilterns with the Steiners, Amiel returned to her house in their Volvo estate. Inside they found David Graham, his hands bloodied from breaking in. Filled with jealousy, he was reading her diary. 'Oh my God,' exclaimed Amiel, clearly upset. Her life was high drama. A brief and pointless discussion followed. There was no hope of reconciliation. Weidenfeld was delighted. By early 1987 he was thinking of marriage.

At a party at the American Embassy on 9 March 1987, Amiel was introduced to Woodrow Wyatt, a newspaper columnist and former Conservative MP. Wyatt recorded in his diary meeting 'a strange woman' who made no mention of a sexual relationship between herself and Weidenfeld. Nevertheless, that summer Weidenfeld told many friends about his marriage plans.[5] 'She's a washed-up orphan,' he explained to London society. 'She had a terrible childhood.' Some applauded his intentions; others, including Evangeline Bruce, the wife of a former American ambassador to London, were appalled: 'If you marry her, I'll never speak to you again,' she said. Weidenfeld was undeterred. To help Amiel's career, he obtained Jacob Rothschild's agreement to be interviewed by her for *The Times*. The subsequent article amused the banker and led to more introductions. Irritated by her habit of working through the night in her house, Weidenfeld bought a flat below his own and installed furniture including a desk costing £15,000. She refused his offer. 'I don't like going to bed with him,' she told friends. Weidenfeld's portly form was one reason. Laughingly she told of a night when he became hungry in bed. On his doctor's orders, the kitchen had been locked by the staff to prevent his excessive eating. Desperate for food, he eyed Amiel and coaxed her to slither naked through the serving hatch to retrieve his sustenance.

Amiel's distaste for Weidenfeld's physique – he was twenty years older than her, and thirty-nine years older than Sam Blyth – and her love for his social life were complicated by their similarities. Both demanded attention, yet both were unable to give the consideration the other craved. That incompatibility was causing arguments. To ease the tension, they flew to the Caribbean. The holiday ended in disaster. After arguments, Amiel flew back to London early. Distraught, Weidenfeld telephoned friends, asking, 'How does one cope with a neurotic?' On his return, they were reconciled and agreed to stay with Paul Getty in Salzburg for the music festival. Weidenfeld flew to Austria and awaited her arrival. To his embarrassment, she did not appear, and failed to telephone to explain her absence. Once again, Weidenfeld called friends in London, admitting his fascination and his despair. He had never, he moaned, experienced similar behaviour. He returned to London resolved to end the relationship. Unexpectedly, Amiel telephoned him at his home. During the call she spoke sexually, and she later appeared at his flat dressed only in a coat, to 'reawaken his interest'.

Weidenfeld's bewilderment was matched by Amiel's apparent desperation. There was feverish gossip that she had theatrically threatened to commit suicide by jumping off the Albert Bridge, within view of Weidenfeld's flat. In the course of her confessions, friends recognised two different personalities. On the one hand there was the heartfelt journalist asserting her contempt for rich society. In that guise, other journalists suited her need for non-glamorous confidants offering stability and sanity. But on the other hand there was an ambitious player, planning her intellectual and social ascent. 'Do you want to come with me to Malcolm Forbes's house for a bridge tournament?' she asked Gina Thomas in 1987. 'He's hosting a load of American multi-millionaires.' By February 1988, Weidenfeld's urge to marry Amiel had gone.[6] Soon after, they agreed to end the relationship. 'But please do continue to invite me to your parties,' she soothed him. He admitted his devastation. No other woman had outmanoeuvred him in that fashion. 'She's wicked,' he told Peter Brimelow, reflecting his hurt feelings about a woman he had loved. 'George Weidenfeld,' Amiel told *Tatler* magazine shortly after, 'started out as a good intellectual friend . . . He allowed me to talk about Zweig and Schnitzler – things that matter to me. He's been a bit of a shoulder through my divorce.'[7] At the same time, her friendship with Gina Thomas also ended. Thomas complained about Amiel's 'manipulation'. 'Barbara Amiel has left a nasty taste in my mouth,' she explained.

The end of the affair with Weidenfeld struck some as Barbara Amiel's self-liberation. Over lunch in Knightsbridge she told

Judith Steiner, 'I need a make-over.' She was to receive a crash course in British politics from Douglas Eden, a political analyst, and she would also undergo more cosmetic surgery. 'I think I need my neck done,' she explained. Steiner also noticed a slight change in her accent, which was becoming less Canadian.

In the scramble to re-establish herself, she sought help from Peter Munk. Over drinks in Toronto, she explained her wish to be launched in London as an individual. 'I need the right sort of publicity,' she explained. Munk offered to help. He called David Wynne-Morgan, a charming public relations expert with a wide range of contacts. In her honour, Wynne-Morgan organised a dinner party at Mark's Club near Berkeley Square for ten people, and then another at Harry's Bar with Mark Birley, the founder of both Mark's and Annabel's. Amiel, delighted to be the centre of attention, dressed in an expensive, tight-fitting top, spoke memorably as a coy seductress and a tough polemicist, and won admiration. The personal cost for Wynne-Morgan was about £10,000. His reward was a gracious letter of thanks from a woman who was by then being compared to Pamela Harriman, the Anglo-American society hostess known as '*une femme horizontale*'.

At subsequent parties, Amiel struck one suitor as 'smouldering, sexual and delicious'. Some described a '*femme fatale*', others 'a sort of intellectual Barbarella doll'. Like wildfire, a story circulated of a man admiring her belt. Taking it off, she dangled it in front of his face. 'Usually,' she said, 'I only wear this.' The invitations were numerous, among them one from Algy Cluff, a buccaneer oil explorer and former owner of the *Spectator*. 'There's one thing I have to tell you,' Amiel reputedly replied in her acceptance. 'I won't be wearing any knickers.' Irritated by her overt sexuality, some women carped that Amiel gritted her teeth throughout sex. Transparently, she was seeking men, sucking in some and disappointing others. During an affair with a rich businessman introduced to her by Judith Steiner, she suggested that they spend the summer in Palm Beach. 'We can see where the billionaires live,' she urged. He rented a house, but at the last moment Amiel cancelled her holiday. He spent the summer alone. On Christmas Day she appeared at the home of David Metcalfe, another admirer. Rhetorically she asked Woodrow Wyatt, who was there as a guest, whether she should get involved with a younger man. 'Give it a try,' suggested Wyatt, aware from Weidenfeld that she was 'very neurotic' and 'complicated'. Amiel's response, Wyatt recorded in his diary, suggested that 'she didn't like the idea – as if it would be the first time'.[8]

The combination of looks, intelligence and strident ultra-conservatism attracted increasing interest in Amiel. She presented herself as a passionate Thatcherite. 'There may be a woman in history whom I admire as much as Thatcher,' she wrote, 'but one does not easily come to mind. Nor a man.' Her cogently argued and stylishly written opinions attracted praise. 'She has the looks of Gina Lollobrigida and writes like Bernard Levin,' wrote one commentator, 'and do remember to get it the right way round.' (Levin was a brilliant but physically unattractive journalist.) Naturally, the enthusiasm was not universal. After accusing Germaine Greer of suffering from 'terminal self-absorption', Amiel was in turn described by Greer as having 'great hobbit feet, a breakfront bosom and effusing patent insincerity'. Any criticism from such a quarter only enhanced Amiel's status.

To her satisfaction she was dubbed 'Wapping's Own Iron Lady' for consistently criticising political correctness, multi-culturalism and single-issue groups. She was keen to outrage. Courting unpopularity, she opposed the state's financing of abortions: 'People who wish to terminate a potential human life for their own convenience should bloody well pay for it themselves,' she wrote. 'Homosexuals,' she suggested, 'have the right to their freedom of choice in sexual predilection, but not the right to my moral approval – or my tax money to promote it.' She added later,

'I suspect homosexuality is rather like having a hunchback . . . we are all now required to pretend that being deformed or "gay" is ordinary.' Homosexuals suffering from AIDS, she insisted, should not be allowed to enter Britain, nor should they be allowed to proselytise in classrooms. The feminists' 'reign of terror' was another hatred. While 'gender should not encumber anyone', she argued against the 'mass myths' extrapolated from the experience of one woman. She disparaged those seeking excuses because they were unsuccessful, ugly, had suffered a deprived childhood or endured adverse 'psycho-social conditions'. Value judgements, she insisted, were legitimate. There was nothing wrong in saying someone was 'good' or 'beautiful'. More important, considering her fate twenty years later, was her constant advocacy of self-help and personal responsibility. 'We have long ago abandoned the idea,' she wrote, 'that people may in any sense be responsible for their shortcomings or needs.' A 'consequence-free culture', she argued, would lead to society's destruction. She opposed 'mindless egalitarianism' and favoured segregating the underclasses, because the alternative was a society based on 'rules appropriate for a zoo'. Her conclusion was uplifting: 'It is not our morality that is growing, only our cowardice and hypocrisy.'[9]

In November 1987, Amiel's advocacy of personal responsibility was uncompromising. Six days after the New York Stock Exchange crash of 'Black Monday', she mocked New York's rich, especially the women at the previous night's 'exclusive party' at the Metropolitan Museum of Art, preoccupied with their diamonds, 'wrapped in the delirium of beautiful gowns by Oscar de la Renta'. Her attitude towards that class's 'unthinking pursuit of wealth' was coruscating. 'The newly rich of the 1980s want something for nothing,' she wrote. 'The most amount of money with the least amount of effort . . . All that one needs is a good broker and some insider information.' She attacked those greedy hustlers who spent more than their income: 'One spends one's way out of difficulties created by character flaws – by an eye that is bigger than the stomach or by an appetite that is bigger than the wage cheque.' Returning to the guests at the glittering party at the Metropolitan Museum, she noted: 'Underneath the patina of gloss and jewels was a moral vacuum that must be filled once more . . . What appalled many of us was the new American fascination with wealth without any matching concern about the process that generated it . . . The materialism of America . . . has grown into a national obsession, a killing addiction.'[10] In summary, Barbara Amiel was a conservative with a social conscience, disgusted by mindless, ostentatious avarice.

Two years later, having enjoyed the hospitality of plutocrats in London and New York, her opinion had fundamentally switched. Shameless wealth had become admirable, and its critics were damned. The women at the Metropolitan had become her heroines. Influenced by Tom Wolfe's novel *The Bonfire of the Vanities*, Amiel was persuaded that white entrepreneurs were being persecuted by prejudiced state prosecutors chasing capitalist scalps to justify their imprisonment of drug addicts and other social misfits. She wrote sympathetically about Keith Best, the Conservative MP who had illegally submitted multiple applications for BT shares, and in support of the imprisoned Wall Street junk bond dealer Michael Milken who, despite his guilty plea, was in Amiel's opinion innocent. Both, she argued, were victims of envy, mistrust of big business and the 'cancerous growth of regulatory agencies'. Justice in the spotlight aroused her suspicion. The prosecution of the famous, she believed, was victimisation. By 1989 her columns were regularly advocating the cause of the super-rich, although she occasionally relied on erroneous information.

The conviction and imprisonment in 1989 of Leona Helmsley, the New York property developer and hotel owner, for evasion of $1.2 million in taxes provoked Amiel's anger. 'Even after you've paid £38 million in taxes, as she did,' wrote Amiel, 'the impulse to withhold the last £678,000 cannot be alien to any of us.' Helmsley's fortune was worth over $5 billion, and she was found guilty of thirty-three counts of tax evasion and conspiracy. While openly admitting ignorance about the facts surrounding Helmsley's crimes, Amiel explained in a most prophetic sentence, 'Many entrepreneurs find it difficult to see the distinction between personal and business expenditure.'[11] Amiel's second prophetic thought was her belief that 'personal responsibility', her previously vaunted theology, should not apply to the rich. Helmsley and her breed, she complained, had become 'scapegoats', ogled in the courtroom by 'the same journalists who recently had swallowed her Veuve Cliquot at parties to promote her hotels'. In those circumstances, 'justice' for the rich, she wrote, was simply 'show business'. Helmsley, Amiel believed, was a sixty-nine-year-old first offender who had been spitefully singled out. 'Aren't we all a bit like Helmsley?' she asked. 'The object lesson of these stories is that in this world of institutionalised envy, if you are rich, successful, beautiful (or once beautiful) and worse, presently bejewelled . . . it's best to err on the side of self-effacing politeness.'[12] Her argument, she admitted, was near-hopeless: 'Trying to arouse public sympathy for rich people denied justice, particularly a rude, flamboyant, rich Jew such as Mrs Helmsley, is a thankless task.'[13] In fact it was only 'thankless' among non-millionaires, and Amiel had moved into social circles where self-interest influenced the interpretation of the truth, and her sympathy for the likes of Helmsley attracted endless admiration.

Unusually for a Jew, she used the Second World War as a platform to argue that the rich and famous should not be accountable for their responsibilities. 'The Second Word War,' she wrote, 'was a fight, as I have written so often, to create a world in which people were presumed innocent until proven guilty.'[14] From that truism, she opposed the trials of Nazi war criminals and damned the critics of Kurt Waldheim, the former UN Secretary

General and Austrian President, for failing to satisfy the normal 'standards of proof' about his wartime activities. In 1986 documents had been discovered showing that Waldheim had deliberately concealed his participation in various war crimes, including 'cleansing operations' to kill partisans in the Balkans and Greece. Despite Waldheim's signature appearing on incriminating documents, Amiel wrote that he was the victim of 'a campaign of smears' because, she asserted, there was no evidence against him.[15] Eventually, Waldheim admitted that he had concealed his actions in the Balkans during the war, and conceded that the documents were authentic. Until then Amiel had been credited as a columnist who based her opinions on careful research, but her mistaken assumption that Hitler's profession as a 'painter' meant that he had been a decorator rather than an artist suggested that her support for Waldheim was based on a shift towards sympathy for fashionable right-wing causes, rather than an understanding of the Third Reich.

In that vein, Amiel attacked Harold Macmillan, the former Prime Minister who in June 1945 had been Britain's political representative in occupied Austria. In 1986 Nikolai Tolstoy accused Macmillan in his book *The Minister and the Massacres* of ordering the unlawful repatriation of 70,000 Cossacks to the Soviet Union, knowing that they would probably be killed. Tolstoy had attracted support from many conservatives, including extreme anti-Communists who were critical of Britain's decision to declare war on Nazi Germany. They dismissed the reality that, in the post-war chaos, Macmillan was a small cog in an enforced decision. The facts were indisputable. During the war the Cossacks had voluntarily fought with the Nazis against the Soviets, outclassing their German allies in their butchery of Russian civilians. In 1945 they fled to the British forces for sanctuary, forgetting that Britain and Russia were wartime allies bound by the Treaty of Yalta, which stipulated that they, as Soviet citizens, would be repatriated to Russia after the war. Amid terrible scenes the Cossacks were handed over by the British Army; most of them were to die, either by execution or during imprisonment. Amiel called Tolstoy's book 'compelling proof' of Macmillan's 'direct responsibility in crimes against 70,000 human beings'.[16] In reality, the documentary evidence about the British Army's operational crisis in Austria in July 1945 and Britain's obligations under the Anglo-American agreement with Stalin at Yalta earlier that year meant that there were doubts about Macmillan's 'direct responsibility'.[17] During a subsequent libel trial in London after the Tory peer Lord Aldington had contested allegations in the book, Tolstoy's evidence and the chaotic circumstances of the repatriation were exhaustively examined. He lost the case, and was ordered to pay Aldington huge damages. By implication, Macmillan was somewhat exonerated. Amiel's strident journalism never admitted the possibility of harsh judgements about individuals without fully considering the conditions. She had travelled a long way from her earlier assumption that morality would suffer if politics and prejudice overrode laws. In her opinion, some Nazi war criminals should have been protected from international law, and Macmillan should have deliberately ignored the Cossacks' butchery and Britain's obligations under the Treaty of Yalta.

In a much later piece Amiel once again acted in alliance with the rich against the law, extending her sympathy to Swiss bankers who had stolen the deposits of foreign Jews who it was assumed had died during the Holocaust. Amiel stated that the Swiss, like those in other countries, were 'unaware of the details of the Holocaust' during the war.[18] She was mistaken. In July 1942 Swiss nationals and Gerhard Riegner, the Secretary of the World Jewish Congress based in Switzerland, publicly presented the evidence of the Nazis' mass murder of Jews to the Swiss people.[19] Undisputed investigations in the 1990s revealed that the bankers had deliberately lied to Jewish claimants after 1945, denying that their families' wealth had been deposited in Swiss banks. The Swiss Bankers' Association eventually admitted its members' guilt in personally profiting from the Holocaust, and established a $5 billion fund to compensate the victims. Amiel nevertheless defended the bankers. She had become susceptible to a predilection she had identified more than a decade earlier. 'The True Believer,' she had written, 'won't abandon a good plot for lack of supporting material.'[20] That tendency would encourage her to write in 2003, shortly after the invasion of Iraq, 'To deny the existence of [WMDs in Iraq] because they cannot be produced would be silly.'[21]

Barbara Amiel's eulogising of the rich, sometimes with a rose-tinted view of the facts, appealed to Conrad Black. Over the previous thirty years Amiel had moved across the whole political spectrum to reach the position of supporting, alongside him, patricians' privileges. His praise for his fellow-traveller was unconditional: 'Beautiful, brilliant, ideologically a robust kindred spirit, a talented writer and galvanising speaker, chic, humorous, preternaturally sexy, a proud though not religious Jew, tempest-tossed in marriage, disappointed in maternity, a fugitive from Canada assuredly making her way from and towards poles not unlike my own.'[22] During October 1991 the kindred sprits spent much time together. On 17 November Black resolved his fate. He arrived at Amiel's latest home, a duplex off Walton Street in Chelsea, en route to Covent Garden. Scattered around her living room were letters from notable admirers extolling her beauty and intelligence. When she was out of the room he read pledges of love, evidence of her social engagements and praise for recent articles. Propped up on a shelf was the photograph of her father in uniform. In her bedroom, he knew, the walls were covered with peignoir nightdresses. 'They turn Conrad on,' Amiel told Judith Steiner. Black gazed at Amiel's voluptuous figure. Compared to his ex-wife, her throaty voice making brilliant observations was thrilling. 'A man led by his dick,' one of Black's London bankers would conclude, unsurprised by his attraction to 'a reactionary glamourpuss'. Before leaving the house Black declared his love to Amiel, and made an offer of marriage. In his version, Amiel successively expressed bemusement, amazement, and then suggested a visit to a psychiatrist. It appears that she was concerned that Black had not recovered from the breakdown of his marriage. After a single session at the Tavistock Clinic in Hampstead he was assured of his sanity.

Barbara Amiel considered her options. Months earlier, she had described Black in an article as a 'role model'.[23] Previously she had written, 'I have never noticed how he handles knotting his tie or washing behind his ears, but because he handles words with such considerable skill . . . I have always been intrigued by the manifestations of Conrad Black. He understands power.' In Amiel's lexicon, 'power' and 'wealth' implied lifelong 'protection', which, now aged fifty-one, she earnestly sought. His offer fitted her definition of a 'good marriage', although some would undoubtedly suspect her of being a gold-digger. Amiel's ambitions for social advancement had reached a plateau, and Black offered new prospects. Everything she still wanted from life coalesced in a tycoon who she judged to rank among the world's truly rich. He matched her claim that 'a person possessing power has an indefinable mystique'.[24] She accepted his proposal. Once the decision was made, William Goldman was dismissed.

On the day Conrad Black and Barbara Amiel secretly agreed to marry, she celebrated at Manolo Blahnik by choosing pairs of the world's most expensive shoes, as usual with high heels to minimise her big feet. There seemed no reason to stint on expenditure. In previous weeks she had complained that Black spent hours during his visits to her flat on her telephone to Canada and America. 'Oh, don't worry,' he replied. 'I think you'll find that I'll be a profitable cost centre.' Despite her reputation for thorough research, she had not investigated the precise origins of his fortune. She judged Black on his terms, and she loved what she saw. 'A bluebird has landed on my window,' she told her friend Krystyne Griffin. 'Am I not so lucky?' The prospect of marriage to Black resolved her fear of continued rootlessness. The guaranteed security offered by a besotted nabob eager to be her idol was the answer to her prayers.

Among the first to suspect their secret was Andrew Knight. In a chance encounter, he smiled at Black: 'I remember you trying to get me to hire Barbara, and now I hear you're seeing quite a lot of her.' 'Yes I am,' admitted Black. 'And I can tell you, Andrew, she has a wicked body. Quite pulchritudinous,' he added, unable to resist, even when talking about his future wife, challenging his audience's need for a dictionary.[25] Amiel had more than a body, Black reported to others, she also had a mouth.

Early in January 1992, the news of their impending marriage leaked. Not all the comment was favourable. Some would exclaim that the 'huntress', permanently on an upwards trajectory to satisfy her dream, had finally reached the top. The match was described as being between 'Lord Con and Lady Barbarella', or 'Mr Money and Attila the Honey', the right-wing media queen, the Madonna of ultra-conservatism. Black, one wag laughed, was the first tycoon to ditch his first wife for an older model. By trading up, someone said, they would 'spice up their CVs. He needs sex for his image, she needs power.' Black blamed such bitchiness on envy of 'Barbara's great talent and beauty'.[26] Journalists who telephoned Amiel for a statement encountered hell. 'Absolutely no comment. I have nothing to say,' snapped the woman who previously could rarely resist self-revelation. Those still hunting for quotations about the couple landed on Frank Johnson. 'Barbara is marvellous,' he said, adding that the only people who hated Amiel were women resentful of her looks and brains, and men whose advances she had spurned.[27] Eventually

Amiel agreed to comment on the 'horrendous' publicity: 'You must forgive one for being snappish,' she sighed. 'Now the knives are drawn. My marriages and even a cup of coffee I had with a friend have become "an item" in my Past . . . The upside of all the nasty remarks that peppered the Canadian press about my friendship with Conrad Black is that, speaking for myself, happiness is an elusive bird, and all the screechings in the world can't make its song sound any less sweet.'[28] To her sister she admitted her vulnerability, saying, 'I hope this one lasts.'

Others recognised something more profound. Regardless of the stark difference in their backgrounds, the ambitions of Conrad and Barbara had merged. There was a unique community of interest, a natural symmetry to their union, which neither had found in previous relationships. Both loved language and power, were immersed in newspapers and politics, and regarded the other as brilliant. Both shared a need to be respected, accepted and admired in the spotlight. Their inferiority complexes were partly personal and partly those of the inhabitant of Toronto towards Londoners and New Yorkers. Together they could break out of those shadows. There was, however, an added ingredient. They shared the legacy of fathers who had committed suicide, a link which only they could understand.

7

Demons

Robert Maxwell's death on 5 November 1991 provoked unusual sympathy from Conrad Black. 'Don't be too hard on Bob,' Black told Max Hastings, mistakenly assuming that Maxwell had committed suicide. 'I know he was a crook, but he was a not uninteresting character as well. He had his moments.' Hastings was reluctantly persuaded to 'err on the side of generosity'. Black was pleased with the *Telegraph*'s lenient obituary.[1]

Black's compassion for Maxwell surprised Hastings, who was unaware of his employer's empathy with other members of the rich men's club earning their fortunes by dancing on the edge. Only months earlier Black had consoled Paul Reichmann, the near-bankrupt Canadian property developer, by re-endorsing his directorship of Hollinger. Black admired Reichmann's reckless but ultimately successful gambling. In recent months he had also expressed his dismay at the treatment of Gerald Ronson, the British tycoon who had been convicted and imprisoned for secretly propping up the price of Guinness's shares during a take-over bid. In Canada he would support the theatrical impresario Garth Drabinsky, wanted on fraud charges in America. He had also suggested the appointment as a Hollinger director of Adnan Khashoggi, the controversial Saudi middleman released in July 1990 from a New York jail after his acquittal on fraud charges. Black's sympathy for falling stars, regarded by many as shady, was inexplicable to those unaware of his own history, but consistent with his loathing for authority and prosecutors, the little people in his Gulliver's world. His affection for the anti-hero was matched by his own desire for popular acclaim.

Black had met Maxwell at the Savoy in July 1986. The owner of Mirror Group Newspapers had complimented the newcomer for 'landing history's largest fish with history's smallest hook'. Flattered by Maxwell's praise, Black had discussed plans for a joint printing plant, but Maxwell's unreliability ended their cooperation. Like Black, Maxwell was distrusted by the stock market because he profited from inter-company trading at the expense of minority shareholders. Just as there was a 'Black Factor' in Canada, London had its 'Max Factor'. In both cities there were doubts about newspaper proprietors who brazenly promoted their own opinions, and tycoons who aggressively used the libel laws to suppress criticism. To Black's dismay, as the revelation of Maxwell's frauds unfolded after his mysterious death, some people noted a number of similarities between himself and Maxwell. The comparison tarnished Black's magic, discounting the value of Hollinger's shares. Others also suffered. United Newspapers' share price fell, and Black would lose £21 million when he sold his stake in 1992.[2] He would also lose a substantial sum on a 13 per cent stake he accumulated in Trinity International, another British newspaper group, because its share structure prevented a takeover. In Canada, Hollinger's share price also fell. The revelation of Maxwell's frauds had spurred researchers to discover that Black's restructure of his companies in 1990 had been completed at the expense of the minority shareholders. Black had perceived the risk to his reputation in July 1991, when the *Globe and Mail* had reported the comment of James Cole, a Toronto broker, that Hollinger's structure and accounts were 'misleading' the market. 'That is absolutely preposterous,' screamed Black.[3] A few days later, the same newspaper described Black as a 'mutant' and a 'shabby intellectual traitor' for suggesting that Canada surrender its sovereignty to America. Black's opinions were harmlessly lampooned, but he nevertheless issued a writ claiming C$1.25 million damages.[4] A new bout of criticism, he now feared, was about to explode. Ann Finlayson, writing in the *Globe and Mail*, cited the Dominion pension saga and suggested that some still criticised Black's 'corporate banditry'. Black issued another writ. The revelations following Maxwell's death increased his sensitivity. *God's Dominion*, a respectable book examining religions by Ron Graham, a lapsed Catholic, contained a single sentence implying that Black believed greed and ego added to the sum of human misery. Graham assumed that Black was a friend, and would appreciate a favourable exposition of his humanity. To his surprise, Black interpreted Graham's sentence as defamatory, because he did not believe that 'ego and greed . . . have produced human misery'. He believed the opposite, and instructed his lawyer Peter Atkinson to issue a writ demanding C$1.5 million in damages and an injunction preventing the book's further sale. Graham was horrified. Rejecting mediation and negotiation, Black spent huge sums pursuing him, demanding total capitulation for accusing him of being an egoistic, greedy, ruthless, predatory tycoon and 'responsible for causing human misery'. Terrified by the escalating costs, Graham and his publisher arranged for a grovelling apology to be printed in the *Globe and Mail*.[5] The surrender confirmed Black's belief in his own invulnerability. Once again he had avoided cross-examination under oath. No one, he implied, could presume to understand his mind or character except in the most favourable light, and even that was subject to his approval. Performing as the virtuous grandee, Black even wrote letters publicly attacking the *Telegraph*'s columnists. Stephen Robinson was criticised for predicting Bill Clinton's victory over George Bush; Edward Whitley for predicting that the Reichmanns would lose their fortune at Canary Wharf;[6] Richard Dorment was nearly dismissed for criticising Walter Annenberg, an American billionaire and former ambassador to London whom Black particularly worshipped; and another unfortunately accurate writer was lambasted for highlighting Lord Carrington's limitations as NATO's mediator in war-stricken Yugoslavia.[7] Black expected his newspaper to protect, not criticise, the rich and famous.

His own collection of celebrity admirers expanded following the appointment as a director of Hollinger Inc. of Allan Gottlieb, Canada's former ambassador in Washington. While serving in Washington, Gottlieb had satisfied Black's request for introductions to famous Americans. Among those he attracted to the dinners at the Canadian Embassy was Richard Burt, a senior American diplomat. Gottlieb assumed that the purpose was to improve Black's understanding of American politics rather than to aid his social climbing, but Burt was also recruited to Black's galaxy. Black's offer of a directorship to Gottlieb was gratefully accepted. The ex-ambassador was reliant on a small government pension after other prospects did not materialise. Black had told Gottlieb soon after his appointment that he wanted an annual Hollinger dinner in Washington, attended by opinion-makers. On Gottlieb's recommendation, Hollinger employed the event organiser Carolyn Peachy to arrange the dinner. Her task was to find a suitable location, supervise the caterers, florists and lighting, and recommend the guest list. Using Gottlieb's Rollodex and her own sources, Peachy persuaded 150 notables to accept the invitation at the Folger Shakespearean Library, specially chosen to reflect the host's interests. Black selected the wines and spent many hours arranging the seating plan. On the night, to the organiser's embarrassment, most of the guests asked, 'Who's Conrad Black?' Oblivious to his anonymity, Black was intoxicated by the evening's success. Social triumphs fuelled his commercial ambitions.

The most succulent target in the summer was the Fairfax

Group in Australia. Another person's misery was once again Black's opportunity. The group, led by thirty-year-old Warwick Fairfax, owned a clutch of Australia's most prominent newspapers, including the major broadsheets the *Sydney Morning Herald* and the Melbourne *Age*, reaching about 20 per cent of the country's readership. A family dispute in 1987 had wrecked the company's stability. To resolve the crisis Warwick Fairfax had borrowed a huge sum to buy out his rivals, but by 1990 he had run out of money, and the administrators of the insolvent company were seeking new owners. Ranking as a major media player, Black was a natural candidate. The disadvantage was travelling to Australia, a greater burden, he complained, than crossing the Atlantic. The opportunity, however, was too good to miss, and Dan Colson volunteered to mastermind the bid.

Black's social life eased his introduction into the competition. Through James Goldsmith he had met Kerry Packer, the Australian billionaire. In May 1991 the two joined forces to overcome substantial legal obstacles to a bid for the Fairfax Group. Firstly, Packer was barred from owning more than 15 per cent of a newspaper because of his television interests. Secondly, foreign nationals were not permitted to own more than 15 per cent of an Australian newspaper. The third barrier was Australians' dislike of foreign tycoons, and in particular of Black himself, after local journalists had reproduced critical reports from Canadian newspapers. The final hurdle was the rival bidders, principally the Tourang group, a consortium of junk bond holders led by Malcolm Turnbull, a prominent Australian lawyer, and another group led by Tony O'Reilly, the Irish chief executive of Heinz. O'Reilly's Australian ex-wife had introduced him to the owners of local newspapers and to Australian politicians, including Prime Minister Bob Hawke. With that background, O'Reilly was the favoured candidate.

Even before Colson arrived in Australia, O'Reilly's team had launched a venomous campaign to characterise Black as a fascist, feudal press baron. In reply, Black dubbed O'Reilly's 'hysterical' onslaught as the product of a 'ketchup salesman'. Black issued writs for defamation, especially against the members of the Friends of Fairfax.[8] 'Serve the writs at their homes,' he ordered his lawyers. 'It was necessary to make the point that defaming me had its risks,' he would say with satisfaction.[9] Black's trust in writs to intimidate his critics was short-sighted. O'Reilly smelled blood. He won the regulator's support and sought popular sympathy, accusing Black of being 'an interventionist, right-wing pro-Thatcherite owner'. The following month, political pressure forced Packer to withdraw. 'O'Reilly and his pimps are to blame,' raged Black, attacking the official support for O'Reilly as 'sleazy, venal and despicable'.[10] Just as all seemed lost, Colson produced a formula to secure the government's support. In collaboration with the Tourang group, Black would agree to buy just 15 per cent of the company, but would take full responsibility for its management. The take-over was sealed. In theory, the investment appeared to be a good bet. Buying from a receiver, Black knew, rarely meant overpaying. For Au$1.425 billion (£638 million), the business was annually producing a $190 million cash flow. With good management, Black and the banks which loaned him the money expected the annual flow to increase to $250 million. The defect was that while he would be 100 per cent responsible for the company's management, he would receive just 15 per cent of the benefits, and none of the cash flow or assets could be incorporated into Hollinger's accounts. 'They can't hold us to 15 per cent,' Black predicted. 'It's an iniquitous law and a nonsense.' Ignoring reality, he headed to Sydney to claim his prize after the bloody public battle.

A bank of cameras and a crowd of journalists awaited Black on 13 December 1991. Australia's summer sun, he believed, was especially shining upon him. Glory required special phrases, and every word he uttered was intended to be judged by posterity.

'Contrary to widespread rumours,' he said with exquisite delivery, 'it is not the plan of Mr Colson or myself to erect a guillotine at Broadway [where the *Sydney Morning Herald* was based] and move journalists through it on a random basis.'[11] Like the old British Empire, he boasted, the sun would never set on his publishing kingdom. His new audience applauded, and the world hailed Black's coup. In the shorthand beloved of journalists, Black was described as the new rival to Murdoch. Reading those newspaper articles fed his self-glorification and his appetite for further expansion.

Top of his list were Maxwell's *New York Daily News* and Channel 5, a new television station in Britain. A telephone call from Rupert Murdoch on 14 February 1992 confirmed Black's rising eminence. Maxwell's private possessions were being auctioned at Sotheby's in London by the administrators of his insolvent estate. Murdoch had for years regarded Maxwell as a dishonest Soviet agent, and wanted to share his relish of his rival's final humiliation. Black swelled with pride that Murdoch had chosen to share his pleasure with him, and laughed loudly as Murdoch recounted Maxwell's folly in regarding himself as an equal of the world's biggest media tycoon. At the end of the call Black's self-esteem soared, but on reflection he knew that he shared few of Murdoch's values. He disliked Murdoch's merciless satirising of British institutions, his newspapers' profiteering from the invasion of privacy, and his appetite for trashing human dignity. Black wanted to build a rival global newspaper chain, but he lacked the energy, expertise and vision to emulate Murdoch's diversification into television, film, satellite, cable, and exhibitions and trade specialities. Newspapers were the only business Black understood and, unlike his adversary, his finances were vulnerable to changes of government. In early 1992 he had good reason to fear the anticipated election of a Labour government in Britain.

The atmosphere at midnight on 9 April 1992 in the Savoy's

Lancaster Room was electric. About three hundred people, Conrad Black's guests, were staring at the projection of BBC Television's election-night programme on a huge screen. The second result declared was Basildon, a Conservative marginal seat in Essex. Loud cheers greeted the surprise Tory victory, seemingly confounding the predictions of defeat for John Major. 'More champagne!' shouted the astonished guests, enjoying a generous buffet.

Conrad Black arrived at his own party with Margaret Thatcher after midnight. Like an emperor he circulated among the Tory faithful, suggesting that he and other newspaper proprietors, rather than the Conservative Party itself, had defeated Labour. 'I told Hastings to promote the party's interests, not Major's,' he told his audience. 'I wanted unity, not arguments about Maastricht.'[12] He was referring to the treaty signed by Major in December 1991, committing Britain to further integration into the European Union. Major's signature had provoked bitter divisions among Conservatives. No other proprietor of a national British newspaper would have criticised his editor as Conrad Black did that evening, with the exception of the late Robert Maxwell; and to Black's irritation the aftermath of Maxwell's death clung like glue to his own reputation.

Black's increasing debts, a familiar feature in his operations, had raised embarrassing questions about whether he was a serious businessman intending to consolidate his newspapers within a normal corporation, or, like Maxwell, simply a deal junkie. The purchase of Fairfax and over three hundred small newspapers in Canada and the USA, incurring loans of C$727 million, and his ill-considered attempt to become a media mogul in Britain by investing in United Newspapers and Trinity International, were the curtain raisers to his appearance in New York promoting his bid for the *Daily News*, a loss-making tabloid formerly owned by Robert Maxwell. None of his activities promised substantial profits to fund repayments to the Canadian Imperial Bank of

Commerce, his principal banker. Although he remained a director of the bank, Black sensed an intolerance among the senior staff towards the loans to him. To strengthen his position he invited Don Fullerton, CIBC's retiring chairman, to become a director of Hollinger Inc. Fullerton, he calculated, would strengthen his relationship with the bank although more support was required.

The flotation of the *Telegraph* group on the London stock exchange, Black decided, would be the best solution to repay his debts and fund his aggrandisement. There was, he understood, a risk. The British regulators vigorously scrutinised companies seeking public money. He was unconcerned. His verbal performance, he trusted, would suffocate any doubters, and the sums were too enticing to ignore. Between May 1985 and July 1992, Black had paid £119 million for his 83 per cent stake in the *Telegraph*. He intended to sell 13 per cent of the shares for £85 million and keep 68 per cent. The remaining 19 per cent of the shares were held either by his staff or by shareholders from the Hartwell era. The prospects were magnetic. In 1991 the *Telegraph*'s profits were £40.5 million, 35 per cent more than Black had paid for the newspaper six years earlier, and there was no reason to expect the income to fall. The bankers and brokers visiting Black's fifteenth-floor office were impressed. Uniquely in London, the tycoon's shelves were full of books he had read, his walls covered with paintings and drawings he understood, and his mastery of nineteenth-century European and American history kept them spellbound. All of which confirmed their client to be an extraordinary, erudite and amusing man.

Black's honesty was endorsed by the City institutions promoting the flotation. Evelyn de Rothschild, a Hollinger director and the chairman of N.M. Rothschild, agreed to underwrite the share price that was agreed with Cazenove's. David Mayhew, John Kemp-Welch and Anthony Forbes, Cazenove's senior partners, began negotiations with David Montagu about the share price and the terms of the prospectus. Within hours, however, the Maxwell legacy was haunting their discussions. In 1991 Maxwell had floated Mirror Group Newspapers, but had insisted that he retain the majority of the shares. Distrust of Maxwell had caused the sale to flop. Over the following months his plundering of the Mirror Group's pension funds had been facilitated by his control of the company. Memories of Maxwell prompted Cazenove's directors to ask David Montagu how potential shareholders could be reassured that Black would not resort to similar ruses. The brokers sensed that just as Black delighted in using convoluted vocabulary to baffle his audience, so he chose complicated corporate structures to obscure his business affairs.

At the same time, unknown to Montagu, Cazenove's researches into Black's activities in Canada had unearthed several startling similarities to Maxwell. Black had been criticised for shuffling debt between companies and disregarding his minority shareholders. Just like Maxwell, as Black was chairman of all the companies, the possible conflicts of interest were glaring. Black's corporate structure seemed similarly confused to Maxwell's. Ravelston, a private company, owned 78.2 per cent of Hollinger Inc., a public company in Toronto which would, after the flotation, own the majority of the *Telegraph*, a public company. But by then keeping the majority of the *Telegraph*'s shares, Black could discriminate against the minority shareholders, using Hollinger Inc. as his personal company. To prevent Black from secretly profiting from inter-company trading – namely by arranging a deal so that his own private company profited at the expense of the *Telegraph*, the public company – Rothschild's and Cazenove's imposed an embarrassing condition. If the *Telegraph*'s directors declined to complete a deal but Hollinger Inc. proceed with the same deal, then the *Telegraph*'s minority shareholders would have to be asked to approve the deal – and Black could not vote.

Black appeared discomfited. Posing as the Titan, outraged that his integrity could be doubted, he complained with familiar bluster that 'The capricious imposition of ridiculous and unjust measures suggests that the company has been overtaken, dominated, subverted, suborned and kidnapped by a bunch of get-rich-quick parvenus, and that's just not true.' His audience was impressed by his fluency, but knew that investors would require more than words for protection. The discussions between Rothschild and Black were peppered by arguments. 'I'm no Maxwell,' Black told a young banker whose questions he deemed to be insolent. The bankers remained silent, waiting for the air to clear. 'I understand that is a natural comparison,' Black eventually said, 'but it would mean that I am doing things that would lead straight to a jail cell.' Trusting the strength of a blatant untruth, he asserted, 'Unlike Maxwell, I have no real debt and my financial ethics have never been questioned.' The SEC 'consent' and the Manos judgement, he believed, were deeply buried. To squash the last doubters, he added with a deep sense of self-righteousness, 'Any link with Maxwell is absolutely outrageous, scurrilous and demonstrably untrue.'[13] Irritated that for every ten people who praised him there was always one who damned him as a crook, Black asked a prominent Canadian to approach the SEC informally and negotiate the removal of the 'consent'. 'Negative,' Black was told. 'They won't play.' With no choice, he agreed to accept the restrictions. He needed the money to play in New York.[14]

Owning the *Daily News* would be a succulent visiting card for Conrad Black among Manhattan's elite, the identical motive which had spurred Maxwell's purchase in 1991. During his brief ownership Maxwell had failed to break the Mafia's grip over the business, and the newspaper was still losing about $750,000 a month. Black proposed to fire seven hundred of the 2,100 employees and move the editorial offices from 42nd Street in Manhattan to a cheaper location. To prove his manhood in the negotiations with the trade unions, he composed an attractive quip: 'I have no interest in coming to New York to clasp my lips around an exhaust pipe,' and he sniped contemptuously at his rival bidder Mort Zuckerman, a property developer and the proprietor of *US News and World Report*. Zuckerman, he proclaimed, had a vulnerable ego spawned by a doting mother. The judge responsible for saving the bankrupt company nominated Black as the preferred bidder at $75 million. Black was ecstatic. Big in Toronto and London, he was on the verge of being crowned in New York. But as so often, Black's words failed to match his deeds. Ponderous and unperceptive, he could not forge a working relationship with the coarse trade union officials. Zuckerman, faster and shrewder, derailed Black by promising better terms, including the re-employment of men condemned as criminals. Black walked away, caricaturing Zuckerman as 'a well-to-do amateur making non-economic deals to get into the glamour and influence business'. Zuckerman's recklessness, Black proclaimed loudly, was unsustainable: 'He will be on his knees every day before the head of the pressmen's union and the drivers' union to get his paper printed and delivered. He will not have the ability to manage anything.' To relieve his disappointment, Black agreed with Radler's suggestion to buy the *Chicago Sun-Times*, a troubled newspaper dominated by the superior *Chicago Tribune*. Owning that paper would at least be a recognised status symbol in Palm Beach and Manhattan.

The purchase agreement in Chicago coincided with bad news from London. On 9 June 1992 the prospectus for selling the *Telegraph*'s shares had been issued by Rothschild's. Days later, the brokers and bankers discovered Black's loans of £33 million from the *Telegraph* since 1986, taken out without the approval of the minority shareholders. Nerves were strained. 'Those arrangements,' soothed Black, 'were inadvertently overlooked.' The ruffled feathers did not trouble Black, immersed in a hectic symmetry of diverse events. In the midst of the flotation of the *Telegraph* in London, the disappointment in New York, the purchase in Chicago and finalising the secret arrangements to marry Barbara Amiel, he hosted Hollinger's annual dinner in Toronto. The guest speaker was Richard Nixon. Ten years earlier, Black had said the discredited former President was 'sleazy, tasteless and neurotic', and 'deserves the compassion due to sick people'. But in the intervening years, recalling his own narrow escapes, Black's attitude had mellowed into appreciation of a man determined to re-emerge on his own terms. As the two sat with Henry Kissinger, Black felt a kinship towards a politician who, like himself, had defied his critics and survived by an overwhelming sense of self-righteousness.

Black was uninterested in Nixon's lies and crimes. Watergate, in his opinion, was 'sanctimonious pseudo-legalistic putschism'.[15] Like the rich, the President deserved to be protected from mere mortals' laws. With familiar sensitivity towards the reviled, Black regarded Nixon in 1992 as a hero, the victim of an emotional witch-hunt against 'a profoundly and widely esteemed figure, an elder statesman'.[16] He condemned the loathsome media outright. 'Richard Nixon's resignation,' he wrote, 'was not . . . a triumph of the free press, it was a triumph of Nixon's neuroses and his enemies' vindictiveness over the national interest'. Black's hatred of retribution pleased Henry Kissinger, by then a close associate. During the dinner, the host could not resist parading his knowledge of American history to Nixon. He even recited some the former President's speeches. 'You were the victim of spite and envy,' he pronounced, his recurring explanation of any criticism. With insightful self-analysis, he would later praise Nixon's self-preservation: 'In the end only Richard Nixon could and did defeat and humiliate Richard Nixon. Nixon was illustrative of the truth of the old adage that for every ten men who can stand adversity, only one can stand success.'[17] Black counted himself among that minority.

Conrad Black's hectic schedule presented the image of a man

capable of withstanding adversity and enjoying success. From Toronto he jetted back to London to enjoy, on 25 June 1992, a late-night celebration at 11 Downing Street of Chancellor of the Exchequer Norman Lamont's fiftieth birthday, and then, early the next morning, he arrived in the City to finalise with his bankers the *Telegraph*'s flotation, due on 1 July. Black's advisers had become nervous. The *Independent* newspaper, quoting Black's secret diversion of £33 million in loans, repeated the familiar allegation that he had deliberately manipulated his Canadian company assets to enrich himself at the expense of minority shareholders. To suppress further speculation, Black issued a writ; he would eventually receive an apology and damages, but the harm was done. The shares' sale price was reduced to £3.25, valuing the company at £470 million. 'Rock bottom,' muttered a member of Black's team. Minutes after the shares were launched, the price tanked to £2.80. Black pocketed £84 million, showing no concern for the losses borne by Rothschild and the underwriters.

Equally unconcerned were the personalities, including seven peers, who had accepted Black's invitation to join the *Telegraph*'s board of directors for a celebratory lunch at Canary Wharf with Black's advisory committee. Henry Kissinger, the former President of France Valéry Giscard d'Estaing, Lord Hanson, Sir Martin Jacomb, Paul Volker, Jacob Rothschild and Margaret Thatcher listened to their host's lengthy analysis of world affairs without revealing any impatience. On the contrary, they appeared impressed. Searching for a metaphor, one observer would compare the newspaper owner to a Spanish bullfighter – a large upper body with spindly legs. After the applause each guest was invited to contribute to the discussion. All departed having enjoyed a well-paid day, untroubled that their presence would be used by their paymaster to endorse his assertion of honesty.

The only voice of doubt was Hal Jackman's. The rich Canadian sent his old friend several books about Hitler and Napoleon's disastrous invasions of Russia. 'I find his appetite somewhat large, maybe insatiable,' sighed Jackman. 'That always presents dangers.'[18] Black was not listening. Luck, he believed, was on his side. In the midst of a recession, the value of his original investment in the *Telegraph* had increased by 1,500 per cent. He was on a roll, confirmed later in the month by his investiture as a Privy Councillor of Canada by the Queen during a state visit. The Queen, he would later say, had thanked him for the *Telegraph*'s 'tasteful coverage of the marital difficulties of the Royal family', and he would claim that the Queen Mother repeated the royal gratitude three weeks later.[19] There were no eyewitnesses to confirm these comments.

On a high, Black flew in August to Australia to meet Paul Keating, the new Prime Minister. Black needed political support to remove the 15 per cent limit on foreign ownership of the Fairfax Group, which, as predicted, was a financial handicap. His earlier meetings with Bob Hawke, the former Prime Minister, had suggested a possibility of change. Keating confirmed that the limit would be raised to 25 per cent. Any further increase, he said, would depend on Black's performance over the following years. Black was not pleased. Impatient to rank as a major global media tycoon, he returned to Toronto to finalise the purchase on 13 November 1992 of 21.5 per cent of Southam, the Canadian newspaper company that owned eighteen daily Canadian newspapers. The price was C$259 million. Black appeared once again to be profiting from another's misfortune. Over the years the Southam family had invested millions of dollars on buildings and their newspapers' editorial content without increasing the profits. Crippled by age, illness and factionalism, the family's hopes were sinking. There was an undisclosed purpose in Black's impatient attack on the company. Southam possessed substantial cash deposits, but they were only accessible with 100 per cent ownership. If Black bought the company outright he could have the cash, and he would also own a total of one hundred daily newspapers and two hundred weeklies across North America, making him Canada's leading newspaper publisher. Many of those newspapers were earning 30 per cent net profits. His complete success depended on an agreement with Paul Desmarais, a Canadian billionaire who owned 19 per cent of Southam, just a small part of his C$25 billion assets. Black was to be disappointed. Desmarais had never quite trusted him since he had leant over during a dinner party and asked, 'Tell me, Paul, what's it like to be a billionaire?' Desmarais mocked Black's desire to play in the big league: 'I bought into Southam at C$14, Conrad joined the party at C$18.10.' Black's pleasure was not quashed by the older man's churlishness. His purchase in April 1993 would be a significant event in Canada, and to Desmarais's dismay he used it to promote himself. 'Conrad's a little too big for his boots,' Desmarais told a friend. 'He's behaving like a spoilt child.'

As a wise man, Black could have reflected upon the importance of this milestone, and sought to persuade his critics that their past suspicions were unfounded. Instead, he remained consistent. He committed the *Telegraph* to buying the Southam shares without first notifying the *Telegraph*'s directors, and then abused Southam's directors. 'By his deceptions,' one of them emotionally alleged, 'he's using his total force to try to demolish us.' Desmarais was shocked. 'Conrad's a bully, not a businessman,' he complained, 'and he's got away with it for too many years.' To aggravate Black, Desmarais voted with Southam's old guard to dilute Black's stake in the company and deprive him of any serious influence. Hal Jackman was again bewildered: 'He's riding too fast, too high and beyond reality,' he said, surveying the Southam conflict. Expansion and huge debts were a well-trodden formula for the ambitious heading towards the graveyard. 'The problem with Conrad,' said Jackman, 'is that he's always looking to the next deal and not carefully managing his assets.' Such piety irritated Black.

'Absolute crap,' he shot back, scathing about Jackman and his family. 'He's very suspicious of everything that isn't very slow-moving and very deliberate, following upon his father.' Black derided the Jackmans as being embroiled in a fifty-year plan, unappealing to a man in a hurry.[20] 'Glory is but fleeting,' replied Jackman.

8

Bliss

Conrad Black celebrated his marriage to Barbara Amiel in London on 21 July 1992. Seated between Margaret Thatcher and Sarah Ferguson, the Duchess of York, Black had collected some loyal supporters along the single table in Annabel's private dining room. Lord Weidenfeld, Jacob Rothschild, David Frost, Richard Perle, David Radler and David Metcalfe had been invited for the coronation of the 'power couple' after the legal ceremony at the Chelsea Register Office witnessed by Brian Stewart and Miriam Gross. All had been entertained by Max Hastings's speech and a wedding cake modelled on the *Daily Telegraph*'s front page. The mood was festive, but towards the end of the evening several guests were reconsidering their host's character. 'What on earth is the Duchess of York doing here?' asked a surprised David Metcalfe. 'Conrad's a starfucker,' replied another, irritated by Black's social climbing and trophy wife. 'Like hydrogen and nitrogen,' whispered another guest, eyeing the two newlyweds. 'Safe by themselves, but explosive when combined.' Others noted a melancholy aspect. The Blacks were well suited, but marrying so late in life suggested missed opportunities. 'Previously she always liked oddballs,' said one, unaware just how unconventional Black's business practices were. One woman, suspecting Amiel's material motives for marriage, questioned her love for Black. 'Oh yes, it's real love,' she laughed, 'but I bet he's terrible in bed.'

Any lingering remnants of Amiel's reticence about her new wealth and status had been replaced by a desire to be known as rich and influential. Seven years after her fateful marriage to David Graham, she had properly married up. Among those surprised not to receive invitations was Fred Eaton, the Canadian High Commissioner in London since 1991. Over the previous months Eaton had hosted lunches and dinners at Black's request for those passing through the capital who could be helpful to his ambitions. Just before the wedding the Blacks had attended a party at the High Commission. Eaton painfully noticed how Amiel had ignored his greeting, turned and walked away from himself and his wife. Just as some men swooned at receiving Amiel's full attention, Eaton was crushed by her snub. Amiel's blacklist extended to her old college friend Ellie Tesher, her school friend Louise Lore, whose television programme she had unkindly criticised in a newspaper, and Irene Buckman, her father's sister, and all other members of her family.

The following day the Blacks flew on Concorde to New York for dinner at La Côte Basque with the conservative newspaper columnist William F. Buckley Jr, his wife Pat, and the journalist John O'Sullivan. Over dinner the newlyweds argued about the decriminalisation of drugs, which she supported and he opposed. 'Some people might say Conrad's starfucking,' Buckley later reminisced, 'but he's a very curious man – one has the feeling that essentially he's taking things in all of the time.'[1] Their next stop was to join Black's three children at a cottage in Maine rented from David Rockefeller. The opportunity for Amiel to build a relationship in difficult circumstances was not a marked success. Then it was on to a celebratory dinner in Toronto and a flight to Wakaya, a private island in Fiji owned by Peter Munk. The Blacks expected that their week at the 5,500-acre resort created for just six couples, with a golf course, excellent shooting and a first-class chef, would be a romantic climax. Instead, Black stepped off the aircraft and complained of the heat and boredom. They departed for London after three days.

Their marital home was Black's house in Highgate. Inheriting the suburban home chosen and decorated by Joanna understandably depressed her successor. 'It's all so cheap and tacky,' Amiel complained to Judith Steiner, visiting on a hot August weekend. 'Look at these borders,' she said, pointing at the walls. 'They're stuck on. They should be painted on.' In bad weather, she added, the long walk from the house to the waiting car would ruin her hair, and the drive to her haunts in Knightsbridge and Chelsea took at least forty minutes.[2] In compensation, her relationship with her new husband, she disclosed, was perfect. Sitting in the garden, Steiner noted that Conrad Black was on heat. 'If I walked past him,' she told a friend, 'I would have had to step over his tongue, literally hanging out. He was smitten by her sex.' Steiner was looking at a man enslaved by his wife's worship of him. Placed on a pedestal, Black felt a hero. Since the marriage his depression had lifted, life had become perfect. Amiel took care of his diet, insisted that his tailor fashion less stuffy suits, and loved arguing about politics. They were, he prided himself, a team. By understanding his vanities she could enable his ambitions. In turn, relaxed and smiling, he sought to satisfy his new wife's dreams.

Despite appearances, Barbara Amiel was not wholly secure. 'He will leave me,' she told a friend. 'I'm making plans for when it all goes wrong.' Just weeks after the marriage, she was tense and pessimistic. Miriam Gross, a generous friend, explained Amiel's predicament: 'She is very aware of the danger of taking advantage of the luxuries of life, and how things can change from one moment to the next, as any intelligent person would be. She will guard against and consciously fight against being spoilt. That is why being married to a rich man won't change her. She won't let herself become dependent. She will be prepared for any eventuality.'[3] Amiel's angst surprised Black. Marriage, he had assumed, would lighten the dark side of her life. His remedy, which also satisfied his own desires, was to initiate fundamental changes. There was, he intimated to Amiel, no limit to his finances. It was agreed that they would move nearer to central London.

In December 1992 Conrad Black bought 14 Cottesmore Gardens, a terraced nineteenth-century townhouse in Kensington, from Alan Bond, the disgraced Australian businessman. The price was £3.5 million. Soon after, he bought the adjoining house for a similar amount. The rich set in Toronto were amazed. 'He's competing with Galen Weston,' suggested Peter Munk. 'Just move the decimal point two places for Conrad's wealth,' another smirked, assessing Black's fortune at no more than C$80 million. While Weston's wealth could be accurately assessed every day by checking his company's share price, Black's finances were as clear as mud. 'He's bought the houses with borrowed money,' one concluded. 'And from a crook.'

Assuming that her husband's wealth was truly immense, Amiel vowed to make the best of her beauty, brains and articulacy to create a palace that would attract celebrity worshippers of a 'power couple'. Without hesitation Black agreed that Britain's most expensive interior designer, David Mlinaric, should be employed to oversee the renovations. Mlinaric, whose previous clients included Jacob Rothschild, John Sainsbury and Paul Getty, was affordable only to the city's richest inhabitants. His brief was to provide designs for ten bedrooms and six reception rooms suitable for entertaining up to 350 people. Part of the first floor was to be removed to create a huge ground-floor reception area. Visitors would enter through a marble entrance hall and walk up the stairs past hand-painted *trompe l'œil* walls covered with curtains and gardens to gaze from a balcony down onto what was intended to rank among the world's most eminent salons. For the Blacks' private use there would be a swimming pool, an underground gymnasium and a mahogany-panelled library. The furnishings would include portraits by Joshua Reynolds and George Stubbs. Naturally, there would also be a bust of Napoleon. 'We needed the right background for laughter and challenging conversation,' Amiel explained. 'We needed the contents to be "high" decoratively, to animate such a large place.'[4] There was one omission. 'We thought these rooms would be suitable for the children,' said Mlinaric. 'We won't need children's rooms,' Mlinaric was told. Black's children would rarely visit the house.

The rebuilding would take over a year. In the meantime the Blacks rented a house in Chester Square, Belgravia. Marking his first steps away from his former modesty, Black encouraged the joint cultivation of new images for himself and his wife. Barbara Amiel's accent became more refined. By contrast with her previous search for publicity, she refused interviews with magazines whose attention she had once sought. Discretion, she decided, was temporarily advantageous. The new style was no longer casual and cool, and she dispensed with some old friends, including Judith Steiner: 'You remind me of a person on a step exercise machine, always going up but never getting anywhere,' she told Steiner. 'I have a new friend. Miriam Gross. I don't need you any more.'

Chester Square was a laboratory in which to learn social graces. At an early dinner party, Amiel had fussed about the use of fish knives and the appropriate dress to wear. Paul Johnson was surprised that all the men were grouped at one end of the table, and the women at the other. Lessons were soon learned. At a dinner party for Henry Kissinger, Stella Rimington, the director of MI5, was seated to the American celebrity's left, and another woman on his right. She would be told later that evening by Amiel, 'If I hadn't fallen for Conrad, perhaps I would have fallen for Henry.' Black was oblivious to the mood. Dinner parties were often organised for him to deliver lectures, to score points, and to display the power of his memory by quoting from books and poems. While most hosts expected their guests to sing for their supper, Conrad Black expected his to listen for theirs. In the grander environment, Black's self-confidence, even swagger, increased. He was holding court in his own home, beating the English language into submission. He demonstratively showed his gratitude to the 'little woman', as he began calling his aspiring society hostess. The witticism was not appreciated by everyone. 'No joy for you in those wedding bells, my boy,' John Fraser, the editor of *Saturday Night*, had been told by his wife. Years earlier, the diminutive Fraser had hotly disputed Amiel's allegations of left-wing bias in Canada's media. At the climax of the feud, Amiel announced at a book club meeting in Oakville, Ontario, 'I am the victim of a monstrous lie by a little fellow.' After her marriage to Black, Amiel was appointed as a director of the *Spectator* and *Saturday Night*, and Fraser was fired.

In London, under Amiel's influence, Black had become irritated by Max Hastings's 'incorrect political thinking'. At her direction, Black protested about an article by the *Telegraph*'s fashion editor about the popularity of long dresses. 'It is bunk to claim that long is in,' Black asserted. 'Short is out and anything above the knee, as the *Daily Telegraph* wrote of the Princess of Wales, is dowdy.' Amiel's interference was obvious. In the *Sunday Times*, to which she had been appointed as a columnist by Andrew Neil in 1991, she explained the psychology of the hemline: 'Fashion offers a woman an opportunity to make a statement: following fashion requires assets. Those that can discard old clothes and buy new are making a status assertion. But they are also making a sexual assertion . . . an indication of her intensity and readiness for sexual negotiation.' Fashion, she concluded, was 'biology', and skirts would remain high.[5] Dismayed by Amiel's influence, Hastings commissioned a new article humorously reflecting Black's point of view with a photograph of Amiel in a mini-skirt.[6] Amiel's nit-picking intensified until, some months later, Black telephoned Hastings from Palm Beach in the middle of the night. He had read an editorial criticising the NHS for giving IVF treatment to women over fifty. '*Daily Telegraph* readers are liberal,' said Black, 'like my wife, and would not agree with your leader.' 'Conrad,' replied Hastings, 'you're speaking as if Barbara had a revolver at your head.'[7] Black unconvincingly denied his wife's influence: 'I was aware that there was a myth that had floated around . . . that my wife was exercising some Mephistophelian influence on my relations with the editor. I can assure you, none of that is true.'[8]

Amiel now began to reveal herself as an anti-journalist, especially intolerant towards those expressing unacceptable opinions. Her target in the *Sunday Times* on 17 October 1993 was Vicki Woods, the editor of *Harper's & Queen*. In an article in the *Spectator*, Woods had made use of her presence at a photo shoot of Margaret Thatcher to describe the former Prime Minister's behaviour and comments. Undoubtedly the report could have been interpreted as a breach of etiquette because Thatcher was not being formally interviewed, but after forty years in the business, she knew the rules. If Woods had similarly embarrassed a Communist politician, that would have been justified by Amiel, but embarrassing comments about one of her heroines were condemned as an outrageous breach of Thatcher's privacy. Woods was compared by Amiel to '*canailles*. Today that means rogues, but I understand it in the sense of scum or sewers . . . We journalists may live in the sewer, but our sewer has a genuinely important social function. It actually prevents an even worse sewer.' She meant political tyranny. Living as she did with a man who hated the profession of journalists, Amiel's justification of journalism as a necessary evil to protect democracy was hardly convincing. She certainly did not want journalists prying into her own or her husband's life – he had called investigative journalists 'swarming, grunting masses of jackals' – nor would she condone any criticism of her increasing army of rich friends. As a journalist, she wrote, 'I think we are all made of *merde* and the craft is *merde*'. Each time she wrote an article, she claimed, she was compelled to ingratiate herself with people she disliked and adopt 'ruses', producing 'a host of smarm and iffy relationships that bring me out in spots half the time. After each profile I write, I vow never to play the game again. And then the vow is broken. Why?' The answer to her rhetorical question was that the sewer of journalism prevented the greater evil of 'star chambers and secret power-holders in high places'.

Amiel's attack on journalists provoked a contributor on BBC Radio 4's *Start the Week* programme to describe her as a 'rich bitch'. Gleefully she responded: 'One of the differences between me and my sisters in the women's movement is that I do not regard my money as my own. Having married very wealthy men before my current husband, I can guarantee that I parted from them leaving both their fortunes and my opinions intact . . . I have been a bitch all my life and did not need the authority of money to be one . . . My detractors were calling me a "fascist bitch" long before I had a penny. I come to this status pure and untainted by money . . . I continue to be moody, opinionated, a bit driven and all the things that rubbed people the wrong way before I met Conrad, and rubbed some the right way, which was responsible for my getting a column and other jobs . . . Ultimately I am a north London Jew who has read a bit of history. This means I know this: in a century that has seen the collapse of the Austro-Hungarian, British and Soviet empires, reversal of fortune is this rich bitch's reality: one might as well keep working and have the family's Vuitton suitcases packed.'[9] Previously Amiel had sought acceptance and admiration. Now the shrill of her delight in posing as the survivor of a harsh life was cultivated to create fear. Despite her claims, her purity was no longer intact. She was spending a huge amount of her husband's money, and any inconvenient principles were discarded in the cause of self-interest. Their gilded life in the grandeur of Cottesmore Gardens encouraged an aristocratic loftiness.

The 'power couple' invaded the conservative establishment, yet instead of focusing on academics, civil servants, bankers and industrialists, Barbara Amiel preferred entertaining celebrities. Among the cast list invited to dinner were Princess Michael of Kent, Prince Andrew, Joan Collins, Roger Moore and Mary Soames, the daughter of Winston Churchill. 'Can I call you Mary?' asked Black. 'No, you cannot,' Soames stiffly replied, irritated by a host she later called 'that boring man'. Black was undeterred, and associating with famous names remained a priority. Fellow guests at a concert in Buckingham Palace to celebrate the conductor Sir Georg Solti's eightieth birthday in 1992 had been astonished to see Black and Amiel, after a reception, race ahead so as to sit behind the Prince and Princess of Wales.[10] Having made their acquaintance, Amiel appeared to take the relationship for granted when she later encountered the Prince of Wales at the Royal Opera House, Covent Garden, both being the guests of the American bank Morgan Stanley. Standing at the crush bar with Prince Charles, Amiel announced, 'Will you excuse me? I must work the hall.' Walking away in her blazing red dress, her bosom spilling out, the belle of the ball sought out an acquaintance. 'We don't know each other well,' she said. 'We must get together. Shall we do that through music?' 'I don't like music,' replied the man. 'Oh dear,' said Amiel. 'What shall we do, then?' Her attempts to spread her network had provoked the journalist Simon Heffer to observe, 'Barbara has turned Conrad from an *homme sérieux* into a society petal. He's besotted with her, like a spaniel.'

During her celebrity dinner parties Amiel sat at the mahogany table with her hand hovering over a button, occasionally appearing unrelaxed, not quite enjoying her husband's jokes. Her syrupy voice and stiff manner were contrived, some guests felt, in the mistaken belief that the rich were expected be lordly. At the appropriate moment her finger pressed the buzzer firmly, and two butlers with supporting liveried staff appeared. One guest claimed, mistakenly, that a butler carrying a telephone message to Black on a silver plate actually murmured, 'My Lord.' The same visitor was equally critical of the architectural mishmash of Cottesmore Gardens, which resembled a show house rather than a home. Black's huge house was certainly feeding imperial ambitions, brazenly suggesting the wealth and influence of a billionaire.

A lack of punctuality, always a congenital problem for Conrad Black, was compounded by Amiel's own tardiness. Often at the last moment she was indecisive about her clothing, making the Blacks arrive late even for dinner at Clarence House. Dresses were strewn across her room while she deliberated. Black was unashamed. 'I'm Conrad Black. I own the *Telegraph* and I'll turn up whenever I like,' appeared to be his attitude, belying his considerable efforts to receive invitations from the royal family. Arriving as the last guests, the Blacks' entrance was conjured for dramatic effect; heads would turn and the attention of London's principal power-brokers would be aroused. Everyone, Black assumed, would be impressed as he worked the room, exchanging smiles and shaking hands while Barbara stunned them all with her own magic, bestowing upon those whom she deemed worthy a dashing smile, dismissing those she regarded as too lowly with a blank stare or by turning her back. For their part, the audience took the Blacks' impersonation of billionaires seriously, and only wondered whether Amiel would be 'off the boil' that night, prickly to those she encountered. One couple, however, were distinctly unamused by the spectacle. The Blacks had been their house guests for the weekend, and after their departure Conrad Black had telephoned to explain that inadvertently both he and Barbara had left tips for the staff. 'Could you return one of the gratuities?' he asked.

Barbara Amiel was not oblivious to her critics. Like her husband, she assumed that it was her wealth and status that attracted envy. Together, they were members of the rich man's trade union.

No moral point of view was acceptable other than promoting or defending the interests of the well-heeled. Only one bauble was missing: a peerage. Amiel had predicted in 1989, 'The fact is that he's going to have to get one. He's the most credible, intellectual and erudite publisher in England. And he is a Thatcher supporter of considerable enthusiasm. There's just no way Mrs Thatcher can leave office without giving it to him.'[11] Three years later she told a London newspaper that the 'brilliant, courageous and wonderful' newspaper baron had been 'sure to get a peerage from Mrs Thatcher'.[12] The Blacks consoled themselves that it was only Margaret Thatcher's abrupt demise that had deprived them of the honour. Those close to Thatcher knew the truth. Despite lobbying in Downing Street, Black was never considered for a peerage. In Thatcher's opinion he had done nothing to deserve special recognition. Thereafter, his quest for a title depended upon John Major.

Although Thatcher's successor as Prime Minister had sent a handwritten note congratulating the couple on their marriage, he did not feature in the Blacks' social world. Regarded as uneducated and unsophisticated, Major was also disliked for his broadly pro-European policy. In the early months of his premiership Black had concealed his criticism in the hope that Major would agree to offer him a peerage. In 1993 Black had contemplated Jacob Rothschild's suggestion that the *Telegraph* group buy Winston Churchill's papers for the nation. 'It could significantly accelerate my peerage,' Black told Max Hastings, but he rejected the idea after being persuaded that shareholders would object to the misuse of their money.[13] Major's anger at Black's support for Michael Portillo's plots to snatch the party leadership ended his early hopes. 'My patience is exhausted,' Black said about Major, echoing Hitler's ultimatum in 1938 before signing the Munich agreement and annexing the Czech Sudetenland. In the *Spectator* Amiel attacked Major's government for intellectual pusillanimity and capitulation to feminist thinking. Major, she wrote in October 1992, was in thrall to the 'matriarchy' and Europhiles. The following year Black approved more overt criticism of Major in the *Telegraph*. Hyper-sensitive to opposition, Major was thereafter not minded to grant Black a peerage, and the *Telegraph* group's antagonism towards the Prime Minister increased.

This disappointment was a minor irritation in the Blacks' remarkably agreeable domestic life. Both tended to work late into the night and rise at noon. Drinking ginger tea and eating chocolate biscuits made by his chef, Conrad Black spent hours on the telephone to Canada and the USA, while Barbara Amiel struggled with each column for the *Sunday Times*, sometimes taking three days to complete 1,300 words in her modern office on the top floor. Her food was sent up from the kitchen or stored in her personal fridge. Their staff included the chef, three butlers, three Portuguese cleaners, Ben, Amiel's personal trainer, and Penny Phillips, her assistant. On one occasion an outburst by Amiel prompted Phillips to offer to resign, but she was lured to remain. Outside were two chauffeurs, tending to a Rolls-Royce and a Bentley (the *Telegraph* would contribute $380,000 annually to the costs of the Blacks' staff[14]). Black's lifestyle prompted Hal Jackman to call him 'a parvenu drifting away from reality. I can't understand his priorities. He does too much entertaining and not enough business.' Black would resent that criticism. Neither he nor Amiel cared to compare their lifestyle with Rupert Murdoch's. While they sought glamour in palaces, the world's leading media baron could be found eating dinner at the Electric Club, a medium-priced restaurant on the Portobello Road, one of London's colourful street markets. The symbolism was appropriate.

9

The Torpedo

Like a shark, Rupert Murdoch had followed his prey, and he struck on Monday, 6 September 1993. The news, delivered while he was resting in Palm Beach, disturbed Conrad Black's placid features. His rival had exploited a glaring weakness. As a historian, Black might have compared Murdoch's unexpected attack with Hitler's surprise invasion of Russia in June 1941, except that Black would not have appreciated any comparison with Joseph Stalin. He would also not have welcomed historians identifying the bombshell as the beginning of his ultimate ruin.

News International, Rupert Murdoch's corporation, announced that the price of *The Times* would be cut from 45 pence to 30 pence. Since *The Times* was losing about £20 million every year, Murdoch's self-inflicted wound seemed inexplicable to Black. After all, *The Times*'s daily sale of 350,000 copies was dwarfed by the *Telegraph*'s 1.1 million copies at 48 pence.

Murdoch had aspired for years to topple the *Telegraph*'s dominance. Until that day, Black had assumed the existence of a cosy, informal understanding that *The Times* would remain a low-circulation broadsheet subsidised by Murdoch's other, profitable, newspapers. To sustain their relationship, Black, as a champion of capitalism, had regularly defended Murdoch and attacked his critics for their 'spite and envy'. Given the loyalty he had shown, Black was astonished by Murdoch's price cut, which he calculated would add an estimated £30 million a year to *The Times*'s losses.

High-profile price wars were foreign to the champion of raw capitalism. In North America, Black's newspapers were either monopolies or competed in small leagues. Murdoch had astutely assessed Black as a cost cutter and never a price cutter, and as expected, his challenge provoked irrational obstinacy. Self-interest influenced Black to misjudge the impact of Murdoch's initiative. 'We won't cut the *Telegraph*'s price,' he told Max Hastings and his other executives. 'Rupert doesn't know what he's doing.' Implacably, Black repeated, 'We'll compete on quality, not price.' The *Telegraph*, he reasoned, was the market leader, with a loyal readership that appreciated a better newspaper. There seemed to be no argument for *Telegraph* readers to switch to *The Times* just to save 90 pence a week. He preferred to ignore Hastings's warnings that the *Telegraph*'s price increases since 1989 were akin to 'trying to milk the cow three times a day'. In 1989 the *Telegraph* had cost 35 pence, but, anxious for more cash, Black had abandoned Lord Camrose's philosophy of selling a broadsheet at a tabloid price. 'Undisguised greed' was Hastings's judgement of the latest price increase.[1] 'Rupert's got deeper pockets than us,' warned Jeremy Deedes. Black hated any suggestion that Murdoch was richer than himself: 'Let's just say that he has greater access to borrowings. He's made a mistake.' Black's single consolation was the fading comparison of himself with Maxwell. The new challenge – 'Murdoch vs Black', the clash of the Titans – enhanced the minnow's status.

Black concealed his true dilemma. As a capitalist, he should have instantly cut the *Telegraph*'s price and spent money on improving the newspaper's editorial content and promotional campaigns to blast *The Times*'s challenge into oblivion. The cost excluded that option. Unlike Murdoch's media empire, which generated $7.5 billion a year, Black's kingdom was dependent on the *Telegraph* for more than half its annual profits, and despite the income, Hollinger had accumulated debts rather than cash. Without any capital, Black relied on the previous day's cash flow to survive. Matching Murdoch's price cut, he knew, would not only jeopardise his finances, but would break a lifetime's habit. Black was fighting a war on unfamiliar terrain.

As a student at Oxford, Murdoch was renowned as a poker player. Ever since, his commercial career had been marked by risking huge sums to win, and occasionally bearing a loss. Black did not understand a game of chance among equals. He could only win if his opponent was in trouble and the odds were stacked in his favour. If he had gathered around himself serious advisers and directors rather than relying on Dan Colson, David Radler and Jack Boultbee, he would have understood this new battle. But openness was anathema to the cabal, a weakness spotted by Murdoch, who smelt blood.

The price war ruined the honeymoon of Black's commercial life. Five months earlier, in April 1993, he had completed the purchase of Southam Newspapers. 'We have bought half a loaf for the price of a quarter of a loaf,' he had boasted, describing his victory over Canada's old guard as another 'watershed' similar to Argus, the *Telegraph* and Fairfax.[2] He now controlled over 50 per cent of the country's print media, including fifty-eight of Canada's 104 daily newspapers. Those characterising his new empire as a threat to Canadian democracy were rebutted with relish. Hollinger, he puffed, with six hundred newspapers, had become the world's third-biggest newspaper owner.[3] David Radler, alias 'the human chainsaw', was as usual expected to sweat the newspapers, cutting costs to produce the profits to repay the loans. 'It's my intuition,' he smiled about dismissing employees. 'I rely on my tummy.'

The price of the trophy was high. Paul Desmarais had sold his shares to Black for C$294 million, pocketing $60 million profit. This had plunged Black deeper into debt, and he still lacked total ownership. The remaining shares were owned by funds managed by Stephen Jarislowsky. 'I'll give you $26 for your shares,' offered Black. 'I want between $32 and $36,' replied Jarislowsky. 'I could make it interesting for you if you help me,' countered Black. 'No way,' said Jarislowsky, amused by Black's tactics. 'I'm only seduced by beautiful women. I'll let you off at $32.50. It's a fair price, and that's it.' Jarislowsky's obduracy irritated Black, provoking insulting letters. Southam's share price earlier that year had been a mere $15.

Jarislowsky was puzzled by Black's approach. To discuss Hollinger's management, he called at Black's home in Bridle Path one weekend. Black's eldest son Jonathan, aged fifteen, was talking with the staff while their discussions continued. By then Jarislowsky had reread Hollinger's latest accounts. 'They're Byzantine,' he told Black. 'They're convoluted. Any mortal would find them hard to read.' Black attempted to soothe him with platitudes. 'You can earn more money by building up the company and improving the share price than by taking huge fees,' Jarislowsky told him. Black was uninterested. 'Right,' he said, curtailing their discussion. 'I'm off for dinner to Washington.' 'What about the kid?' asked Jarislowsky. 'You're leaving him here? That's terrible, Conrad. The family's more important.' Black stared back, unconcerned.[4] He expected his children to care for themselves. He had forsaken any thought of building a dynasty. 'He's just out for himself,' thought Jarislowsky with mounting outrage as he drove away from the house. 'It's going to lead to a well-deserved fall, and Conrad's going to get what he deserves.'[5] With bad grace, Black accepted Jarislowsky's counter-offer. 'Conrad's a bully,' concluded Jarislowsky. 'I don't like his threats.' At the Southam board meeting to approve the purchase, Jarislowsky abstained from the vote. 'At the risk of causing your displeasure, Conrad,' said Barbara Amiel, 'why is Stephen abstaining?' Amiel, it became apparent, did not understand the term 'conflict of interest'. Soon after, Jarislowsky resigned his directorship of Black's company. He would later discuss his concerns with the Ontario Securities Commission, but they were not interested.[6] The deal cost Hollinger $70 million, propelling the company's debts towards $1.4 billion. To mitigate the burden, Black persuaded the *Telegraph*'s directors to recommend that the London company buy some Southam shares for an inflated price of £72.3 million. The shareholders agreed.[7] Their submission to his scheme emboldened Black. He misjudged his engineering as an adequate defence against Murdoch's exploitation of Hollinger's rising debts. Bursting with self-confidence, he believed that no one, including Rupert Murdoch, could undermine his realm.

Black's fifteenth-floor office in Canary Wharf, with its yellow silk upholstery and pictures of battles, model battleships, a bronze of Cardinal Newman, a portrait of Nelson and Napoleonic memorabilia, didn't match the mood of the times. Getting up at lunchtime, taking long holidays and attending celebrity conferences rather than hitting the telephones at 7 a.m. to scrutinise the accounts and his employees' performance, reflected Black's interpretation of business challenges in military terms. The symbols of his virility were Napoleon and General Douglas MacArthur. His heroes' victories, he knew, had not depended merely on stubborn resistance, but on cunning counter-attacks. He could endlessly recite examples. In a recent aside he had compared an unimportant commercial venture as akin to 'the jungles of Guadalcanal, the beaches of Tarowa, the sands of Iwo Jima, the caves of Saipan and hand-to-hand combat ending only with the incineration of the enemy by flamethrowers'. For years his verbal power had slaughtered the opposition. In the price war, he believed, words would again deliver victory. 'Murdoch's going to take a pasting,' he told his directors. '*The Times* is giving away millions of copies,' he would say to anyone listening. 'We're doing brilliantly.' Naturally, he sought an apt military epigram for his destiny: 'Wars are expensive,' he quoted General Dwight D. Eisenhower. 'The cost of victory may be high, but the price of defeat is everything.' Black never sought to explain the similarities between the invasion of Normandy in June 1944 and selling newspapers on the high street. Vicariously reliant on history books' descriptions of military manoeuvres and political manipulations, the connoisseur's dead heroes shared little in common with Rupert Murdoch, a modern-day media legend.

In his frustration, Black became suspicious of anyone enjoying Murdoch's trust. One target was Tim Bell, the lobbyist and publicist who met Murdoch regularly. Bell's loyalties became suspect once Barbara Amiel breathlessly reported how he had recommended at a public meeting that any Tory wanting to understand Britain should read the *Sun* rather than the *Telegraph*. To the Blacks, this observation by a Thatcherite Tory who shared their political philosophy was akin to treachery. 'Murdoch's a crook,' Black declared to Bell. 'He doesn't pay his taxes.' The publicist was ostracised for some months.

Three months after Murdoch's challenge, in December 1993, the purchase of the *Chicago Sun-Times* for $180 million was completed by the American Publishing Company. Black's latest acquisition resembled the walking wounded. While enjoying the city's biggest circulation, the *Sun-Times*'s revenue from advertising aimed at Chicago's poorer citizens was low compared to the *Chicago Tribune*'s huge advertising income, targeted at its suburban middle-class readers. Nigel Wade, the new editor seconded from the *Telegraph*, was expected to relaunch the newspaper as pro-Republican in a solid Democrat city. No one explained how those contradictions could be reconciled. Over lunch in David Radler's office, Wade was struck by Radler's extraordinary meanness. Eating a hot dog with green pickles wrapped in a foil wrapper, Radler spoke only about cutting costs and trimming the editorial comment to suit the advertisers. 'Nothing about Bloomingdales until they advertise with us,' ordered Radler, whose company apartment was above the department store. 'I won't let Rona shop there until they advertise in the paper.' 'You know the reason they won't advertise?' replied Wade. 'They say our readers are their shoplifters.' Radler scoffed. 'We don't have that problem in Calgary.' In Radler's vision, Calgary was the formula for success in Chicago, and everywhere else.

Radler was charged by Black with finding a solution in Chicago just as Kerry Packer surprisingly united with Murdoch to threaten his investment in Fairfax by bidding for some of the outstanding 75 per cent of shares not owned by Black. In the rollercoaster ride, Black assumed that salvation would emerge. But unlike Murdoch's constant micro-management of expansion and profitability, Black the scholar was devoting his time to planning the next Bilderberg Conference in Toronto. Over four days he would welcome about two hundred influence-peddlers, including George Soros, Henry Kravis and Henry Kissinger. Instead of discussing Rupert Murdoch's threat, he would dissect the diplomatic skills of Count Metternich, Austria's nineteenth-century master diplomat. To win further recognition as a literate historian among those whom he admired, he also began writing his autobiography, to be called *A Life in Progress*.

Depression encouraged Black's decision to write the book. Despite his good physical health, he was convinced that his life would end prematurely. Vulnerable and insecure, he resented being lampooned. He sought to be taken seriously, and wanted his life to be recorded on his terms, rather than allowing others to paint a false picture. He intended his autobiography to provide answers, but inevitably it provoked questions. 'I'm not interested in popularity,' he told Richard Siklos, an approved biographer. 'I just don't want to be synonymous with something that is a magnet for public hatred.'[8] To justify the hours he spent writing in longhand, he spoke about 'setting the record straight' and 'owing my countrymen a statement of why I am not mainly resident in Canada'. In reality, he wanted 'to get something off my chest' about those critics who had dared to compare him with cheap crooks, to expose the 'self-serving fiction' and 'disingenuousness' of those engaged in conspiracies against him.

In Black's autobiography, published in Canada by Key Porter Books in December 1993, R. Howard Webster, a former owner of the Toronto *Globe and Mail*, was described as 'erratic', and as having a drink problem which resulted in his standing on the stairs of the Toronto Club with his trousers around his ankles. Black mentioned telling the banker Sigmund Warburg's wife about her husband offering a woman a job on condition of a sexual relationship; he boasted of telling a Canadian minister, 'You look like a perfect asshole'; Lord Hartwell, alias 'the ultimate misanthrope', was categorised in his final days by Black as 'irksomely . . . waffling and fishtailing'; and he described Nicholas Berry's principal qualification for directing the *Telegraph* as 'surviving childbirth'.[9] Laurier LaPierre, a Senator and former teacher at Upper Canada College, was described by Black as 'one of the more enthusiastic flagellators' who enjoyed violently assaulting 'the comfortable derrieres of Upper Canada's scions' during his time there. LaPierre, Black later realised, was not teaching at the school during his era. As an apology, Black invited LaPierre to an expensive restaurant. 'You are homosexual, aren't you?' asked Black. 'Of course,' replied LaPierre. Black excused himself and left the table. Fifteen minutes later, the waiter told him that Black would not be returning. 'Bring me the menu,' ordered LaPierre, and chose the most expensive wines and food, to be enjoyed at Black's expense.[10]

Conrad Black was delighted by his book. Each review was carefully studied. Some were generous, others critical, including one comment that it 'read as if translated from the original Czech'. Unpublished were the scathing comments about his distortion of events, and the hypocrisy of a profligate issuer of libel writs indulging in unbridled abuse of his opponents. Joanna Black uttered the most pertinent observation. 'I wouldn't call Conrad a liar,' she said in the tone of a liberated bystander. 'I would call him a revisionist historian.'[11] Black looked forward to the book's publication by Lord Weidenfeld in Britain in the spring of 1994. Nicholas Berry would claim credit for preventing that event. 'After all the work you've done with my father,' he wrote to Weidenfeld, 'how could you publish this book?' Malcolm Turnbull would also claim credit for blocking the book's overseas publication after reading Black's mischievous repetition of the libel based on ill-founded Sydney gossip that after an argument with a girlfriend Turnbull had 'sneaked' into her home and dropped 'her kitten into the freezer, transforming a frisky pet into a well-preserved corpse'.[12] Black was willing to repeat such libels, despite his own practice of suing those he felt had libelled him. By way of contrast, missing from the book was a lengthy history of Black's depression and self-destructive tendencies. On the advice of Anna Porter, his publisher, most such self-revelation was removed. In appreciation for her work and friendship, Porter would be appointed two years later as a director of a Hollinger company, joining, after his retirement from the Church, Cardinal Carter.

Emboldened by his autobiography's publication, Black felt empowered to destroy those he cast as unhelpful. In April 1994 his frustration with the Australian government's refusal to allow his ownership of Fairfax to increase beyond 25 per cent was exhausted. His debts were too great to sustain his investment, and he disliked Australians, especially their politicians, for denying him what he regarded as his entitlement. Since his childhood, when cornered or dissatisfied Black's response had always been to throw a verbal grenade. Writing in the *Sydney Morning Herald* and the Melbourne *Age*, both owned by Fairfax, he alleged that during the original negotiations Paul Keating, the Prime Minister, had made him an unusual offer. Sympathetic to Black's complaint about the limitation of foreign ownership of Australian newspaper groups to 15 per cent, Keating allegedly offered a deal. In return for 'balanced' coverage in Black's newspapers during the forthcoming election campaign, he would consider raising the ceiling. Keating was re-elected, and the ceiling was raised to 25 per cent. Suggesting a grubby secret deal, Black wrote that Keating had even offered to consider raising the limit to 35 per cent, an allegation that Keating denied. As intended, this provoked a political storm, and Black was summoned to give evidence to an Australian parliamentary inquiry. Before he appeared on 21 April 1994, he had been damned as an untrustworthy liar by Malcolm Turnbull, and accused of 'distorting events through the prism of his own self-interest' by Bob Hawke, Keating's predecessor as Prime Minister. Delighted by the attacks and protected from libel writs by parliamentary privilege, Black added to the brew by alleging that Hawke had asked Dan Colson to pay him $50,000 to act as a secret lobbyist. In reply, Hawke insisted that he had not asked for the money, rather Colson had made the offer. One of the two was not telling the truth. Black called Hawke 'pathetic', but in a later peace settlement he withdrew his allegation. In public, Black laughed that the saga was 'a scream', failing to realise his mistake. Australia's politicians and media condemned him as unreliable and unstable. The headlines describing him as 'a liar' bounced around the world, reaching London just as *The Times*'s eight-month price war was torpedoing the *Telegraph*'s sales.

By May 1994 *The Times*'s circulation had risen from 350,000 to 545,000. The *Telegraph*'s sales had fallen just below one million, compared to 1.2 million when Black bought the paper. Black's entourage had not foreseen that newspapers could be so price sensitive, and had underestimated Rupert Murdoch's mastery of the business. In Canary Wharf, Black's executives were fretting. Despite a popular but costly subscription offer to readers, the *Telegraph*'s sales continued to haemorrhage. If Murdoch's success continued, Black was warned by Hastings and Jeremy Deedes, the paper's sales could fall in October to 900,000. The only cure, he was told, was a price cut, reducing the *Telegraph*'s net profits by about £15 million. The loss, Black replied, was too great. He vetoed the suggestion.

In Palm Beach, Black pondered his options. Enjoying his marriage and new lifestyle required money. Unfortunately, his empire was failing to produce the required cash for himself. The obstacle was Hollinger's $1.4 billion of debt and the limitation on the money he could extract from the *Telegraph*. The solution, he agreed with Jack Boultbee, was to raise more money in New York. As a preliminary move, he decided to float American Publishing, the owner of his American newspapers, on NASDAQ, the alternative stock market, at $13 a share. Their company, later to be called Hollinger International, could be used to borrow more money in the future. Black's additional need for cash could be satisfied by Max Hastings's success at the *Telegraph*. Fortunately, despite Murdoch's aggression, the *Telegraph*'s share price was £5.87, a healthy rise over the offer price of £3.25 in 1992. Black still retained 68 per cent of the *Telegraph*'s shares. He called the broker Michael Wentworth-Stanley at Cazenove's and told him that he had decided to sell 12.5 million *Telegraph* shares. On 19 May 1994 Wentworth-Stanley, in consultation with Mark Loveday, a senior partner, sold the shares to clients, and Black pocketed £73 million in pure profit. Unable to resist boasting, he told Hastings: 'I have just been obliged to make some calculations about the current state of my own affairs, Max, and I must say that the numbers achieved a heart-warmingly satisfactory consummation.'

That huge sum of money persuaded Black to realise his old ambition and launch himself and Barbara Amiel among New York's A-list celebrities. First, rather than stay in hotels, they needed a home in the city. In May 1994 they found a second-floor apartment in a co-op at 635 Park Avenue, near 66th Street.

Hollinger International, the public company, paid \$3 million for the lease. As the company's chairman, Black then authorised himself and his wife to live in the expensive location without paying rent.[13] The apartment had not been redecorated for forty years. After considering various local designers, Amiel again chose David Mlinaric to create a home. The cost would be shared between the company and themselves. Pending the redecoration, they flew to Palm Beach. The telephone calls Black received from Canary Wharf were increasingly desperate. 'If we don't cut the price,' Hastings told him, 'the outlook is bleak.' To Hastings's surprise, in early June Black finally agreed. Murdoch's challenge would be repulsed on 1 July 1994. There was to be no announcement until Black returned to London.

The Blacks' arrival in London in June celebrated Barbara Amiel's new prominence. At Hollinger Inc.'s annual general meeting that month, shareholders had approved her appointment as a director and vice-president, responsible for editorial matters in Hollinger's newspapers. Consistent with her new status, Amiel asked Carla Powell, the wife of Thatcher's former foreign policy adviser Charles Powell, whether she could join her in hosting a party being planned at the Ritz in Piccadilly on 14 June with Tessa Keswick, the director of the Centre for Policy Studies. Two hundred guests were to be invited to celebrate James Goldsmith's election to the European Parliament and the sixtieth birthday of his wife Annabel, and as thanks to both Goldsmiths for their hospitality to the Keswicks, the Powells and other guests at his home in Mexico. For the Blacks, the party was an opportunity to display their rank as natural members of London's A-list. Amiel's participation was welcomed by Carla Powell, who despite her limited finances was renowned as a political hostess, entertaining the famous including Margaret Thatcher and Tony Blair for dinner in the kitchen of her comparatively modest home. Casting an envious eye at that reputation, Amiel hoped that Cottesmore

Gardens would also become a hub of 'power' hospitality.

The three hostesses agreed that each would invite a third of the guests, plus the Princess of Wales. To Amiel's surprise Carla Powell, a fiery Italian, dominated the organisation. Powell declared that she, rather than Amiel, knew London's most desirable bankers, developers, politicians, men of letters, celebrities and assorted billionaires. 'You're a hack who wants to be a hostess,' she effectively told Amiel. 'You don't know how to host a party.' In retaliation, Amiel suggested that they buy hugely expensive flower arrangements. 'No,' said Powell, 'I'll get the flowers at Covent Garden in the morning.' Drawing attention to Powell's limited finances was Amiel's weapon. 'It's a matter of style,' said Powell, whose popularity appeared to irritate Amiel. 'I won't be treated as a skivvy,' Amiel declared angrily. 'I'm not coming to the party. I'm staying at home.' She was finally coaxed to appear. 'She's got a generous heart,' Powell half-soothingly told her friends, 'but she's tricky. I've been treated appallingly by Barbara. The party is my idea and she wanted to come in.' The night was a roaring success. '*Tout* London' awaited the speeches from the three hostesses. At the last moment Carla Powell decided not to speak, and Amiel presented herself as the leader. On her late arrival, the Princess of Wales was escorted by Amiel towards Kerry Packer, who was engaged in conversation with Petronella Wyatt, a seductive journalist. 'Would you like to get up and move elsewhere?' Amiel asked Wyatt. 'Princess Diana is going to sit here.' 'Oh no, you stay,' ordered Packer. 'I don't want to sit next to that old bag.' Eventually Wyatt sat elsewhere. Amiel appeared humiliated, and at the end of the evening she was unforgiving towards Carla Powell.

The following day Conrad Black chaired a meeting to plan his retaliation against Rupert Murdoch. Those summoned to his office included representatives of Cazenove's. Black described the *Telegraph*'s predicament and his intention to announce the next day, 16 June, that the *Telegraph*'s price would be cut from 48 pence to 30 pence. The senior journalists and executives were relieved. The representatives from Cazenove's were silent, although Black had previously given no warning that he was considering cutting the *Telegraph*'s price. 'Murdoch is a Darwinian. He wants survival of the fittest and that's what he's going to get,' Black declared, convinced that his would be the last word. Hours after the *Telegraph*'s triumphant announcement, *The Times*'s price was cut from 30 pence to 20 pence. Black was sent reeling by Murdoch's seeming willingness to 'bet the company' in order to win. 'Apparently Rupert said, "It's time to teach Conrad another lesson,"' one of Black's informants reported. Black imagined that words would restore his credibility. 'You shouldn't listen to the propaganda of our rivals,' he replied. 'We have our foot on the windpipe of our principal competitor.'[14] But few could envisage him winning a price war against his richer opponent. With rumours that the *Telegraph*'s annual £40 million profits would disappear if *The Times*'s circulation hit 700,000, the *Telegraph*'s share price began to fall towards £3.49, a full £2.28 less than Black had received from his private sale through Cazenove's in May. The scenario was familiar to Black's critics, and so was the recrimination.

Cazenove's directors were outraged. Six weeks earlier they had sold Black's shares to clients without warning that the *Telegraph*'s price could be cut. Those clients had suffered substantial losses, and were demanding an explanation. 'I think we might have been misled by the chairman,' agreed David Mayhew, Mark Loveday and Michael Wentworth-Stanley. Conrad Black had not behaved illegally, but his way of doing business left a sour taste, explaining the epithets 'the Black Factor' and 'Conrad Tricky'. Cazenove's announced its resignation as the *Telegraph*'s brokers. 'You'll never be able to have lunch in this town again,' Black was told by a Cazenove's director. 'Nor will you ever be able to raise money in the City again.' Categorised by London's most prestigious brokers as untrustworthy, Black's carefully cultivated reputation in London was threatened by their criticism of his 'entrepreneurial arrogance'. He appeared to be standing on the edge of a precipice. 'Don't they trust us, or what?' he pouted. 'The famous firm just scuttled out of the back door into the tall grass.'[15]

Gratifyingly, Black's entourage sprang to his defence. The *Telegraph*'s directors unanimously attacked the brokers. 'Cazenove's,' Rupert Hambro told Black, 'are unfair. You've been badly treated.' Max Hastings agreed. Black's treatment, he wrote, was 'a cynical gesture . . . to appease angry clients'.[16] Black's calm dismissal of the snub reassured his circle of his innocence. 'It was an orgy of self-righteous English hypocrisy,' he explained. 'I mean the fact is, I naturally had [Cazenove's] in and consulted with them the day before we cut the cover price. They didn't offer a word of dissent. You know, it's a bit rich of them to carry on the way they did. I don't think they did themselves any favours in this thing. I gave them a pretty good shot on the way out, which they richly deserved.'[17] The 'rich shot' was defiance. Cazenove's, he said, were to blame for mishandling the sale of his shares on 19 May. 'You can't make war and peace at the same time,' he told the *Financial Times*. 'You can't suck and blow at the same time.' His comment to the *Wall Street Journal* was less obscure: 'The act of investing is not risk-free. Sometimes people stub their toes, and sometimes they catch cold and die.'[18]

But clever words could not repair the damage. Under fire from Murdoch and the City, Black's commercial opportunities in Britain had vanished. 'In an ideal world,' he mused, 'maybe I would have no peer. I'd own everything I wanted to own and there wouldn't be anyone else to have the effrontery to have a different view or a different interest. But that's not the way the world works, so you've got to deal with who's there. It creates issues, but you know, what the hell am I paid for? I've got to do something for a living.'[19]

Lord and Lady Black at their home in Palm Beach, Florida, in May 2003. The previous year, Black had been called a 'liar' by angry shareholders at Hollinger's annual general meeting.

On 14 July 1977 Black married his former secretary Shirley Walters. The Canadian media had just labelled him 'Man of the Year' and 'Boy Wonder' after he had completed an audacious coup placing him in control of a conglomerate worth $4 billion.

On 21 July 1992 Black married Barbara Amiel in London. During their celebratory dinner at Annabel's, one guest admitted his irritation at Black's social climbing and trophy wife. 'Like hydrogen and nitrogen,' whispered another guest, eyeing the two newlyweds. 'Safe by themselves, but explosive when combined.'

'Marrying up' had been one of Barbara Amiel's ambitions. Her second husband was George Jonas (*above*), a Hungarian writer whom she married in October 1974. During the marriage Amiel enjoyed several affairs, including a hectic one with Sam Blyth (*left*), thirteen years younger than herself.

Barbara Amiel was famous in Canada for her smouldering sexual allure, and she was equally eager in London to pose as an aggressively opinionated journalist.

Among those Barbara Amiel relied upon during the break-up of her third marriage was Lord Weidenfeld. Their stormy relationship exasperated the publisher, who was famous in London for his smoothly cultivated seductions.

Conrad Black and Barbara Amiel shared an unqualified admiration of Margaret Thatcher. The British Prime Minister however was irritated by Black's monologues, lassified him as 'low profile' and refused to nominate him for a peerage.

Margaret Thatcher, while Prime Minister, refused to recommend Conrad Black fo a peerage. His consistent lobbying was finally rewarded in 1999, but the nominatio was stymied by the Canadian Prime Minister Jean Chrétien. After abandoning hi Canadian citizenship, Black became a peer in 2001. His nominees were Margare Thatcher and Lord Carrington, a loyal director of Black's company. Henry an Nancy Kissinger witnessed the investiture. Hollinger's employees in New York however, refused Barbara Amiel's request to address her husband as 'Lord Black'.

The Blacks' appearance in summer 1999 at a fancy-dress picnic at Kensington Palace hosted by Prince and Princess Michael of Kent, as Cardinal Richelieu and Marie Antoinette, was later used by critics as an illustration of Amiel's confession, 'I have an extravagance that knows no bounds.'

Using the company's Gulfstream IV jet, Black and Amiel regularly swept across the Atlantic and America to party in London, New York, Palm Beach and Toronto.

Launching the *National Post* in Canada in 1998 had won Black unusual popularity and applause. But his dream quickly lost over $100 million, propelling his empire and his personal fortunes towards the abyss.

At Christmas 2002, Conrad Black unexpectedly arrived at the annual party held by Lord Rothermere, the chairman of Associated Newspapers. 'We should work together as friends,' Black suggested to him. Not surprisingly, Black did not explain to those present the gravity of his problems in New York. From left: Tom Bower, Conrad Black, former *Telegraph* editor Max Hastings, Lord Rothermere.

(*Top*) In New York Laura Jereski (pictured with Christopher Browne), an analyst at investment fund Tweedy Browne, was digging up embarrassing revelations about the running of Black's commercial empire. Her demands for answers during telephone calls to Paul Healy (*bottom left*), Black's corporate relations manager, were causing increased friction among Hollinger's executives. One of those who would be criticised for pocketing excessive income was Richard Perle (*bottom right*), a former member of President Reagan's administration.

Since 1969 Black and David Radler (*centre*) had been partners but never close friends. From scratch, they created the newspaper empire. As their finances unravelled in 2002, they were pressured to appoint Richard Breeden (*top, left*), a former chairman of the Securities and Exchange Commission, and Gordon Paris (*top, right*), a banker, to investigate their commercial conduct. Breeden's damnation of Black's 'kleptocracy' led to a Delaware judge describing Black as 'evasive and unreliable'. Black (*above*) was shattered. Radler eventually confessed to having perpetrated major frauds.

During October 2003 Conrad Black ignored the criticism and investigation of his conduct, and toured bookshops promoting his massive biography of Franklin D Roosevelt. Finally the scandal forced both Black and Amiel to retreat from public life

However, on 15 November 2005 they made a deliberately sparkling appearance at a Toronto party. Later that week, both knew, Conrad Black would be indicted to face charges in Chicago. Ever since, he has refused to hide from the cameras. Posing in public, he believed, would help prove his innocence and secure his acquittal at his trial, set for 5 March 2007.

The crisis gave Black a chance for unexpected profits. He began buying back *Telegraph* shares at their reduced price. 'It's basically buying dimes for nickels,' he boasted, insensitive to the disgruntled shareholders. The institutions criticised Hollinger's offer to buy the shares back as a device to raise the *Telegraph*'s share price, and refused to oblige.[20] Unconcerned, he plotted his exit from the London Stock Exchange. Being listed in London, he decided, was too onerous. He didn't like sharing the profits with shareholders. He wanted the cash for himself. The Stock Exchange imposed too many restrictions, and explaining his policy to analysts was irksome. He decided he would move to Wall Street. Robert Gemmell at Merrill Lynch in New York had assured Black that he could sell 70 per cent of the company but keep 76 per cent of the control. That ruse was unavailable in London, especially with a British board of directors. In New York, Black knew, he could hire more malleable personalities as main board directors, including Henry Kissinger, Lord Weidenfeld and Shmuel Meitar, an Israeli businessman; everyone knew that Hollinger was Black's company, and the directors were to be obedient or resign. He wanted, however, a good price for his departure. Ignoring the fact that he had received £5.87 per share in May, he offered to repurchase all the shares for £4.50. 'I'm an honourable man,' he said, 'but commerce is not the welfare system.' To his surprise, the *Telegraph*'s directors, led by David Montagu and Rupert Hambro, refused to help. 'The shareholders must be treated fairly,' he was told. Black bristled. 'Conrad doesn't like being defeated,' said Montagu, 'but no doubt he'll come back.'

For months Black haggled about the price for his exit. He organised a presentation by Radler and Merrill Lynch to show how shareholders would benefit from a combination of cash and the shares to be issued in New York. Radler's performance underwhelmed his audience. 'We think cash is more attractive,' said Montagu politely. In mid-1995 Black surrendered, agreeing to pay

£5.70 a share for the outstanding 36 per cent of the company. The cost was £273 million, wiping out his windfall in May. As a consolation, the *Telegraph* group was valued at £770 million, compared to the £119 million he had originally paid. As usual, Black was one step ahead of his creditors. The valuation provided some comfort to the banks concerned about his debts, although the consolation was limited. Lucky breaks, Black acknowledged, struck only once in a lifetime. Rupert Murdoch could smile. His move to Wapping had made Black rich. Now his price cuts were making Black poor.

Black was sensitive about the significance of his relocation from London to New York. Disillusioned by John Major's government, his interest in mainstream British politics was declining. Occasionally he sat quietly listening to political discussions among the *Telegraph*'s journalists, saying nothing but resembling an elephant in a drawing room. Only on rare occasions could he applaud a *Telegraph* leader, as in June 1993, for his newspaper's support of President Clinton's Cruise missile attack on Iraq, but generally he found Hastings's reluctance to share his interpretation of Washington politics tiresome. Although Black was a middle-of-the-road conservative, he supported Bill Clinton's Democratic presidency. His increasing enthusiasm for America's neo-conservatives provoked Hastings's irritation. The editor was growing tired of walking a tightrope, balancing the criticism from both Blacks and the expectations of the *Telegraph*'s readers. After ten exciting years, he wanted relief from harangues at ungodly hours by an employer posing as a great man, on a heroic scale, dispensing and demanding wisdom. Black's imposition of a reshuffle among his senior staff prompted Hastings to accept the offer of the editorship of the London *Evening Standard*. Hating the implied criticism of himself, Black could not resist sniping: 'Max bottled out . . . The price war [with *The Times*] got to him and he lost his nerve. He invoked a lot of pretext, but his real fear was that he'd run out of steam and he was afraid I was going to sack him. Which I wasn't.'[21] In reply Hastings explained, 'I thought Conrad had lost the plot: about the price war, about his desire to push the *Telegraph* to the right again, and in suddenly wanting to influence senior editorial appointments. In a sense, I did "bottle out", because I was given a chance to escape from what was becoming a very difficult relationship with him, just when it stopped being fun.' Andrew Knight and Max Hastings, the architects of the *Telegraph*'s revival, had both gone. Initially, Black and Amiel were certain that both were replaceable. Black would now be judged on his own talent.

Hastings's departure had made the Blacks more in demand than ever. Every ambitious, opinionated and talented right-wing journalist clamoured for the editorship of the *Telegraph*. John O'Sullivan, Frank Johnson, Simon Heffer and others interpreted Black's smiling approval of their pitches to be a cast-iron promise. Others relied on Barbara Amiel's assurance about her influence over the outcome. 'Dominic Lawson will never be the editor of the *Sunday Telegraph*,' Black had told Frank Johnson. Dan Colson agreed. The lawyer wanted Lawson, the editor of the *Spectator*, sacked, but suspected his move was being frustrated after Amiel became friendly with Rosa Monkton, Lawson's wife. 'Dominic promises to overtake the *Sunday Times*,' Black was told by Amiel, who began to change her husband's opinion. Anything Colson wanted was opposed by Amiel, who had become irritated by what she felt were his wife Suzanne's social airs and her considerable expenditure on antiques and marble for their home in Regent's Park. It was whispered that Charles Moore, the editor of the *Sunday Telegraph*, was being dismissed as a contender for the editorship of the *Daily Telegraph* by Black for being uncommercial and woolly. 'We'd better see what the little woman thinks about that,' was Black's frequent response when asked for his opinion. 'The *Telegraph*,' Heffer complained, 'is being run like a cocktail party in a banana republic.' Days passed, and the lack of announcements was puzzling. Unknown to all, Black thought he was persuading Paul Dacre, the editor of the *Daily Mail*, to become the *Daily Telegraph*'s editor. But at the last moment Dacre was lured by a huge pay increase to remain at Associated Newspapers. Within hours all the promises and denials had been forgotten. Dominic Lawson was appointed editor of the *Sunday Telegraph* and Charles Moore of the *Daily Telegraph*. Although Moore had described Black's prose style in 1990 as 'grand, rolling, adjectival, slightly old-fashioned, neither rapier nor bludgeon, more like some huge medieval siege engine', he had become an admirer of his employer's support for journalists.[22] For the Blacks the erudite intellectualism of Moore, a committed Thatcherite and pro-Republican, made him an easier companion than his predecessor. Moore and the Blacks agreed that the *Telegraph* should veer sharply to the right just as the country, including many middle-class Tories, was inclining to vote Labour at the next election. In his speech to the staff on 24 October 1995, Moore was critical of his inheritance. Nearly every part of the newspaper displeased him: 'The direction is not clear and nor is there enough wit, originality or surprise.' He continued, 'My aim is to replace a culture of fear with a culture of achievement. I shall certainly punish failure, but I do not believe in unnecessary bloodshed.' His appointment was accompanied by casualties. The loudest of them was Simon Heffer. On Amiel's insistence, Frank Johnson had been appointed the *Spectator*'s editor. Heffer was furious that Black had reneged on his guarantee of the job. He resigned in disgust, blaming Amiel.

An aura of potency hung over Amiel, sealed by a social coup. The Princess of Wales had accepted the Blacks' invitation for dinner. The successful enticement was compensation for Conrad Black's failure, despite considerable effort, to be invited to a dinner hosted by Douglas Hurd, the Foreign Secretary, in honour of Henry Kissinger. Princess Diana had been among Hurd's twenty-two guests. Hurd's refusal to invite him and Amiel had caused Black much pain. Diana's arrival at Cottesmore Gardens, witnessed by a gaggle of photographers camped on the doorstep, thrilled Amiel. Days later, dressed impeccably, she walked into Annabel's private dining room, where a Canadian businessman was hosting a dinner party to which she had been invited. 'Who's the hostess?' Amiel asked his wife with notable insouciance. Before she heard the reply, she moved towards the table. 'I'm so glad to be sitting next to you,' her host said with a big smile. 'Well, I'm sorry, I've got laryngitis and can't speak,' replied Amiel as she sat down. Turning her back on him, she engaged in an animated conversation throughout the evening with the Scotsman on her left. 'Conrad probably needs a Lady Macbeth to get ahead,' concluded the snubbed victim.

Barbara Amiel's successful king-making at the *Telegraph* had been followed by an animated debate between the Blacks. Conrad wanted to end his wife writing as a popular columnist in the *Sunday Times*. Charles Moore agreed to employ her, albeit, he would say, 'on her merits'. Although Amiel was initially reluctant to move, the change had the advantage that she would be free to write without the normal restrictions imposed by an editor, and would guarantee her influence on the *Telegraph*'s opinions. To establish her special status, she arrived with her husband at an executives' conference in the Royal Berkshire Hotel at Ascot to discuss the *Telegraph*'s overall editorial strategy. She said little, but, enthralled by her presence, Black appeared to his employees like putty in her hands. No one doubted that everyone's contribution would be dissected later that evening, and that Amiel's agenda would be implemented. 'She's nasty to those who can't answer back,' complained some journalists, who formed a strange alliance with the taxi drivers employed by Trident who were contracted to drive the *Telegraph*'s staff. 'You're fired,' appeared to be Amiel's favourite line to the drivers. She could be similarly uncompromising towards the journalists appointed to edit her column. Instead of submitting 1,100 words as stipulated, she sometimes presented as many as 1,600. 'Run it in full,' she would say, knowing the problems she was causing the sub-editor. To her apparent pleasure, the 'small people' were not allowed to forget her rank.

Among that category were Fred Eaton and his wife. Conrad Black's loyal friend had just retired as Canadian High Commissioner in London, and was appointed a director of Hollinger Inc. The Eatons had fondly anticipated their visit as the Blacks' guests to the preview of the Chelsea Flower Show, always an exciting occasion. After speaking to Conrad Black, Eaton spotted Amiel and walked towards her. To his surprise, she turned and darted away. Nearby, Dan Colson watched the rebuff and laughed. 'She feels,' the Eatons concluded, 'she's better than anyone else, and doesn't need to speak to us.' Thereafter, whenever they were noticed by Amiel, she would turn her back. 'Surgery changed Barbara, not life,' rued Fred Eaton, disappointed that Conrad Black had become infected by his wife's arrogance. There was no apology or explanation. Neither of the Eatons realised that in Amiel's mind, having risen from the lowest to heights she had never imagined, she believed herself entitled to say 'Fuck off' to those she deemed unimportant. Aptly, his lifelong sense of entitlement emboldened Conrad Black to offer a similar message to his new American investors.

10

The A-List

SECURING THE FRIENDSHIP OF Henry and Marie-Josée Kravis was important to the Blacks. Among Manhattan's A-list socialites, the Kravises ranked as a 'most-sought-after couple'. In 1988 Henry Kravis, a joint founder of KKR, a private equity house, had been the legendary hero of America's biggest take-over battle, the leveraged buy-out of RJR Nabisco, immortalised in the book and subsequent film *Barbarians at the Gate*. Since then he had become one of America's richest men. Marie-Josée, an attractive, intelligent economist and a Fellow of the Hudson Institute, was a director of two multi-billion-dollar corporations, Ford Motors and Vivendi. Manhattan's 'power couple' were pivotal to the Blacks' social and commercial aspirations for stardom. They shared nothing in common other than the Blacks' hunger for the Kravises' wealth and status.

Conrad Black's desire to please Barbara Amiel never faltered. An uncanny chemistry bred a mutual understanding about life's priorities. Black wanted to appear as a billionaire, and Amiel was an eager accomplice to his desire. During their discussions about grander houses, more clothes, increased staff, travel and her jewellery, Amiel barely thought to enquire whether her husband actually possessed sufficient millions to afford those luxuries. The woman who flaunted herself as ranking among the world's most perceptive journalists, the extremes of suffering and elation she had experienced bestowing special authority to pontificate about society's ills, preferred to delegate the responsibility for providing the money to fund her lifestyle to her husband. As a director of Hollinger and Ravelston, Amiel could have discovered that her husband's income was insufficient to finance their ambitions, but she preferred not to investigate.

To rank among Manhattan's A-list required power and wealth, implying the unencumbered possession of at least $1 billion. Such a fortune, and the appropriate contacts, secured invitations to meet other members of the clan at charity events, cocktail parties and dinners. The *Wall Street Journal* assessed Conrad Black's wealth at $600 million, but those encountering the Blacks were unaware that because of his debts, this estimate was an exaggeration. In fact, presenting himself alongside his friend Henry Kissinger as a Renaissance man, Black gave the impression of much greater wealth than the *Journal*'s assessment. His vast business as an international media mogul, he casually suggested, was a means for him to display his brilliance as a polemicist, historian, confidant of the powerful and conversationalist. In a city obsessed by leanness and fitness, his plump torso and lugubrious movements were seen as the amiable eccentricities of a witty raconteur accompanied by a knockout wife. To those enjoying the Blacks' company, there was no reason to doubt their credibility as members of the international billionaires' club.

Before their decision to reinvent themselves in New York as members of the super-rich, the Blacks had frequently met Norman Podhoretz, the conservative commentator and a former speechwriter for President Reagan, and his wife Madge. On Amiel's apparent insistence, the Blacks abandoned intellect and cultivated instead the Kravises, Alfred Taubman, the chairman and major shareholder of Sotheby's, and his wife Julie, the socialite and Republican fundraiser Georgette Mosbacher, and others who fluttered around the Palm Beach hostess Jayne Wrightsman.

Among the casualties were Amiel's friends in London. Miriam Gross and others felt abandoned, and complained about her failure to return calls. A relationship with Amiel, they concluded, was akin to picking up water. Oblivious to such grumbles, the Blacks sought closer relations with the Kravises. Their mission was not difficult. Conrad Black met Henry Kravis at the Bilderberg Conferences, and Marie-Josée was an old friend of his from Toronto. Some even speculated that he had considered Marie-Josée as his second wife before choosing Barbara Amiel. The two women shared a sophistication that their husbands lacked. Just as Marie-Josée had introduced Henry to Picasso's art, and had persuaded him to buy several masterpieces to decorate their home, Barbara had introduced Wagner's operas to Conrad. To some, the women's friendship seemed tainted by rivalry; others would observe Barbara's envy. But any such emotions were hidden in 1995, while Black sought an important coup. After careful persuasion, Marie-Josée agreed to become a director of Hollinger International when the new company was transferred from NASDAQ and floated on Wall Street in January 1996. Her presence on the board, Black knew, would reassure investors. Gratifyingly, she was untroubled by the complexity of Black's proposed company, or by his motives. Her trust in him was shared by Robert Gemmell, a Canadian, and others at Merrill Lynch.

Black's negotiations with the brokers and bankers in New York were in stark contrast to the atmosphere in London. Merrill Lynch's representatives had no qualms about dealing with arrogant media tycoons. Black spoke the language of entrepreneurship, and, they decided, he had delivered. He told them he wanted to buy a flagship paper in New York. Such an acquisition would be a valuable addition to his global media empire, and New York, he said, was the natural magnet for his ambitions. To Robert Gemmell, that sounded eminently plausible. Media shares were popular on Wall Street, and convoluted company structures which took huge amounts of money from shareholders but left control with the 'owner' were quite acceptable. 'Media is in vogue,' Black was assured by Gemmell. 'You'll get a ton of money. Shareholders don't care about Byzantine structures so long as the company's sound.' That was music to Black's ears. He loved America and American capitalism. Gemmell appreciated that Hollinger's complicated structure, while common in Canada, needed to be sold in New York, but he had no doubts about Black and Boultbee's honesty. 'Conrad is too smart and too experienced not to know how it works in New York,' he concluded, convinced by Black as a 'strong leader, well respected in the community'. All understood that Black's sole reason for floating in New York was to take the public's money but to keep absolute control of the company. If he was successful, Merrill Lynch would earn huge fees. The only losers could be the public shareholders. Gemmell's warm assurances were not endorsed by all the bank's analysts. 'Clean this up,' Gemmell's staff were told. 'The Black Factor is going to work against you. His company structure is too complex.' The bankers agreed to discuss the obstacles with Jack Boultbee, the mastermind holding everything together. Boultbee was their guide through the intricacies of Hollinger's smokescreen.

Among the manoeuvres which would eventually provoke litigation against Black was the alleged transfer of newspapers owned by Hollinger Inc. in Toronto to the proposed New York company at below market value. The object was to depress the value of Hollinger Inc.'s share price, and to squeeze out other shareholders. In 2006 Hollinger Inc.'s directors, claiming $700 million in damages, would allege that Black's scheme transformed the Canadian company from 'a thriving operating business into a non-operating shell'. Those questionable transfers were easily overlooked in New York. The mood soured, but eventually, in order to satisfy every objection by the bank's lawyers and accountants, Boultbee produced a seal of good housekeeping from

Torys, Hollinger's lawyers, and KPMG, the company's auditors. 'Nothing in this is going to be plain vanilla,' one banker sighed after yet another screaming match with Black, Radler and Boultbee. 'They're a bunch of bumpkins. Not as sophisticated as outsiders think. We mustn't let others see the worst.' Finally, the prospectus was agreed. The next obstacle was David Radler, chosen by Black to make the presentations to potential investors. 'Radler's got the bedside manner of a pitbull,' groaned one banker, weary of Radler's disdain for those giving their money. 'He thinks he's got an entitlement to their cash. He doesn't want to tell the truth.' The bitterest arguments were about the price of the shares. The cabal wanted top dollar, and expected the bankers to deliver. 'Do something for your fees,' snapped Radler. He sweated his newspapers for every cent, and expected the same from Merrill Lynch.

The result was only partially pleasing to Black. The public were offered 68 per cent of the shares in Hollinger International, while he retained 32 per cent. Ostensibly, the division suggested that Black was a minority shareholder, removing the doubts about his alleged profiteering at shareholders' expense. But there was a sting. Within the small print, Black preserved complete control. Hollinger International in New York would be controlled by Hollinger Inc., the public company based in Toronto, in which Black retained 77.8 per cent of the voting rights. Those buying shares on Wall Street were, despite the appearance of their owning 68 per cent of the shares, automatically minority shareholders, because Black's 32 per cent stake actually represented 77.8 per cent of the votes. To completely nail down his control, 78.2 per cent of Hollinger Inc. in Toronto was owned by Ravelston – and Black owned 65.1 per cent of Ravelston, while Radler owned 14.2 per cent. As chairman of Hollinger International in New York, and Hollinger Inc. and Ravelston in Toronto, Black exercised complete control. He could choose every director; and there was an added twist. Hollinger's executive directors – Black, Radler, Boultbee, Peter Atkinson and Colson – were not employees of Hollinger International in New York. Instead, Hollinger International would pay management fees to Ravelston for the directors' services, albeit the size of those fees was subject to the control and scrutiny of Hollinger International's audit committee. The unusual arrangement did not arouse any alarm among the potential investors. Within the agreement between Hollinger and Ravelston, however, a critical clause was inserted at the bank's insistence. If Black and the other directors believed their conduct was creating a possible conflict of interest between Hollinger International and Ravelston, they were bound by law to declare that conflict to Hollinger's independent board of directors. In 1995 the fee Ravelston charged to Hollinger International was $4.1 million, a reasonable amount. No one realised that the sum was set by Black, Radler and Boultbee to suit their personal requirements rather than to reflect the market rate. In 1995 their agenda was to reassure the public of their modesty and probity.

To Black's satisfaction, several pertinent questions were left unanswered once the flotation was agreed. Firstly, no one asked why Hollinger was floating in New York although the company's principal sources of income were Britain and Canada. Secondly, Black was not obliged to reveal Ravelston's accounts. Thirdly, no one asked him to explain his empire's complex structure. Investors could however rely on the laws of Delaware, the state where Hollinger International was incorporated. Under Delaware's laws, any transactions between companies and their subsidiaries required a standard of 'entire fairness', and Black would also be expected to abide by the standard of 'entire fairness' towards the company's shareholders. By law, he was obliged not to do anything for his personal benefit without explaining his intentions properly and in full detail, and obtaining the approval of independent directors. Since Black's plan was to retain absolute control as 'the proprietor', empowered to ignore the shareholders, he might have reflected on the potential risks. Instead he laughed as Radler roared, 'Throw in their asses right now,' referring to the public shareholders. 'I get a piece of the action, Conrad gets a piece and the shareholders get a piece.'

On 16 January 1996 Hollinger International was formally floated in New York at $9.75 a share. The flotation valued the company at about $2 billion, but since Hollinger Inc. in Toronto had debts of $1.4 billion, the shares in New York were effectively worth only $600 million, meaning that Black's own shares were worth about $200 million. That gross wealth was reduced by the personal loans he had raised against those shares. By the standards of New York's A-list, Black was comparatively poor.

A few days after the flotation, at a board meeting of Hollinger Inc. in Toronto, Marie-Josée Kravis might have suspected the dangers of associating with Conrad Black. Around the table were Fred Eaton and Doug Bassett, Black's childhood buddies who he unkindly assumed would jump as ordered; Don Fullerton, the retired banker, who sat in silence; and Allan Gottlieb, whose gratitude towards Black was unconcealed. All four regarded Black as 'brilliant', and volunteered that serving on his board was 'absolutely an honour'. The only internationally recognised heavyweight was Peter Munk, who was on the way to transforming a $100 million investment in Barrick, the gold company, into a $20 billion goliath. Munk was the type of star Black adored, despite his irritating independence. 'You're not the proprietor of Hollinger,' Munk joked to Black. 'This is a public company.' 'Bullshit,' replied Black. 'I'm the proprietor.' Munk, a director since 1994, examined Black's new corporate structure. Everyone including himself, he saw, was Black's puppet. During the board meeting after the flotation Munk noticed Marie-Josée Kravis and Barbara Amiel, recently promoted as a director of the company with a salary of nearly $300,000, exchanging notes about fashion, parties and social gossip. This, he decided, was not the place for a serious man. Shortly after, he resigned.

Sensitive to appearances, Barbara Amiel took control of decorating the corporation's new Manhattan headquarters on the eighteenth floor at 712 Fifth Avenue. The office was rented from a company belonging to Alfred Taubman, the chairman of Sotheby's, whom Black regarded as a friend. Neither of the Blacks would have welcomed anyone drawing attention to the symmetry of the fact that Taubman was at that moment crudely defrauding his clients by price fixing. The budget to redecorate the office was set at $400,000. At Amiel's insistence, David Mlinaric was hired and flown first-class across the Atlantic to create a gem. 'Mlinaric!' exclaimed a genuine Manhattan billionaire on hearing the news. 'We couldn't afford him.' The office walls were covered with silk, the boardroom was filled with a massive mahogany table and twenty-four matching chairs with stark blue fabric, and the designer recommended a blue-rimmed Limoges china dinner service. Mlinaric's bill was $4 million. Black placed a photo of Al Capone in the boardroom. 'A Hollinger shareholder,' he liked to joke.

Barbara Amiel was getting into the rhythm and mastering the pressures of membership of the A-list. The Blacks were now the owners of four substantial homes, and their ambition to match the Kravises swelled. Their new domestic staff in New York expected accommodation, and Black decided that Hollinger would buy another flat in the same block on Park Avenue, ostensibly to provide somewhere to stay for visiting Hollinger executives. Once again David Mlinaric was flown from London to prepare the plans. At the same time the Blacks became dissatisfied with their home in Toronto. Builders were commissioned to improve the chapel, extend the library and build a new swimming pool. Her status as the employer of about seventeen butlers, cooks, chauffeurs and cleaners influenced Amiel to re-evaluate her lifestyle.

'I'm never going to a public cinema again,' she told a friend. 'The smell is too awful.' During a dinner in Manhattan with the Kravises, the discussion swung around to the inconvenience of flying across the Atlantic on commercial airlines. 'It's so much better to fly on our own plane to Europe,' remarked Marie-Josée. 'You leave when you want, and can sleep in your own bed.' Amiel shot a familiar look at her husband. 'Aren't you ashamed you haven't got a bigger private jet?' she later asked him. Conrad Black knew that that was a trophy too far and remained silent.

Soon after, the Blacks were having dinner in Manhattan with two couples. 'We'd better go,' said Black. 'We've got to check in.' Amiel froze. Once in the limousine en route to JFK airport, she turned on Black. 'I've never been so humiliated in all my life. Why haven't we got our own jet?' Black did have a jet. His Gulfstream II could fly around the United States, but not cross the Atlantic non-stop. Some weeks later, Amiel's Concorde flight from Heathrow was delayed. In a fit of anger, she tried to reach Lord King, the British Airways chairman and a Hollinger director. When that attempt failed, she decided to vent her spleen through a *Telegraph* employee. 'Tell Lord King,' she declared, 'that I'll never fly commercial again. I'm finished with British Airways, public transport and the lot of them.' Black leased a Gulfstream IV previously owned by Coca-Cola. 'Nice plane, terrible interior paint,' the Blacks and Gerry Smith, their senior pilot, agreed. The annual cost charged to Hollinger, including three pilots, would be between $3 and $4 million. Radler took Black's old Gulfstream II, but on reflection he resented using Barbara's cast-offs and bought a Challenger 601 worth $11.6 million. At last the Blacks could eat dinner on the same day on both sides of the Atlantic. Both were ecstatic. If they tired of the Kravises in New York, they could pop down for dinner with Kate Graham in Washington or with Jayne Wrightsman in Palm Beach. Eagerly they sought an invitation from Walter Annenberg to spend the weekend on his spectacular estate in Palm Springs, and flew overnight to London to prove their membership of the jet set to Europe's aristocrats. Although there was no hope of repaying Hollinger's excessive debts, there was sufficient cash passing through the *Telegraph* to create the appearance of matching the lifestyle of the super-rich; but two old friends were not convinced.

During the summer of 1996 the Blacks were invited with Charles Bronfman, the heir to the Canadian alcohol empire, and Galen Weston to a gala concert at Covent Garden starring Placido Domingo. Bronfman was uncomfortable in Black's company. He doubted his integrity, and disliked the *Jerusalem Post*'s opposition to Israel's reconciliation with the Palestinians. He agreed with the Thomsons, both Ken and his son David, that it was safer to steer clear of Black. Beyond Black's hearing, he compared his fellow Canadian to Robert Maxwell. The Blacks appeared unaware of the billionaire's disdain as Barbara Amiel, dressed in a shimmering red dress, posed for the photographers. Neither Bronfman nor Galen Weston approved of the flashy display. Others were baffled by her behaviour.

A week later, Amiel offered two friends a lift on board the Gulfstream from Luton airport to Salzburg, where at Lord Weidenfeld's suggestion she was visiting the music festival. As usual, the packing had taken Amiel several hours. Twenty-four dresses, set out on a rail in her dressing room, had been packed flat for the three-day trip. Included were clothes from a favourite shop on the Place Vendôme in Paris. She had arrived at the airport in the Bentley at 11 a.m., and the luggage followed in an estate car. While Captain Ridley worried how to pack all the suitcases into the hold, Amiel apologised to her friends about the aircraft's inadequate appearance. Over the next years, she explained, she planned to install new leather seats, two divans and an extra lavatory. 'We've got to have two toilets,' she explained, 'because I don't want the crew coming through our cabin to use the one at the back.' Unfortunately, she continued, Marshall's, the fitters, were so busy that the improvements could not be undertaken until 2000. The cost would be $3 million, including $250,000 for the second lavatory. That did not include the cashmere blankets purchased from Leron in New York, or the china dinner service. Watching Ridley coping with the luggage, Amiel asked her friends if they would like some caviar. 'Eleven o'clock in the morning is a bit early,' replied one of them, who had seen the airport caterers deliver Conrad Black's favourite peanut butter and jam sandwiches. 'How about a sandwich?' he asked. 'I've forbidden Conrad to eat those,' said Amiel. Finally the plane took off at 2 p.m., the Blacks' notion of a morning departure. The unravelling of the plans began at Salzburg airport, where the two cars that had been ordered to transport Amiel and her luggage to the Goldener Hirsch hotel failed to arrive. Amiel's voice rose, and her anger did not subside until she returned to London. Dissatisfied with much throughout her stay, and undecided about which clothes to wear, the trip, despite the Gulfstream, had not been enjoyable. Combining all her different responsibilities – social hostess, professional writer and the manager of four homes – was more burdensome than she had anticipated, and she also needed to arrange adequate time to fulfil her statutory duties as the director of a public company.

Conrad Black was finalising Hollinger's financial safeguards. One important chore was the appointment of an ambassador to attract more fund managers to invest in his company. He had selected Paul Healy, a banker whose family background gave him access to Manhattan society. There was some urgency in Healy's appointment. Hollinger's relocation to New York had coincided with a stock market boom. The Dow-Jones index had soared from 3,000 to 11,700 points. Media shares had risen in anticipation of huge profits from the dotcom revolution. Yet Hollinger's share price, having shot up to $14, was inexplicably sliding back towards $11. The reason, Healy heard, was the 'Black Factor'. For his part,

Black assumed that Healy's reputation for honesty, combined with his own performance, would sway New York as he had been able to do in Toronto and London. Knowing that Hollinger's turnover would peak in 1997 at $2.21 billion, Black's sense of well-being was fortified in his approach to the company's audit committee, a critical protector of the shareholders' interests.

James 'Big Jim' Thompson, appointed by Black as chairman of the audit committee, appeared to be a paragon of diligent virtue. Elected four times as the Republican Governor of Illinois, he had previously won fame as a US Attorney, a crime-buster targeting corrupt policemen and politicians. In recognition of his fame and to satisfy his vanity, Chicago had named a monstrous glass building in the centre of the business district 'The Thompson Centre', and adorned the entrance with an ugly fibreglass structure. Since his retirement from politics Thompson had become one of Chicago's most prominent lawyers, but his weakness, spotted by Black, was his comparatively modest wealth. Chicago's big rainmaker was desperate to attract business to his law firm. Despite his image, Black reasoned, Thompson was for hire, and he hoped he would not ask embarrassing questions. The second member of the audit committee chosen by Black was Richard Perle, the former US Assistant Secretary of Defense. Over the years Black's relationship with Perle, alias 'the Prince of Darkness', had become especially close, partly influenced by Barbara Amiel's reliance on Perle's expertise about Israel and the Palestinians for her newspaper column. Ambitious to become rich, Perle hoped to use his relationship with Black to exploit the vogue for new technology.

'We should get into Netscape,' suggested Mathew Doull, the stepson of Monte Black, who was employed by Black to work on corporate development, referring to the start-up of an unknown software company. Black, scornful of the young, scruffy geeks in Silicon Valley, refused. Those unsophisticated technicians, he scoffed, were little more than witch-doctors. Doull was advised to find some better investments. Black's lackadaisical 'no' lost him over $100 million in pure profit. Black was only attracted to businesses subject to his total control. With the flotation complete, he began transferring cash from Hollinger International to himself and his collaborators. Doull was directed in August 1996 to create Hollinger Digital, a technology company, with Richard Perle as chief executive. Despite Perle's lack of business expertise and the incongruity of a newspaper company investing in unrelated technologies, Black was unusually keen to help the neo-con academic. Hollinger Digital, he reasoned, would be a useful conduit to enhance his cabal's income. As CEO Perle was paid $300,000 per year, plus $50,000 as a director of Hollinger. Even before Hollinger Digital was earning any money, it began paying bonuses to its directors under an unusual incentive plan. Black, Radler and Colson started transferring $5.3 million in bonuses from Hollinger Digital to Argent News, a tax shelter in Barbados.

A further payment of $3 million was made to Holcay Ltd, a company registered in the Cayman Islands. By 2003 Hollinger Digital would have lost $65 million, but the directors had paid themselves a total of $15.5 million in bonuses. Perle's income was $5.1 million.[1] That self-reward was not disclosed to Hollinger's public shareholders. The largesse was extended to Barbara Amiel. In 1997 she received over $1 million in dividends, options in 370,000 Hollinger shares worth over $4 million, and fees paid to Black-Amiel Management Inc., another company based in Barbados to avoid taxes.[2] Amiel's earnings were not immediately disclosed to Hollinger's public shareholders or the company's independent directors.[3]

Richard Perle was no doubt grateful to Black. Black may not have been surprised by Perle's understanding when Ravelston submitted its 1997 accounts for its management fees to Hollinger's audit committee, of which Perle was a member, for the services of Black, Radler, Boultbee and other executive directors. Eating a tuna sandwich, Radler told 'Big Jim' Thompson that Ravelston's fees to Hollinger International had increased. Instead of $4.1 million in 1995, the charge in 1997 would be $26.5 million.[4] Radler's calculation of the fees, he would later admit, was 'back-of-the-envelope', with no analysis other than what the Black group desired. So far as he and Black were concerned, Hollinger was Ravelston's client, rather than a company to which they owed statutory duties. To Radler's satisfaction, neither Thompson nor Perle asked for any explanation for the sixfold increase, or how the money would be spent.[5] No independent consultant was hired for advice about the market rates, nor were there any negotiations. Without debate, the two members of the audit committee approved the demand. None of Hollinger's other directors, nor the shareholders, were told the details of the account. The independent directors, including Henry Kissinger and Marie-Josée Kravis, also failed to request any detailed explanation from Black. None of the directors had spotted the conflicts of interest introduced into Hollinger at the time of the flotation at the shareholders' expense. 'That's the bullshit,' exclaimed Radler, gleeful about the unpenetrated façade covering the company's finances. The $26.5 million was transferred to Ravelston.

Days later, pleased with Perle and Thompson's lack of opposition, Black and Radler created the 'executive committee', the final component of their machinery to avoid scrutiny of their financial management. The committee was empowered to act on behalf of the board of directors on any issue.[6] Decisions could be made by the committee in some secrecy by 'unanimous written consent'. Black and Radler were appointed, and they made Richard Perle the committee's third member. Perle confirmed his reliability when the unusual procedure was first invoked in September 1997. To cover its debts, Hollinger Inc. in Toronto needed money. Black and Radler decided that Hollinger International in New York should lend $42.5 million to Hollinger Inc. for ninety days. The interest rate was an unreasonably low 1.25 per cent.[7] Wanting to avoid any scrutiny or discussion about the loan by the non-executive directors on Hollinger's board in New York, Black and Radler 'summoned' the 'executive committee'. Perle was given documents authorising the loan by the company's lawyers. Without reading, understanding or discussing their content with anyone, he signed it off. To Black's financial benefit, with the public shareholders remaining unaware, the loan would be extended for two years at the uncommercial rate of interest.[8]

Conrad Black's 'proprietorial' attitude towards Hollinger's finances, and the dramatic increase in management fees, coincided with the first signs of decline in Hollinger's empire. Black's position as a minority shareholder in Fairfax had become untenable. Rather than improving his personal relations and maximising profits, he had reinforced his unpopularity in Australia by repeating the allegations of corruption he had made two years earlier. Treating Australians as inferiors had cost him any hope of raising the 25 per cent threshold. With limited income from his investment, he had insufficient money to repay the loans which had funded the purchase. Under pressure from the banks, he sold his 25 per cent stake for Au$544 million (£260 million), compared to the Au$1.39 billion he had paid for the whole company. Having pledged to defeat Murdoch in his own country, he had been driven out. To outsiders it appeared that Black's exit was a profitable coup. Black himself, however, realised the truth. The 'proceeds' were used to repay loans. His only comfort was refusing Murdoch's offer for his shares. Although their price war in London was over, Murdoch had won. The circulation of *The Times* had doubled to 766,000 and the *Telegraph* was financially weaker, having restored its circulation to one million by offering readers a cheap subscription rate. Only words could console Black in defeat. 'The proceeds of the sale,' he said in a final flourish to Australians, 'will be better applied in jurisdictions where foreigners are not treated with official bad faith and insurmountable suspicion.' His dream of building a global empire had been halted. 'You can't build an empire by selling things,' Fred Eaton told him. 'It was too tough,' replied Black. 'There were too many fights in Australia.'

The building engaging most of Black's attention in 1997 was another house in Palm Beach. Since he had first visited the resort in the 1960s, the old mansions had been demolished and replaced by palaces. Their inhabitants were no longer the rich, but the super-rich. The billionaires demanded even bigger living areas, cinemas, walk-in humidors, temperature-controlled wine cellars and the transformation of bedrooms into apartments. The world's top designers were hired to provide the most expensive furnishings and to find precious paintings to cover the walls. Anti-Semitism remained entrenched in Palm Beach's private clubs, which excluded Jews not only as members but as guests.

Although Barbara Amiel did not always enjoy Palm Beach, she was certain that 150 Canterbury Lane, Black's house there since 1980, was inadequate. 'How can we invite the Kravises and Jayne Wrightsman here?' she asked. To set off from such a nondescript house for morning coffee dressed in the resort's uniform of Chanel casuals and half a million dollars' worth of jewellery was, she implied, too embarrassing. Ever since she had driven through the resort in 1989 just to gaze at the billionaires' mansions she had known that size mattered. Conrad Black agreed. Since buying Canterbury Lane he had coveted 1930 South Ocean Boulevard, a 14,000-square-foot house overlooking the sea. By chance, in 1997 it was for sale at $9.9 million. Included was a two-storey guest house, a heated pool, gym, cinema and tennis court and, most dramatically, a tunnel under the road linking the house to a three-hundred-foot private beach. Before buying the house, Black might have considered the fate of successive previous occupants, united by premature death and bankruptcy. Convinced that he was charmed, he ignored the house's unlucky history and agreed that

David Mlinaric should once again be hired, along with the expensive New York architects Richard Sammons and Anne Fairfax.

The famous interior designer and the architects knew that Palm Beach's truly rich would have demolished the outdated building, which had been damaged by seawater, rather than renovating it as the Blacks chose. Nevertheless, the Blacks' shopping list was not unduly modest. Amiel briefed them to produce 'quiet elegance' rather than ostentatious extravagance. Their plans included the complete gutting and reconstruction of the buildings, adding 6,000 square feet to the house to create five bedrooms, eight bathrooms, a cinema, a library and a vast living area, all linked by a black onyx double staircase. 'This will be Henry Kissinger's bedroom,' Amiel explained, 'and this one will be for the Kravises.' There was an elevator costing $4.4 million, a fountain featuring a marble statue of Poseidon, crystal chandeliers, expensive rugs and stylish carpentry. 'Why are you building such a huge house?' Black was asked by a visiting English banker. 'I hope you think it suits my position,' he replied.

Membership of the A-list, the Blacks knew, required more than merely grand homes. Tycoons were expected to contribute to charities on a generous scale. Manhattan celebrities like the Kravises annually gave millions of dollars to museums, orchestras, art collections and worthy causes. With those contributions came tickets to dinners, concerts and parties. The Blacks decided to join in. At Hollinger's expense, they began giving hundreds of thousands of dollars to New York's opera houses, museums and libraries. Black also contributed $1.2 million over four years to support *The National Interest*, a foreign-policy quarterly which he co-chaired with Kissinger and Perle; he gave a further $275,000 to the Nixon Center, and $375,000 a year to the Institute of Strategic Studies, a London think-tank. To win similar kudos, Radler began giving to charities in Canada and Israel. On reflection, the Blacks and Radler decided that they wanted more permanent recognition, and both began negotiations to contribute money to public buildings which would bear their names. The cost of these personal acknowledgements, including the 'Black Family Foundation Wing' added to a Toronto hospital, would be $6.5 million. Radler began negotiating to endow a building and scholarships in Toronto and Jerusalem using Hollinger's money. His pretensions to equal status irritated Black, but he was silenced when his partner pointed at the photographs of Conrad and Barbara at social events. 'You should be happy with all the money I've earned to pay for your parties,' said Radler, appreciating better than anyone the financial reality.

The Blacks' flamboyance aroused sniggers among the few who understood Hollinger's finances. 'I don't understand why Conrad wants to be the poorest billionaire in America,' commented one observer, noting that Black's standard of living, which he could ill afford, was higher than that enjoyed by the two richest men in the world, Bill Gates, the founder of Microsoft, and the investor Warren Buffett. Black never considered that the son of Katharine Graham, the owner of the *Washington Post*, travelled to work on the subway, or that Ken Thomson, controlling an $18 billion empire, anonymously dressed in jeans, shopped in his local supermarket. Oblivious to those comparisons, Black's self-confidence during summer 1997 was soaring to new heights. With great pride, during Elizabeth II's visit to Canada in June, Black dressed himself in the uniform of an honorary colonel of the Governor General's Foot Guards and greeted the Queen in Ottawa. He never contemplated that his critics would parody his display of loyalty as the parade of an obsequious doorman. Rupert Murdoch, *New York Times* owner Ochs Sulzberger and Ken Thomson joked about his imperial posture as a member of the Canadian Privy Council. Others queried his conduct as Canada's biggest newspaper owner, and Barbara Amiel's influence over Southam Newspapers. Among the casualties during those weeks was James

Travers, the editor of the *Ottawa Citizen*. Despite six successful years, Travers was fired and replaced by a friend of Amiel's who shared her political ideas, prompting a media outburst against Black as a menace to Canada's freedom of expression.[9] Unpopularity in Canada no longer bothered Black. The embrace of New York and London was so reassuring.

The squeeze of the famous into Cottesmore Gardens at the Blacks' summer party in 1997 reflected their importance among a particular group of writers, journalists, politicians, businessmen, playboys, actors and elder statesmen. Even though some criticised their house as 'an expensive, ugly monster', the hosts adored the spotlight among the crowds in the specially constructed two-storey reception room. The sight of Henry Kissinger at one end, supermodel Elle MacPherson at the other, and dozens of other famous faces in between generated electric excitement. Welcoming celebrities to their home inflated their self-importance. Only days earlier, during a discussion over dinner at the Garrick with Lord Weidenfeld and Norman Lamont, Frank Johnson had disputed an assertion by Black. 'Don't speak like that,' Black shot back. 'Don't forget, I sign your pay cheque.' There was no jest in his voice. Respect was due to a couple who were equally thrilled by the list of those excluded from their celebration.

Barbara Amiel could be harsh towards those she deemed to be valueless. Now fifty-seven, but boasting the looks of a woman ten years younger, she was indulged by her proud husband. Two dressing rooms of their Kensington home resembled an emporium. Clothes, handbags and shoes costing hundreds of thousands of pounds were amassing in the cupboards designed by David Mlinaric. Amiel never appeared to question whether her husband was making a clear distinction between Hollinger's and his own personal money, and occasionally items bought by her staff were inadvertently charged to Hollinger. There was no reason for Amiel to question her husband's ability to fund her love of clothes. She had every reason to assume he was as rich as his posture indicated. 'What men will do to keep high-maintenance wives,' carped Dan Colson about Amiel's trips, flying on the Gulfstream, from New York to Paris to buy dresses, and then, after a three-hour visit, continuing to London. 'All for "the little woman",' mimicked Colson. 'Barbara's calling the shots on everything.'

Amiel's behaviour suggested the vulnerability of a woman hurrying to compensate for lost opportunities. Medicine and drugs kept her exterior youthful. Surgery to her face and body had tautened her skin. She described fat being extracted from her buttocks and injected into her face as preferable to Botox. The corollary of pleasure was pain. Unseen, she was suffering from dermatomyositis, a rare auto-immune disease causing muscle inflammation and degeneration. Every two to three months she required three or four days of treatment, including blood transfusions. The occasional fragility of her health was matched by sporadic attempts to re-engage with some of her family. From time to time she met her mother and stepfather, living in a top-floor flat in an ugly tower block in Kitchener, Ontario. Despite disagreements she was reconciled with her sister Ruth, and very occasionally she arranged a meal with the Buckman family. Her own illness made her sympathetic to other sufferers, especially her brother-in-law, who was dying of cancer. In a search for her roots, she had even telephoned David Bentley, a first cousin, to offer an invitation to a charity concert at St James's Palace. Bentley, a lawyer in the Civil Service, was surprised. He had not heard from Amiel since they met in a pub off Whitehall ten years earlier, and was unaware of her new status. They would not see each other again for several years. One emotional consolation for the childless woman was shopping. Expensive clothes, she admitted, were a 'personal sickness'. To justify the fortune she was spending, she invented a political explanation. Fashion, she wrote, is 'a subtle expression of status and rank in a society . . . a counterbalance to the relentless march of feminism'.[10]

Clothes, however, were no longer enough. Amiel had never forgotten the night she arrived in her bedroom, filled with expensive designer items – a scented Manuel Canovas candle, a shagreen 'temple' made by David Lindley containing a gold comb, perfume from the Santa Maria Novella chemist in Florence and a copy of Gale Hayman's *How Do I Look?* in the bathroom – to find on her pillow an enormous natural-pearl and diamond brooch. Despite Conrad Black's pride and generosity, she decided that it was too big to wear. 'I simply can't carry it off,' she declared, and placed it permanently in a safety deposit box.[11] That modesty appeared to have vanished during a jewellery night at Annabel's in September 1998. A representative of Laurence Graff had placed a hundred-carat diamond in her hand. Even in the dim light, the stone's sparkle was captivating. The salesmen had identified his quarry, although he was unaware of an earlier embarrassment. In 1986, David Graham had examined a bracelet at Graff. While considering whether to take out his credit card, he overheard a salesman sneer, 'It's too expensive for him.' Sheepishly, Graham had left the shop.[12] Times had changed. Then, jewellery had been unimportant to Amiel, but after socialising with the Kravises and others in New York, she appreciated that her new friends rarely appeared in public without displays of huge stones set in white gold. Jewellery, she acknowledged, was 'a defining attribute' among that class, 'rather like intelligence or the number of references you have'. Her erstwhile prejudices were abandoned. 'All that stuff I believed about big stones just being vulgar,' she wrote, 'went into ether.'[13]

Gossip spread among jewellers that Amiel was a big spender. After one lunch in Victoria, she encouraged her female companion to drive to Bond Street. Stepping from the Bentley, she was welcomed like royalty by the manager of S.J. Phillips. A huge nineteenth-century necklace displayed in a special box was ready for her inspection. 'I'll have it,' she announced. The manager knew the procedure. He was to telephone Conrad Black and reveal that his wife would be pleased if he could make the purchase. Stepping back into the Bentley, she urged her friend to travel to Theo Fennell, the jewellers in Chelsea. 'We've got a very high-powered dinner tonight,' announced Amiel, 'and I need some presents for the guests.' Her friend understood that she herself was not sufficiently grand for the dinner or a present. Indeed, when they arrived at the shop, she was asked to remain in the car: 'Wait here. I'll be five minutes inside.' Forty minutes later, Amiel emerged with several boxes and barely uttered an apology. In the car, she telephoned a friend. 'Have you decided what to wear for Imran [Khan] and Jemima [Goldsmith]'s wedding?' she enquired breathlessly. Little was omitted in her quest to prove her importance. Before every occasion she tried on a succession of dresses, some costing over £20,000, regardless that her indecision would mean a late arrival. Many garments would never be worn. Conrad Black waited indulgently. Before the Princess of Wales's funeral at Westminster Abbey he had shown remarkable patience as she tried on more than a dozen hats, fussing about the appropriate colour and shape and mentioning her star appearance on Sky News. Amiel sensed no discrepancy in the juxtaposition of her own extravagant behaviour and regularly carping about the world's ills in her journalism.

Under the control of senior butler Andrew Lightwood, second butler Peter Wilson and a succession of third butlers, Amiel's life in Kensington had become what her constantly changing staff called 'bizarre'. Each recruit was taken by Lightwood on an introductory tour of the house, ending on the roof. 'Make sure the landing lights are on at all times,' instructed Lightwood solemnly, 'because Madame takes off from here on her broomstick looking for cats. She needs the lights to guide her return.' His face would crack into a smile. 'Most important, take care that she never sees you. She hates seeing any of us.' Amiel's eccentricity demanded that her staff hid whenever she approached, diving into cupboards if necessary, and never entered her quarters when she was present. The beginning of her day after twelve noon was signalled by the lights blinking on the telephone. Breakfast – ginger tea for Black and coffee with Coronation milk for Amiel – was prepared and taken to the floor below the main bedroom. Listening to the creaks on the floorboards above, the butlers could assess just when the trays should be deposited in the Blacks' offices upstairs without the delivery being spotted. Thereafter, again listening to the floorboards, the butlers tracked the Blacks into their offices and ordered the cleaners to quickly enter the bedrooms.

Every day, all the bedlinen was changed and subjected to 'the penny test'. A coin was dropped onto the sheets. If it failed to bounce, they were not drawn sufficiently tight. Every cushion was arranged to a precise pre-ordained position, and each towel placed exactly as Amiel had predetermined. 'Andrew!' she screamed down the telephone on one memorable occasion, 'the towels are in the wrong place!' Lightwood, as Amiel knew, was in New York, but he was expected to telephone the staff in the house in London to rectify the error. 'You fucking pillock!' she yelled at another member of staff for reading her *Daily Mail* before it had been delivered to her. 'Where's Andrew?' Telephones throughout the house were ringing as she attempted to find the head butler. Eventually, he picked up a handset. 'Where the fuck were you?' screamed Amiel. 'I was in the toilet, Madame,' replied Lightwood. 'You're never there when I need you!' shouted Amiel. 'You're always cocking things up!' Increasingly, there seemed no rhyme or reason to her moods, and no one was quite sure how to satisfy her requirements. On one occasion she had demanded Paula, a maid. 'I'm afraid, Madame,' explained Lightwood, 'that Paula has taken Adelia [another maid] to hospital. She collapsed.' 'Why couldn't Paula just put Adelia in a taxi and send her to the hospital?' asked Amiel.

Lightwood did not reply. Amiel, he realised, was clearly having another bad day. The butler considered entering a monastery.

Amiel's unconventional domestic behaviour remained unknown beyond a small circle until a dinner party at Cottesmore Gardens in June 1998. The Blacks had invited about thirty people. As usual, there would be two tables, Conrad's and Barbara's. Late in the afternoon, Amiel was told that one woman would be unable to attend. In a panic to ensure equal numbers of men and women, she asked her husband to invite a suitable female from the *Telegraph*'s staff. On his behalf, Charles Moore chose Eleanor Mills, a writer. After rushing home to change, Mills was welcomed by Black at the house and offered a glass of wine. Fifteen minutes later, Black reappeared. The placement at his table, he had been told by Amiel, was again awry. A late cancellation meant that there was now an extra woman. Mills had become more than superfluous, she was a positive embarrassment. Amiel wanted her to leave immediately. 'Why don't you finish your drink and skedaddle?' Black told the puzzled Mills. 'Finish your drink and run along. Barbara will sort out a taxi.' Mills's humiliation was compounded by finding Amiel chatting with Petronella Wyatt, a rival journalist who was clearly favoured to stay. Directed by Amiel to depart through the kitchen, Mills did not wait for Penny Wilson, Amiel's personal assistant, to order the taxi. She merely stood in the street and vowed revenge.

Long before the dinner was over, both Blacks had forgotten the incident. In their new assumption of superiority, neither understood that few Londoners cared about equal numbers at dinner. Only those irredeemably permeated with provincial values could treat a guest in that manner. Neither imagined, as they congratulated themselves on another successful evening, that their behaviour would outrage even their closest admirers as, over following days, Mills revealed the story of her embarrassment. When he did hear the criticism, Black called Charles Moore. 'She was treated very rudely,' Moore told his employer. 'I think you should apologise.' 'I'll do that,' replied Black. Mills never received an apology.

Black failed to do anything about his wife's bad manners. Weeks earlier in Toronto, Barbara had invited a journalist to lunch, only to exclaim loudly on the doorstep, 'Oh, you're not who I thought you were,' and close the door. Journalists, in her opinion, were dispensable. Her close girlfriends blamed her bad behaviour on insecurity. Pledged to fighting age 'until the end', she expressed a fear of younger women chasing her husband. 'If he leaves me, at least I've had a good run,' she sighed. The relationship between the Blacks had become fraught. At a weekend party in Wiltshire the previous month, Black had said to a glamorous young journalist, 'If it ends with Barbara, are you up for it?' The woman was puzzled by the crass approach, which confirmed the gossip about Amiel's apprehensions. The strain had also been noticed at a party hosted by James Goldsmith in Paris. Amiel spotted Black engrossed in conversation with Nicola Formby, an attractive writer. Glaring, she stood behind her husband until, as an observer noted, the hairs on his neck were 'receiving electric messages to tell him to leave'. Shortly after, Black was again speaking to Formby. 'Beat it,' Amiel said to her. 'You've been with my husband long enough.' The tension continued during the dinner. Undeterred by the public nature of the occasion, Amiel spoke coldly to Black, causing eyewitnesses to be 'frightened' that he would be mentally wounded. That night, they suspected, she would, hard as nails, withdraw within herself like a wild animal.

Barbara Amiel had become too rich, regal and respected to be dismissed on account of her behaviour. Those employed by the Blacks were expected to bear her variable moods silently. In the summer of 1998 Conrad Black sensed a recurrence of her sulks during the preparations for the annual Hollinger dinner for three hundred guests at New York's Metropolitan Club. As usual, he had asked Carolyn Peachy to organise the event, endlessly discussing the guest list and the seating arrangements. 'I want a great mix,' he explained. Since the writer Tom Wolfe was the guest of honour, Barbara Amiel insisted on becoming involved, 'to shine', it was said, 'in the spotlight'. Samples of the tablecloths, napkins, cutlery and menus were sent to London for her approval. A 'final' draft of the invitation list was faxed to Kensington for her endorsement. Half an hour later, her hysterical curses were winging to Peachy's office in Washington. The fax machine, Amiel screamed, was on the ground floor, while she was upstairs, 'and there's no butler to bring it up, and I'm not going down'. Her frenzy towards Peachy's assistant was similar to that shown in a recent outburst on the street in Manhattan. At the end of a lunch for the board of directors arranged by Peachy's office, a fax addressed to Amiel had been placed in a box for shipping to Canada. 'I need that fax!' Amiel had yelled in anger, knowing that the miscreant's expectation of the Blacks' fees guaranteed that he would not dare to bite back.

Conrad Black was surprised by his wife's attitude. So often she lost her temper, screaming about trivialities. Whereas he would sometimes take a maid out for dinner to show his gratitude, or, if a waiter dropped a glass, bend down to help clear up the mess, Amiel scolded hapless people for the slightest mistake. Everyone suffered her moods. Regularly, he had to make excuses for what he regarded as a single flaw in an otherwise perfect wife. Soon after the public explosion in New York he had telephoned from his plane. 'I apologise for Barbara,' he said, 'she's not feeling well.' The recipient of Black's apology was grateful. Amiel, she decided, was 'a negative influence on Conrad'. There was no such apology for Amiel's outburst from Kensington about the faxed guest list. 'She flips her personality and mood every day of the week,' her assistant explained. 'Her enemies even joke that she pretends to be a dog when some British aunt visits her.'

The 1998 Hollinger annual dinner, costing about $1 million,

was a seminal moment for the Blacks. Tom Wolfe, the famous author of *The Bonfire of the Vanities*, intoxicated his fans. The author's exposure of the victimisation of rich whites by politically biased and colour-prejudiced state law enforcers was a favourite theme among Manhattan's A-list, enthralled that year by Wolfe's latest book, *A Man in Full*. Wolfe's fiction gratifyingly portrayed wealth-creating capitalists as the victims of society's spongers and their patrons in the government. Among Black's Manhattan friends, the conviction in 1990 of Michael Milken, the junk bond dealer, was regarded as a travesty of justice. Milken's confession, they insisted, had been extracted by blackmail. Academic studies had proven to Black's circle that state prosecutors had become laws unto themselves, and were beyond control. In their opinion, the state was persecuting a handful of rich whites in order to justify the simultaneous prosecution of deprived blacks. Wolfe had become the hero of those American capitalists, and Black was among the cheerleaders. In Wolfe's term, he counted as 'a big swinging dick'.

The headlines that year justified the soubriquet. Hollinger's turnover was over $2 billion, and its gross profits were nearly $200 million. Unseen was the downside. The profits were insufficient to repay any of the $1.4 billion debt, and barely funded the dividends, interest payments and Ravelston's increasing management fees. 'The debt is not our fault,' Black told Paul Healy. 'We're undervalued on the market because the banks don't realise how much our assets are worth.' Black's concealment of his fragile finances, cocooned by the lack of interest among the company's non-executive directors, was a lifebelt. Reality could be ignored. In the presence of Tom Wolfe and some of Manhattan's cleverest, richest citizens, Black wistfully pondered how he could achieve his elusive destiny as an author, statesman and political panjandrum. The remedy, he believed, was not far off. He was on the brink of a gamble that would permanently change his life.

For years Black had been frustrated by what he saw as Canada's politically correct, socialist governments. He was outraged by the 'complacent, back-scratching . . . soft-left orthodoxy' among the major newspapers and CBC, the national broadcasting corporation. He owned newspapers everywhere in Canada except Toronto, where it counted. In his own city he had to tolerate Allan Fotheringham and his ilk describing him as 'a bloated, bullying megalomaniac'.[14] He particularly loathed Toronto's *Globe and Mail*, which he regarded as a lacklustre newspaper and which Ken Thomson refused to sell to him. Thomson's rebuff was partly motivated by Black's unwillingness to pay a high enough price, and also in anticipation of the government's displeasure if the prestigious newspaper was sold to a critic. Unspoken was the legacy of Black's libel writs and his conduct towards the Argus widows. Toronto's patricians had not forgotten his pitilessness. Black's ultimate threat to launch a rival newspaper against the *Globe* failed to persuade Thomson to sell. Efforts at brinkmanship against an empire worth C$22 billion were forlorn. In a final attempt to outmanoeuvre the *Globe*, Black made a bid for the *Financial Post*, a Toronto newspaper with a healthy daily circulation of 90,000. He was spurned.

Over brunch during Easter 1997, Black had mentioned his dissatisfaction to Ken Whyte, editor of his *Saturday Night* magazine. 'Canadian newspapers are boring, reading them is a chore,' said Black. 'We need to stir things up.' Canada's media, he felt, lacked a dynamic conservative voice featuring the best journalism, of the type he read in London and New York. Hating mediocrity, he wanted to shock those stuffed prunes at the *Globe* with original design, brilliant journalism and scintillating writing. Newspapers, he believed, could create a powerful right-wing opposition to Jean Chrétien, the re-elected Liberal Prime Minister who had laid waste the parliamentary Conservative Party. Black's ambition was to finance a revolution in Canadian journalism. Breaking the habit of a lifetime, he wasn't going to cut costs to make money, but would spend to score points. He was, he told Whyte, thinking of creating a newspaper to destroy the socialists and encourage the opposition. This was not only a business but a political crusade for the right to proclaim 'It's OK to be rich.' Whyte, who some saw as congenial but bland, lacked any national newspaper experience, but as a loyal employee he nodded in agreement. 'See you on the boat,' Black told Whyte.

Their discussions continued in late spring 1998 on board Black's beautiful forty-five-foot wood-strip launch moored in Toronto's harbour.[15] As his plans materialised, Black convinced himself that a new national newspaper to be called the *National Post* would be a memorial to his talent and would entrench his political influence. His destiny, unlike Beaverbrook's and Thomson's, was to fulfil an intellectual's political mission. At their regular meetings in restaurants during those months, Black, drinking immoderately, held forth loudly, summoning the waiters to discuss his ideas. Whyte thought his employer, swaying in his seat or as he stood, resembled a tall tree in a stiff breeze. Like many others, he doubted whether Black would actually take the gamble. The arguments against a new Canadian national newspaper seemed compelling. Every English-speaking community in the country supported at least two daily newspapers; in Toronto, there were three major daily newspapers as well as some commuter sheets. More pertinently, Black owned over 50 per cent of Canada's press, and the *National Post*'s success would depend on luring readers away from his own thirty-three daily papers. Few could understand the business logic of risking $100 million to compete with himself. Ignoring those arguments, Whyte was ordered to launch a bidding war for the best journalists across the country. He was authorised even to plunder Black's own Canadian newspapers for printing and distribution facilities, and to offer higher wages to journalists employed on Black's other newspapers to encourage them to switch to the *National Post.*

Black's enthusiastic cannibalisation of his own papers aroused Radler's scepticism, so he was kept away. This was Black's business.[16]

At the age of fifty-four, Black was launching a new product for the first time. Other media groups had diversified into advertising, exhibitions and broadcasting. By then Rupert Murdoch had relaunched the *Sun* newspaper in London, established Sky TV across Europe and Asia and Fox TV in America, and was the owner of Twentieth Century-Fox, one of the world's largest film production companies. Players like Murdoch understood the huge cost of funding start-ups. Newspapers were a mature business which Ken Thomson was abandoning, yet Conrad Black in June 1998 was proposing to risk $100 million in that declining industry. Previously some of his speculation had been on the edge of morality, but this time he was taking a wager on innovation. Spare no expense, were his orders to Whyte.[17] All the lessons from his expensive battle with Murdoch in London were ignored. He even forgot that the *Telegraph*, the source of his fortune, had only fallen into his hands because of Lord Hartwell's failure to predict the financial costs. Black believed his destiny was glory, regardless of the odds.

Conrad Black was hiring journalists, not because he liked them – on the contrary, he still damned that disreputable breed – but because he needed their talent to promote his political agenda. He and Amiel had convinced themselves that they could attract readers to agree that Canada would remain a lousy, second-rate country until it espoused conservatism. Even while he proposed ridiculing his potential readers' ideas, he expected their support for his newspaper. No one warned him that alienating his audience was rarely a successful sales pitch. Black did not employ independent sceptics.

In those heady early-summer days, jetting between dinners and parties in London and New York and billionaires' estates across

North America, Black assumed a new omnipotence. In June 1998 he paid $18 million for a 5 per cent stake in Livent, a theatre company run by Garth Drabinsky. The money was taken from Southam Newspapers. Just six weeks after Black applauded 'an attractive diversification opportunity', Livent filed for bankruptcy and the American authorities targeted Drabinsky in a fraud investigation. Black's investment was lost, yet he remained Drabinsky's loyal friend, and promised to fund the criminal defence lawyer Eddie Greenspan to act on his behalf.

Throughout that year, Barbara Amiel's mood towards the *National Post* gyrated. Initially, she had told her husband that Canada's newspapers were a lost cause, an unexpected attitude considering that Black owned more than half the country's titles. 'I don't see how it can make profits,' she said pessimistically. Her gloom disappeared once Canada's Sun Media group, fearing competition from Black's new paper, finally agreed to sell the *Financial Post* to him for C$110 million. Instead of declining the offer as a sign of desperation, Black paid the full price. The *Financial Post*, he decided, would be inserted inside the *National Post*. Overnight, the cost of his investment had doubled. By selling 300,000 copies a day, he pronounced, he would break even within one year. 'Buying the *Financial Post* is a great thing,' Amiel excitedly told Ken Whyte.[18]

Throwing herself into the venture, Amiel agreed to host with her husband a dinner to woo Canada's major advertisers. One hundred and fifty chief executives and their wives and partners were invited to a party in the garden of their Toronto house. Just hours before the first guests arrived, Amiel rushed home to discover a huge marquee on the lawn. 'This is horrid-looking,' she shuddered. For six hours she toiled to add, as she would later describe them, 'decorations, the whimsy, and the clever touches that make a large event intimate'. During those hours she consoled herself about the value of her efforts, because the guests were, as she wrote in a magazine article, 'potential underwriters for next spring's wardrobe'. In publicly confessing her brazen materialism, Amiel was immune to the irritation of her guests. By contrast, during the dinner Black smelt failure. His audience, he realised, represented precisely the things he disliked about Canada. They were smug, fearful of change, and saw little reason for another newspaper except to force down advertising rates. Their animosity towards him was tangible. Unwilling visibly to support Black personally, they found his aggressive pep-talk just as discomfiting as their wives did Amiel's majestic appearance. Her diva-like poise froze the potential advertisers' hearts and wallets. The majority of women departed seeking either reassurance to restore their self-confidence, or alcohol to calm their irritation.

Only Barbara Amiel herself remained unaware of the consequences of her performance. Days later, she sat in her office, thoughtfully writing her regular column for *Maclean's* magazine. 'I am married to the chairman of Southam Inc.,' she wrote, 'which is launching a new national newspaper in Canada later this month. I may also write for the said paper, and if that paper is a financial success, I'm hoping my husband's income from it will subsidise my obscene dress bills.' On reflection, Amiel realised how offensive many would find that sentiment. But from the top of her mountain she had become scornful of poorer people. They were all, she agreed with her husband, motivated by spite and envy. Accordingly, she added an afterthought: '(Of one thing you can be sure: someone will take that last sentence out of context.)'[19] There was no need. Observers were accustomed to reading Barbara Amiel's mind like a book.

During the countdown to the newspaper's launch, a truth dawned on Amiel. Conrad Black's certainty of success was questionable. Excluded from considering the financial quagmire, she fretted about the newspaper's design. 'It's very vertical, isn't it?' she asserted in a rising voice. With just days to go before the launch,

Ken Whyte, Martin Newland, the British editor, and others feared the explosion of a hysterical outburst. 'Are readers going to like that?' Amiel jittered. 'Perhaps we should consider something else . . .'[20] Only buckets of water, some suggested, could restore calm before the volcano erupted.

On the evening of 26 October 1998, John Fraser hosted a drinks reception for Black at Massey College on the University of Toronto campus. That night the *National Post* would be launched. Even those with grievances against Black, including Fred Eaton, Hal Jackman and Peter Worthington, attended to express their goodwill. To capitalise on his moment of stardom, Black presented each guest with a copy of his massive Maurice Duplessis biography, specially republished that week. 'Congratulations on the newspaper,' said the British journalist John O'Sullivan. 'Ken has done a great job,' Amiel replied, adding an unexpected reality check: 'But I wish we had got the other papers right before we went in.' At 9.30 p.m. the party moved to Don Mills, a Toronto suburb, to watch Black press the button and start printing across five time zones. Four hours later came the first bad news. The newspaper was printing perfectly in eight plants, but the machines in Toronto had crashed. Amiel passed on her husband's anger to Pat Brennan, the production manager. 'Tell him that things are running smoothly in all other areas,' said Brennan. 'I'm not sure that will do,' snapped Amiel icily. Eventually, the first copies were presented. After critical scrutiny, dozens of *Post* employees surrounded Black and Amiel demanding autographs, giving praise and cheering. 'He's at his best,' thought Ken Whyte, 'rightly proud of what he's accomplished.' By daybreak, Black was experiencing a rare sensation. Rivals were impressed with the *Post*'s combination of 'tits and analysis', and journalists praised him for paying high salaries and encouraging good writing. By comparison, the *Globe and Mail* looked dreary. Unusually, Black was a hero.

Overnight, a newspaper war erupted in Toronto. Four major

papers were seeking readers among the city's 4.5 million population. Three months later the *Post*'s circulation hit 270,000, close to the *Globe*'s 300,000. Ken Thomson was alarmed. Black's challenge coincided with the beginning of a financial squeeze and a decline in advertising. Although the *Post*'s advertising income was poor, its circulation was artificially inflated and there were piles of unread newspapers cluttering Toronto's subways and shopping malls, Black's challenge bore the imprint of success. Only money and new talent, Thomson decided, could rescue the situation. Philip Crawley, an experienced British newspaper manager, was hired to overhaul the *Globe* and defeat Black. Considering Thomson's superior financial resources, Black's fate was precarious. He was determined to win, and welcomed Amiel's help.

Amiel had become Black's key editorial adviser, at the *Telegraph* and Southam. Confident of her expertise to direct improvements at the *National Post*, she regularly lectured Newland and Whyte about hiring, redesign and the newspaper's content. At the hint of any reluctance to obey, she was transformed from serenity into a screaming fit. Conrad Black chose to ignore his wife's behaviour. Her tantrums were familiar at home. His beloved Barbara, he knew, was temperamental, but nevertheless a remarkable woman. Six years of marriage had bonded them. Amiel's advice and support were invaluable. The two agreed that in 1999 she should be paid in 1999 an annual salary of $285,000 by the *Chicago Sun-Times* for her services as an editorial adviser to the whole group. Under American law, they knew, that payment should have been disclosed to Hollinger's audit committee. But Hollinger's executive directors decided to conceal the payment. Thereafter, Nigel Wade, the editor of the *Chicago Sun-Times*, received notes with the inscription 'Dictated by, but not read by, Barbara Amiel.'

Launching the *Post* created a financial crisis. Barbara Amiel became aware of its gravity after a flight to Palm Beach to inspect the progress of rebuilding their new home. Boarding the

Gulfstream in New York with Henry Kissinger, the Blacks announced their plan to drop Kissinger in Washington and then fly on to Florida. 'There's a snowstorm in Washington,' said the pilot. 'We won't be able to land.' 'I'll take the train,' said Kissinger. 'How can Henry get to the station?' asked Amiel. 'Quickest way is by helicopter,' advised the pilot. Swivelling towards Conrad Black, Amiel snapped, 'Why haven't we got a helicopter, Conrad? The Kravises have one.' Black's smile froze: 'We're not rich like the Kravises.'

Down in Palm Beach, Amiel carefully inspected the plans for perfect acoustics and lighting in her office and her husband's library, while Black tried to find out why the local contractors were proving more expensive than anticipated. 'Charging through the nose,' he complained. His ambition to provide a palace for his princess was proving troublesome. 'Lord Macbeth', local wags guffawed, was not pleased. The workers had nevertheless gone to some trouble to provide refreshments for their employers. Amiel was given a plastic bottle of water. 'What am I meant to do with this?' she asked. 'Where's the glass?' The Blacks departed disgruntled. Sitting with friends later that day, Amiel reflected upon her lifestyle. 'I don't deserve these things,' she admitted. Her audience stared back. Was this the same woman, they wondered, who had dispatched the Gulfstream from New York to collect a handbag from Palm Beach; and who, while walking in Worth Avenue, Palm Beach's shopping centre, sighed as she passed a woman, 'I'll never be like that beautiful blonde.' Amiel was, they concluded, an enigma.

Before their return to Toronto, Conrad Black decided that he could no longer afford the development. He found a reason to argue with architect Richard Sammons's accounts, and withheld payment. 'He's invented an excuse,' Sammons told several friends in New York. 'He's a bad man.' Black was not intending to abandon the project entirely. Rather, he was looking for additional income from the sale of Hollinger's newspapers.

11

Sliding Towards the Edge

The financial pressures were inescapable, and the cure was crude. 'It's time to get out,' Conrad Black announced. 'We've got the maximum value from our community newspapers. Let's sell.' David Radler agreed. 'Project Wishlist' was the name given to the sale of large parts of the empire to repay their debts. In the name of capitalism, there would also be what others would perceive as shortcuts. Jack Boultbee was to work behind the scenes with Peter Atkinson, the lawyer, to plan the delicate path towards the secret self-enrichment of the four.

Conrad Black had understood the fundamental weakness of his finances for some months. Hollinger's debt could not be repaid, the haemorrhage at the *National Post* could not be sustained, and the profits were inadequate to fund his lifestyle. Although his threat of writs suppressed damaging comments about his predicament, he appeared to be just a few steps ahead of his creditors. Unlike Rupert Murdoch and Henry Kravis, the pontificating champion of capitalism could no longer make the system work to his advantage. Buying cheap and squeezing profits, his trusted formula for wealth, was a formula from a bygone age.

The pressure did not improve relations among the inner circle. Radler and Black spoke frequently but saw little of each other. United by their desire to make as much money as possible, each tolerated the other's interests while observing the pecking order, which rewarded Black with more. In return, Black respected Radler's interests in Chicago and Jerusalem, although both were financially unsuccessful. While excelling as the cost-cutting manager of small-town, monopoly community newspapers, Radler was hopelessly adrift as a big-league player.

Radler's draconian cuts and editorial somersault at the *Jerusalem Post* had undermined the newspaper's popularity, propelling the accumulated losses towards £15 million. The predicament at the *Chicago Sun-Times* was worse. In the face of a fall in advertising and sales, Radler ordered massive cuts. The best employees were the highest-paid, and to save money they were fired. As the quality of the newspaper's management and content deteriorated, the income fell. 'I want you to open all the employees' mail,' Radler ordered Nigel Wade. 'I want you to check if anyone's disloyal.' Wade ignored the instruction. 'I want you to fire anyone with a betting slip,' decreed Radler. 'They've gotta be crooks.' Again he was ignored. Radler even ordered the dismissal of a postroom clerk who left 35 cents for a stamp he had taken for an urgent letter to the Revenue. 'He's certain to have taken other stamps without paying for them,' snapped Radler. Operating from his dirty office in Vancouver, the awkward, squinting man who ended each sentence with 'OK!' pathologically loathed journalists. 'Fire the music critic,' he told Wade. 'We don't have one in Calgary.' 'David,' replied Wade patiently, 'our newspaper's only got its credibility to sell. Without that, we're finished.' In frustration, to save money Radler shut down escalators and began overstating the newspaper's sales to maintain advertising revenue. By 2002, the circulation would be exaggerated by nearly 20 per cent. The *Sun-Times* was becoming a byword for bad management and decline.

The financial problems led the relationships among the cabal to deteriorate. Mutual respect was replaced by mutual distrust. Radler and Colson had always disliked each other, but were united by their disdain for Amiel, especially after she began drawing a secret salary and enjoyed a billionaire's lifestyle at Hollinger's expense. The Blacks' extravagance irritated Radler's instinctive abstemiousness. 'Crossharbour strikes again,' he scoffed on each occasion he spotted evidence of the Blacks' unbridled expenditure, referring to Black's anticipated title once he received his peerage* – Amiel was known as 'Very Crossharbour'. In response, Radler decided that his two daughters and his wife should also benefit from the company. One daughter was employed at an inflated salary as the New York correspondent of the *Jerusalem Post*, the other was hired on normal terms by Governor Thompson's law firm in Chicago; while his wife Rona was paid to act as the chairman of the *Chicago Sun-Times*'s charitable trust. Those limited advantages were poor compensation for a man increasingly displeased by his partnership with Black. The sell-off, he agreed, would make life easier. Instead of focusing on improving the business or recruiting new executives to revitalise the corporation, Black and Radler focused on financing their personal lifestyles and creating a new business.

Before embarking on 'Project Wishlist', Black, Radler, Atkinson and Boultbee consulted lawyers and accountants to discuss the legality of various scenarios. In the game of words and interpretations, they planned their possible responses to questions from the independent directors, the SEC and even prosecutors in a court. 'If we do this,' those involved in the discussion asked, 'can we successfully argue our innocence and rebut any incriminating allegations?' In their scenarios, the 'truth' was what could be proven; the rest was open to interpretation. That grey area defined their proximity to the edge. The conclusion depended on obtaining relevant letters of approval from their lawyers and accountants.

* Crossharbour is the Docklands Light Railway station near the *Telegraph*'s London print works at South Quay.

Eventually that authorisation was granted, sanctifying a master-stroke dreamed up by Boultbee.

The four men in the inner circle, it was agreed, could personally profit from each sale of Hollinger's newspapers by including in the contract a 'non-compete fee' – money that is normally paid by the purchaser of a business to ensure that the seller is forbidden to use his expertise immediately after the sale to set up another business in competition with the company just sold. There was an added bonus to the ploy. Under Canadian law, non-compete fees were tax-free. Conventionally, Black knew, non-compete fees were paid to the employers, in this case Hollinger, and not to the employees.[1] An exception would be permitted if Black, after submitting all the information, obtained the approval of Hollinger's board of directors. In email exchanges after the plan was agreed, Black knew he could rely on Boultbee to direct David Radler, the mechanic, to execute the sales and arrange for the payment of the non-compete fees. He himself would remain aloof from the details, satisfied that Torys, Hollinger's lawyers, would provide a seal of probity and hence, he believed, sufficient protection against any allegation of wrongdoing. A subsequent investigation on behalf of the company would report that by serving Hollinger Inc., Hollinger International and Ravelston simultaneously, Torys 'gave them the legal advice they sought that these inconvenient rules did not apply to large portions of the cash transferred to Black and Radler through Ravelston'. Torys, the investigators continued, did not reveal that it 'had a conflict in giving this advice'.[2]

The first sale was conventional. On 30 November 1998, Black and Radler revealed to the board of Hollinger International in New York that forty-five American newspapers were to be sold to Community Newspaper Holdings (CNH) based in Birmingham, Alabama. The price to be paid to Hollinger International was US$472 million. The sale, for a good price, was approved, but Hollinger's directors were not told about the twist introduced into the deal at the last moment.[3] The directors of CNH were asked by Radler to label $50 million of the purchase money as a non-compete fee. CNH's directors were surprised. Hollinger's newspapers were monopolies distributed in small communities, so a non-compete clause was irrelevant. However, since there was no extra cost and no loss to CNH, they agreed to Radler's request. At the last minute, Radler directed CNH's directors to send $12 million of that fee to Hollinger Inc. in Toronto. The destination was significant. Hollinger Inc. was a shell company without employees, not party to the deal, and would be unable to 'compete' with CNH. After the money was deposited, the directors in New York who were selling the newspaper were not told of the arrangement by Radler or Black.

Once the $12 million was deposited, Radler used the money to partly repay the $42.5 million debt which the Toronto company had owed the New York company since 1997. In other words, Hollinger International in New York was being 'repaid' with its own money, and no one at Hollinger's headquarters on Fifth Avenue was told or noticed.[4] The remaining $38 million of the non-compete fee was paid to Ravelston, fulfilling Radler and Black's decision to receive a 'cut' out of the deal. Again, the directors in New York were not told.[5]

Black and Radler were also planning a second, more audacious operation. At the same Hollinger International board meeting in New York on 30 November 1998, Radler proposed that a further thirty-three small American newspapers owned by sixteen companies should be sold for US$43.7 million. The purchaser, he announced, was a newly incorporated company called Horizon Publications whose headquarters was in Marion, Illinois.[6] Radler disclosed to Hollinger's directors that he and Black would 'take equity positions' in Horizon. Radler explained that his small investment was an act of charity to help Todd Vogt, a former Hollinger employee, establish a business. Not one director asked for the details of Radler and Black's relationship with Horizon, or challenged the potential conflict of interest. Henry Kissinger was too busy to read the notes, while Marie-Josée Kravis was not paying attention. Neither they nor the other directors discovered that 48 per cent of Horizon was directly owned by Black and Radler; and that 24 per cent of the company 'owned' by Todd Vogt was held under a secret agreement in trust for Radler. So Black and Radler owned 72 per cent of Horizon, which had been established in anticipation of the two men's exit from Hollinger. In praise of his new company, Black wrote to potential investors that he and Radler had 'bought and sold hundreds of these little American newspapers . . . and have never failed to make a handsome profit on them'. He continued, with remarkable candour, that he was 'buying them back now for our own account, knowing their profit potential intimately'.[7] He appears to have neglected his obligations to Hollinger and its shareholders.

Nor did Hollinger's directors query the price. Trusting Black, neither Thompson nor Kravis appears to have read the formal documents carefully. Neither imagined that Black was no longer a commercial trader, but a trader in faith. Witnessing the directors' docility, Radler ordered Todd Vogt to tell the employees of the thirty-three newspapers (two of which were eventually excluded from the sale) that Horizon was an independent company with no connection to Hollinger, and to manipulate the price of the newspapers sold to Horizon downwards in Horizon's favour.[8] Later calculations suggested that Horizon had possibly paid $18.1 million (or 29 per cent) less than Hollinger could have obtained on the open market. To pay for the purchase, Radler arranged that Hollinger would loan the entire purchase money to Horizon at a low rate of interest.[9]

Having loaned the money to Horizon, Radler organised a final twist. Horizon 'demanded' a 'non-compete clause' in the contract from Hollinger International. Radler agreed, and Horizon paid

$1.2 million of the purchase money to Hollinger Inc. in Toronto, rather than to Hollinger in New York. That payment was completed without the approval of the directors in New York. Black and Radler could not believe their good fortune. Not one of Hollinger's directors, nor the company's lawyers or auditors, had objected to an astonishing fact. Horizon, owned by Radler and Black, was paying $1.2 million to Hollinger Inc., controlled by Radler and Black, to prevent Radler and Black competing with themselves – and the money all came from Hollinger's own funds in New York. An added element of genius to the plan was that Black's shareholding in Hollinger International had fallen to 19 per cent, yet his super voting shares gave him complete control over the whole arrangement.[10]

The paperwork for the transaction was completed by Mark Kipnis, Hollinger's in-house lawyer. A kind, unmalicious family man, Kipnis had been hired from a small law firm with a big increase in salary. Whether in order to be part of the in-crowd, or to pursue his burgeoning ambition, he did not appear to question Radler or Boultbee's instructions. Sharing an office with Radler in Chicago, he understood precisely what was happening. Boultbee was also profiting from the deals. He bought a large new house in Toronto, a ski chalet and a house by a lake. Among his new cars was an Aston Martin.

Encouraged by their success, Black, Radler and Boultbee decided in January 1999 to take more money out of Hollinger, using what they called the 'Template' of non-compete fees. Eight months earlier, *American Trucker* magazine had been sold. Despite the completion of the deal, Radler ordered $2 million from the proceeds to be diverted to Hollinger Inc. in Toronto as a non-compete payment, although the shell company would be unable to compete with *American Trucker*.[11] The New York directors were not told about this transfer. Thereafter, every sale of Hollinger's newspapers would be subject to the 'Template'.

Conrad Black and David Radler knew the value of the newspapers they were selling and their potential profits better than anyone. The *Naugatuck Daily News* was sold by Hollinger to Horizon in March 1999 for $78,000. Six months later, Radler resold the newspaper for $673,314, a profit of nearly 900 per cent.[12] By the end of the year Horizon had bought another fifteen newspapers on the open market. In some communities, Horizon newspapers were competing with Hollinger's. Conrad Black decided not to reveal that conflict of interest to the other Hollinger directors. Instead, he said of his involvement with Horizon, 'I own a few shares because they needed a balance of sale but I have nothing to do with it.'[13] In truth, he and Radler controlled the company. Beyond that, they had also neutralised the safeguards to prevent insider deals.

The independence of Hollinger's lawyers Torys, based in Toronto and New York, had been contaminated by seeming conflicts of interest. At their client's request the lawyers agreed to simultaneously advise Ravelston, Hollinger Inc. and Hollinger International. Black and Radler's second success was their debilitation of the audit committee. By law, the committee was required to investigate any transaction that had been seemingly contaminated by conflicts of interest. In early 1998 Black was told that Richard Perle's employment by Hollinger, for which he would be paid $757,962 during that year, disqualified him as an independent committee member. Perle was replaced by the retired American diplomat Richard Burt and Marie-Josée Kravis. Together with Governor Thompson, these three were the shareholders' bulwark against any wrongdoing. Married to an outstanding investor, Marie-Josée Kravis preened herself on the belief that she possessed similar talents. Her directorships of major corporations had, she reckoned, proved her individual importance. But beyond Kravis's swanky performance Black perceived a scatterbrain, precisely the quality he required if he was to avoid rigorous scrutiny.

Perle's resignation was also a mere matter of appearance. He remained as a member of the crucial executive committee. Burt seemed out of his depth. Finally, Black resorted to outright concealment. Under federal and Delaware laws, the company was obliged to reveal to the SEC that Horizon was owned by Hollinger's directors. Their control was not disclosed.

Like an adulterous husband, Black's first experience of the charade might have been tinged with fear of exposure, but each successive act of deception reduced the fear and the guilt. Greed had driven Black to approve transactions which, if not criminal, were clearly unethical. After embarking on his chicanery he gave an interview to Bill Hagerty, a British journalist who he vaingloriously felt would present the image of him as an honest newspaper proprietor. In the past, Black had damned those who failed to appreciate his talents as being consumed by 'a sadistic desire, corroded by soul-destroying envy, to intimidate all those who might aspire to anything in the slightest exceptional'. On this occasion he presented a more emollient tone. 'I don't want to sound self-righteous,' he told Hagerty, 'but I don't know that it's ever been alleged that I have ever failed to keep my word. Ever, on anything, I always do – I think even my opponents would grant me that . . . I don't think moral standards are so much in peril.'[14] No one in London, Toronto or New York bothered to question Black's self-congratulation.

Pocketing the non-compete fees relieved Black's personal cash crisis, and the reconstruction of the house in Palm Beach was resumed. However, Black and Radler understood that over the longer term Hollinger's financial predicament remained difficult. Newspaper circulations were falling and advertising revenue was dipping. Despite the sales of the newspapers, Hollinger's debt in June 1999 increased to $1.62 billion, and was destined to increase by another $100 million during that year. The reason was that Hollinger was selling its most profitable newspapers in the United

States. The beneficiaries were Black and his group.[15] Their success encouraged Radler to adopt a more brazen strategy in Kelowna, a lakeside town in Brtitish Columbia, 1,700 miles from Toronto and safely isolated from any unwelcome enquiries from the east coast.

Until spring 1999, Radler had counted the *Capital News* in Kelowna, a free three-day-a-week newspaper, among Hollinger's successes. Over the previous three years Paul Winkler, the publisher, had transformed a jaded newspaper into such a success that its rival, the *Daily Courier*, owned by Thomson Newspapers, had admitted defeat and announced its sale. Spotting an opportunity, in April 1999 Radler told Todd Vogt to purchase the *Courier* on behalf of Horizon for $11 million, a good price. Radler had not told Hollinger's directors of the profitable opportunity.[16] 'Welcome to Kelowna,' Winkler said to Vogt, unaware of Horizon's relationship with Hollinger. Vogt did not volunteer to remove any confusion, not least because soon after 1 May 1999 he offered the *Capital News*'s key employees tempting sums to work for the *Courier*.

Winkler's irritation disappeared on hearing that the *Courier*'s printers intended to strike against their new employer. The *Capital News*, he smiled, would be the only paper in town. His pleasure was short-lived. In a telephone call, David Dodd, Radler's senior executive, ordered Winkler, 'I want you to print the *Courier*.' Winkler was incredulous. 'Help the competition?' he choked. 'You must be joking. Absolutely not.' 'Bullshit!' yelled Radler. He flew to Kelowna to issue an order to Winkler: 'It's our policy to help competitors when threatened by trade unions.' Winkler laughed, 'I've never heard of that before.' 'Sort him out,' Radler ordered David Dodd. Radler's emissary arrived unannounced in Winkler's office. 'You either learn to like the way we operate,' Winkler was told, 'or you leave.' Dodd concluded, 'Just enjoy your family and do some skiing, and don't get involved.'

The strike did not materialise, but Winkler's suspicions were aroused. Canada's competition laws outlawed the common ownership of Kelowna's two newspapers, and the country's criminal laws forbade the executive directors of a private company (Horizon) undermining their own publicly-owned company (Hollinger). 'Just tell me what's happening,' Winkler asked Dodd. 'It's a shame,' he was told. 'You're just too pure.'[17] Winkler and his wife, a journalist on the *Capital News*, were dismissed. Denied any income to support his four children, Winkler became distressed. The solution, he decided, was to appeal to Conrad Black. 'Dear Mr Black,' he started his letter. 'I'm still not sure why I've been treated this way... It's hard for me to believe that you would condone the treatment I have received.' There was no reply. Shortly after, the *Capital News* was sold by Radler. To Winkler's amazement, the price was $5.4 million. 'It's worth $15 million,' Winkler gasped. His incredulity soared with the revelation that the purchaser was Todd Vogt's stepfather. Still unaware that Radler and Black were Horizon's owners, Winkler sued Hollinger for wrongful dismissal. In the meantime, unemployed and determined to establish the truth before he sought other employment, he alerted local politicians, the Ontario Securities Commission and journalists on the *Globe and Mail* about the inexplicable events. Depressingly, no one was interested in the sale of a remote newspaper.[18]

Conrad Black was unconcerned about Paul Winkler's fate. His attention was concentrated on the *National Post*. By May 1999 the advertising revenue was paltry, and the circulation was only maintained by giving large numbers of copies of the newspaper away free. Black finally understood the folly of his enterprise. He was competing with his own regional papers for advertisers and readers; and there was worse – readers were resistant to buying a newspaper so obviously influenced by himself and Barbara Amiel. Proprietors as propagandists were distrusted, especially those with a history of eviscerating critics with writs and demands for humiliating apologies. 'My image,' Black confessed, 'is of a Frankenstein monster that's been lurching about for twenty-five years, and I have no idea what animates it at times.'[19] Unlike Murdoch, Black refused to adopt a low profile or enhance the appearance of his editors' independence. Unashamedly, he was in the business to change the world, especially Canada. By an unexpected quirk of fate, his newspaper began to pursue a scandal which epitomised Black's principal aversion.

Jean Chrétien, the Canadian Prime Minister, was accused in the *National Post* of awarding a loan from government funds to support a bankrupt hotel owned by a friend. The so-called Shawinigate affair consisted of allegations that Chrétien, before he became Prime Minister, had owned a share in the hotel and had transferred his interest to his friend, an allegedly corrupt businessman. Initially Chrétien denied any involvement in the loan, but he would eventually admit influencing government officials to make the loan, although he denied any wrongdoing.[20]

The *Post*'s relentless pursuit of Chrétien was good investigative journalism, a genre which Black despised. For Shawinigate, he was prepared to make an exception. The *Post*, Black was content to boast, was fulfilling its purpose of exposing the shortcomings of the left. For once, he believed, the cosy relationship between the media and liberal government politicians was disrupted.[21] Chrétien, a seasoned streetfighter, was convinced that the *Post*'s campaign was inspired by Black, a conviction that was reinforced after his personal protests to the proprietor were ignored. Black, always believing that in verbal combat his last word would silence the critics, approved a trenchant editorial which asserted: 'This and many other incidents show that the Liberal government plays fast and loose with public money . . . Canadians deserve better. They deserve honest and competent management of their money and government.'[22] Black gloried in his public role as the honest newspaper proprietor. Only the cabal would have noticed the double standards between his attitude to the public's and Hollinger shareholders' money.

In the heat of the battle, in May 1999, Black heard unofficially from London that Tony Blair had agreed to grant him a peerage. After all his efforts, Black was not surprised. Twelve years after buying the *Telegraph*, he desperately wanted a title. John Major had refused outright to grant it, both in punishment for the *Telegraph*'s hostility towards his government, and latterly because he suspected that Black was not entirely honest. Since Major's departure following his defeat in the 1997 general election, several senior Tories, especially Lord Carrington, had urged William Hague, the new Conservative leader, to propose Black for a peerage. The 'sustained whisper' had preceded Black's invitation to Hague for dinner in Kensington with Henry Kissinger and Margaret Thatcher. Black regarded Hague as a 'kindred spirit' in politics, particularly in opposing closer association with Europe in favour of a strong partnership with Washington. The admiration was mutual, although Hague was mildly surprised by Black's confession, 'I'm not really interested in business.' As intended, Hague was impressed by the dinner party, at which he was reminded that the *Telegraph* had supported his candidature as party leader. In February 1999, after substantial lobbying, finally by Margaret Thatcher, Hague submitted Black's name to Downing Street for Tony Blair's approval.

Since John Major's defeat in 1997, Black had built bridges with the Labour government. In recognition of his importance, Tony Blair, accompanied by his media adviser Alastair Campbell, had visited Black in Cottesmore Gardens. The Prime Minister recognised Black as a natural Tory, but sought sympathetic coverage for his new government. To seal their relationship, Blair agreed to address 350 guests at Hollinger's 1997 annual dinner at the Wallace Collection in central London, which had cost $1.2 million to stage. Since then, Black had given no reason for Blair to regret his commitment. Once Black heard that Hague had put his name forward he called Jonathan Powell, Blair's chief of staff, to seek a guarantee that the Prime Minister would offer no objections. Powell's reassurance was accompanied with the news that the formal announcement would be made on 18 June. Black was ecstatic. Finally, he would rank with Beaverbrook and Thomson.

At the beginning of June, Black was in London. Besides his own annual summer party, he had accepted invitations from his many British admirers and friends. To a few he confided his exciting secret, while others, including Lord Carrington and Lord Cranborne, knew about the appointment because they had signed his application for dual citizenship, which Black believed was an acceptable arrangement under Canadian law to enable his assumption of a British title. With the help of Downing Street officials, that application, lodged on 11 June, was processed in just eight hours. Three days later, the Queen's office was formally advised of Black's nomination. The Blacks excitedly awaited the formal announcement. Both anticipated the thrill of making a grand entrance as a colourfully-attired master of ceremonies loudly announced, 'Lord and Lady Black.'

On 17 June, while flying to Germany, Black received the staggering news that his nomination for a peerage had been cancelled. In a message to Downing Street and Buckingham Palace, Jean Chrétien had objected to the honour, citing a parliamentary resolution from 1919 requesting the British government not to confer honours on Canadians who were resident in Canada. As a resolution was not law, and over thirty Canadians had accepted British honours since 1919, Black was doubly astonished. Tony Blair had no alternative but to remove Black's name from the list. Black's telephone call to Chrétien was received with pleasure. 'Remove that block within forty-eight hours,' ordered Black. Chrétien smiled. Black, it appeared, still misunderstood politics. He assumed that the *Post*'s Shawinigate campaign had prompted

Chrétien's veto. 'Do you know what the bastard has done?' Black exploded to Ken Whyte during a telephone call from Germany. Chrétien, he cursed, was mean and vindictive. Canada was truly unkind to him.

Over the following weeks, seeking to negotiate a solution, Black was rebuffed by Jonathan Powell in Downing Street and told to resolve the impasse in Canada. In Ottawa, Black danced forlornly around the obstacles until, to Chrétien's pleasure, he fell into the politician's trap. Consistent with his philosophy to always attack and never to take hostages, Black ignored his own scepticism about Canada's liberal establishment and issued a court writ alleging an abuse of power by the government. The line was drawn for his ultimate challenge to a society he criticised for its socialistic, multi-racial worship of dishonesty and egalitarianism. Just how he reasoned that Canada's judges would defy public sentiment and find in favour of a plea based on a colonial, snobbish passion to parade in ermine in an undemocratic foreign institution was inexplicable to his critics, and even to some of his friends. 'Conrad believes in an eye for an eye,' was the conclusion of his friends. 'He will not be dragged down.' News of the writ unleashed a mocking campaign in the newspapers he loathed. 'Lord Nearly-Nearly', 'His Tubship' and 'Lord Tubby of Fleet (Pending)' was caricatured for wanting either to own Canada or to rule the world. A cartoon showed Black saying, 'So at a very early age I had to make a decision . . . Did I really want to be Prime Minister? "Shit, no," I thought, "I'd much rather be powerful."' Canadians were unlikely to sympathise with an anti-hero attacking their own country.

As the dominant owner of Canada's newspapers, Black considered himself too powerful to be snubbed by Chrétien, a man he laughably regarded as a charlatan and a thug who might not be above lining his own pockets. With Amiel's encouragement, he planned to mark the *Post*'s first anniversary in October 1999 with a challenge to the Prime Minister. He would stage a spectacular party at the Royal Ontario Museum to counter the government's smear about the *Post* as Black's mouthpiece and to celebrate the paper's circulation of 305,000, about equal to the *Globe*. Every journalist employed by the *Post* was invited to travel to Toronto for what was billed as a royal gala. On the night, few had ever seen an open bar of such a size, such amazing food, or a sight and sound equal to the bands and artists who had been hired to entertain Black's guests.

Stung by the ridicule over the affair of his peerage, Black had composed the speech of his life. Impassioned and succinct, he commanded attention, especially from journalists who were enduring sacrifices to make the *Post* successful. Crush the *Globe*, he urged his audience, and attack the government. 'We will triumph!' he exhorted with a Churchillian flourish. 'Give 'em hell, Conrad!' the crowd screamed back. Black smiled. He loved the unexpected popularity. That evening, everything seemed possible. For once he did not appear as the ugly, money-grabbing capitalist, but as the impassioned romantic hoping to convert his country to his political ideal. He was heroically trusting the power of the word to defeat corrupt politicians. He had stimulated debate about taxes, race and other issues that had been buried beneath political correctness. Single-handedly he had improved Canada's media. He'd run up the flag and everyone was saluting. Their cheers were ringing in his head. Just like Napoleon at his imperial peak, Black appeared impregnable, fuelled by a radiant self-confidence. Days later his employees would still be cheering him, and not only because of the generous entertainment.

London was the natural venue for the Blacks' exuberance. Later that summer they were invited to a fancy-dress picnic party at Kensington Palace hosted by Prince and Princess Michael of Kent. Conrad Black appeared as Cardinal Richelieu and Barbara Amiel as Marie Antoinette. Most Canadians scorned their appearance as foolish conspicuousness, but the British appreciated personalities having fun. The Blacks' were delighted by the photographers' cameras clicking, the eager heads craning for a view, and the thought of their appearance in fashionable gossip magazines. Barbara Amiel might never reign supreme in New York, but the city's aristocracy were more tolerant of her soaring regal airs than were their counterparts in Toronto, while in London opinion was mixed. Conrad Black, many noted, was becoming more relaxed, more amusing and less pompous. By contrast, the London *Evening Standard* asked facetiously of Amiel, 'Is this London's most powerful woman?' In contrast to Conrad Black's new good humour, Amiel's new friends on both sides of the Atlantic carped about displays of brittleness which even she, in retrospect, found hard to explain. Her hunger for the spotlight during the summer aroused suspicions, but offered no immediate explanation.

At a dinner party for eighty guests in Cottesmore Gardens held to celebrate the publication of Simon Courtauld's history of the *Spectator*, Amiel had as usual organised two tables. Conrad Black had asked that Minette Marrin, an attractive, intelligent journalist, be seated next to himself. Marrin was good company, and they enjoyed common interests. The sight of their animated conversation and laughter was spotted with amusement by Amiel at the other table. During her speech from the balcony praising the *Spectator*, she jokingly said, 'Conrad, have you seen Minette's cleavage?' Marrin was upset; Black smiled wanly. Any embarrassment was concealed by bewildered laughter and the resumption of conversation. Fear of their hosts prevented the guests from reporting the incident. Most were grateful for the Blacks' patronage. The lavish entertainment, at a time when editorial budgets were being cut and expenses slashed, masked their hosts' financial problems.

The *National Post* was draining Hollinger's cash, compounding the continuing damage caused by Rupert Murdoch's attack on the

Telegraph. While in the same period Murdoch's gamble on Sky had bequeathed a new empire worth $10 billion, Black's effort had not even earned $10. The result was brutal. The circulation gap between *The Times* and the *Telegraph* was again narrowing. The *Telegraph*'s daily sale occasionally fell below a million, while *The Times* regularly hit 700,000. 'He's got a knife to our throats,' Black admitted about Murdoch.[23] Wall Street's investors looked upon the champion of the free market as jaded. In 1999, Hollinger International's share price fell from $18 to $11.

In New York, the managers of Tweedy Browne, an investment fund controlling assets worth US$8.6 billion, noted the fall and wondered whether Hollinger was undervalued. Many investors, the managers knew, regarded newspapers as unfashionable compared to the new media. The tip to buy Hollinger had been offered by Laura Jereski, a thirty-six-year-old analyst hired the previous year after an unfortunate experience. As a Wall Street journalist, Jereski had criticised a company and lost a libel action. Eventually her accuracy was vindicated, but the distress she had suffered encouraged her criticism of Wall Street's acquiescence in corporate greed and apparent inability to detect wrongdoing. While researching Hollinger she had spotted nothing untoward in these areas, but nor had she delved into Black's personal history, or carefully studied the small print in the company's annual reports. As a run-of-the-mill investment, she assumed that Hollinger was managed in the normal manner, belying the fall in its share price. Tweedy Browne had already made money out of the *Telegraph*'s shares in London, and so, applying a standard valuation to the stock, Jereski believed that the company was worth at least $2.3 billion. Beyond committing 2.5 per cent of the funds under the company's management, there was no ulterior motive. Since Black controlled 78 per cent of the votes, there was no possibility of a take-over bid, which in any event was contrary to the fund's mandate.

Jereski's advice had been accepted by Christopher Browne, the fund's joint founder. Browne had built his fortune by discovering gems ever since the partnership had unearthed the Nebraska insurance company Berkshire Hathaway in the 1960s while employed by the legendary Warren Buffett. Hollinger struck Browne as undervalued and potentially profitable. The understated manager epitomised a breed whose support Black sought. Familiar among the city's personalities, including their mutual friends Oscar and Annette de la Renta, he sat on the board of several major charities, including Rockefeller University. During his encounters on those boards with Henry Kravis and Nancy Kissinger, neither had ever mentioned anything negative about Conrad Black.

Tweedy Browne's pronouncement that Hollinger was undervalued, and their purchase of about 17 per cent of the shares, delighted Black. If other major investors similarly recognised his success, the share price would rise. He welcomed a meeting with Jereski and Browne in his office arranged by Paul Healy, his executive responsible for investor relations. Over a cup of tea, Black was ebullient. 'The stock price does not represent the real value,' he chimed. 'We'll soon have colour presses in Chicago and we'll be in better shape. If the price doesn't rise, we'll take the company private.' At the end of thirty minutes, Browne reflected that Black had 'made the right moves'. In Black's opinion, the quietly-spoken New York socialite had accepted his representations. Overlooked by Black were the values Browne shared with Wall Street's regulators.

Millennium night, 31 December 1999, was a poignant moment for the Blacks. They had flown in their Gulfstream to the Dominican Republic to stay for three days as guests at Casa de Campo, an estate owned by Oscar and Annette de la Renta. The invitation to the party celebrated their acceptance onto the Manhattan A-list. Barbara Amiel's appearance was acknowledged to be exceptional even by men weary of her affected manner. Her gaze, they noticed, had been transformed from remote to imperial, demanding that others look up to her. Women, she had written, should make men 'afraid', and it appeared that she intended to render women afraid too. Several guests were disenchanted by her melodramatic performances. Like the Blacks' past hosts in country houses in Britain and elsewhere, their fellow guests in Dominica were puzzled by their unusual hours. Never seen in the mornings, they appeared for lunch, and thereafter seemed content to live according to their own rules. As she made her entrance, Barbara Amiel, unlike Conrad Black, showed little consideration for the domestic staff. Whereas Black was noticeably considerate towards servants, Amiel gave the impression of aloofness. Her impatience appeared to be worn as a badge of honour.

Soon after the Millennium, Paul Healy was startled by a message on an answering machine. 'You're all fired!' Amiel was screaming hysterically on the tape. 'Every one of you is fired!' She had telephoned just as the switchboard was overwhelmed by calls. Instead of a personal answer, she heard an answering machine. The tape was played repeatedly among the staff. 'She's a mean and nasty person,' said Healy. 'A Park Avenue bitch with an attitude.' The palatial homes, the Gulfstream and the staff appeared to have changed her understanding of reality. Black summoned his employees. 'I apologise,' he told them. 'Barbara's not well.' Few believed the excuse, but they agreed to Black's suggestion that 'we put a sunset on this'. Barbara's moods had become notorious. John Cruikshank, the editor of the *Chicago Sun-Times*, was a victim of her fury for failing to respond to her criticism that the front page was badly designed, with too many advertisements. 'What do you want me to do?' Cruickshank asked Radler. 'Tell her to fuck off,' replied Radler. 'That is not one of the roles I signed on for,' replied Cruikshank. He had already encountered Amiel at a restaurant in Vancouver. 'I'd like a hamburger,' she told the waiter, 'and I'd like that very rare.' 'I'm sorry,' replied the waiter, 'health regulations prevent us serving rare meat.' 'My God, I get my blood changed four times a year. I'm not going to be killed by a hamburger,' Amiel exclaimed.[24] Besides the anecdotes, according to editor Nigel Wade she left no legacy in return for the $295,000 she received every year as an editorial adviser. However, her imprint was more discernable at the *Telegraph*.

By 2000, Amiel had become a passionate supporter of aggressive Zionism and an uncompromising critic of the Palestinians. The climax of her regular articles denouncing the enemies of Israel came in a lengthy attack on 7 November on the Palestinians and their supporters. Spread over two pages of the *Daily Telegraph*, it was four times longer than her usual contribution. At the end of the article she challenged those readers who linked her extensive exposure in the *Telegraph* to her husband's ownership of the newspaper. She was, she wrote defiantly, a famous columnist long before her marriage to Conrad Black. As the article wended its way up the editorial chain, no one dared to warn the proprietor's wife that the postscript was professional suicide. As usual, there was reluctance to edit or question her work. Amiel was treated with the deference she expected. Previously, the cost of her entitlement had included an apology published in the *Telegraph* to the moderate President of the United Arab Emirates after Amiel had inadvertently accused him of urging his followers to kill Jews and Americans. No one had questioned her research then, and once again the staff knew better than to trifle with Amiel's outbursts concerning Israel. Only Charles Moore, the staff knew, could save Amiel from herself. After what Moore would later call 'a full discussion', Amiel agreed to omit the postscript. The article attracted the anticipated ridicule from her critics, but also praise from her admirers.

While Amiel exulted in one field, Conrad Black fretted in another. He knew that his gambles had failed. The profits of three successful deals – the *Telegraph*, Fairfax and Southam – had been wasted. His financial plight was serious. Hollinger's debts were rising towards $1.8 billion, the cost of the interest payments that year would be $143 million, the *National Post* had irrecoverably lost over C$100 million, and his personal expenditure was increasing. He had reached another Rubicon, the moment to acknowledge that his bid to rival Rupert Murdoch as a global media player had failed. After making that realistic assessment, he decided to sell the bulk of Hollinger's newspapers in North America. Although Radler opposed the sale, Black began searching for a buyer with the promise that he had three priorities. First, Horizon would be the foundation of a new business; second, they would extract as much money as possible from Hollinger for themselves; third, they would retain the *Telegraph* and the *Chicago Sun-Times* as sources of healthy income.

Superficially, Black's income from Hollinger was a modest £290,000 a year, but ignored by outsiders including Tweedy Browne was Ravelston's receipt of nearly $200 million in management fees from Hollinger since 1995. By carefully selecting and seducing Hollinger's directors, Black and Radler had secured a tenfold increase in fees since 1995 – from US$4.1 million to $40.98 in 2000. Without telling the audit committee, Black also charged the annual $4 million expenses of his Gulfstream to Hollinger rather than Ravelston. Black and Radler might have feared that Thompson, Kravis and Burt would demand to see Ravelston's accounts, and would discover that the private company's costs for twenty employees and office overheads was less than $1 million a year.[25] But the three directors had not questioned any of the management fees, or queried why the payments of non-compete fees were made to Hollinger Inc., a shell company, rather than Hollinger International, the operating company in New York. Comforted by that carelessness, Black and Radler constructed the sell-off without fear of retribution.

Conflicts of interest, Black had learned thirty years earlier from Bud McDougald and the Argus cowboys, could be profitable. After careful thought, he and Radler executed a succession of self-interested deals involving newspapers enjoying profitable monopolies and good advertising revenue. Two small sales in early 2000 personally profited Black through the 'Template', the tested formula. A group of newspapers were sold to Forum Communications for $14 million; $400,000 of the purchase price was labelled as a non-compete fee. Another batch of newspapers was sold to PMG Acquisition Corp. for $59 million, of which $2 million was labelled as non-compete payment. The $2.4 million was paid to Ravelston and Hollinger Inc. rather than Hollinger International, the newspapers' owners in New York, without full disclosure to the board of directors.

More profitable was the sale of four newspapers for US$37.6 million to Bradford, a new company established in 2000. Fifty per cent of the company was owned by Black and Radler. To help finance the deal, Black and Radler arranged for Hollinger International to grant Bradford a ten-year interest-free loan of $6 million, without Bradford offering any security to repay the money. Classified as a 'non-competition payment' this would be paid in instalments over an indefinite period. Hollinger also signed a guarantee covering Bradford's existing $22 million bank loan. Effectively, Black and Radler were buying four newspapers from themselves with money they lent to themselves.[26] To avoid the directors' scrutiny, they arranged that the executive committee should approve the deal by signing a 'unanimous written consent'. Securing the approval of the committee's three members was not difficult. Black and Radler as members signed the documents, which were then presented by lawyers to Richard Perle. Without reading, understanding or discussing their content with Black and Radler, Perle also signed. The market value of the four newspapers was later assessed to be at least $4 million more than Bradford paid.[27] 'A useful idiot' was the subsequent description of Perle's role by a critical investigator.

In April 2000 Horizon exchanged five loss-making newspapers for three profitable newspapers owned by Hollinger, and the following month Hollinger sold the *Skagit Valley Argus* and the *Journal of the San Juan Islands* to Horizon. The price paid by Horizon was 50 cents for each title, about the cover price of one copy. The deal included what was described as 'working capital adjustments', namely a payment by Hollinger to Horizon of $162,000, allegedly to repay the two newspapers' debts. The deal for $1 was submitted to Hollinger's board of directors. In the accompanying letter, the board was told that the two newspapers were in debt, and that to avoid publicity it was better for Horizon, rather than Hollinger, to eventually sell them. That submission was inaccurate. Six months earlier David Dodd, the manager of the *Argus*, had revealed to Radler, with whom he worked closely, that the newspaper was profitable, and more recently Radler had received news from Todd Vogt of an offer of $750,000 for the *Journal*.[28] Fortunately for Black, none of Hollinger's directors questioned the transaction. Henry Kissinger could not have done so because he did not attend the board meeting; Barbara Amiel was unlikely to challenge her husband; Governor Thompson, Marie-Josée Kravis and Richard Burt remained silent; Richard Perle, with an annual salary of $300,000 and a bonus that year of $2 million, did not query Black's arrangements, possibly because he had just asked Black to invest $2.5 million in a new company of his own. At the end of the twenty-minute board meeting, none of the directors other than Black and Radler was aware of the newspapers' true value, and only they were aware of Horizon's true ownership. To Black's satisfaction, the directors accepted that 50 cents for each paper was a 'fair market value'.[29]

The deal was dressed up to appear innocuous, with Hollinger's shareholders being told that the newspapers had been sold for 'net working capital'. Soon after, the *Argus* was resold by Horizon for $450,000, and the *Journal* for $280,000. Hollinger's shareholders had not only lost $730,000, but in addition had given Black and Radler $162,000 for taking over the 'unprofitable' newspapers. Black must have been chortling as he confided to Radler in an email about 'the splendid conveyance of the non-competition agreements from which you and I profited so well'.[30] Two years later, Black would be asked about the deal. 'The shareholders,' he said, 'got a better deal than we did.'

None of the guests arriving at the Blacks' summer party in London in 2000 could have imagined the financial turmoil preoccupying their hosts. Although the group's profits would soar towards a record £70 million, the *Daily Telegraph*'s circulation had permanently fallen below the magic one million, undermining Hollinger's finances. The guests at Cottesmore Gardens, including Elton John's partner David Furnish, Imran Khan, Margaret Thatcher, Peter Mandelson, Jonathan Aitken and Claus von Bülow, whose eventual acquittal on charges of murdering his wife was the subject of the book and film *Reversal of Fortune*, were flattered to be identified by *Tatler* as representing 'power and glamour'. There was a frisson among those personally greeted by Barbara Amiel's sparkling green eyes. Amiel glowed, delighted to have been recently described by Paul Johnson as 'a dazzling, formidably intelligent figure in her own right, as well as being a leading political hostess'.[31] Despite her fame for fearless offensiveness, most guests craved Amiel's approval. She represented the aspirations of so many under her roof – fashion, four homes, a private jet, influence, professional success and international fame. Her recent justification of Hollinger's ownership of two executive jets – 'It's always best to have two planes, because however well one plans ahead, one always finds one is on the wrong continent' – overwhelmed those under her spell. Her indiscretions and sometimes curt behaviour contrasted with her genuine warmth towards those she identified as friends. The majority, however, were deemed insufficiently important to engage in conversation, or even greet. Her attention was exclusively directed at the super VIPs and a handful of soulmates who, that day, included Leonie Frieda, a writer and former drug addict. Frieda had welcomed Amiel's support and friendship after laughing too heartily at a host's joke during a dinner party. 'The art of conversation,' Amiel had told her, 'is like holding a beautiful bird of paradise in your hand: you should whisper to it and stroke it – not guffaw so much it wants to fly away.'

Across the room was Conrad Black, his appearance very different from the unshaven and tieless Sunday-morning visits he had begun making to Brompton Oratory to seek comfort from priests and the Almighty. Very few suspected him of any wrongdoing, or understood that his conversations with God gave him a justification for his behaviour. Those who did would have agreed with an unusually candid banker: 'We're all prostitutes, mesmerised by his money and loving to roll with him.' But even that guest did not query whether the silver platters of drinks and canapés were funded from honest earnings. The sight of the elegantly dressed Conrad Black uttering defamatory gossip about other well-known personalities despite his sensitivity to attacks on his own reputation, delighted those hungry to hear a mogul's intrigues. 'By the time I get through with Chrétien, you'll be able to squeeze him through an eyedropper,' he smiled.[32] Few cared to imagine the consequences of Black's defeat in his court case against Chrétien the previous March to compel the Canadian government to allow his peerage, or the background to the unexpected question from sceptical journalists in April of whether his financial plight would compel a sale of the *Telegraph*. 'There'll be no sale of the *Telegraph*,' he had angrily retorted.

No one at the summer party was aware of Black's negotiations with Izzy Asper, the chairman of CanWest, a Canadian communications company. The deal agreed during July between Black and Asper was for the sale of all Hollinger's Canadian newspapers and half of the *National Post* for $2.1 billion. Black, it was agreed, would keep nominal control of the *Post*. Hollinger would be reduced to owning a few community newspapers in the United States, the *Chicago Sun-Times*, the *Jerusalem Post* and the *Telegraph*. As a gross sum, the price Black extracted was high.

The decision to sell half of Hollinger's assets had been opposed by Radler. 'Why dismantle everything?' he asked. 'And then I won't be allowed to work in Canada.' Eventually, the 'mechanic' was induced to agree to the sale with the promise of a generous non-compete payment. If the amount was big enough, Radler reasoned, it would be a restorative farewell from the Blacks, especially Barbara Amiel. He could focus on Horizon and his jewellery business. Once the payment was agreed with Radler, Black successfully insisted that he was entitled to the same, and the sale to CanWest was presented by Black to Hollinger's directors during a teleconference on 26 July 2000. Among those listening were Henry Kissinger, Richard Perle, Alfred Taubman, Richard Burt, Lord Weidenfeld and Shmuel Meitar. Black's tone was upbeat. The purpose of the sale, he explained, was to reduce Hollinger's crippling debt. 'Izzy Asper,' he said, 'was the last train leaving the station.' All Hollinger's debt, he said, would be expunged and the company would be 'cash rich'.[33] Black was mistaken. CanWest was paying US$972 million in cash and $1.38 billion in CanWest shares valued at $25 each. Since Hollinger could not sell the shares, Hollinger's debt would be reduced by barely $1 billion, leaving $812 million of debts. The discrepancy was not challenged by any of the directors, nor did they ask why, within the past three years, Black had also sold the profitable community newspapers and not savagely cut costs, thereby transforming a major media corporation into a rump with revenues halved to $1.1 billion. Instead, Black was pleased to note, his audience applauded his conclusion: 'These guys at CanWest are taking a huge gamble, but the debts are too big for us.' With the board's approval, the sale was to be announced on 31 July 2000. By then, Black and Amiel had flown in the Gulfstream to Bayreuth in Germany to attend, at Lord Weidenfeld's invitation, the Wagner festival. The jet had become an essential element of their way of life. The list of their passengers – including Henry Kissinger, Barry Humphries, Margaret Thatcher and Helmut Kohl – proved their importance.

The weekend in Bayreuth coincided with Monte Black's sixtieth birthday party in Toronto. Most of those who had grown up with the Black brothers, including Conrad Black's own children and other family members, had accepted the invitation to celebrate at the York Club. Conrad Black, however, had told his brother that he would be unable to attend. Barbara Amiel, as Monte, his second wife June and Black's first wife Joanna knew, was often 'unwell' whenever a Black family event was organised. All three nevertheless remained convinced that on this occasion the younger brother would make a dramatic entrance. Any wife, they reasoned, would have ensured Conrad's return. Amiel was different. She was not enamoured of the Toronto crowd, and appeared equally unloving towards Monte. They were peasants compared to the glitterati, and whenever possible she avoided visiting Monte's house. 'It was probably the saddest party I've ever been to,' said Joanna Black after listening to Monte give his own birthday speech.[34]

Seemingly oblivious to his brother's distress, Conrad Black was more preoccupied with his personal finances. Since Hollinger had shrivelled, Ravelston's income would inevitably drop. For weeks he had been discussing with Radler and other members of the cabal the size of the non-compete fee to be extracted from the CanWest deal for themselves. During his early negotiations with Izzy Asper, Black had not mentioned the 'Template' addition to the non-compete clauses. All the purchase monies, it was assumed, would go to Hollinger International in New York. At the last moment, in July 2000, Black requested that an additional clause in the contract should quantify the non-compete fees. Asper did not protest; he expected a clause in his contract to prevent Black and his experts establishing rival newspapers. So long as the purchase price remained the same, Asper replied, there was no problem. Pleased with that outcome, Black proposed that CanWest label $51.8 million out of the total cash payment as a non-compete fee. Asper considered the suggested sum enormous, but there was no reason to protest so long as the clause was valid.[35] Black knew that the amount was audacious. The cabal was proposing to take $51.8 million belonging to the shareholders, with the extra windfall of avoiding tax. Black did not fear exposure. He had survived so many scrapes – the theft of the school exam papers, Argus, Norcen and Cazenove's resignation – that any sense of fear or guilt had vanished. Habit produced a performance of charm and conviction oiled to perfection.

Black added another twist to the deal. Asper wanted some help with managing the newspapers in the early stages. Black agreed, and demanded $12.3 million a year for his services. When Asper questioned the amount Black retreated and proposed that Ravelston would charge CanWest US$3.9 million (C$6 million) in perpetuity, with added conditions. If the annual management fee was cancelled, CanWest agreed to pay Ravelston C$45 million (US$29.1 million) in compensation; and if Ravelston cancelled the agreement, CanWest would pay C$22.5 million (US$14.6 million). Asper agreed. The management service contract, worth $39 million, was deducted from the proceeds of the sale price, adding to Hollinger's losses. Thompson and the other members of the audit committee accepted the arrangement without posing any queries. Black was so confident that he never paused to consider a potential embarrassment. In 1999 Ravelston had charged

Hollinger a management fee of $40.3 million, yet during 2000, after the sale of half the company, that $40 million fee would remain the same. On that basis, Ravelston's management fee to CanWest should have been $20 million, yet Black only charged $3.9 million.[36] By his own deeds, Black revealed that Hollinger's fees to Ravelston were excessive.

Black and Radler understood the conflict of interest they had invented. As employees of Hollinger International, they had sold most of the company's Canadian assets to CanWest. The non-compete clauses were agreed between CanWest and Hollinger International. Yet they intended, while continuing to take a salary from Hollinger International, to divert the US$51.8 million (C$80 million) non-compete fees from Hollinger International's shareholders to Ravelston. Each would personally take US$11.9 million from that sum. Their safety net was the apparent approval they received from their professional advisers. Boultbee and Atkinson discussed with KPMG, the company's auditors, and Torys, the company's lawyers, the provision of documents to justify the payments. Both firms failed sufficiently to expose any wrongdoing or exceptional behaviour. However, the lawyers, Boultbee and Atkinson, ignored an incongruity. Izzy Asper had never asked for the non-compete clause to be linked to Black and Radler personally. The non-compete clause in the CanWest contract embraced all employees of Hollinger International.

There remained one major hurdle before Black and Radler could each safely bank their US$11.9 million. By law, the non-compete payments to Ravelston needed the approval of Hollinger's audit committee. To help Thompson, Burt and Kravis consider the CanWest non-compete fees, Radler asked in-house lawyer Mark Kipnis to compose a memorandum justifying the $51.8 million payment. To minimise the huge sum, Kipnis ascribed $31.8 million as non-compete fees to be paid personally to Black, Radler, Boultbee and Atkinson, while the other $20 million payment to Ravelston was described as a 'termination' fee for losing the contract from Hollinger International to manage the newspapers. Kipnis also submitted that $2.6 million would be paid to Hollinger International, although that payment was never made. None of the directors apparently questioned why Ravelston should receive any of the non-compete payments when the company's directors had already been paid, and Ravelston as a company was in no position to compete with CanWest.

Less straightforward was Radler's personal submission to the audit committee at its meeting on 11 September 2000. The payments, wrote Radler, were 'required by CanWest as a condition to the transaction'. That was accurate, but Radler went further: 'CanWest originally insisted that Messrs Black and Radler each receive $16.8 million in order to justify their exclusion from Canadian newspapers.' That was inaccurate. Asper had never stipulated that the money was to be paid as a personal fee to Black and the others, nor did he quantify any amount. Radler's lie went unchallenged. None of the three members of the committee asked why the directors should personally receive non-compete payments when they were obliged, as executives of Hollinger, not to break their company's agreement with CanWest. After just fifty-five minutes, the directors approved the arrangement. Black and Radler ought to have known that their order to Hollinger's accounts department to transfer $51.8 million to Ravelston was unlawful.[37]

David Radler remained unsatisfied. As a parting shot, he charged Hollinger a $1.1 million 'interest charge' to compensate for the 'delay' in transferring the $51.8 million to Ravelston. The total cost to Hollinger's shareholders had risen to $52.9 million. In completing that single sale, Black and his group had probably taken over $92 million from them.[38]

News of the audit committee's approval fomented an unusual brazenness in Black's conduct. The committee's decision required ratification by the full board. Black might have hesitated. Hollinger's net trading profits had fallen to $117 million, and the directors might have objected to Ravelston receiving $51.8 million. But he had no fear of rejection. In telephone calls to the directors he boasted that the deal had made Hollinger 'rich'. Content that his audience was persuaded, he excused himself from the directors' meeting and boarded his jet for St Petersburg in Russia, ostensibly to attend a conference. Sitting in Vancouver, Radler was delegated to chair a conference call with a handful of directors scattered across North America to approve Hollinger International's payment of $51.8 million to Black and his group. At that very moment, flying across the Atlantic, Black anticipated saying at a future meeting, 'Hollinger's shareholders can rely on our distinguished group of directors.'[39] And so he could. The only irritation was a complaint by Dan Colson, who griped that his income had not risen. He was awarded a $1 million bonus. The final dénouement was the submission to the Securities and Exchange Commission of the company's accounts in early 2001. To complete the concealment, the directors did not reveal the full details of CanWest's payment to Hollinger's directors in the company's statutory filings. Barbara Amiel's income as an editorial adviser was not reduced despite the sharp cutback of her duties after the sale of the Canadian papers.[40]

Conrad Black's journey to Russia was a remarkable thrill for Barbara Amiel. In St Petersburg they met Mercedes Bass, alias 'Mimi from Geneva', the wife of a Texan billionaire. Bass arrived in her personal Gulfstream from Scotland. Unfortunately, Russian police discovered shotguns on the plane and the pilot was ordered to return immediately to Scotland, and to leave the guns behind. Meanwhile the sightseeing party, which included the American TV interviewer Barbara Walters, began a tour of the city. Curiously, Mercedes Bass had become an icon for Amiel. Her zeal to shop till she dropped, her five hundred pairs of shoes, her passion to change clothes during the day, and her endless chatter about money would have provoked many to consider her vulgar, but Amiel was blind to that criticism. Over five days in St Petersburg and then Moscow, she appeared enthralled by Mercedes Bass's conversation.

On her return to Canada, Amiel was bubbling with excitement. Eager to describe her latest social adventure, she spotted Taki Theodoracopulos, the *Spectator*'s amusing columnist, at a wedding reception in Montreal hosted by the former Canadian Prime Minister Brian Mulroney. The rich Greek hedonist, regarded by many as a life-enhancer, would, she assumed, appreciate her success, although their relationship had been bumpy. They had first been introduced in the 1980s, and Amiel had welcomed Taki's invitations to parties until her marriage to Black. Weeks after the wedding, Taki had spotted the Blacks at Drones, a London restaurant. Surrounded by excited young friends, he approached them. To Taki's surprise, Amiel stared haughtily while he greeted his employer. 'I don't think you know who I am,' she pronounced, recalling her irritation at Taki once pinching her bottom while she was bending over in the aisle on Concorde. 'I've had a little too much to drink,' replied Taki, who assumed the woman was Joanna Black. Relations had not been improved by Taki's attack in the *Spectator* on President Clinton for pardoning Marc Rich, an American fugitive lurking in Switzerland to avoid extradition to the United States on charges of tax evasion and illegal oil deals with Iraq. Black was furious at Taki's criticism of the President and his description of Rich's dishonesty. Aware of that anger, the Greek had been surprised to hear his secretary call out, 'Barbara Amiel's on the phone.' 'Tell that fucking bitch that she has no right to fire me!' Taki shouted back. 'What do you want?' he snapped, picking up the telephone. 'I only wanted to invite you for lunch,' replied Amiel. Their *rapprochement* prompted Amiel to tell Taki about her journey to Russia at the wedding party. 'I was with

Mercedes Bass and Barbara Walters,' she gushed. 'You went with that group?' spluttered Taki. 'I can't think of anything worse than being with Mimi, a Persian ex-girl-about-town.' Perhaps it was Mimi, he speculated, who had influenced Amiel to look down her nose at people. It was the same Amiel who had recently asked him at Annabel's for an introduction to the attractive blonde English fashion writer and socialite Kate Reardon. 'I have a very demanding wife,' Black had smiled across the basement. Some days later, Black's judgement was endorsed. As usual he and Amiel had arrived late at the airport. 'We're flying Conrad Standard Time,' joked Captain Ridley. 'The little lady's fault,' smiled Black as the mountain of suitcases was loaded onto the plane. 'It was not my fault,' said Amiel indignantly. 'Barbara, it is incongruous to lecture me on tardiness,' smiled Black. At the end of their flight they were taxiing across the parkway at Teterboro airport in New Jersey when they spotted a brand-new Gulfstream. 'Could we have one of those, Conrad?' asked Amiel. 'Work harder,' replied her husband.

During Black's visit to Russia he had heard bad news about the reaction to the CanWest deal. Rivals had written him off as a loser and a debt-stricken adventurer. Although Lord Carrington would tell a television interviewer, 'Conrad's an admirable man, in respect that he's straightforward and honest; and he's an amusing companion and he's fun,'[41] Hal Jackman was pessimistic: 'It's going to end badly,' he predicted. 'He wants to be seen as a colossus, not only as businessman but also as a major authority on history and politics. There's something self-destructive about Conrad. A great mystery.'[42] Similar opinions were echoed on Bay Street and Wall Street. Few dealers were interested in buying Hollinger shares. Most resented their losses after responding to Black's earlier sales patter, and were not prepared to risk being burnt again by a man who stated in that year's company annual report that the *National Post* was on 'the cusp of profitability'. The sale of half the *Post* had outraged his journalists. 'We've been betrayed,' complained

Christie Blatchford. 'I'm stunned. I'm furious. I won't forgive him for this. Ever.' Black's conservative allies were equally appalled. Having brandished his banner against the liberals, he was not only selling his newspaper to the enemy – Izzy Asper opposed the Conservatives – but was abandoning the movement he had championed. His legacy was to have launched the *Post* and improved his competitors, especially the *Globe and Mail*. Stung by the vitriol, Black published a counter-attack in the *National Post* on 5 August 2000:

> *I do not choose to reply to those who in the last week have likened me to a jackal, have claimed that I have left no legacy in Canada and that I have stripped little newspapers to feed large ones, declared that I have never added value to a company that I was at the head of, or am guilty of the vast catalogue of Kafkaesque shortcomings that have been alleged against me by my self-declared enemies in the Canadian media. The authors of these lies and smears illustrate perfectly . . . all the weaknesses of the country and the journalistic craft that I have addressed before . . . To my enemies, some of whom have claimed they will miss me, your nostalgia is premature and completely unrequited.*

The only city where no questions were asked about the sale was London, and in particular at the *Telegraph*. Black's trips to London had declined, and the Tuesday management meetings were conducted in his absence. Not one of the executives or newspaper editors understood that the sale signalled Black's financial demise. 'It's a good deal,' the *Telegraph*'s financial experts chimed. Charles Moore knew nothing about Hollinger or the company's activities in North America, and did little to attempt to discover the truth. He was not a business expert, and he assumed that the finances of his employer, who he admired, were sound. Ever since he had published the warning against Black by John Ralston Saul in the *Spectator* in 1986, Moore had assumed that all proprietors were attacked as a matter of course, and since then he had judged Black by his own positive experience. Nevertheless, disconcerted by the canteen's shorter hours, staff cuts and the closure of foreign bureaux, Moore complained to Black that excessive amounts of the *Telegraph*'s money were being remitted to New York. 'Times are hard,' Moore was told, although the year 2000 had been the newspaper's most profitable in its history. Jeremy Deedes was equally puzzled. 'The money's always earmarked for somewhere else before we've even earned it,' he said, 'but I just don't know what's happening in New York.' Black offered no explanation. He simply told everyone beyond Canary Wharf, 'We're sitting on piles of cash.' The two explanations were irreconcilable, but not a single employee took the trouble of undertaking any enquiries. Everyone trusted Conrad Black, and any sceptics would have been condemned as unworthy.

Emboldened by that faith and the ease of obtaining the audit committee's approval of any proposition he put before them, David Radler was encouraged to sell more newspapers and divert more money to Ravelston. In November 2000 another batch was sold to Community Newspapers for US$90 million. Initially $2.25 million was, on Radler's instructions, labelled as a non-compete fee, but at the last moment he directed that the sum should be increased to $11.75 million. Black and Radler each received $4.3 million. The remainder was paid to Boultbee and Atkinson. After the payments, Mark Kipnis, Hollinger's lawyer, mentioned his concern at the size of the non-compete fees, which he suspected were not legitimate. He was placated by Radler's assurance that Governor Thompson had approved them – which was untrue. Radler was aware that Thompson had just approved the payment of $51.8 million from the CanWest deal. Disguising any suggestion of greed, he decided, would be sensible. Any further doubts Kipnis may have harboured were held in check by Radler's approval, as a sign of his appreciation, of a $100,000 bonus payment to him. None of the four recipients of the $9.5 million (which increased to $10.25 million) revealed that income in Hollinger's official declarations. In total, the cabal had taken an additional $16.55 million in unauthorised payments from the company.[43]

Kipnis performed another valuable service by presenting Hollinger Digital's 'incentive plan' to the audit committee. He proposed that Black, Radler, Boultbee and Colson should be paid $5.3 million by the new media company led by Richard Perle. The calculation and justification for the money were unusual. Digital had invested $203 million and lost $68 million. Nevertheless, Kipnis's proposal was endorsed by Thompson and the audit committee. A further $3.1 million was paid to Richard Perle.

Black's personal income had hit a record high. Besides taking unquantified fees from Ravelston and at least $7 million in expenses from Hollinger, covering his apartment, jet, staff in four homes and entertainment, he had banked an additional $15.3 million from the non-compete payments, $2.2 million from the Hollinger Digital incentive scheme, and unquantified profits through Horizon. In celebration he bought his wife a twenty-six-carat diamond ring costing $2.6 million from Graff Diamonds. Later, it would be alleged that he paid for the gift from the money he had just received from Hollinger. With that transaction completed, and before Hollinger was completely sold, he nevertheless wanted more.

As a tidying-up operation, he decided to buy from Hollinger the second-floor apartment he occupied at 635 Park Avenue in Manhattan. Since its purchase in 1994 for $3 million, the apartment's value had increased to $5.4 million, due in part to David Mlinaric's design, some of which Black had funded. Under the agreement Black had signed with Hollinger in 1994, he was allowed to purchase the apartment at any time at a 'fair market value'. Black's proposal was ostensibly uncomplicated. He owned the smaller 'staff' ground-floor apartment in the same block, which he had personally bought for $500,000 in January 1998. Since then Hollinger International had paid $1.5 million to renovate that apartment, converting it into three distinct living spaces. In the company's formal accounts, these renovations were assigned to maintaining the Hollinger-owned apartment on the second floor inhabited by the Blacks, partly because the Blacks had personally financed the rebuilding of that apartment. In December 2000 Black proposed a swap of the apartments' ownership. The only issue to be agreed was the value of each apartment. Black declared that the value of his own ground-floor flat had increased since 1998 to $850,000, while the value of the second-floor flat had not increased since 1994, and was worth only $2.85 million. To justify this assessment, Jack Boultbee signed a declaration that a firm of New York 'real estate specialists' had attested that while the second-floor apartment had not appreciated in six years, the ground floor apartment's value had increased by 70 per cent in two years. The board of directors, assuming that Black and Boultbee were telling the truth, approved the swap. In a public company, Black knew, he owed a legal duty to care for the shareholders' money, yet he decided not to disclose his profit of $2.1 million in Hollinger's annual report. Instead, he declared that he had paid a 'fair market value' for the second-floor apartment.[44] Later he would claim that he had personally spent $2.2 million on renovations. Twenty years earlier, Barbara Amiel had written, 'Greed can be held in check by ordinary criminal laws.' About the same time, Conrad Black had lamented society's 'moral torpor'.

By the end of 2000, the cabal had been sated. In the rush some legal formalities, Radler was told, had been overlooked. To cover Hollinger's statutory requirements, documents were prepared to record a meeting of the executive committee on 4 December 2000. The official minutes recorded that the two men had ratified some undefined asset sales. This cursory conclusion was assumed to cover any eventuality.

Black was preoccupied by the surprise party he had organised to celebrate Barbara Amiel's sixtieth birthday that same day. He had invited eighty guests to La Grenouille, one of Manhattan's most expensive restaurants. Weeks earlier, on 7 November, in the midst of celebrating George W. Bush's apparent cliffhanging victory over Al Gore at Bill Buckley's election party, Black issued one more invitation. 'Keep it quiet,' he told Taki. 'It's a surprise.' Before the end of the evening, Taki had drunkenly revealed everything to Amiel. 'It's a secret,' he giggled. 'Don't tell anyone.' Taki had not forgotten the indiscretion the following day, but Black, he decided, could be irritating. At a recent dinner hosted by Taki for a young girlfriend, Black had spent the evening lecturing his hosts about a historical incident and then, just before leaving, had pulled Taki aside. 'You know,' said Black solemnly, 'you should stop having young girls. It's bad for your marriage.'

On the morning of Amiel's birthday, Black told her, 'I've arranged a quiet dinner for the two of us.' Amiel smiled innocently. On her computer that morning she found the usual messages from Conrad. Frequently he typed out immature love sentiments in his office, often with sexual innuendos, and emailed them down the corridor to her room. Her messages in reply revealed constant neediness. 'What time will you come home?' she repeatedly asked. Few outsiders could guess her dependency on her husband. On her birthday, she had lunch with friends. To her relief, Black was waiting on her return to Park Avenue. 'I've just spoken to someone on the Supreme Court,' he said, obviously eager to impress, 'and he says it's going to be all right.' George W. Bush, the insider had revealed, would win the majority of Supreme Court votes that would enable him to clinch the election. Impressing his wife was as important as honouring her birthday.

That evening Manhattan's A-list, including the broadcasters Peter Jennings and Barbara Walters, the businessman Ron Perelman and a delegation of neo-cons from Washington warmly welcomed their hosts. Cost, Black had decided, would be ignored. Caviar and excellent vintage wines had been ordered. Naturally, Henry Kissinger sat near the hostess – Hollinger's internal accounts for the year would list three dinners in Kissinger's honour, costing $28,480 in all. At the end of the dinner, all eyes focused on Black. This was the moment he had anticipated with glee and considerable effort. He had been flattered that some guests had called to check whether Amiel's age on the invitations was not mistaken. Few could believe that she was sixty. In response he had composed a speech not of praise, but worship. Rising and looking at the room full of those he most admired, he launched into an oration of passion. 'The little woman's body,' he began, 'is agile and youthful.' Barbara, said Black in full seriousness, had not benefited from any plastic surgery. 'I've seen her naked, and it's all natural. She looks better with her clothes off than on.' Black might have expected yelps of appreciation and applause, but instead there was embarrassment. The ageing women in his audience did not take kindly to unflattering comparisons and incredible assertions. But their host was undeterred. Asserting Barbara's natural beauty, he had recently told Kimberley Fortier, the publisher of the *Spectator*, was important. It was most unfair, he complained, that Barbara was believed to have benefited from plastic surgery.

The titters were silenced by Black's theatrical cough. 'The little woman,' he continued, glancing towards his conspicuous partner, 'was perfect, vertically and horizontally.' The audience's bemusement did not stop the adoring eulogy, although he would save for a future occasion his praise for her clothes. 'She's got this flair for getting really unusual things,' he would say about a dress made of copper scales. 'I mean, how many women go around in chain mail, and how many look fabulous in it?'[45] Then followed a recitation of poems, including one by Tennyson. He paused. 'For the benefit of my Greek correspondent,' smiled Black, and briefly praised Taki's colourful contribution to life, speaking in Greek. Then, glancing at Alfred Taubman, he assured all his guests that their friend, recently convicted for price-fixing and about to be imprisoned, would always be supported and welcomed by those in the room. 'Conrad loves the sound of his own voice,' muttered a disgruntled guest, noticing Taubman's embarrassment. Polite rather than rapturous applause followed Black's speech. This was not fun, some concluded, but just another social event.

As Barbara Amiel rose to reply, she was scrutinised with unusual severity. New York's judgement was divided. Some were disdainful of her pretentiousness, others were captivated by her beauty and brains. All were checking her face and neck for signs of plastic surgery. The 'surprise' of her party, she immediately disclosed, had been ruined by Taki. The Greek's face froze. Every American billionaire, he suspected, was watching him. Few could remember the remainder of Amiel's speech. Eyes were raised, heads sank and a gentle depression descended. Manhattan's elite, Black discovered, were more demanding and blasé than London's. Days later, he decided that two-thirds of the $62,870 cost of the party would be paid by Hollinger. After all, most of the company's directors were present, along with many other business associates. None of his old friends from Toronto were invited. They would not have been welcomed by Barbara.

Charging the company for the dinner was consistent with Amiel's use of what she called Hollinger's 'slush fund'. To match Marie-Josée Kravis's charitable donations, she had given $20,000 to a breast cancer gala, $100,000 for a dinner fund-raiser for the New York Public Library, and $61,000 for a bursary in her name at the North London Collegiate School. On her initiative, the company had given $14,400 to the Israeli Philharmonic Orchestra and $7,200 to Elton John's AIDS foundation.[46] In the midst of donating so much of Hollinger's money to charity, Black and Radler decided in February 2001 to award another $5.5 million from Hollinger to themselves, Boultbee and Atkinson. The money was described as a non-compete payment. As a novelty, it was approved on condition that the four men agreed not to compete with the American Publishing Company, a dormant subsidiary of Hollinger International itself. In essence, it was a convenient way to take income without paying tax. For tax reasons the payment was backdated to 31 December 2000, but in their haste Black and Radler forgot to amend the minutes of the board's executive committee meeting on 4 December 2000 to show that it was discussed and approved. That reflected the truth. Hollinger's board in New York had not been informed about the payment. The four had taken the money for agreeing not to compete with themselves without the authority of the company's directors and the audit committee. The arrangement would later be described as 'the backdating of a sham agreement'.[47]

Conrad Black was not suffering any delusions. He knew the rules, and in his usual lazy manner, gambled on ignoring them. Obedience to the law was irrelevant to a man whose lack of conscience was tempered by regular prayer. What some would characterise as a charming insouciance was in fact a conviction that if problems arose, his articulate explanations and the professionals' letters of approval would suffice to resolve them. At fifty-six, Black was gearing himself up for dramatic change as Hollinger became a mere shadow of his former ambitions. Enough would remain after the shrinking was completed to support his new project: a biography of Franklin Delano Roosevelt. Black's ambition was to 'rescue' FDR's reputation from that of a man of the left outwitted by Stalin at the end of the Second World War. 'The man had to be emancipated from being a mascot of the moderate left of this country,' he would say, 'and the apostrophisation of the unthinking right.' He set out to prove that Roosevelt was a centrist who rescued the capitalist system from the Depression and helped the poor.

Black's scenario was neither farce nor tragedy, but greed was sapping his chance of survival. While he indulged his fantasies as a historian and casually ignored the problems besetting his business, he was unaware that about four hundred yards south of his Manhattan home on Park Avenue, the seeds of his undoing were maturing.

'Have you never heard about the "Black Factor"?' a rich Canadian investor asked Chris Browne. Browne, influenced by his father's dictum 'Don't spend it until you have it,' had assumed that Black's wealth was genuine, but the visitor's warning prompted him to order a deeper investigation of Hollinger. In Tweedy Browne's spartan offices, Laura Jereski was influenced by the new mood spreading across Manhattan. Galvanised by Eliot Spitzer, the city's dynamic Attorney General, significant Wall Street players including Sandy Weill, the chief executive of Citibank, were being embarrassed by the new zeal against corporate greed. Spitzer was playing Jereski's favourite tune. Her new scrutiny of Hollinger's accounts revealed the tip of the iceberg. 'They pocketed US$154 million between 1995 and 2000,' she told Chris Browne. 'As Hollinger's performance declined, the payments increased. And the shares are 30 per cent less than the float price.' Neither realised that Jereski was underestimating. In the year 2000 alone, Black and his group had taken a total of $122 million from Hollinger in management fees, non-compete fees, aircraft costs and general expenses. The company's net income in the same year was $117 million.

Two blocks to the west, in Hollinger's offices on Fifth Avenue, Black and Radler had just decided to award themselves another chunk of money. In April 2001 Black received US$600,000 and Radler US$285,000 as 'supplemental non-competition payments' for newspaper sales in autumn 2000.[48] They had become so sloppy that they did not trouble to create any plausible justification for the payments. In appropriating that money, the two sensed that their access to tax-free income would soon be curtailed. Over coffee, Radler submitted Ravelston's fee for 2001 to Governor

Thompson. Although Hollinger's net losses that year would, for technical reasons, be $337.5 million, and the company was dramatically smaller, Ravelston's fee was $30.7 million, about 73 per cent of the company's net income.[49] Without demur, Thompson agreed to the payments, and he expected Kravis and Burt to defer to his approval. Neither ever carefully read the documents, and Kravis often failed to attend meetings. Hollinger was asked to pay a portion of the fees to Black-Amiel and to Moffat, the Blacks' private companies incorporated in the offshore tax shelter of Barbados. Since the representative of KPMG was present and said nothing, the requests were assumed to be acceptable.[50] Before leaving, Radler did however tell Thompson that Hollinger was still renegotiating its loans with the banks. The Governor nodded, unaware of a serious threat facing Radler and Black.

During that month William 'Bud' Rogers, a lawyer advising Hollinger International about refinancing its debts, was sifting through the company's records. To his surprise, he discovered that the $51.8 million paid by CanWest as non-compete fees had not been properly disclosed by the company to shareholders. He alerted Paul Healy, telling him that the discrepancies in the records required correction. Healy was in a difficult position. Knowing that Black had taken the non-compete fees from the purchase price, he had assumed that the unorthodox payment had been properly declared. Rogers's discovery was a reality check. 'You've got to disclose that money,' Healy told Black. 'We're obliged by law to reveal the full truth to the directors and the shareholders.' After tense discussions involving all members of the cabal and their legal advisers, Black retreated, and under his supervision Mark Kipnis composed a circular to the directors in May 2001. While the payments, explained Kipnis, were 'a critical condition' of the sale and 'in the best interests of all shareholders', there had been an 'inadvertent' suggestion that CanWest had stipulated the amount Black and the other directors should receive. The word 'inadvertent' was included at Black's suggestion. With such expert obfuscation, only the most skilful deciphering of Kipnis's memorandum would reveal that $51.8 million had been deducted from CanWest's purchase price at the shareholders' expense, or that CanWest had never stipulated that any money should actually be paid to Black, Radler and the others. The declaration satisfied Rogers, although the full truth about the continuing contractual relationship between Ravelston and CanWest had still not been disclosed to the directors.[51]

Black might have expected some embarrassing questions about the payment when the audit committee met on 14 May 2001, but the circumstances were tilted in his favour. The twenty-minute 'meeting' consisted of a telephone conference call. None of the three directors had previously consulted each other or was given papers to enable them to understand the critical questions. Beth DeMerchant, the lawyer at Torys responsible for the Hollinger account, did not discover either that Izzy Asper had not insisted that the Black group personally receive the $51.8 million, or that the money was taken from shareholders' funds. The withholding of that information, and Black's placatory responses to the innocuous queries, smoothed his task to win retrospective approval for the payment.[52]

To complete the legal requirements, Black authorised an announcement to Hollinger's shareholders. As an experienced businessman he knew the need for accuracy and honesty. In the announcement he signed, the company explained the background to the fees. The non-compete condition, it was stated, was 'required by CanWest as a condition to the transaction'. The money, the document continued, was paid to Hollinger, which decided that the distribution should be: $26.4 million for Ravelston, $11.9 million each for Black and Radler, and $1.3 million each for Boultbee and Atkinson. The reader was led to believe that the fees had been paid in addition to the purchase price. Conrad Black knew that was inaccurate.

The statement arrived at Tweedy Browne's offices at about the same time as the report of Hollinger International's first quarter results. Conrad Black reported unprecedented losses compared to the previous year's profits. Worse, the price of the CanWest shares received by Hollinger as part-payment for its Canadian newspapers had fallen from C$25 to C$14.25. The sale to CanWest had become a costly mistake, compounded by a cash crisis. Hollinger Inc. in Toronto was receiving insufficient money from Hollinger in New York to repay the empire's debts. The short-term solution, Black decided, was for Hollinger Inc. to borrow money from Ravelston. No other public company would have found itself in the absurd position of its chairman taking money from the company and then lending the same money back through his own private company, yet his unorthodoxy was not investigated by Hollinger's lawyers and auditors. Beth DeMerchant at Torys and KPMG's partners requested changes in the presentation of Hollinger's activities, without sufficiently insisting that the reasons were accurately explained to the shareholders. Conrad Black complied, and was also relieved. Ravelston owned just 19 per cent of Hollinger International shares in New York, yet Black controlled the majority of votes in the company. He was quietly thrilled with the beauty of his profitable scheme. In crude terms, in return for Ravelston investing $19, it received $100 from Hollinger, and that was entirely legal.

Scenting something suspicious from the disclosures, on 15 May 2001 Laura Jereski telephoned Paul Healy. The combination of Jereski's remorseless manner and her grinding determination to secure precise answers to embarrassing questions troubled Healy. 'She's their chief Rottweiler,' spat Black unjustifiably on hearing Healy's report. 'Fired from the *Journal* and with an absolute contemptuous disregard for the facts.'[53] Black's experience in Toronto and London reinforced his dismissal of the Jereskis of New York. The historian and self-appointed political sage wilfully ignored the calibre of New York's financial community – just as he disregarded the change of atmosphere introduced by Eliot Spitzer. The following day, Chris Browne signed a letter drafted by Jereski. After mentioning Hollinger's excessive payments to Ravelston, Browne requested a meeting with Hollinger's directors 'to voice our displeasure and hear your remedies for our company's underperformance'. Simultaneously, a letter was sent by Federal Express to Hollinger's directors asking for an explanation of the company's huge payments to Ravelston.

Black received the letter on 17 May. Subtlety was abandoned. Outraged and uncontrolled, he vented his spleen to Healy, acting like an authoritarian monarch, all guns blazing with no consideration of the consequences. Browne's letter, he ranted, was 'histrionic', 'righteous', 'self-pitying' and an 'arithmetical travesty'.[54] Demolishing facts with vocabulary was Black's talent, but his description of himself as a proprietor not subject to shareholders, 'When it's your money, you run things better than when it isn't,' was deliberately inaccurate.[55] To Healy's bewilderment, Black was unwilling to understand the other point of view. Even Healy's practised speciality of stroking Black's ego failed to mollify his employer. Healy did not understand that self-preservation dictated Black's refusal to permit a meeting between Browne and Hollinger's directors, who he advised to ignore Tweedy Browne's letter. The line was drawn. 'That's pretty outrageous,' Chris Browne muttered. 'They think we're just another pesky shareholder.'

Convinced that Tweedy Browne was permanently sidelined, Black focused on the important issue, his peerage. The battle against Chrétien had been lost. The supreme court had ruled in the government's favour, and as over 60 per cent of the population supported the Prime Minister, it seemed that Black's only choice if he was to secure his longed-for ennoblement was to renounce his Canadian citizenship and be fast-tracked for British. 'With regret but without rancour', he announced on 18 May 2001 that he was formally cutting his ties with his country. But he wanted the last word, so as to display his anger. The venue was arranged and the text printed for circulation. An audience was invited to hear Conrad Black damn Canada as a 'one-party state doomed to mediocrity'. He blamed his countrymen for forcing his renunciation of Canadian nationality: 'Having opposed for thirty years precisely the public policies that have caused scores of thousands of educated and talented Canadians to abandon their country every year, it is at least consistent that I should join their dispersal.' Abandoning Canada, Black admitted, was 'a victory of sorts' for his enemies, 'though an eminently endurable defeat for me too'.[56] He could not resist one item of revisionism about his quest for a peerage: 'I have not lifted a finger to achieve this honour,' he said with apparent sincerity, 'and to become a member of what is certainly the most talented legislative chamber in the world. But the honour having been offered, I wasn't disposed to be deprived of it in this outrageous way.'[57] 'Lord Almost', or 'His Lardship', was too unpopular to win much sympathy. Canadians had consistently voted for an egalitarian society, and disliked anti-Canadian snobs. Neither Conrad Black nor Barbara Amiel felt much regret as they prepared to fly to London for the summer season and the introduction to the House of Lords. Amiel seemed to admire her husband's parting quip: 'You're not going to see the end of me until the undertaker tells you I've gone.' While in London she suddenly rang her cousin David Bentley and invited him for a drink. Bentley was suitably impressed, but could not understand the reason for the unexpected honour. He was not invited to that year's summer party, which was charged to Hollinger at $24,950, nor would he ever see Amiel again.

Some suspected that Conrad Black's imminent peerage had

pushed Amiel 'further up the mountain' away from mortals. Others assumed that her sixtieth birthday had caused fears of visible ageing. 'One third of my waking hours,' she told a friend, 'are devoted to making myself look beautiful.' Daily she covered her body in creams and lotions, especially the anti-wrinkle treatments Crème de la Mer and Retin-A. She regularly visited a New York dermatologist, she mentioned frequent trips to California for unspecified treatments, and her admission that the formula for eternal youth was the extraction of fat from her buttocks, to be frozen and injected at intervals into her face, seemed to explain her remarkable looks. Her occasional sighting in a wig was assumed by some to be an attempt to hide new scars from plastic surgery. Her obsession about her appearance had also unleashed remarkable spending on clothes. 'My sexual armour', she called them. Many beautiful middle-aged women seek the reassurance of perfect clothes to prove their elegance, but Amiel's spending suggested insecurity, and perhaps regret for being childless. At fittings she was nervous, strangely helpless, and stumbled over her instructions. Armoury or allure, aficionados of fashion did not acclaim her as chic, but as the Queen of Excess.[58]

In Cottesmore Gardens, two rooms were assigned as dressing suites for the storage of Amiel's clothing. Each cupboard was allotted to a different garment. Sweaters, furs, T-shirts, shirts, gloves, belts, handkerchiefs, underwear and tights each had their designated wardrobe or drawer. Hanging on thin brass rods were shawls made of cashmere, chiffon, pashmina and silk. In a cupboard for handbags were dozens of spotless models, of innumerable shapes and colours, manufactured by Hermès, Renaud Pellegrino, Manolo Blahnik and Chanel, some plain, others bedecked with jewels. Another cupboard stored countless shoes, including over fifty pairs designed by Manolo Blahnik, each preserved in a clear box for easy selection. In another section were stacks of brand-new shoes in unopened boxes. The most important collection was the dresses – evening gowns and daytime dresses, suits and skirts from the best couture houses in Paris and New York. Some had cost $75,000 but remained unworn. All were suspended on padded hangers from a custom-built rack. Perfectly sewn small cushions were placed on the clothes carrying explicit orders: 'To be ironed', 'To put away', 'Alterations' and 'To try on'. While Amiel personally paid for the cheaper ready-to-wear clothes, the expensive dresses were financed by Black. The life that required couture, in Amiel's opinion, was his world. Perceptively, Margaret Wente of the *Globe and Mail* wrote that year, 'Only a few hundred women in the world can afford to dress like Mrs Black, and Mrs Black may not be among them.'

The Blacks treated such criticism as contemptible. In response, they flaunted their wealth. On 30 July 2001 they flew on the refurbished Gulfstream to Bora Bora in French Polynesia, intending to enjoy a week's holiday. After refuelling in Seattle and Honolulu, they completed the eleven-hour flight and checked into the best hotel. When they awoke, both admitted their mistake. 'It's beautiful but boring,' said Amiel. 'It's worse,' said Black grumpily. 'There's nothing to do here.' After two days Rosemary Millar, Black's secretary in London, called Captain Ridley, who was staying in a cheaper hotel on the island. 'I'm sorry,' she apologised, 'Mr Black wants to get out.' They left after four days. On the journey they ate with silverware recently purchased at Hollinger's expense for $3,530. The total cost of the flights was $530,000. Half was charged to Hollinger. Other personal costs charged to the company during the year included Amiel's claims of $2,463 for handbags, $140 for 'jogging attire', $2,083 for exercise equipment, $2,057 for a 'T. Anthony' leather briefcase and $828 for stereo equipment in the New York apartment. Their addiction to consumption was to be abruptly halted by reality.

On 3 September 2001 both Blacks, clearly emotional, sat in the sunshine of their Toronto garden. Ken Whyte had been invited on Labour Day weekend for coffee to discuss a turning point in their lives. Unsustainable losses had compelled Conrad Black the previous week to sell the remaining 50 per cent of the *National Post*. The announcement had sparked more anger among the staff, already depressed that the newspaper's anniversary party was billed as 'sausage rolls at the Hard Rock Café'. 'What are the staff thinking and saying about me?' asked Black, as usual concerned about his image. The truth was unpleasant. To Black's relief, Canadian newspapers would not risk reporting the worst of the complaints. Intimidated by the threat of libel writs, his critics did not publish details of Paul Winkler's legal case against Hollinger for his wrongful dismissal as publisher of Kelowna's *Capital News*. Winkler had departed for a new job puzzled that no one in Toronto considered it worth reporting that the *Capital News* was sold by Radler in April 2001 to a company partly owned by Todd Vogt's stepfather for $5.4 million, although Hollinger had received offers of about $8 million. Indeed, it would be resold in July 2003 for $13.7 million. Those murky relationships and transactions had been ignored, along with Radler's surprising testimony during the trial. In his testimony, Radler had testified that he and Black owned 48 per cent of Horizon, although the true figure was 72 per cent. Unable to interest anyone in Toronto or Ottawa about the deceit, Winkler simply wanted justice for himself. He would have to wait nine months before he knew the outcome of his case: he would be awarded $160,495 compensation, the maximum amount possible.[59]

Conrad Black remained phlegmatic about the potential risk. Past successes, a lack of conscience and his sense of entitlement immunised him to any sense of danger about Horizon's growth at Hollinger's expense. Having started the transfer of assets from one company to the other, he and Radler agreed that the process should be completed. During the summer Hollinger sold the *Mammoth Times* to Horizon for just $1. Hollinger had bought the newspaper two years earlier for $1.75 million. Hollinger's directors and audit committee approved the deal after hearing from Radler and Black that the paper was losing money, and there were no other potential buyers. The directors were unaware that the company had recently been offered $1.25 million for the profitable newspaper, and that Radler had earlier acknowledged receiving another offer of $2 million.[60] By the end of 2001 Horizon owned twenty-five newspapers. During that year Ravelston and the Black group received $45.1 million in fees and non-compete payments.

With no concern that prosecutors would one day allege that his conduct amounted to 'textbook money laundering', Black concentrated on his biography of President Roosevelt. To his delight, he heard that FDR's papers and memorabilia were for sale. Grace Tully, Roosevelt's secretary, had died, and the administrators of her estate had sold the collection to Glenn Horowitz, a dealer, for $4.5 million. Black could not resist owning the papers and mementoes, including the flag which had flown over the White House at the time of Roosevelt's death. Horowitz sensed his enthusiasm. 'I can get $12 million to $14 million,' he told Black at one point during his six-month seduction, knowing that there was no other buyer. Eventually Black agreed to pay Horowitz $8.9 million, and ordered the collection to be delivered to his homes in New York and Toronto. $8 million, he decided, would be paid by Hollinger. He did not ask the Hollinger directors for their approval. '$8 million,' he would later explain, 'was not something I was prepared to spend.' In response to Peter Atkinson's unease, he asserted that the collection's value 'will go straight up from here'. Asserting his expertise as a historian and businessman he added, 'I will be happy to guarantee personally against any downside from our purchase price.' He would later claim that any suggestion that he had bought the collection because he was writing FDR's biography was 'a lie unsupported by any basis in fact'.[61] Convinced that Hollinger was rich after the CanWest deal, he never considered how he could further justify the purchase, especially in the light of the company's increasing debts. Advertising at the *Telegraph* and the *Chicago Sun-Times* was falling, the *Telegraph* was only selling 560,000 copies at full price and the remaining 480,000 copies at a crippling discount, and CanWest's share price had fallen further to C$10, compared to $25 when the deal was struck. Black's sale of the Canadian newspapers would never repay Hollinger's debts. Hollinger's share price had fallen to $13. Black was unconcerned. Over the previous years he had encountered too many crises to be disturbed. Rather, in anticipation of Downing Street's announcement of his peerage on 11 September, his purchase of the FDR collection seemed reasonable, simply because he desired to be the owner with possession.

Disappointingly, Downing Street's announcement was overshadowed by the terrorist attack on New York. In the aftermath, Black hoped for some respite from Tweedy Browne, but he was disappointed. After the mayhem had calmed down, Chris Browne and Laura Jereski re-examined Hollinger's accounts. In the wake of 9/11, Hollinger's share price had fallen to $9, and the company's income was threatened by a dearth of advertising. Considering those problems, Browne dispatched a letter on 16 October 2001 asking Black to justify Ravelston billing Hollinger International for $154 million in fees.

Two blocks across the city, Black had reason to pause. The mood in Wall Street had changed significantly following the collapse of Enron in Houston amid allegations of extraordinary frauds. The banner newspaper headlines reporting suspicions about Enron's multi-millionaire executives were accompanied by references to suspected dishonesty at the communications companies Adelphia and WorldCom. John Rigas, the chairman of Adelphia, was accused of using the company 'like a private ATM', living off it at the expense of shareholders; Bernie Ebbers, the founder of WorldCom, was accused of having carried out an $11 billion fraud by false accounting. Black had great sympathy for the creators of both businesses. Their shareholders, he believed, should either have been grateful to them or sold their shares. The new antagonism towards alleged corporate greed was repugnant to Black, who felt at ease among swashbucklers and convicted businessmen. He had already decided to visit Alfred Taubman in jail. 'Other than in cases of legal or moral necessity, which have not arisen here,' he would explain to justify his eventual visit to Taubman's Minnesota prison, 'we do not desert our friends.'[62] Recently he had been irritated by the *Daily Telegraph*'s criticism of Buckingham Palace for allowing the Queen Mother to meet Gerald Ronson, who had served a prison sentence after conviction for conspiracy to defraud. He had met Ronson several times, and had planned to cooperate with him in a property deal. In protest, he sent a letter to his own newspaper for publication. There should, he argued, be no 'prolonged social persecution of convicted lawbreakers after official justice has fully run its course, or the vilification of wives whose only perceived shortcoming is to stand by their husbands through terrible times of adversity'.[63] Corporate governance, he scoffed, smelt of political persecution. He had created Hollinger, and there was no reason for deference to lawmakers or fund managers seeking to compel his obedience to spiteful laws.

In the same spirit, Black dictated a confident reply to Chris Browne's letter. He assured Browne that the payment of the management fees had been approved by Hollinger's directors, but he did not reveal that significant information had been withheld from them. 'Given your evidently aggrieved baronial references to me,' he wrote with relish, 'you will be relieved to learn that when I am inducted into the House of Lords at the end of this month, that will not dilute my profound commitment to egalitarianism, in shareholding as in other matters.' Presenting himself as an 'egalitarian', Black may have smiled, was a wonderful stroke which Barbara would undoubtedly savour.

Alone in London, his wife was captivating guests at the seventieth birthday party of the historian Hugh Thomas with her glittering jewellery and a flamenco dress designed by Oscar de la Renta. The total cost of her accoutrements, everyone agreed, must have been well over £1 million. Her close friend Miriam Gross confided, 'She enhanced the evening. She dresses always for the occasion. I think it comes not from trying to call attention to herself but out of a wish to get into the spirit of things. Most people are frightened of overdressing, but she risks things out of generosity, I think.'[64]

Equating Barbara Amiel with generosity was a matter of opinion. The more perceptive would say that while those of Amiel's class dressed to look chic and expensive, she just looked expensive. Her combination of jewellery and clothes was as questionable as her choice of outfits. Her harshest critics would say that her appearance was vulgar, and that was reflected in her expression of dissatisfaction with the Rolls-Royce Silver Wraith which her husband enjoyed using in London. Amiel did not understand his sentimental attachment to the old car purloined by Bud McDougald. She had little understanding of McDougald's importance in Black's life, but she did know that the car needed modernising. Black agreed. The refurbishment, costing an estimated $90,000, was billed to Hollinger. Soon after the work's completion, Peter Munk spotted the car after having dinner with Black in Mayfair. 'My God,' Munk thought. 'That's the most beautiful car in the world.' He said to Black, 'Have you seen this car?' 'It's mine,' replied Black. 'But it's got purple leather. It's like the Queen's. How can you afford it?' asked the billionaire Munk. Black smiled. The car was appropriate for a couple about to become ennobled.

As she sat in the gallery of the House of Lords on 31 October 2001 watching Conrad Moffitt Black swearing the oath to become

Baron Black of Crossharbour, Barbara Amiel could have been forgiven for thinking of how the shop assistants in London, New York and Paris would thereafter address her as Lady Black, and how the butlers opening the front doors of their four homes would ask, 'Do you wish to see His Lordship or Her Ladyship?' Even ersatz nobility appealed to the woman from Watford. Professionally, of course, she would retain her maiden name, but in other circumstances she would expect the appropriate respect for 'Lady Barbara Amiel Black', rather than the accurate 'Lady Black'. Everyone would grant her additional respect. Seated nearby were Henry and Nancy Kissinger, Lord Hanson, Lord Weidenfeld, Dan Colson, Lord Deedes and the former Conservative leader William Hague. Some of the credit for Conrad Black standing in the chamber below between his proposers, Lady Thatcher and Lord Carrington, was, Amiel believed, due to her skills. The induction would have different consequences for Lord Black, who appeared unusually relaxed. 'Our right trusty and well beloved Conrad . . .' chimed the voice of the clerk, confirming the title. As a member of this exclusive club, Baron Black soon after explained, his speeches would be followed by four field marshals, which never occurred in the Canadian Senate. John Fraser, his school friend, offered a different scenario. Unlike Black's rich and powerful friends, said Fraser, a number of the members of the House of Lords appointed by the Labour Party came from underprivileged backgrounds. 'It will be Conrad's first opportunity to meet ordinary people,' he quipped.

At the celebratory lunch after the ceremony, the Blacks seemed to reflect the accuracy of the label attached to them three months previously by *Harper's & Queen* magazine as the 'fifth most influential people' in London. The Conservative Party's leadership race following William Hague's defeat at the general election in June had been decisively influenced by the *Telegraph*. After successfully campaigning against the pro-European Kenneth

Clarke, Black and Amiel were undecided about who to support. Amiel favoured Michael Portillo, while Black leant towards Iain Duncan Smith. Briefly believing that Margaret Thatcher supported Portillo, they wanted to add their own endorsement, but after hearing from Charles Moore about Thatcher's disdain for Portillo, the Blacks switched to Duncan Smith, their editor's choice. The victory of Iain Duncan Smith, the weakest candidate, confirmed the Blacks' influence. Few of those looking at Lord Black, seated between Lord Carrington and Henry Kissinger in the sombre peers' dining room, could have imagined his involvement in financial chicanery. Both Carrington and Kissinger had staked their reputations on Black's honesty, and Kissinger's evident enthusiasm for his friend had reassured shareholders about Hollinger's probity. The exception was Laura Jereski at Tweedy Browne. Just how, she wondered, had Black's directors tolerated such huge payments to Ravelston while the company's performance deteriorated? Her repeated questions increased Paul Healy's own concerns. 'We're going to have to meet them,' Healy told Black on his return to New York. Black's instinctive resistance wavered. He could, he reasoned, charm his way out of trouble once again.

On 17 November 2001, Black and Healy arrived at Tweedy Browne's offices in Park Avenue. Their object, they had agreed, was to 'smooth over everything' and persuade the critics that Hollinger's retained profits would rise. 'You've got to reduce Ravelston's fees,' said Chris Browne, 'and understand that your task is to act in all the shareholders' interests, not just your own.' Black nodded in agreement, playing his hand to placate a critic. 'Don't worry,' he replied. 'There'll be beneficial changes in the future.' Browne and Jereski smiled. Lord Black, they believed, should be trusted. 'That went well,' Black said to Healy as they left the office, pleased with his performance. He had had the last word. All would be well. The incongruity between being scolded by a fund manager in a frugal office and the opulence of his own social life blinded Black to Browne's potential threat. His self-congratulation appeared justified. Browne and Jereski accepted his assurances at face value, and put Hollinger out of their minds. Black also put Browne out of his mind. After a hectic social round in Manhattan, he was flying back to London with Amiel. Before he departed, he might have considered settling one grievance with Healy which arose after his ennoblement.

On their return to New York, Barbara Amiel had sent a memorandum to Hollinger's staff asking them to address her husband in the future as Lord Black. To her surprise, they refused. She also asked Paul Healy to organise a business lunch of caviar and champagne. 'I won't do that,' Healy replied, complaining to friends that Amiel was a 'social-climbing bitch'. The relationship between Healy and his wife, Black knew, had deteriorated after someone reported that Healy had denounced her as 'an actress unable to sustain her phoney upper-class English accent while coquetting powerful men'. (Someone else mentioned that after Amiel had created a huge fuss in London about preparing a kosher dinner for two rabbis, and had then asked for a Parma ham sandwich after their departure.) Antagonism at the heart of his business was not new, but these latest spats were unhelpful. The disputes in New York remained unresolved, and two weeks before Christmas Black departed to London to host a buffet dinner at Cottesmore Gardens in honour of Boris Johnson, the *Spectator*'s successful editor.

Boris Johnson had been elected as a Conservative MP in June 2001, and hoped to remain as the *Spectator*'s editor despite his promise to Black that he would resign after the election. Black was hosting the party to celebrate Johnson's betrayal of his pledge. One hundred and fifty personalities had been invited to celebrate the 'Boris Phenomenon', and Barbara Amiel had filled the reception rooms with large cardboard cut-outs of Johnson and hired a comedian to poke fun at him. Flattered to be the centre of attention, Johnson mingled with the guests, barely noticing Daniel Bernard, the French ambassador, engaged in a provocative discussion with Black about the Middle East. After the guests had gone, Black told Amiel that the ambassador had said about Israel, 'Why should the world be in danger of World War III because of these people?', and had also referred to Israel as a 'shitty little country'. These were inflammatory sentiments for the Blacks. In recent years they had become renowned as passionate Zionists, interpreting any criticism of Israel as anti-Semitic. Bernard's remarks, they agreed, were beyond the pale. Amiel pledged vengeance. She would, she declared, quote Bernard's bigotry in her *Telegraph* column. She barely paused to consider the breach of convention. First, it was an abuse of hospitality to quote without permission a guest's private comments expressed in her own home; and secondly, since she had not personally heard Bernard, she should have asked him to confirm his actual words. Conrad Black could have intervened to prevent his wife violating those conventions, but he did not. Although he had previously denied interfering in his newspapers, recently he could not resist foisting his pro-Zionist opinions on the *Telegraph*. Few doubted that Amiel had influenced his conversion.

Both had changed substantially since their marriage. In October 1994, under the headline 'Hollywood's New Jewish Establishment', William Cash had described in the *Spectator* the power of Jews in America's film industry. The organised uproar on the West Coast swamped Black's office in Canary Wharf. Encouraged by the Simon Wiesenthal Centre, famous stars including Steven Spielberg, Barbra Streisand and Kevin Costner complained to Black about his magazine's anti-Semitism. Max Hastings was in Black's office when Jack Valenti of the Motion Picture Association called. 'It was one of the few moments in my time with Conrad,' wrote Hastings, 'when I saw him seriously rattled.' Black was nervous, and confessed his concern: 'You don't understand, Max. My entire interests in the United States and internationally could be seriously damaged by this.'[65] Black, it would appear, feared Jewish influence. In a *Sunday Times* column six months previously, Amiel had attacked Hollywood's Jews for taking 'McCarthyism to [their] bosom', adding, 'I find it absorbing that so many Jews are involved in the film industry.' Two years later, she no longer found the topic 'absorbing'. She expunged any doubts about Israel's treatment of the Palestinians.

Barbara Amiel's writings in the *Telegraph* hardened the perception of the newspaper as an uncritical propagandist for Zionism. A *Spectator* report in September 1994 by William Dalrymple about Israeli extremists' desecration of the graves of Christians had incensed Black. Dalrymple, he ordered, should be banned from writing for the *Telegraph*. His demand was ignored, but few doubted the influence of Amiel and, behind her, Richard Perle. In March 2001, Black's partisanship for Jews and Israel was attacked by critics who noted his fierce reaction to a *Spectator* column by Taki attacking President Clinton's pardon of the Jewish white-collar criminal Marc Rich. The combination of a Jew and a criminal was a double whammy for Black. Rich, he declared was a friend, and Taki's attack on him resembled Goebbels at his worst. Battle was declared. The former Tory MP Ian Gilmour, a well-known Arabist, attacked Black for suppressing criticism of Israel in his newspapers. Black retorted that Gilmour was a Jew-baiter. The mixture of emotion and politics was potentially explosive.

During the evening on which the 'Boris Phenomenon' was celebrated, Barbara Amiel appeared to be unusually preoccupied by what some called her 'Middle Eastern sensibilities'. She had confided to a guest, 'As a Jew, I can never feel comfortable. I'm never sure if people like me or not.' She could not even decide whether she belonged to London or New York, she explained. To other guests, she displayed her acid temperament. A woman friend expressed surprise after receiving an ice-cold rapier greeting, and another mentioned that their hostess had ceased returning her telephone calls. Some journalists complained about her influence, not least in preventing the promotion of women in the *Telegraph* group. 'She's always irritated about something,' Charles Moore had previously commented. Unkind people would describe her condition as paranoia, but undoubtedly her personal insecurity and nomadic existence inflamed her attitude towards Daniel Bernard's criticism of Israel. Most hosts would nevertheless have restrained their anger. After all, what a guest said at a party might not accurately reflect the sober opinion of an ambassador who was well known among senior Foreign Office officials as sympathetic towards Israel, not least because he himself was Jewish. The Blacks did not consider those possibilities. Both regarded themselves as unfettered by conventional rules. Since his failure against Chrétien, Black had publicly chastised a bishop as 'a jumped-up little twerp', criticised the BBC as 'pathologically hostile to most British institutions', and issued a writ against Britain's ambassador in Berlin for suggesting that the *Telegraph* was unobjective about Europe. Black, the self-appointed pillar of the British establishment, enjoyed causing outrage in public. Lacking inhibitions, he encouraged Amiel to shame Bernard.

In her *Telegraph* column on 17 December 2001, Amiel wrote: 'Recently, the ambassador of a major EU country politely told a gathering at my home that the current troubles in the world were all because of Israel.' The ambassador, she continued inaccurately, 'told me' that the world was dangerous because of 'that shitty little country Israel'. Warming to her theme, she wrote that the ambassador's sentiments were echoed at another lunch where 'the hostess – the doyenne of London's political salon scene' asserted her dislike for the Jews and said she believed that they were to blame for their own misfortune.

Within hours of the article's publication, Daniel Bernard had been identified as the ambassador. Although he insisted that

Black had distorted his words,[66] he was withdrawn from London and posted to Algeria. He died in April 2004. Fingers were also pointed at Carla Powell as 'the hostess', an accusation she denied in a letter to the *Telegraph*. Just as she had not personally heard Bernard's remarks, Amiel had not been at Powell's lunch – which Powell denied had even taken place. Considering Amiel's damnation in 1993 of Vicki Woods's reporting about Margaret Thatcher during a photoshoot, her display of double standards in her treatment of Bernard and Powell to serve her own personal agenda accurately characterised those 'journalistic' transgressions so often decried by Lord Black.[67]

In the short term the Blacks were victorious, yet neither considered how their personalised use of the *Telegraph* damaged the newspaper. In Charles Moore's opinion, Amiel, initially an ally of journalists, had become 'tricky, and gave the impression of constantly playing games.' Her conduct echoed her own criticism of *The Kiss*, an autobiography by a daughter explaining her incestuous relationship with her father. 'To consider dropping one's pants in public as a liberating experience,' Amiel wrote, 'is the sick aspect of this book . . . and, if the culture demands and rewards it, then our culture is sick as well.'[68]

The Blacks had transformed themselves and their newspapers into sources of amusing gossip rather than influence. Unlike Rupert Murdoch, whose papers could genuinely threaten governments, the *Telegraph* had moved to the periphery. While Tony Blair had shifted the political agenda towards the centre, the *Telegraph* had marginalised itself by supporting Iain Duncan Smith's right-wing agenda, perpetuating the Conservative Party's divisions. Eccentric and out of touch with Blairite Britain, the newspaper was deterring potential young readers, and its circulation declined. Its owner was consumed by his crude scrabbling for cash, and his authority was diminishing just as Murdoch was consolidating a vast empire. Unable to beat Murdoch, Black lampooned his rival following his prostate operation as 'a biological wonder in addition to a great businessman'. Black's absence of subtlety provoked a rumour that he was planning to purchase Napoleon's penis. 'He thinks it is so outrageous and unbelievable, it made him almost speechless,' responded Rosemary Millar, his assistant.[69] On the eve of the storm, the introduction of ridicule gave some symmetry to the Blacks' lives.

12

'Thief!'

Christmas in Toronto was traditionally marked by a huge party at the Blacks' home in the Bridle Path. In 2001 the guest list included, as always, the city's celebrities and a large contingent from Ottawa and Montreal. On the long driveway leading to the house, the chauffeured limousines waited in line for their passengers to be received by an army of servants offering excellent food and drink. Canada's elite enjoyed their moment of indulgence, spotting famous faces and commenting on those who were no longer invited.

As usual Barbara Amiel had devoted hours to selecting her dress and jewellery. Long after the first guests arrived, she made a grand entrance down the stairs. To her horror she spotted the English journalist Michael Coren, who had been hired by Conrad Black to write for *Saturday Night* magazine after writing a favourable review of his autobiography. The job did not materialise. She had also enjoyed Coren's company until he showed anti-conservative tendencies. 'Just like Dracula,' thought Coren, transfixed by the sight of Amiel's descent. With an aggressive stare, Amiel walked brusquely past. 'We won't be invited again,' mumbled Coren's wife accurately. 'Well, let's fill up our pockets with their lovely sweets,' replied Coren. 'The kids love them.' Cutting and dropping people was Amiel's style. 'Barbara always gets a headache when the plane enters Canadian airspace,' Black said jovially to Coren later that evening, unaware of the guest's 'execution' by his wife.[1] Since becoming Lady Black, her remoteness had grown.

The following day Black and Amiel, dressed in another dazzling costume, were seated at a charity dinner. Nearby, Peter Munk had taken a table. Among his guests was the British publicist David Wynne-Morgan. As the dinner ended, Munk went over to greet Black, and Wynne-Morgan moved towards Amiel. Thirteen years earlier, when she was alone in London, Wynne-Morgan had hosted at Munk's request two dinner parties in her honour. 'Hello, Barbara,' said Wynne-Morgan. Amiel's face was stony blank. 'I'm David Wynne-Morgan. Remember, I gave some dinner parties for you in London.' 'No I don't remember,' said Amiel disdainfully, and turned away.

Amiel's irritation appeared to increase as Christmas approached. Some believed her mood was connected to Conrad Black's regular visits to his brother Monte, who was dying of cancer. Since the diagnosis nine months earlier, Monte had forlornly placed his hopes on experimental drugs produced in Europe, but his fate was irreversible. On Christmas Day, it was agreed, Conrad and Barbara Black would come for lunch to Monte's home. Black arrived two hours late. 'Barbara can't come,' he announced. 'She's ill.' One hour later, Amiel arrived. Amid the misery for June, Monte's second wife, who had enjoyed a blissfully happy marriage, and his four children, no one challenged the lack of consideration shown by Conrad and Barbara towards the stricken family. Days later, Monte was transferred to the Sunnybrook hospital. Conrad Black visited his brother regularly, dissipating the gloom with warmth and humour. Tragically, Monte's children from his first marriage were also caring for their mother, who was also dying of cancer in the same hospital. Monte's death, announced on 13 January 2002, was expected. 'I hope we're going to be very Anglo-Saxon about this and not get emotional,' Black cautioned June.[2]

The wake was held at Conrad Black's house. Throughout, Amiel, dressed in black and wearing a wig, sat in the library with her sister Ruth. No one could understand why she remained hidden and had not overtly offered her condolences to the widow. Nor could Monte's family understand why Conrad chose that moment to take out his diary and recite his engagements for the following weeks. 'We only do A-list dinners,' he explained to the other mourners. Shortly after, Conrad Black fainted. The family assumed that he had finally succumbed to the blow of Monte's death.

After the funeral Amiel flew to London. Her preoccupation with status had encouraged her agreement with *Vogue* magazine to feature in an article entitled 'The Style-Setters from Sixteen to Eighty'. In agreeing to the magazine's suggestion, Amiel undertook a substantial commitment involving hours of make-up, endless changes of clothes and the patience required to pose for the photographer. That inconvenience was tolerable for a woman anxious to become an icon herself and who suffered another concern: she was now aged sixty-one.

Draped across expensive furniture in the house at Cottesmore Gardens, dressed in garments by Chanel, Oscar de la Renta and Yves St Laurent, Amiel radiated wealth and sexuality during her interview with *Vogue* journalist Julia Reed. With the coquettish allure of a starlet in a tabloid newspaper, she confessed to suffering from a persistent anxiety: 'I'm always worried about cleavage,' she said. 'I seem to keep spilling out of things.' Her attempt to retain her dignity while coping with her big breasts was, she admitted, self-defeating. 'I know I shouldn't like sexy looks, but I'm not quite ready to play dead and play safe.' Even more than twenty years later, Amiel still could not resist wanting to be admired for her brains while still pushing her breasts into men's faces.

Keen to show her full armoury, Amiel invited Reed to inspect her dressing rooms. Amid the cascade of dresses, shoes, handbags and accessories, Amiel was not oblivious to the impression she was creating. Quite deliberately, as she selected her jewellery for the photographs, she mentioned the natural-pearl and diamond brooch Black had bought her six years earlier which was so big that it remained unworn in a safe. She justified the uncounted fortune she had spent on clothes by describing a humiliating incident as a student. She had been wearing a second-hand dress for a date when the boy's mother identified it as one discarded by her daughter. After that embarrassment, said Amiel, 'I sort of never forgot it.' As with so many of Amiel's emotional descriptions of her impoverished youth, the veracity of that story was hard to judge. Then, with a slight pause, she added a sincere confessional conclusion to Reed: 'And now I have an extravagance that knows no bounds.' With over thirty years' experience in the media and as a director of a publicly owned company, Amiel understood the impression of wealth and power she had created.

During those first weeks of 2002, Conrad Black sensed the increasing gravity of Hollinger's debts. Hollinger International's accumulated losses in 2002 – engineered by Jack Boultbee to avoid taxes – would be $238 million, compared to the previous year's losses of $337 million. The combination of financial engineering, the cabal's sucking of cash from the company and Hollinger's complicated structure had created a vicious circle that was slipping beyond Black's control.

The income of Hollinger Inc. in Canada and Ravelston depended entirely on management fees and dividends paid by Hollinger International in New York. As Hollinger International's profits declined, Hollinger Inc. in Canada could only survive on loans from Ravelston. To maintain those loans, Black ordered that Ravelston's management fees for 2002 should be set 'as high as possible'. Radler submitted an account to Hollinger for US$23.7 million (C$31 million) which the audit committee approved without protest. The total paid to the Black group during those two years in management and non-compete fees and expenses, despite the losses, was $110.6 million, including a salary to Black of US$6.5 million and a further US$1.9 million for Black-Amiel Management, transferred to their offshore account in Barbados. Hollinger's unorthodox finances were themselves endangered by Black's strategy. As he sold off newspapers and Ravelston's fees were cut, Ravelston had less money to lend to Hollinger Inc. Black could have chosen to economise on his lifestyle, but he deemed that solution unacceptable. Instead, he arranged that the *Telegraph* should pay Hollinger International a dividend of £54.8 million in 2002, £15 million more than its pre-tax profits. To no avail, Charles Moore protested about the squeeze, which denied the newspaper vital investment. Seeking an explanation, Jeremy Deedes could only repeat: 'I don't know what happens when the money gets to New York.'

Some of the money taken from the *Telegraph* was required by Black to fund Trireme Associates, a new venture capital company established by Richard Perle and specialising in the defence industry, an unusual investment for a newspaper company. In February 2002 Perle was asking Black to commit $25 million to Trireme. Black's quandary was whether he dared to snub the director who had helpfully approved the non-compete payments without appearing to read the documents. Perle's reward for that chore, Black believed, was already generous. Every month he was spending up to $6,000 on his Hollinger American Express card to buy groceries and meals in restaurants, and in 2000 and 2001 he had received $3.1 million under the Digital incentive plan, despite the company's losses. Nevertheless, he seemed to want more. There was, Black complained to Peter Atkinson, 'a good deal of nest-feathering being conducted by Richard', and his demands were increasing. Perle had promised Henry Kissinger $25,000 plus expenses for attending each meeting as a director of Trireme.

Kissinger had accepted the offer, and Perle was awaiting Black's agreement to invest before he finalised the details. Even Black baulked at Perle's demand. 'I am,' he told Atkinson, 'well aware of Richard's shortcomings [as] a trimmer and a sharper.' But eventually Perle's 'repertoire of histrionics, cajolery and utilisation of fine print' persuaded Black that Hollinger should invest $2.5 million in Trireme without consulting the Hollinger board. Having invested the money, Black was sore. Perle had recorded a $25 million commitment by Hollinger. 'My instinct told me,' Black admitted, '[that Perle was] trying to smoke one past us . . . but [he] should treat us as insiders with our hands cupped as the money flows down, and not as outsiders pouring in the money'.[3] After hearing that Perle had awarded himself an annual salary of $500,000, Black pledged that he would not invest any more money. He had little choice.[4]

In the last weeks of March 2002, as Hollinger's financial results were being computed, Black was irritated by Paul Healy reporting that Tweedy Browne was asking more questions about Ravelston's management fees. The atmosphere, Black knew, had changed. The public's demand for the punishment of corporate greed among America's banks, insurance companies and mega-corporations was inflicting fatal wounds. Among the latest targets were over twenty executives at Enron; Dennis Kozlowski, accused of plundering Tyco International of $600 million to fund his lifestyle; Frank Quattrone, a prominent investment banker in the high-tech industry, accused but later acquitted of obstructing justice; and Martha Stewart, the TV lifestyle guru, accused of insider trading. Black preferred to dismiss such prosecutions as reminiscent of Michael Milken's persecution in the 1980s. Once again, just as Tom Wolfe had so brilliantly exposed in *The Bonfire of the Vanities*, low-paid state prosecutors, motivated by 'spite and envy', were seeking wealthy scapegoats to please the rabble. Any hint of reassessment or retreat in front of Tweedy Browne, Black reasoned, might be interpreted as surrender or, worse, an admission of his own guilt. 'It's an epidemic of shareholder idiocy,' he impatiently scoffed to Healy about the fund manager's questions. Tweedy Browne, like the other complainants, he protested, were 'a bunch of self-righteous hypocrites and ingrates, who give us no credit for what has been a skilful job'.[5] Rather than consider how to placate Chris Browne, he relied on insults and flew to Palm Beach.

The house on South Ocean Boulevard had not proved quite the attraction he had envisaged. Although Donald Trump, Brian Mulroney, Ronald Lauder, Alfred Taubman and Al Haig were interesting neighbours, Amiel was an unenthusiastic visitor to the resort. However, Black himself found the lazy, luxurious life in the sunshine blissful. Writing the biography of Roosevelt in his study, occasionally gazing through the sunlit palm trees at the ocean, was idyllic. While the cook prepared lunch, the gardener tended the lawn and the cleaner was removing every speck of dust from the paintings and artefacts, he mused about money and power. The book, he reassured himself, was a palliative while others plotted Hollinger's fate. Some years earlier he had condemned Bud McDougald for being 'a prisoner of his dreams' while living in Florida, but there was, he reasoned, little equivalence between his own and McDougald's life, other than the fact that they shared a great talent.[6] The only irritating interruptions were calls from Jack Boultbee and others who were completing Hollinger International's annual report to the Securities and Exchange Commission. A complication had arisen. To avoid trouble in the future, Torys, the company's lawyers, were suggesting that the directors offer more disclosures to the SEC. Hollinger would need to reveal that following the sale of the remaining US newspapers for $215 million, Black and his group had received $15.6 million in non-compete fees. The payment, the report would state, had been approved by the independent directors. That was inaccurate.

The payments had not all been fully approved by the independent directors, and the payments were, as usual, not genuine. But the beauty of the plan was the apparent imprimatur of Torys. Black believed that his defence against any criticism for the mistakes was in place.[7] More worrying was the requirement, for the first time since 1999, to reveal that 'certain members of the board' owned a controlling interest in Horizon and Bradford;[8] and, Black was told, the company would need to divulge Barbara Amiel's accumulated income of $1.1 million from the *Chicago Sun-Times*. At KPMG's insistence the annual report also stated, 'Lord Black is our controlling shareholder and there may be a conflict between his interests and your interests,' and added: 'Entities affiliated with Lord Black and other officers and directors of the company engage in significant transactions with the company, which transactions may not necessarily be consummated on an arm's-length basis.' After considerable argument, Black also agreed that the report should disclose the receipt by Ravelston of $6 million, that Radler received $3.1 million and Colson $1.8 million. He forbade KPMG to verify those payments independently. 'They weren't invited to inspect the accounts,' he would say, furious that 'KPMG made it look like we diddle our shareholders. That's not what you pay auditors for.' The disclosures irritated Black. Unknown to the SEC, he and Radler had never revealed their income of $226 million in management fees from Hollinger between 1996 and 2003, or how they had finessed the CanWest non-compete fees. That information remained firmly concealed.[9] Each bit of extra information was a gift to his critics, and he feared that their numbers were increasing.

Leon Cooperman, a maverick investor, was one of those malcontents. On a trip to Palm Beach in late March, Cooperman asked for a meeting. Over lunch he warned Black to change his game. 'Everyone knows,' said Cooperman, 'that you're pumping money from Hollinger to yourself. You're just a minority shareholder with special voting rights. If the relationship between Ravelston and Hollinger isn't ended, the share price will carry on falling.' Black smiled. There was no need to worry, he assured Cooperman. The company's performance was improving, the dividends would increase and costs were coming down. The share price, he insisted, would rise. Cooperman appeared to be satisfied. Black, he decided, was trustworthy. After all, a rise in the share price was in everyone's interests. He looked forward, he smiled, to the shareholders' meeting on Tuesday, 23 May 2002 at the Metropolitan Club in New York.

In the weeks before then, Black realised that he would fail to beat Bud McDougald's record of a thirteen-minute shareholders' meeting. Laura Jereski was inundating Paul Healy with questions about the management fees paid to Ravelston and the CanWest non-compete fees. Mistakenly, she believed that the four Hollinger directors had received $23.8 million from CanWest, rather than the actual figure of $51.8 million. 'We must do the right thing,' Healy repeatedly told Black. Keeping Tweedy Browne pacified, Black realised, depended on retaining Healy's trust. Under the heading 'Epidemic of Shareholder Idiocy', he sent an email to Healy: 'I am assembling material to rebut these foolish questions. I don't think it will be particularly difficult to do so.'[10] He also offered to meet Browne and Jereski again. 'I see it as an opportunity as much as a challenge,' he wrote, 'to present the answers Laura wants pre-emptively, thoroughly, plausibly, truthfully and courteously. Much as I would like to just blow their asses off, I don't want to sour the atmosphere at the shareholders' meeting.' The invitation was rejected by Browne. Black understood that there would be a public showdown with shareholders, a unique experience in his career. Keeping all his supporters in line would require as much effort as answering his critics. In particular, he was concerned by Peter Atkinson's doubts about the non-compete fees. The opportunity to restore Atkinson's nerve would arise at Hollinger Inc.'s annual general meeting in Toronto, before the more crucial shareholders' meeting in New York.

Glancing at his watch to note that he was unusually punctual, Conrad Black arrived at the AGM with Barbara Amiel, and spotted Peter Atkinson on the dais. Nearby were Radler, Colson, Boultbee and Kipnis. Leaving Amiel to sit in the front row of the audience, he walked towards Atkinson, smiling his greeting. Close up to the lawyer, Black's face remained benign as he hissed in monotone anger, 'You're an absolute wimp, a wimp. I've never seen such wimpishness.' 'We'll talk about it,' replied Atkinson, 'because it's accurate.' 'Courage,' interrupted Black, terminating the exchange.[11] The public meeting passed uneventfully. Led by a bodyguard, the Blacks were walking together towards the exit when Amiel, staging an exchange for the cameras, laughingly whispered in Black's ear, 'You couldn't resist, could you, Conrad?' 'Resist what?' he smiled, bewildered. 'A few pungent remarks about Canada.' Black replied appreciatively, 'Oh no. If you want pungent, I'll give you pungent.' Here was abiding proof of pure teamwork.

Lunch for his directors afterwards was a jolly occasion. Fred Eaton, Don Fullerton and Allan Gottlieb were joined by Maureen Sabia, a new director and an old school friend of Amiel's whose family had welcomed the homeless girl before she went to university. Sabia proclaimed herself an expert in corporate governance, but over lunch she did not raise any questions about Black's conduct. Only Gottlieb was slightly discomfited as Black launched into an hour's discourse about international trouble spots. During a trip to London, Gottlieb had noticed in British society magazines the Blacks' appetite for publicity and social climbing. Troubled, he commented to another director that Barbara appeared to be eager for wealth on any terms, but nothing was said to Black. The directors were paid to keep quiet about their powerlessness. By the end of the lunch, as intended, Black's lecture had prevented any discussion of the company's affairs. Satisfied, he departed.

One month later, Amiel was sitting in the front row of the audience at the Metropolitan Club in New York for Hollinger International's annual meeting. On the platform, Conrad Black appeared calm. He had persuaded Kissinger, Kravis and the other independent directors that their attendance was unnecessary. Accustomed to public speaking, he was unruffled by the unusual sight of stern-faced fund managers below. His speech had been carefully crafted. Reflecting his Byzantine corporate structures, it would be full of convoluted, jargon-infested sentences. Density rather than clarity was his apparent objective. By confounding them with a blanket of smog, he expected the experts to be placated.

Reassuringly, Amiel seemed impervious to the mood. She had never doubted her entitlement to over $3 million of the shareholders' money. While she could write eloquently about the iniquities of those who relied on state benefits, she unquestioningly assumed her own right to satisfy her desires. The sentiments of the shareholders surrounding her were best ignored. Amiel gazed at her husband as he spoke, and despite her intelligence had as much difficulty in understanding him as did his professional audience. After fifteen minutes, Black interpreted the hush across the packed room as evidence that the dissidents had been squashed. Defiance, he decided, was an appropriate defence.

Nothing interrupted the silence except his voice. Everything, he told the shareholders, had been disclosed; everything had been approved; and all the internal deals had benefited shareholders. 'You bet *they* benefited,' said one man in the audience loudly, jerking his head towards Radler and the other executive directors sitting on the stage with Black. Envy and spite, Black thought, looking at the muttering disbelievers among his audience. Rather than suppressing his anger and offering emollience, he impulsively turned on his critics. 'You're charlatans,' he scoffed, 'with a talent for agitation.' The echo of his last words, normally a moment of self-satisfaction, had barely faded before he spotted Laura Jereski walking towards the microphone. As she spoke, he became increasingly consumed by irritation at the woman's nagging voice.

Why, asked Jereski, had $23.8 million of non-compete fees been paid to Black and Radler personally in the CanWest deal, and not to 'our company'. The phrase stung Black. Hollinger, she continued, was after all the only company that could actually compete with CanWest. Black smiled. Fortunately, Jereski did not realise that the non-compete fees had been taken from the purchase money. That was not the moment to retreat, he felt, but to counter-attack, regardless of the dangers. Izzy Asper of CanWest, said Black, had 'demanded' that Hollinger's directors sign non-compete agreements and personally accept the fees. The whole arrangement, he continued, 'was not a matter negotiated directly by us. And, I suppose there's room for debate here, but in all circumstances, the independent directors did what they thought best.' Black knew the dangers of uttering that misinformation. Izzy Asper had never stipulated that Black should personally receive the fees, nor had CanWest fixed the amount, nor had Hollinger's independent directors negotiated the payments. Black was relying on bluff. Summoning the image of the famous independent directors would, he hoped, silence the doubters. He was disappointed.

Chris Browne was the next to step to the microphone. Why, he asked, did Ravelston take such hefty management fees? Why didn't Black just take a salary from Hollinger, the company which employed him exclusively? Black smiled. There was nothing illegal in overpaying himself, and his directors had unanimously approved Ravelston's fees, but it would be wise to remain circumspect. Obfuscation, he believed, would again succeed. 'I've only received a couple of million,' he replied, ignoring the $6.6 million he had admitted receiving that year from Ravelston. 'We are assured,' he continued, 'by independent advisors that the [Ravelston management] fee is at the conservative end of the range of practice . . . The normal cost for outsourcing these services . . . is two-and-a-half-times cost. We are paid much less than that, and a substantially smaller percentage of our corporate revenues than most media businesses managed in this way.'[12] Black knew that between 1997 and 2003 Hollinger had paid Ravelston $218.4 million in management fees, and a further $200 million for directors' fees and expenses. He also knew that independent advisers had never properly investigated the fees, and that 'two-and-a-half times cost' was a fantasy figure plucked out of the air to conceal the fact that Hollinger was being charged twenty-nine times the estimated real costs. Browne remained suspicious, but said nothing. Others, he knew, would press the point.

The next question again raised the CanWest non-compete fees. That money, Black said with a dismissive wave, was 'not a matter directly negotiated by us . . . we effectively handed it to the independent directors to determine'. This was, Black knew, piling one fiction upon another, but no one among his audience could puncture his fairy tales.[13] The tension was rising. In a biting Bronx drawl, the next questioner told Black to strip out all the sweetheart deals and conflicts of interest. Black rose. Over the years he had consistently remained cool under fire. Operating under pressure was not unusual for him. He intended to profess his innocence with a smile. The suspicion, he replied, about his 'unethical' behaviour was unjustified: 'I realise that I seem to be swimming upstream here against a current of opinion, that this is a complete scam and is just a back-door payoff to the executives of the vendor company. That isn't the case . . . You're not dealing with greed here, and you're not dealing with sneakiness.'[14] Warming to his declaration of purity, he continued, with an air of injured innocence, 'We haven't been sitting here feathering our nest.' Black's self-protection became theatrical. 'I would be shocked, I would be shocked, if I thought either you or Chris Browne were trying to suggest there was anything unethical about what we're doing.' Whatever had been done, he said with pained sincerity, 'has not been done unethically – or even greedily'.

Black's repeated assertions of innocence only aroused suspicion, and the mood soured. Edward Shufro, an investment manager, ambled to the microphone to deliver a body blow: 'I've been listening to what my distinguished colleagues have been saying to you. They're trying to be polite about it, but what they're telling you is that they consider you to be a thief, and I can't say that I have any disagreement with that whatsoever.' The electricity sparked. 'Thief' hit Black in the solar plexus. 'Then you shouldn't be here,' Black shot back, attempting to arouse some sympathy as the victim of an undignified smear. 'Well, I'm here,' countered Shufro. 'Sell your shares and get out,' said Black, his fury mounting. In Canada or Britain he could have sued Shufro for slander, but in New York the law offered him no such protection. His final remark was lame: 'If you think I'm a thief, go. I'm not going anywhere.' In that embittered atmosphere, the meeting ended. Black was under no illusion. Wounded, he needed to gauge his vulnerability. He rushed over to Chris Browne. 'I can't believe he suggested I was a thief,' said Black plaintively. Sensing Black's weakness, Browne played an unrevealing poker hand. 'I'm not ready to call you a crook,' he replied, adding, after a brief pause, the word 'yet'. Without expression he concluded, 'I'll keep an open mind.'[15] He suspected Black of greed, not crime.

Black drove to Hollinger's headquarters for lunch with the company's directors. Too upset to attend, Amiel returned to the Park Avenue apartment. In the afternoon she was linked by telephone to a conference call of all the directors including Perle, Thompson, Taubman, Kravis, Kissinger and Richard Burt. Sitting in the boardroom with Radler, Boultbee and Atkinson, Black directed his comments towards the tiny microphones inlaid into the surface of the mahogany table. 'The shareholders' meeting was perfectly in order,' he reported, 'but I hope you will all attend next year.' Healy suppressed his agitation, but soon after the teleconference he rang Mark Kipnis and David Radler. Governor Thompson, he said, should be told about the shareholders' questions. Both agreed, but did nothing.

To Black's relief, the *Wall Street Journal* and the *New York Times* only briefly reported the meeting. Both newspaper groups, like Hollinger, were controlled by minority shareholders with specially weighted votes, and the editors of both papers deemed the publication of any unsubstantiated criticism of Black to be undesirable. Irritatingly for Black, the *New York Post*, owned by Rupert Murdoch, was not similarly constrained. With Murdoch's blessing, the *Post* revealed Black's embarrassment in gory detail.

Black flew to London, where his problems remained unknown. From there he called Healy to protest. 'This is my company,' he said, in a slurred voice suggesting too much white wine. 'I will decide what the board knows and when they know it.' Emboldened in his sanctuary, he railed against the 'rabble rousers' seeking a quick profit by 'shaming or bullying, or aggravating us into a liquidation'.[16] The shareholders, he reassured Healy, were too weak to overthrow him: 'They will have to live with it.' On sober reflection, Black realised the dangers of Healy's honesty. 'Paul's trying to be a boy scout,' Radler had told Black, and placating him would be more sensible than chastising him. Black agreed. He believed in the self-fulfilment of his prophecies. With total conviction, he spun an illusion to Healy: 'The drama will change from *King Lear* to *Julius Caesar* (minus the last act, one dares to hope). So be of good heart . . . Profits will rise, borrowings will wither and loyal shareholders will flourish.' He knew it was untrue, but he trusted in his powers of delusion. By pretending to commit Hollinger to a more conventional future, he hoped the past could be ignored. There was no alternative script. He had no intention of curtailing his excesses. To his good fortune, Healy succumbed to his performance. 'Fine, no problem,' Healy replied. Few of Hollinger's employees could withstand Black's ability to suck the air out of the room.[17]

Peter Atkinson's complaints, however, were less easy to dismiss. The lawyers had been warning Black for many weeks that the New York shareholders would not be satisfied by long words and caustic reprimands instead of cost-cutting. 'Cut all the useless clubs,' Atkinson wrote to Black, 'the unnecessary tables, the investments that are fun to be in but useless to the bottom line.' He suggested abandoning the Gulfstream and reducing the management fees. Black was unconciliatory. Even, he replied, if he was justly accused of 'running a gravy train and a gerrymandered share structure', he had no intention of 'making excessive concessions to the Rod "Hysteria" school of corporate governance', an ironic reference to Rod Ashtaryeh, a banker who was asking searching questions about Hollinger's costs.[18] The Gulfstream, he admitted, was an unjustified luxury, but, he insisted in an email on 5 August 2002, 'I am not prepared to re-enact the French Revolution renunciation of the rights of nobility.' Black's florid prose concealed a sharp calculation. If he succumbed to his critics, he would lose face, social status and possibly his wife. Far better to maintain the fiction that, as the founder-builder-manager of the business, he could perform as a proprietor. Surviving on the edge was his strength. His self-esteem was sustained by his contempt for critical shareholders. All he wanted was to use their money. Atkinson, he feared, was wavering. Survival depended on all the cabal singing from the same hymn sheet. 'We are proprietors, after all,' he told his lawyer, 'beleaguered though we may be . . . We have said for some time that [Hollinger International] served no other purpose as a listed company other than the relatively cheap use of other people's capital.' Recording such opinions in emails showed either naïvety or recklessness, but changing a lifetime's habit had become impossible for Black. 'We have a certain style,' he wrote to the cabal and Colson, 'that all these shareholders were well aware of when they came in. We should fine-tune that style, not revolutionise it with a Damascene conversion to vows of poverty.' While accepting the need for 'minor adjustments', he rejected any 'intolerable adjustment' and insisted that he would not 'abdicate and declare all perquisites to be corrupt'. Hence, he concluded with a flourish, Atkinson's request that he refund the cost of his trip to Bora Bora was unacceptable.[19]

Atkinson would not let go. Chris Browne, he reported, had again asked for details of the special payments. 'What right,' replied Black, 'does Browne have to pry his nose into those payments? Just because he's a shareholder is irrelevant.' Atkinson was unmoved. Black knew the rules and the laws. The lawyer insisted that his employer retreat. To show willing, Black agreed to reduce Ravelston's fees by $2 million, from $24 million to $22 million, and to send Browne an emollient note. The letter, delivered on 11 June, promised transparency in the future, and no more surprises.[20] Browne assumed that Black had noted that the recent Sarbanes-Oxley Act imposed onerous new duties upon directors of public companies to disclose their activities and open their company to scrutiny. He was mistaken.

London immunised Black to Manhattan's harshness. The flock of guests attending his annual summer party had not bothered to read the reports from New York about Hollinger, nor were they aware of the controversy over the funding of their food and drink. None of them, in the infatuated atmosphere, could have imagined that Black had charged the *Telegraph* $380,000 in expenses that year, and would add another $24,950 for that evening's party. Andrew Neil, the former editor of the *Sunday Times*, was the exception. Over lunch he said to Black, 'You've got to be careful now with the Sarbanes-Oxley law.' Black's immaculate reply doused Neil's concern: 'All my shareholders love me, and no one has ever lost money with me.' There would be no change in their lives, Black later reassured his wife. During those early summer days Barbara Amiel had telephoned Jacob Rothschild about their invitation to Jayne Wrightsman's birthday party. She suggested to the banker that guests contribute £5,000 towards a painting as a present for Wrightsman. 'No, thank you,' replied Rothschild. 'She's an old friend, and I'll make my own arrangements.' Amiel had also urged Black to buy the American *Spectator* magazine and appoint John O'Sullivan as editor. Black's negotiations failed, but Amiel's sense of limitless wealth remained undiminished.

Ecstasy spread in the Blacks' household in early July as Black and Amiel excitedly looked through *Vogue*'s glossy pages showing Amiel shimmering in an Oscar de la Renta ballgown and dripping with diamond and amethyst jewellery bought from Fred Leighton and Graf. Black's pride swelled, especially as he read the description of himself as 'one of the world's wealthiest men'. Two days later, after the magazine had gone on sale in New York, the couple appeared at a $1,000-a-plate charity dinner at Cipriani's in SoHo, a restaurant famous for 'Eurobabes air kissing'.[21] Amiel greeted friends more enthusiastically than usual, ceaselessly seeking congratulations for the article promoting Lord and Lady Black. The millions spent on her clothes and jewellery, their smiles confirmed, had been clearly justified.

Fifteen blocks south of the Blacks' apartment on Park Avenue, Chris Browne reread Amiel's confession – 'And now I have an extravagance that knows no bounds' – several times. He was staggered. 'The happy ending to the story,' Julia Reed, the *Vogue* interviewer, concluded, 'is that these days she can easily afford such extravagance.' To Browne, Reed's judgement was as irritating as her description of Conrad Black as 'one of the world's wealthiest men'. Reed's apparently heartfelt belief that Amiel had 'had the last laugh' on her critics was provocative to the disenchanted.

Across the city, the non-believers compared Amiels' extravagance to that of Imelda Marcos, the widow of the former Philippines dictator, whose profligacy notoriously included the purchase of thousands of pairs of shoes. Even those who were unsuspicious of Hollinger's finances were jolted by Amiel's vulgarity. In Canada, Hal Jackman decided, 'Barbara is sort of an absurd person.' John Fraser's criticism was more subtle: 'Barbara's just doing what Conrad wanted out of life.' Amiel tried to excuse her assertion as 'irony', and Julia Reed was belatedly summoned to agree that she had spoken 'not without irony', but there was no escape. The derision was haunting.

Attempting to extinguish that fire did not distract Black from a more important chore. The Canadian Imperial Bank of Commerce and the Toronto-Dominion Bank, his traditional lenders, had refused to renew their loans to Hollinger of $120 million. Since Don Fullerton's retirement Black's relationship with CIBC, despite his own directorship, was strained. A short-term loan of £90 million at a high interest rate now needed to be repaid, and for some weeks Black had searched for new banks. 'I'm Conrad Black,' he told Healy. 'Why aren't the banks agreeing to lend me the money I want?' The reality was unpalatable. Tweedy Browne's criticism had reduced Hollinger's rating to junk. To borrow money, Black would be compelled to pledge his own shares as security. Effectively, he had become a prisoner of the banks. Unable to control his destiny, on Healy's suggestion he assigned the task of finding new lenders to the Wachovia Bank, based in Charlotte, North Carolina.

Black was in a curious position. Hollinger owned genuine assets and was a good business, yet it was mistrusted. The solution, he agreed with Healy was to raise a loan using high-yield bonds. 'We'll just hedge it,' smiled Healy. Black nodded, not quite understanding the technical process. 'To get the market's support,' continued Healy, 'all that's necessary is to reduce the management fees. We've go to stop the leakage. The limit will be $25 million, and then it'll be OK.' Reluctantly, Black nodded his agreement.

To secure the loans, Black was dispatched by Wachovia's bankers during August to brief investors and analysts that Hollinger's profits were rising and that the management fees would be reduced. 'It's going well,' he told Healy, wondering whether he should draw any conclusions from newspaper reports about the imminent indictment of Dennis Kozlowski, the chief executive of Tyco International, whose lurid excesses had included a birthday party for his wife in Sardinia funded by the company and centred around an ice sculpture of Michelangelo's *David* with pure vodka squirting from its penis. On reflection, Kozlowski's plight did not cause Black to ponder his own exposure. Rather, he assured himself of divine protection. After all, no one in Toronto or New York had bothered to report Paul Winkler's success against Hollinger in the British Columbia courts. After the case was concluded Winkler had tried to interest the media in Radler's duplicity, but he found no response.

The moment seemed appropriate for Black to restore confidence among his clan, and more importantly to justify his own conduct for posterity. In early September he sent a memorandum to Ravelston's executives praising their success despite the critics, and reasserting their credo: 'These companies have always been run in the Argus tradition of proprietary businesses where the controlling shareholders take reasonable steps to ensure their comfortable enjoyment of the position they (we, in fact) have created for themselves. Care must be taken not to allow this to denigrate into decadence, as it did in the old Argus. But nor should we allow the agitations of shareholders, amplified by certain of our colleagues discountenanced at the performance of their stock options, to force us into a hair shirt, the corporate equivalence of sackcloth and ashes.'[22] Considering the prevailing turbulence in Wall Street, Black wisely avoided defining 'decadence'.

Shortly after, a representative of the Wachovia Bank, searching through Hollinger's accounts, discovered Black's purchase of the FDR papers. Black was asked to provide evidence of his authority to spend $8 million of Hollinger's money. He replied that the purchase had been authorised at a meeting of the company's executive committee – Perle, Radler and himself – in December 2000, and added that his offer to buy the papers himself at 'a bargain price' had been rejected by Hollinger's directors. News of the exchange between Black and the banker flummoxed Paul Healy, who knew that the board of directors were unaware of the purchase. 'There's no alternative,' insisted Healy. 'You must get retrospective authorisation by the board of directors.' Potentially, the procedure was embarrassing for Black, but the board's minutes on 13 March 2003 recorded the directors' 'unanimous' approval of 'a corporate investment of no benefit to the chairman', with no independent valuation of the papers. Two years later the papers would be sold by Christie's for $2.4 million, but at the last moment the National Archives intervened and declared that the collection was possibly property belonging to the US government.

The successful camouflage coincided with a fall of Hollinger's share price back to $9. Accurate rumours began circulating that TD Securities had withdrawn from negotiations to lend $500 million to the company with Black's shares as the security. The bank's reason was Hollinger's accumulated losses of US$576 million by the beginning of 2003. Although these were not all cash losses but some write-downs to gain tax advantages, the rumours of a crisis reached Richard Desmond, the owner of Express Newspapers in London. Desmond shared a printing plant with the *Telegraph*, which had led to an argument and a court case two years earlier between himself and Black. At the end of the trial the judge, Sir Andrew Morritt, had declared Desmond's evidence to be unreliable and found in Black's favour.[23] Now Desmond ordered the *Daily Express* to report that Hollinger was 'facing its biggest crisis ever' after a 'credit facility was cancelled by its bankers'.[24] Black was horrified. TD Securities had withdrawn because they were suffering a succession of bad debts from other clients and were unwilling to disentangle Hollinger's finances. Nevertheless, the unease, as Black knew, was justified, although he was relieved that no one in London was aware of his problems. Even the famous personalities on his advisory board, including Lord Carrington, Lord Weidenfeld and Sir Evelyn Rothschild, appeared to have ignored the American newspaper reports about Hollinger's plight. To protect himself and to suppress the truth, he sued Desmond and the *Express* for libel. 'There is no cash crisis, nor any prospect of one,' he said in a short statement. To rapidly defuse the row, a mediator was appointed, and Black and Desmond were told to go into a room and hammer out a deal. 'I'm looking forward to your book on Roosevelt,' said the mediator as the two men stood up, 'because I did my university thesis on FDR.' Black stopped and began a thirty-minute speech about Roosevelt, while Desmond sat bemused. The tension was broken and a settlement was agreed, accepting Black's insistence that there was no financial crisis. Victory against Desmond, a tough operator, vindicated Black's remorseless pursuit of challengers. Grinding his critics into the dust had never failed.

At the beginning of 2003 Black set off on a flying tour across the USA with the Wachovia bankers to sell Hollinger's bonds to other banks. Even in that desperate cause, he could not shrug off his habits. Congenitally unpunctual, to the bankers' surprise he showed a meagre grasp of detail during the presentations. Too lazy to master his brief, he dismissed problems with a kneejerk response: 'We can get around that.' By March, nevertheless, the bank had secured a loan of $120 million, although the interest rate was a massive 13 per cent.

Black flew to Palm Beach to finish his book. Sitting in his beautiful study overlooking the sea, he did not doubt the certainty of survival. America and its allies had invaded Iraq, and during his regular conversations with Charles Moore in London and all his famous friends including Henry Kissinger and Richard Perle, Black was reassured of his own importance. A lifetime of wealth and privilege had immunised him to fear. In anticipation of their success he invited Wachovia's bankers and Hollinger's executives to celebrate in Palm Beach. Thankfully for Black, the bankers had arranged the loan despite a fundamental flaw in Hollinger's finances. The loan was given to Hollinger Inc. in Toronto and the security was Black's shares; Ravelston guaranteed the annual repayments to the banks; but Ravelston could only pay the money on receipt of income from Hollinger International in New York; and Hollinger International survived thanks to loans from its Canadian parent company, Hollinger Inc; and that company relied on loans from Ravelston. The circle was completed because Ravelston only had money if it was paid by Hollinger International in New York. Black had about one year to resolve the conundrum by reducing Ravelston's fees and expenses. He and Amiel decided to ignore that option.

To maintain his social status in New York, Black paid $100,000 at Hollinger's expense for a commemorative chair in his honour in the Hyde Park auditorium of the Franklin and Eleanor Roosevelt Institute. Funding Amiel's desire to play among Manhattan's A-list, he authorised at Hollinger's expense a $283,000 contribution to the New York Metropolitan Opera, a commitment to pay $100,000 for a gala in aid of the New York Public Library, and a continuing subsidy to the *New York Sun*, an unread conservative newspaper which had already consumed $2.5 million of Hollinger's dwindling funds. In addition there was Amiel's expenditure on four homes and in international fashion houses all linked by the Gulfstream. The Black group's total charges to Hollinger in 2003 would be $32.7 million, including $4.7 million for the use of the two aircraft. The total cost of the planes since 1995 had been $61.3 million. Black apparently never paused to reflect that Ravelston's annual fees in 2003 – $26 million – were $5 million more than the combined total paid by America's five biggest newspaper corporations to their chief executives, and the combined turnover of those five corporations was seven times bigger than Hollinger's. Since 1997 Black, Radler and the rest of their group had taken $401.7 million from Hollinger International, which was 95 per cent of the company's total adjusted net income. The total amount paid to Ravelston since 1997 equalled 76.3 per cent of the company's total adjusted net income.[25] In the same period the senior executives of the *New York Times* received 4.4 per cent of their company's net income, while those of the *Washington Post* took 1.8 per cent.

Peter Atkinson could no longer tolerate Conrad Black's refusal to taper his expenses. On 17 February 2003, he resigned from Hollinger. Black was horrified. The negotiations with Wachovia Bank to refinance Hollinger were in their final stages, and Atkinson's resignation would alarm the bankers. Beth DeMerchant was asked to broker a reconciliation. Within twenty-four hours she had steered the lawyer back into the fold, and the refinancing agreements were signed.[26]

The forty bankers and Hollinger executives who gathered at Black's home in Palm Beach for cocktails on 28 March 2003 were among the few not deluded by his image. Black could only afford to pay the interest on the loan. He had no cash to repay the loan itself. More important, everyone knew of the real difficulty he would have in finding $60 million by April 2004 to repay preferred shareholders. Only by dramatically cutting his expenses and fees could he hope to survive that time bomb. The truth was irrelevant to bankers earning healthy profits from Black's distress. Inevitably, the Blacks revealed no concern to their guests. Both had chosen to dress in elegant casual style – he in a blue jacket and light khaki trousers, and she in pale cargo slacks and a light brown top.

Sensitive to the importance of the occasion, Amiel was on full gush, cutting no one however unimportant; a welcome contrast, Black noted, to her unexplained refusals to attend lunches and dinners among Palm Beach's community. To humour his guests, Black gave them a conducted tour of the house, explaining the importance of the framed American flag – 'This flew over the White House on the day Franklin D. Roosevelt died,' he said solemnly – and then suggested that the party head for dinner at the Ritz-Carlton. The bill, he was pleased to note, would be paid by the bank. 'Conrad's still masquerading as a billionaire,' Dan Colson sighed to Paul Healy as they drove to the hotel. 'His spending is profligate,' he added grimly. At the end of the evening, Black contemplated a few weeks of peaceful writing beside the ocean before Hollinger's next annual general meeting in May. His only chore was to approve the annual accounts to be submitted to the SEC. As a result of the bankers' scrutiny, some costs and payments could no longer remain undisclosed. He relied on David Radler, Jack Boultbee and Peter Atkinson to comply with the stringent laws, and assumed that SEC officials would remain discreet.

Black's assumptions were wrecked on about 12 April 2003. To his horror Peter Lane, the newly appointed chief financial officer responsible for filing Hollinger's returns, had included a mass of confidential information about the company's debts. Instead of a 150-page submission, eight hundred pages were published on the web; included were details of the company's debts, the fees to Ravelston and, on page 633, the purchase of the FDR papers. That bombshell had not yet been spotted by Laura Jereski and other analysts wading through the mass of unexpected information, but enough had been disgorged for the financial village to shred Hollinger's reputation. The telephone calls to Black were ceaseless. Restraining his anger, his eyes rolling, he rocked in his chair. 'Things are tight,' Healy said to Black. 'Don't use that sort of expression,' Black reprimanded him, 'unless you're referring to women's stockings.'

Denying the truth was Black's talent. His response, he decided, would be flat refutation. The company, he told callers, was in 'rude health'. There was, he insisted, 'no bank debt'. While he admitted that there were difficulties about paying some operating costs, 'these are small problems raked over by people who simply don't understand the business'. His smokescreen was destroyed by Laura Jereski and Chris Browne, whose examination revealed the five directors drawing huge fees and expenses from a hugely indebted company. Their interest was no longer about profit, but principle and probity. On 16 April Tweedy Browne declared war on Conrad Black. Journalists were briefed about the fees paid to Ravelston and the conflicts of interest. In turn, they telephoned Black in Palm Beach for comment. The call from the *Sunday Times* was particularly threatening; Black assumed that Rupert Murdoch was personally interested in demolishing his rival. Black's options were limited. He could have replied that he was addressing the problems. Instead he chose to fuel the flames. Jereski, he told the *Sunday Times* journalist, was 'ludicrous'. All the deals between Hollinger and himself, he said, had given the shareholders 'an advantage over myself'. Shareholders, he intoned solemnly, could rely on 'our distinguished group of directors', and to those who disapproved he offered his wisdom: 'We are not running a Christian Science meeting here, where we all have to sing from the same hymn sheet. Anyone who complains can take a hike.'[27] The *Sunday Times* report on 20 April sparked speculation in London about Black's imminent demise. 'Conrad's become a bully, strong meat, wooden, and a bulldozer,' a banking friend commented.

The next callers to Black from Toronto were greeted with a more careful performance: 'I'm sitting here in Palm Beach watching the majestically swaying royal palms in my garden, and I do not feel cornered and I am not against the wall.'[28] The truth was the opposite. Hollinger's revenues were too small to repay the debts. In conversations with the cabal, Black refused to consider that his run was nearly exhausted. Backdating documents to take money, he scoffed, had been normal in the Argus days, and he was not going to succumb to corporate terrorism and change his ways. Boultbee agreed. 'I think we should concentrate on taking steps to keep the management fees as high as possible,' he emailed on 1 May 2003.[29] Laziness clouded Black's imagination about the endgame. For the moment he would just talk and see how the cards fell. One person he could no longer wholly rely upon was David Radler. 'He took the glory on the way up,' Radler told Healy, 'so he can take the shit on the way down.' Under the pressure their relationship was nearly shattered.

In New York, Chris Browne was unimpressed by Black's refusal to be cowed. There was sufficient contempt in Black's responses to encourage the fund manager to delve further into the small print of Hollinger's past annual statements. He found reports of US$73 million of non-compete payments since 2000, some backdated, Hollinger's $2.5 million investment in Perle's company, and the sale of newspapers to Horizon. The independent directors taking Black's dollar, Browne concluded, appeared to have failed in their duty.

His suspicions were confirmed by Herbert Denton, the manager of Providence Capital, a small fund that owned 3 per cent of Hollinger's shares. After examining the company's annual corporate reports to the SEC, the '10K Filings', since 1999, Denton had noticed that Hollinger's unusually complex description of its activities had changed every year. 'You just get the feeling,' he told Browne, 'that he's skating right along the edge of every line imaginable. There's tension between himself and his lawyers.'[30] For example, he explained, after the sale of Hollinger newspapers to Bradford Publishing in 2000, Black signed a statement that some Hollinger directors 'are shareholders' of Bradford. But in 2003 Hollinger disclosed that some of its directors were 'significant shareholders'.

Chris Browne had no appetite either to orchestrate a campaign against Black or to institute legal action. That would be too costly. One option was to fan publicity about the failure of Kissinger, Kravis, Thompson and Burt. Those self-important personalities would scream about the embarrassment, compounding Black's predicament. Another option, which he chose on 7 May, was to leak Black's investment in Perle's company to a journalist, suggesting accurately that Hollinger's directors had not been consulted. 'Our purpose,' said Browne emolliently, 'is in no way meant to impugn the integrity of the current independent directors ... However, the facts known to us do not pass our smell test.' Governor Thompson and Marie-Josée Kravis were embarrassed. Three days later, Browne formally asked the SEC – under a procedure called Section 13D – to investigate the non-compete payments. The request was accompanied by a letter to Hollinger's directors asking for an investigation. If they refused, Browne hinted, they would be vulnerable to costly lawsuits. At the same time, Browne also suggested to Black that Bert Denton should examine Hollinger's payments to Ravelston. 'That's deliberately provocative,' Black snorted. Browne and Denton, he said, merely wanted to enrich themselves at Ravelston's expense: 'The notion of an antagonistic forensic scavenger hunt [by a] total stranger ... with public allegations posturing in a tendentious media circus' was, he replied, unacceptable. Nevertheless, he did agree to an inquiry, albeit not 'to rummage through the past', but strictly restricted to the future. Each concession was too little, too late. Black, Denton concluded, was protecting his cover-up.

Similar thoughts struck Governor Thompson and Richard Burt. Voices were suddenly warning members of the audit committee about the risk of legal sanctions. Marie-Josée Kravis was particularly vulnerable. She and her husband were social friends of the Blacks, and Henry Kravis had endorsed Conrad Black as honest. In common with the other directors, she grappled to understand what was amiss. Conrad Black, the brilliant raconteur, she and her husband reassured themselves, was utterly trustworthy. Their combined judgement, the Kravises concluded, could not be faulty. Nevertheless, in calls to Black they sought explanations for the backdating of the non-compete payments. The questions unsettled Black. The directors, he sensed, were no longer as trusting as previously; some were even searching for a chance to escape. He needed to defuse the attack. Back in Manhattan, he composed his defence. While crafting a letter to his directors, he began to secretly negotiate the sale of his Hollinger shares to Southeastern, an investment fund, at a fire-sale price. There would be nothing in writing, he decided, just a handshake, but it would be enough to make an announcement at the appropriate moment, to buy time. He knew, of course, that he could not easily sell his shares to Southeastern, because they had been pledged to the Wachovia Bank as security for the $120 million loan, but Southeastern's managers appeared to be conveniently trusting.

Conrad Black's letter was written with the passion of an artist. He mentioned the 'sharp reduction' of Ravelston fees (the amount was $2 million); Bradford and Horizon, he wrote, had bought newspapers from Hollinger because 'there were no other buyers for these assets at sensible prices'; and he criticised Chris Browne as an 'antagonist' seeking to impose 'contemporary standards to past actions that were judged appropriate and fully disclosed at the time'. After a pause for thought, Black could not resist venting his spleen against the potential danger. Browne, he added, was a man in 'a very agitated condition' who had 'launched a systematic campaign of denigration' because he wanted to 'grasp at anything to find evidence of sinister practices'.[31] The letter, sent on 11 May, was received sympathetically. Governor Thompson, Richard Burt and Marie-Josée Kravis could not believe that Conrad Black, their friend and a close associate of Henry Kissinger, was culpable. Browne's proposal for an independent inquiry, they agreed, should be rejected. The appointment of an internal 'special committee' was sufficient. In gratitude, Black volunteered to surrender his controlling shares and fix his annual salary at about US$6.5 million and Radler's at $3 million. 'We'll think about that,' said a committee member. Black was relieved. 'Like all fads,' he replied with the air of a prestigious historian, 'corporate governance has its zealots and its tendency to excess.'

Satisfied that Browne had been neutralised, Black flew down to Palm Beach in a light-hearted spirit. Bob Colacello, a *Vanity Fair* writer, was chronicling an insider's account of life among the super-rich. The team were interviewing and photographing America's aristocrats who dressed in denim and diamonds for parties, revealing the opulence, prejudices and scandals of the enclave, not least the sexual antics, murders and frauds committed by its members. Initially the Blacks had declined to cooperate, but at the last moment they succumbed. On 18 May 2003 Jonathan Becker arrived to take their photograph. Unseen by Becker, Amiel had sampled endless outfits before appearing in the garden. A chair was standing near the statue of Poseidon. Within a few minutes, Becker had his pose. Black was seated, while Amiel, draped across the immaculate lawn, was gazing up at him adoringly. The electrifying image portrayed the couple as the masters of the universe. The atmosphere after the photographs were taken suggested normality. Over coffee, Black betrayed no evidence of anxiety as he charmed the photographer with humorous stories about his biography of Roosevelt.

There was little time to enjoy a house which Black would shortly afterwards describe as 'ridiculous, vulgar and absurd'.[32] In five days, on 23 May 2003, he was due back in the Metropolitan

Club for Hollinger's annual general meeting. The vituperation from the shareholders and the media, he knew, would be inescapable. During the Blacks' flight to New York, Chris Browne had publicly demanded an explanation from Black about his extraction of a particular $73 million from Hollinger; and before Black could even reply, a new complaint had been filed with the SEC accusing him of milking the company. Browne, Black realised, was no longer merely an irate investor. He was enjoying the chase against himself and the directors as a crusade for shareholders' rights.

Barbara Amiel finally understood the allegations facing her husband. As an intelligent woman with strongly voiced opinions on innumerable social and political issues, she had endlessly listened to Conrad Black's angry comments. While not mastering the intricacies of finance, she was satisfied that he was the victim of malice. Dressed in a blue-grey jacket and dark slacks, she entered the Metropolitan Club on 23 May searching for Paul Healy, who she knew had been frantically telephoning regulators and the stock exchange that morning in his efforts to explain Black's offer to sell Hollinger to Southeastern. 'Don't worry, Paul,' she told the distraught man, 'everything will be fine.' Healy had every reason to believe that Amiel, as a director of Hollinger, knew the full facts. 'I hope you're right,' he replied. 'Whatever you're taking,' he said to himself, 'I'd like to take some too, because it's clear where we're heading.'

Conrad Black had now arrived, and was waiting to make his choreographed entrance into the packed room with Amiel. Both knew that Henry Kissinger and Richard Burt had found reasons not to appear at the meeting. Black was unconcerned by the absence of those ornaments. Marie-Josée Kravis, Richard Perle and Governor Thompson were present. The principal celebrity Black produced to offer public support was the entrepreneur Donald Trump, who with his young girlfriend Melania Knauss had been positioned so as to be seen greeting the chairman and his wife on their walk along the centre aisle towards the rostrum. Black's conviction that the presence of Trump, condemned by some as a self-publicist and occasionally wrongly reported to be on the verge of bankruptcy, would reassure observers, created new qualms about his judgement. Like Black, Trump's capitalism ignored the morality of the new era. Those doubts were confirmed by Black's performance in front of his shareholders. In response to Tweedy Browne's request, he announced an internal inquiry by Governor Thompson, and the sale of his Hollinger shares to Southeastern, then paused to await the applause. Instead there was silence, followed by tough questions. 'You don't know what you're talking about,' he curtly replied, 'but you're still welcome as shareholders.'

The meeting was over. At least Black had not been accused of dishonesty. Steadily, he walked through the hall protected by a bodyguard, and emerged into the sunlight. His lines to the awaiting cameras and journalists had been prepared in advance, and he ignored the questions with a smile: 'Best meeting we've had in years. I tried to nominate Donald Trump's girlfriend as a director. Great meeting.' Pretending to be enjoying himself, he added another tease to exult in his phoney triumph: 'The shareholders are happy. It's fine. It was never a real story in the first place. It was invented by you people.' One issue, however, could not be discounted. In a newspaper interview, Peter Atkinson had cast doubt on the Southeastern deal. 'It's a complete myth that the Southeastern deal is in difficulties,' Black soothed, and launched into meaningless jargon to silence the questions. The puzzled expressions on the journalists' faces spelled success. 'You must be bored,' he quipped. 'I gotta go.'[33]

Over the following days, Black and Amiel congratulated themselves. The media were focusing on the sale to Southeastern and the special committee. 'Confession is good for the soul,' he told a caller on 25 May, blaming back-office cock-ups for his taking the non-compete fees without board approval. 'We've done nothing wrong. It'll all get sorted out.' Pleased with his coup he sought to smother his enemy. On 27 May he travelled down Park Avenue to see Chris Browne. 'Would you like to buy control of Hollinger?' Browne was asked. 'No, Conrad, I would not be interested. We invest in newspaper companies, we don't operate them.' Black was expressionless. Browne assumed the question was a charade to test his motives.[34] That night Black had dinner with Henry Kissinger. After sixteen years of friendship, the statesman trusted Black. 'What about Thompson's investigations?' he asked. If necessary, said Black, minimising their importance, he would repay any money owed. 'How much could that be?' enquired Kissinger.' 'At most $5 million,' replied Black, showing no sensitivity for Kissinger's own predicament.

In the early hours of 28 May, Black flew to London with Evelyn de Rothschild in the banker's jet. Rothschild had been a godparent at Black's baptism in London, but he would remain firmly in the shadows for the funeral. British newspapers were now reporting Black's problems in lurid detail. In his car from the airport, at 7.30 p.m. London time, Black read a particularly acerbic feature about himself and Amiel in the *Evening Standard*. The British tabloids were suddenly less restrained than the American press, although his ownership of the *Telegraph* provided some protection. News of his plight had prompted David Barclay, a secretive property developer based in the Channel Islands, to send a fax expressing his interest in buying the newspaper. 'Press accounts of our corporate activities,' Black had promptly replied, 'have been even more wildly inaccurate than usual – conditions are quite manageable. No assets are for sale.'

Walking at 8.30 p.m. into a party celebrating Lord Deedes's ninetieth birthday at the Travellers Club in Pall Mall, Black found the throng of journalists less respectful than previously. Partly it was the news from New York, but there were also doubts among some about the *Telegraph*'s credibility. The previous month, the newspaper had published documents allegedly found in an Iraqi government ministry in Baghdad 'proving' that the Labour MP George Galloway had secretly received money from Saddam Hussein. Outraged by Galloway's anti-Zionism, Black and Amiel had been delighted by his exposure. Neither had considered that he was the victim of gross defamation and sloppy journalism of the kind that had so often aroused their indignation in the past – indeed, Galloway was to be awarded £150,000 damages for defamation. Black's subdued manner at the party reflected his new vulnerability, although few present had heard about him being called a 'thief', and none doubted his honesty. At worst, Lord Deedes's son Jeremy thought, Black might do silly, vainglorious things, but he, like others, assumed the *Telegraph* was safe. No one contemplated telephoning Tweedy Browne for further information. Accordingly, during that week serious journalists continued to sing Conrad Black's praises. Roy Greenslade, the media commentator and former editor of the *Daily Mirror*, said openly, 'I don't think he's in any real trouble. Whatever he does, I'm sure it's going to be a wonderful surprise.' Boris Johnson, the Conservative MP and editor of the *Spectator*, agreed, describing Black as 'an obvious man of destiny, not least because he exudes a sense of purpose, drive and ambition'.[35]

Those qualities were not apparent at dinner in the Carlton Club that evening for friends and family to celebrate Bill Deedes's life. Seated between Margaret Thatcher and John Profumo, the disgraced former Minister, Black was strangely silent. Thatcher appeared incoherent, either because of a drug or mental disorientation. Two days later, Black was back on his Gulfstream. The routine, dubbed by Captain Ridley 'living like vampires', crossing the Atlantic at night, suited the passenger. During his time in London his interest in the *Telegraph* had been limited. The gullible Brits were deluding themselves while he searched for survival.

More important than the *Telegraph*'s fate was a report that day about a judgement by a Delaware court. To take advantage of lower costs and taxes, over half of America's corporations, including Hollinger International, had registered their headquarters in Delaware. The state's courts, conscious of the widespread concern about corporate governance, had already declared that company directors owed a 'duty of care' to their shareholders, who were repeatedly seeking to widen the interpretation of 'duty of care'. In a recent case shareholders had asked the court for the right to sue the directors of the Walt Disney Corporation for excessively compensating Michael Ovitz, the company's former president, with a severance payment of $140 million after just fifteen months' employment. The judge supported the shareholders. Company directors, he declared, could no longer defend their conduct by pleading that they had acted 'in good faith'. The directors' conduct, he found, was subject to censure and reversal by shareholders.

Reading that report, Black had no difficulty in imagining the alarm it would arouse among Hollinger's directors, especially Kravis. He would like to have felt able to rely on Paul Healy to pacify any unrest, but his trust in the former banker had waned. Ever since the public 'thief' accusation at the annual meeting in 2002, their relationship had become uneasy. In the previous weeks Healy had questioned Hollinger's relationship with Horizon, and the bonuses paid by Black and Radler to themselves from Hollinger Digital despite the company's losses. Black had chosen to confront rather than conciliate his employee. 'During the unpleasant developments last year,' he told Healy, referring to the discovery that Hollinger had been secretly charged for the FDR papers, 'I didn't get your wholehearted support. Your attitude implied that I had misappropriated or improperly purchased company property.' This was followed by a reduction of Healy's bonus payments. The battle lines were drawn.

Just three days later, at lunchtime on 3 June 2003, Amiel telephoned Black. Excitedly, she reported that she was eating lunch at Michael's restaurant on 55th Street and had just spotted Paul Healy. 'So what?' asked Black. 'Healy came up,' continued Amiel agitatedly, 'and he introduced me to the man with him. It was Bert Denton.' Foolishly, she said, she had allowed Denton to shake her outstretched hand before she could pull it back, her normal ploy towards those she disdained. 'I know about that,' Black replied. 'Paul told me.' Meeting Black's enemies was Healy's job. Not surprisingly, Black had not forewarned his wife.

Barbara Amiel's apparent self-portrayal as being ignorant of finance and business matters was characterised by her refusal to acknowledge that directors of public companies owed unambiguous legal obligations to their shareholders. In Amiel's philosophy, citizens appeared able to pick and choose which laws to ignore or obey. Just as, in her opinion, some Nazi war criminals were entitled to protection from certain aspects of international law, she appeared on occasion to justify the deceptions of the rich. To assist her husband's defence, she chose that moment to condemn the arrest of Martha Stewart, who had been accused of selling shares on the basis of inside information, in the *Daily Telegraph*. The prosecution was important not just because of Stewart's fame but because she was a director of the New York Stock Exchange. If Wall Street was run by liars, capitalism was surely doomed.

Yet Amiel argued that lying and insider dealing were irrelevant, since the state prosecutors were engaged in a vindictive crusade against celebrities.[36] Stewart, she proclaimed, was the victim of the 'pretty awful' legal process. To many, Amiel appeared to be indulging in special pleading on behalf of extravagance and dishonest tycoons. That did not play well in New York, where people were still gossiping about Amiel's excesses and the allegations against Black. Similarly, in London the juxtaposition of the allegations against Conrad Black and the image of revellers drinking Hollinger's pink champagne in Cottesmore Gardens while the Gulfstream was parked at Stansted airport jarred. Distressed by the antagonism, Black denied any profligacy. 'The opulence of my lifestyle is a myth,' he insisted, 'based on one well-attended cocktail party a year in London, not unlike that given by other newspaper companies in that city, and on one quotation from *Vogue* magazine from my wife, when she was in fact referring to handkerchiefs. My wife never liked parties, dislikes large houses, and prefers to live with a minimum of domestic help and make her own dinners or eat out. She does like stylish clothes, but is happy to pay for that from her own earnings. The attempt to portray her as a Marie Antoinette and me as a supine lovestruck spouse, like most comment on the subject, is a complete fiction.'[37]

The portrait of a modest, retiring wife was contradicted by Amiel's behaviour over the previous thirty years, although a new regime had been introduced by Black. 'Conrad says we've got to cut our spending,' Amiel told friends in London. Some noticed a particularly irritating new trait. At their regular girly lunches, Amiel would choose expensive dishes if her host was paying, but suggested the cheapest if it was her own credit card that would be offered at the end of the meal. Inexplicably, she was also speaking in a more snappish tone. The change became apparent at a party later that month in Fort Belvedere in Berkshire to celebrate the sixtieth birthday of Hilary Weston. Standing upright in a white jacket, Conrad Black was urging everyone to await the arrival of the Queen, Prince Philip and Prince Charles. 'Drop it,' laughed a guest, 'Just get me a drink, waiter.' Black smiled. Amiel, dressed immaculately, looked fierce. Embarrassed by the accusations in New York, she was snubbing more guests than usual, including Black's old friend the journalist John Fraser. Her regal manner sparked discussion about Black's predicament. 'I served briefly on Hollinger's advisory board,' Galen Weston told a group of guests, 'but I wasn't sure where it was going. I wasn't happy and resigned.

I think I made the right decision.' Many nodded. Others remained supportive. 'I hope he gets through,' said Leonard Lauder, a big advertiser in the *Telegraph*. 'Conrad's a wonderful man.'

The surrealism of the evening at Fort Belvedere – the well-dressed aristocrats, the huge firework display, the delicious food and the uniqueness of the spectacle of the former royal home – compounded Black's sense of his plight. Rupert Murdoch had urged that he stop social climbing and focus on his business, but it was too late to change a lifetime's habit. His best hope was a managed retreat, and to launch a counter-attack when appropriate. Surrounded by the orthodox and the honest, the very people whose approval he had always sought, Black was irritated by the advice of the benign Fred Eaton: 'Don't throw gasoline on this, Conrad. Throw a pail of water.' Black smiled wanly. The maelstrom in New York was beyond his control. Allowing an outsider to search through the accounts spelled doom. Yet resisting Chris Browne's demands for an independent inquiry would place his credibility at risk. 'I've got nothing to hide,' he had told Paul Healy and Richard Burt. He hoped he was believed.

Richard Burt had become sensitive to 'the problem' in the hours after the annual general meeting. Black, he believed, was guilty of excessive claims for expenses, and the pledge of his shares to Southeastern 'did not feel right', but he suspected nothing worse than greed. Nevertheless, Chris Browne's formal demand for an independent investigation into the conduct of Hollinger's directors could not be satisfied by Governor Thompson's offer of an internal inquiry conducted by Gordon Paris, a merchant banker and a new Hollinger director. Such an inquiry, as urged by Black, would not comply with the new legal obligations imposed on directors by Delaware's courts. After the annual general meeting, Burt had handed Paul Healy a piece of paper with a telephone number. 'Paul, call Richard Breeden,' he said, naming a former chairman of the Securities and Exchange Commission. 'Send him

Tweedy Browne's filings and ask if he can help Governor Thompson and the internal inquiry.' Three weeks later, the forces of capitalism crushed Black's resistance. Breeden, Black agreed on 17 June, could conduct an independent review under Section 13D. Conrad Black was losing control of his destiny.

13

The Purist

Renowned as a haughty perfectionist, Richard Breeden resented his reputation as a gunslinger famed for collecting corporate scalps. His victims would say that his arrogance was even greater than Black's, while his admirers sang praises to his cool pursuit of purity and perfection. He charged Hollinger $800 an hour.

In an attempt to limit Breeden's hunt for the truth, Conrad Black telephoned Ray Seitz, the former American ambassador in London. Seitz had stayed in Britain after his retirement in 1993 and collected a few non-executive directorships, including the *Telegraph*, until the board was dissolved in 1996. Then he became a member of the advisory board. Like so many respectable citizens, Seitz admired Black's qualities and intelligence, but he rejected his request to join Breeden's inquiry as too burdensome. Black implored him to reconsider, and after Henry Kissinger added his voice, he abandoned his reluctance 'as a favour'. Simultaneously, Graham Savage, a Canadian fund manager, was also persuaded by Peter Atkinson, a friend, to join Breeden's committee. 'It'll last six months,' said Atkinson. Savage agreed, attracted by the chance of meeting Henry Kissinger. Both Savage and Seitz shared Richard Burt and Gordon Paris's assumption that Black's transgressions amounted to little more than excessive private use of the Gulfstream and charging his butlers to the company.

Black could only guess at the committee's activities before its members met for the first time at Breeden's office in Greenwich, Connecticut, on 4 August 2003. The agenda, prepared by Breeden, reflected his quest to unearth corporate malfeasance. His perusal of Hollinger's internal files over the previous six weeks had indicated sloppy record-keeping and headline discrepancies. As he examined the plain paper print-outs, Breeden realised an obvious truth. Lord Black, the multi-millionaire historian, philanthropist, publisher, power-broker and consort of the great and good, had been greedy. All those famous personalities attracted by his hospitality, his erudite knowledge and his power had been taken in by a sophisticated performance. Beyond the theatrics, there was nothing special about Black. He was typical of a common type. The truth would be unearthed by digging through murky records and cross-examining the participants. The investigation was assigned to Jonathan Rosenberg, a New York lawyer and former prosecutor. His team would sift Hollinger's files and question the company's employees and directors, and present a report of their latest discoveries every week.

Two days after the committee's first meeting, Black's worst fears about Breeden were confirmed when he was asked to hand over copies of Ravelston's computer records. Black concealed his alarm. 'Your paramilitaries will discover nothing even slightly controversial,' he reassured Seitz, eager to remain civil and hospitable.[1] But Ravelston's records, he insisted, were off-limits. No one was allowed into the cabal's sanctuary. Similarly, Hollinger Inc.'s archives in Toronto were also barred. The investigation, insisted Black, was limited to Hollinger International in New York.

In mid-August the *Financial Times* exposed the $8 million purchase of the Roosevelt papers. Smoothly, Black complained on 17 August: 'I do not believe this is a matter of legitimate controversy.' The fragile truce fractured on 19 September, when Black and Amiel were asked to allow Breeden's technicians to make copies of their personal computer files in London and New York. 'No one is cloning my personal mail, and I will kill them first,' emailed Amiel. 'The board can take a running jump into well.' She was presumed to have meant 'hell'. Total opposition, Conrad Black, knew would be counter-productive. Their survival depended upon minimising the accusations and the revelations. Accordingly, he told his wife that they had no choice. Her computer would have to be surrendered, although there were safeguards to protect their privacy.

Lifting the curtain proved fatal to Black. As Breeden's team combed through 16,000 emails, they discovered the evidence of Black's crude dismissal of the shareholders' interests, his colourful justifications for his expenses and, most crucially, that the non-compete fees had been obtained without the independent directors' authorisation. Frustratingly, during their interviews with Hollinger's inner group in their efforts to discover the truth, Breeden's staff encountered explanations which were contradictory and unbelievable. Dan Colson, to their surprise, professed ignorance and lack of interest in any of the non-compete payments to Ravelston, although he was a director of both Hollinger and Ravelston. The irritation was compounded by the discovery that Colson's $1 million bonus had been paid to his account in the tax haven of Guernsey, for reasons which the investigators felt Colson had not yet adequately explained. The same forensic accountants had unearthed substantial evidence that in treating tax losses and loans, Boultbee and the others had skewed the advantage, worth millions of dollars, in Ravelston's favour at Hollinger's expense.

Black was not helped by Leonard Asper, Izzy's son and CanWest's CEO. The non-compete fee, he said in September, 'wasn't our idea. It was their choice as to where to allocate it.'[2] Black began voicing his intended defence. David Radler, he told enquirers, handled all the negotiations about Ravelston's management fees with Governor Thompson, without any 'input' from himself.[3] Rosenberg's investigators reported, 'Under every rock we turn up, there's something ugly.' Despite receiving $1.45 million for editorial duties in Chicago, Barbara Amiel had charged the company $20 for a tip to the doorman of Bergdorf Goodman, the fashion store on Fifth Avenue; there were the millions of dollars for the jets, homes, domestic staff and entertainment charged to the company; and the $90,000 for the refurbishment of the Rolls-Royce. At the appropriate moment, Breeden noted, Black could be humbled with the pithy phrase that the profligacy was incurred 'so that Black and Amiel-Black could travel in London in classic style without paying for the ride'. These were trifles, mere foretastes of the tipping point: Rosenberg's discovery of the non-compete payments in Mark Kipnis's files – unmentioned by Kipnis during his interview – and of the fact that the valuations of the Park Avenue apartments were contrived.[4] He and Breeden were familiar with one trademark of white-collar delinquents: they won credibility by combining breathtaking assertions of their entitlement with a dogmatic denial of any misconduct. 'He's wrong if he thinks he can run the train past us,' said a lawyer hired for the investigation. The composite picture was overwhelming. Breeden lost his patience.

Since his childhood, Black had disparaged Toronto's provincialism and praised American capitalism. The aggressive questioning of Hollinger's directors and employees by Rosenberg and Breeden dispelled Black's illusions. New York's culture was like a jungle – only the fittest survived. No matter how hard Black fought, Breeden's challenge would be difficult to defeat. Briefly, however, Black believed in eventual victory. The forty-eight hours beginning on 5 October cleared his vision.

'Black's taken money which he's listed as non-compete fees without the boards' permission,' the special committee were told on 5 October. 'I'm gobsmacked,' admitted Ray Seitz. 'I was sceptical that Conrad did anything wrong, but now I feel like a chump.' His opinion was reluctantly shared by Graham Savage. Black, they were told, had refused to answer any questions, while Radler, Atkinson and Boultbee had all suffered lapses of memory, or as Breeden would say, 'selective viral amnesia'.[5] Breeden concluded that Black was part of a corporate kleptocracy – in effect nothing more than a common thief with a white collar. But Black was no longer the sole focus of the directors' anger. The members of the audit committee, Breeden decided, had been 'ineffective and careless'. The 'ineffectiveness' of Thompson, Burt, Perle and Kravis, he continued, had been 'primarily a consequence of its inexplicable and nearly complete lack of initiative, diligence or independent thought. The Audit Committee simply did not make the effort to put itself in a sufficient position to recognize untruthful or misleading information or even make informed decisions on the issues before it.'[6]

Breeden's anger was particularly directed at Richard Perle, whom he called a 'faithless fiduciary' and blamed for approving transactions which 'unfairly benefited' Black and Radler. 'It is difficult to imagine,' he would write, 'a more flagrant abdication of duty than a director rubber-stamping transactions that directly benefit a controlling shareholder without any thought, comprehension or analysis.'[7] Perle's fate remained undecided. Others understood their predicament. Embarrassed and fearful of lawsuits, Marie-Josée Kravis resigned from Hollinger's board. No one believed her flimsy excuse about a conflict of interest because her husband might consider buying newspapers. Black understood the significance of this latest earthquake. Writing on House of Lords stationery although he was in Manhattan, he accepted her resignation with regrets and thanks. 'You'll be missed,' he concluded, apparently believing that the visual evidence of his peerage would endorse his protestation of innocence.

In the early hours of 6 October Breeden telephoned Kissinger, who was travelling in China. Until that night, Kissinger had been unaware of the detailed allegations against his friend and paymaster. Throughout his directorship of Hollinger he had unwisely refrained from trying to understand the contracts and payments he had approved. Over the next twenty minutes he was introduced to Breeden's criterion for the investigation: 'I'm following the money.' That had been the incentive of Bob Woodward and Carl Bernstein in their successful pursuit of President Nixon after the Watergate burglary. Nixon's tribulations had pained Kissinger, but had not sullied his reputation. In contrast, Breeden's discoveries threatened what an army of journalists and political enemies had failed to achieve in the Watergate era. By the end of the conference call, a shocked Kissinger accepted Breeden's suggestion that the cabal repay $32 million of non-compete fees taken without board approval, and that Conrad Black should retire as Hollinger's chief executive.[8] Kissinger imposed one condition: Black must not be condemned as dishonest. Not only for Black's reputation, but also for his own, Kissinger did not want to be cast as an accomplice to deceit, however inadvertently.

Ray Seitz had participated in this conversation from Hong Kong. Separately, he called Black and urged contrition and a new start, to prevent the danger spiralling out of control. 'Fire the auditors, recruit new people and apologise,' he suggested. His proposals were greeted by Black with stony silence. Hours later, Black and the three other members of the cabal received letters requesting the repayment of $32 million and their resignations. Black had reached a critical landmark. Regaining the initiative, he knew, was important. His lawyer suggested that a deal was possible. Everything depended upon Black's behaviour. In public he brushed aside any suggestion that he would not remain a newspaper proprietor forever. 'All Hollinger is fighting for,' he told *The Times* during a long interview, 'is a reasonable profit. The situation is no more dire than that.'[9]

Events had not quite slipped beyond his control, although his cabal's resolve was crumbling. To Black's dismay, Peter Atkinson made a weeping confession to Richard Burt. 'A kind of broken man,' concluded Burt after Atkinson admitted that there had been a conspiracy about the non-compete fees, and a cover-up. Burt felt betrayed.[10] Similar disillusion spread among the other directors who had trusted Black. Spurred by that sentiment, Breeden issued a deadline. Black should either reimburse his portion of the $32 million or face the consequences. Black understood the threat. Both the SEC and New York's Attorney General Eliot Spitzer were being urged to take an interest in Hollinger. To contain the crisis, Black hoped that Breeden, as a former chairman of the SEC, could be relied upon to broker a settlement. With the goodwill of Seitz, Kissinger and others, there was reason for Black to believe he might escape further retribution. While considering his response to Breeden's ultimatum, he launched with steely determination into a double life.

The Champion of Freedom, his 1,280-page biography of Franklin Delano Roosevelt, was due to be published in November. Proudly clutching his precious achievement, he gazed at the glowing endorsements on the book's cover from Henry Kissinger, George Will, William F. Buckley Jr and Ray Seitz. Hollinger's payroll had encouraged their generous response to his invitation for support. The majority of early readers were impressed by the massive tome's originality and erudition. A minority saw the book as an exercise in vanity, and were critical of Black's shabby research and reliance on secondary sources. Those slurs, trivial compared to the increasing vilification in newspapers for his plunder of Hollinger, would not be allowed to undermine his pleasure in addressing audiences appreciative of his scholarship. November was planned to be a glorious, non-stop, coast-to-coast promotion party. In his daydreams Black had envisaged shining as the guest of honour among historians, politicians, billionaires and celebrities. He refused to completely forsake that image. Among his qualities was compartmentalisation. By sheer will-power and dearth of conscience, he resolved to enjoy authorship.

On 10 November Harry Evans, the former editor of the *Sunday Times* and husband of the former *New Yorker* editor Tina Brown, was Black's host at the prestigious Council on Foreign Relations in New York. For an hour the audience was entertained by Black's fluent, humorous and perceptive description of an American hero. Enraptured by his theme, he appeared to be a man free of all problems. Seated among eighty members of New York's establishment, Paul Healy listened in awe. Over the past weeks he had played a double game, helping both Black and the investors, ensuring that his integrity was retained. That night, he felt great pride in his articulate, clever and amusing employer. At the end, he was puzzled as to whether Black understood his own predicament and would 'do the right thing'. He strode up and shook Black's hand. 'Terrific,' he said in genuine congratulation. His employer, he decided, was the victim of self-delusion. What other explanation could justify both Black's behaviour and his own trust in the man?

On his return to his Park Avenue apartment, Black began composing his reply to Breeden's request for the money and his resignation. Playing for time, he sought an honourable retreat. He would seek forgiveness and propose a quick sale of Hollinger in order to wipe out the debts. In a letter mentioning institutional confusion and the failure of others, he blamed his predicament on a series of unfortunate misunderstandings, legitimate attempts to avoid taxation, and relying on incompetent advisers who had failed to perform their duties. His critics, he hoped, would believe that millions of dollars had flowed into his account before he realised that Hollinger's payments were unauthorised. Among those he blamed were Michael Kipnis, KPMG, Torys and the audit committee for their 'collective responsibility for a regrettable lapse'.[11]

While Breeden and Hollinger's directors considered this self-pitying letter, Black flew down to Washington. On 12 November he stood, relaxed and eager, at the annual book fair of the National Press Club, seeking to sell copies of his book. Nearby, Oliver North, the mastermind of the Iran–Contra scandal, the media sex expert 'Dr Ruth' Westheimer, Tucker Carlson of CNN and the TV film critic Joel Siegel, were competing to sell their own publications. 'You're putting that back?' Black laughed at a browser who was replacing the Roosevelt book on its shelf. 'It's a bargain at twice the price!' Signing books and chatting good-humouredly with the public belied the impression of a beleaguered tycoon. 'FDR was devious,' he revealed to a purchaser. 'Some great leaders are devious.' The surrealism was interrupted that afternoon. A meeting, he was told, had been arranged at Hollinger's offices in New York the following morning, 13 November. Captain Ridley flew him north that night.

At the outset the mood in the boardroom, so carefully designed by Amiel as a suitable setting for a confident tycoon, was polite. Black expected to negotiate a settlement on the basis of his letter, and the expressions of Richard Breeden, Gordon Paris and Governor James Thompson did not undermine his optimism. His hopes were dashed within minutes of Gordon Paris outlining their plan: if the four directors refused to repay $32 million and resign, the committee would seek a court order seeking Black's removal as chief executive and would refer the matter to the SEC. This unexpected ultimatum disgusted Black. The proposal was a patent smear job, he concluded. Nevertheless, he concealed his anger. 'There may have been some paperwork issues,' he began, hoping to preserve the uncombative atmosphere, 'but I had nothing to do with all of this.'[12] Others, he said, were to blame for 'inaccuracies'. The payments to himself, he believed, had been authorised, and he had relied on others to maintain the records. Black was looking for an escape. He was a major shareholder in Hollinger, and he wanted to take as much money as possible from a sale. By conveying his willingness to agree a peaceful resolution, he hoped to avoid a reference to the SEC and the reopening of the Norcen 'consent'. Opposite him were men without any financial stake in the outcome, and nothing to lose by taking the moral high ground.

Gradually, Black gave ground. He offered to repay US$7.2 million, his share of the non-compete fees, in instalments of US$850,000. Gordon Paris, he agreed, would replace himself as the chief executive, helped by Dan Colson. Neither, Black knew, had the faintest idea how to manage a newspaper business. In the trade-off, he hoped that Breeden would pass on the news of his readiness to cooperate to the SEC and save him from the regulator's scrutiny. Exhausted by the process, Black was suddenly overcome by a sense of kinship with his persecutors. He suggested that they have dinner at Le Cirque, an expensive restaurant where Hollinger had an account. Convinced by the end of the meal of Black's sincerity, Breeden proposed that Bruce Wasserstein of Lazards should be invited the following day to make a presentation about the sale of Hollinger, the strategy suggested by Black himself.

On 14 November 2003, the discussion in Fifth Avenue resumed. Black wobbled. Hating his predicament and surrounded by critics, predators and enemies, he lost his self-control. 'If you want to fight, I'll fight,' he exclaimed. 'You can't push me around.'[13] Like an executioner, Graham Savage calmly pronounced that there was no alternative. Black paused and nodded. 'I did my best for all of us,' he sighed to Jack Boultbee. His facial expression did not change, and there was no outburst about his rights as a proprietor, no fantasies about his innocence or cries against victimisation. Suddenly, there was no performance – just the acceptance of exposure and defeat.

All that remained was to draft an agreement. On Saturday, 15 November, Hollinger's board was united in a telephone conference to agree the repayments and resignations. Black was in his apartment. Some words of regret about the circumstances were being uttered when Amiel interrupted. 'Conrad won't be bound by a kangaroo court,' she snapped. 'You don't have to agree to all this,' she told her husband. Agitatedly, she began questioning the agenda – forgetting her comment in her memoirs that 'We are all responsible for ourselves. That is not callous. That is liberation'[14] – but was interrupted by a power cut. The conference was plunged into silence and darkness. Once power was restored, Amiel again urged Black not to agree. He ignored her pleas. Exactly sixteen years before, days after the New York stock market crash, Amiel had ridiculed the 'moral vacuum' which sparked an 'unthinking pursuit of wealth' among the women at the Metropolitan Museum of Art. Since then she had forgotten her denigration of 'an appetite that is bigger than the wage cheque'. She had 'married up' to reap the benefits of wealth and power, and she was damned if she would allow those prizes to slip away. 'Mrs Black, pull yourself together,' said the company secretary, irritated by her hysteria. 'It's Lady Black, you bastard!' shouted Amiel.

At the end of the meeting, Conrad Black pledged to sign the agreement the following day. The document would include his admission that his receipt of $7.2 million in non-compete fees was 'not properly authorised on behalf of the company', and a pledge to repay the money. Radler signed a similar admission and a promise to repay $7.2 million, while Boultbee and Atkinson were asked to repay $602,500 each by 31 December 2003.[15] During Sunday, 16 November, Breeden and his team drafted the restructuring agreement in Connecticut. The document was faxed to Black's Park Avenue apartment in the late afternoon. Black signed everything and faxed the papers to the company's lawyers. The settlement was watertight. As chairman, Black would supervise the sale of a company whose value, following his removal, would increase. After a dance on the edge, he had agreed to retreat. He would be scarred, but would still be a wealthy man.

During the remainder of the day, Conrad Black was transfixed by his predicament. Until the early hours of Monday, 17 November, he failed to grasp the conclusions others would draw from his resignation. Reality arrived with Breeden's announcement of the agreement, highlighting the directors' repayment of $32 million. The telephones in Park Avenue began ringing with critical questions. Black was jolted. He had misjudged Breeden. Instead of an ally willing to effect a gentle transition and bury his embarrassing admissions, he was cold and ruthless. 'Gotcha!' smiled Chris Browne.

Laura Jereski was less enthusiastic. Not only was Black still chairman of Hollinger, but $32 million was a pittance compared to the $200 million in management fees that had been charged by Ravelston; and the conduct of the famous directors – Kissinger, Kravis, Perle, Burt, Weidenfeld, Thompson and so many others – who had failed to prevent Black's plunder had gone uncriticised. As she switched channels, Black's protestations of innocence on TV news programmes magnified her anger. 'I had no idea that these unauthorised payments were made to me,' Black told one interviewer. To another he was saying, 'We'll drive a silver stake through these allegations'; to a third, 'The moment we discovered these payments, we brought it to the attention of the special committee. And we believe they should be repaid.'[16] Bert Denton was one of several bemused by Black's protestations: 'Thirty-two million bucks waltzes out of Hollinger's bank account into Lord Black's wallet and he says, "How was I to know that the guy didn't check the box properly?"' For the moment, Black's excuses were irrelevant. Wall Street's ticker showed that Hollinger's share price had soared above $15. The shareholders' campaign had produced the profits. 'They're crucifying me,' protested Black on another channel. 'I'm the victim of a smear campaign waged by zealots.' On another he was saying, 'I'm being pilloried as a scoundrel and I'm not. It's going to take me two years to retrieve my reputation and show I'm clean. And I will be vindicated.'[17] Following events from Toronto, Hal Jackman understood his old friend's predicament: 'The charisma isn't working any more. Conrad needs to be tempting fate all the time. I just think Conrad has a death wish.'

Reports in Black's newspapers in Chicago and London minimised his plight. In Chicago, Radler ensured that the *Sun-Times*'s minimal coverage was anodyne. At Canary Wharf, Black's employees refused to believe that he was dishonest. They were reassured by the self-interested statement issued by Dan Colson: 'The company has committed nothing more than an unfortunate administrative cock-up.' Colson's denial that 'anything illegal or improper had taken place' reassured Jeremy Deedes and Charles Moore.[18] After seeing Lady Thatcher's disorientation at Lord Deedes's dinner, Moore had resigned as the *Telegraph*'s editor in October to complete his biography of the former Prime Minister, becoming a columnist on the paper. Black would voice little gratitude to him, criticising his politically like-minded acolytes on the newspaper as 'very talented, amusing people, but they rather amplified each other's eccentricities and anachronistic qualities', and consequently propagated a 'medieval monastic tenure'.[19] Despite ten weeks' notice, Black had felt no urgency about finding a successor to Moore. Amiel, he knew, would promote *Sunday Telegraph* editor Dominic Lawson but Dan Colson's veto would be hard to defeat. In the end Martin Newland, the deputy editor of the *National Post*, was appointed at Colson's suggestion. Like Moore and Lawson, Newland was ultra-loyal to his patron.

In New York, Hollinger's directors assumed that Black would resign, repay $7.2 million and help the company to be either restructured or sold. In exchange, the SEC would take no action against him and he could enjoy the countless millions of dollars believed to have been deposited in secret offshore accounts. No one could imagine that just twenty hours after signing the agreement, Black was contemplating reneging.

Champion of Freedom was an odd title for Black's latest book. Black was not an admirer of anyone's rights – people's or shareholders' – except the rich. Ever since its creation, Hollinger had been established solely for his benefit, and he was unwilling to change a lifetime's habit while overseeing its demise, especially the loss of the company's jewel, the *Telegraph*. For some weeks, contrary to his agreement with Hollinger's directors, he had been secretly negotiating the *Telegraph*'s sale. The potential buyers were David and Frederick Barclay, the fifty-nine-year-old English twins renowned for aggressive secrecy and murky commercial origins. Dividing their time between London, a fortress in the Channel Islands and Monaco, they had accumulated wealth from property, shipping and the retail business. Their previous investments in small newspapers had been financial and editorial disasters. The *Telegraph* was a dream opportunity for a family aspiring to improve their social status.

Persistently, Aidan Barclay, the diminutive son of David, had urged his father to pursue their quarry. 'I do not wish to be a bore,' David Barclay had written in a fax sent on 1 September 2003 enclosing another offer to buy the *Telegraph*. Black's reply had been discouraging: 'Our company is in fact prosperous.' If Barclay continued his enquiries, concluded Black, 'you would indeed be transgressing your expressed wish not to be a bore'. During those days, Black's refusal to sell was emphatic. 'Why in God's name would I do that?' he told enquirers. 'Absolutely no. Not now, not ever. It's out of the question.' A few days later, on 16 October, he defiantly told the *National Post*, 'I'll surrender control to the undertaker, but not to anyone else.' Undeterred, David Barclay had on 31 October reiterated his offer. 'Please keep in mind,' replied Black, showing his irritation, 'how tiresome you would find it if every time I saw a negative article about you in the press I wrote of my unquenchable desire to buy an asset of yours that is not for sale. I'm happy to hear from you, but not on this subject again please.' Yet, eleven days later, on Sunday, 11 November, the day before his capitulation to Breeden, Black opened negotiations with the Barclays. There was, he sensed, nothing to lose, despite breaking his agreement with Breeden. The secret discussions continued while Black became the focus of intense attention.

On 18 November, two days after his formal resignation, Black arrived at Indigo Books & Music on Bloor Street, an elegant shopping area of Toronto, where he had an engagement to promote his biography of Roosevelt. He stepped from the car into a mêlée of waiting photographers and journalists, appearing to relish the attention. The rise in Hollinger's share price, the potentially profitable sale of the *Telegraph* and his conviction that he could rebuild his business on the foundations of Horizon appeared to have encouraged his optimism. As he inched behind his bodyguards towards the shop entrance, Black smiled to the crowd and boasted, 'The stock's rising like a rocket, and I made fifty million bucks yesterday. That's a flame-out I could get used to.' His message was plain. Not only was he rich and still firmly in the saddle, but his problems were resolved and shareholders should be pleased. 'Is your empire up for sale?' he was asked. 'No. It's not up for sale. We're exploring a whole range of alternatives.'

Ahead was an escalator. As Black was about to step onto it, the bullet question shot out: 'Are you going to jail, sir?' 'There's no suggestion of impropriety,' Black replied without a glimmer of emotion. 'Read the press release.' The next bullet ricocheted: 'The SEC is investigating.' 'No, I don't know that it is,' said Black, explaining that he was cooperating, not concealing anything, and returning any money that was due. 'Did shareholder activism get you?' 'Yeah, they won. And they deserve to win. A sloppy thing like that, they deserve to win.' Pressed further, he casually acknowledged, 'I take my responsibilities and so must others,' and promised to make good: 'I'll write a cheque for seven million bucks. I'm not trying to steal anybody's money.' His eyes narrowed: 'Don't call me a shirker – I can't stand evasion.' His poise was perfect, concealing his fury. Naturally he did not consider that the sneers directed against himself were the ultimate payback for his own mockery of Lord Hartwell eighteen years earlier, and the revenge of those humiliated by his arrogance. He thought only of surviving by outwitting his critics.

About a hundred people were waiting for him. The journalists hung back while Black spoke for an hour. Unfaltering and captivating, his body language and facial expressions underlined his eloquent description of the life and conflicts endured by Roosevelt. As he spoke, those among the audience who were scanning his book might have spotted Black's admiration of FDR for being 'preternaturally cunning' and 'compulsively devious'. After the applause, the questioning resumed. 'Can you take comfort from FDR?' 'He spent three months on his back just trying to wriggle one toe, so nothing seems difficult. I can take great comfort from him today. I'm chastened by it.' The last question as he stepped into his black limousine was scornful: 'Is the vehicle leased or purchased?' Black smiled. 'Would you recommend an accountant for me?' Watching Black's performance on a news programme in Montreal, fund manager Stephen Jarislowsky was neither surprised nor saddened by his predicament. 'It's good that the bubble has burst,' he told his friends. 'It's great soap opera that will last for years.'

Hollinger's Gulfstream was waiting to fly Black to New York for another book promotion. On the way to the airport he stopped at his headquarters at 10 Toronto Street. The news was dire. The SEC had issued a subpoena demanding his presence to answer questions. His reliance on Breeden had misfired. The puritanical Breeden, he concluded, had never intended to help. Black's strategy had been wrecked. His control over both Hollinger's destiny and his own had weakened. Consumed by the idea of revenge against his enemies, he decided to frustrate Breeden and Tweedy Browne. The two, he suspected, had discussed suing Hollinger's directors for negligence to recover $100 million from the company's insurance policies. Worse, he suspected that they would also divert the proceeds – possibly $1 billion – from the *Telegraph*'s sale to Hollinger International rather than allow it to be shared among shareholders, including himself.

The news required a major reassessment of Black's plans. To ensure that he received the money, he decided to mount a charade. While keeping appointments to meet prospective buyers for his shares, he secretly abandoned his undertaking on 17 November to cooperate with the sale of Hollinger's newspapers by Lazards, and increased the tempo of his own negotiations with David Barclay. No longer trusting emails, he sent a fax inviting a bid for Hollinger Inc., the Canadian company which he controlled and through the super votes, his 19 per cent stake of Hollinger International. Black was seeking a clear profit of $175 million, plus any bonus fee the Barclay twins considered appropriate for the exclusive opportunity. He was interrupted by a telephone call from Ray Seitz. 'Are you sticking to the agreement?' Seitz asked. 'Absolutely,' Black reassured him.[20] If asked, the military tactician would have floundered to explain whether he was advancing or retreating. He justified his deception by a retort: 'Only God will judge me and He will find in my favour.'

Seitz's telephone call was prompted by Richard Breeden, who had been made suspicious and irritated by Black's cavalier disregard for Hollinger's financial plight. Since 1997, Breeden discovered, Hollinger had been charged $1.4 million for Black's personal staff.[21] During Tuesday, 18 November, while Black was speaking at Indigo in Toronto, Breeden urged that his use of the Gulfstream be 'terminated', and Hollinger's payment for the apartments in New York, cars and restaurant accounts be ended. The company's directors agreed. Ravelston, it was announced, would receive just US$100,000 a month for the services of Black and the other former directors. Black interpreted the edict as a declaration of war.

Breeden's assault – the dissemination by his staff of information about the cabal's misuse of Hollinger's funds, first to Hollinger's executives and then to journalists – surprised Black. Overnight, he had become the media's symbol of corporate greed. Accustomed at worst to defamatory disapproval, he had never previously been outrightly ridiculed as a crook. In former times he would have issued writs for defamation to pulverise his critics, but he was suddenly helpless; even the *Daily Telegraph* was publishing critical reports. Among the few remaining loyalists were Dominic Lawson at the *Sunday Telegraph* and others who recalled Black's generosity and support for favoured journalists. To no avail, he told a *Sunday Times* correspondent, 'I urge you, no matter how addicted you are to representing me as shamed, disgraced and a keystone to scandal, to contemplate the possibility that I might be innocent.' His mellifluous phrase-making was wasted. The rumours spread that without their huge income, the Blacks could no longer afford their homes in London, New York and Palm Beach. Hunkered in his Park Avenue apartment, Conrad Black had indeed instructed agents to sell the house in London for £14 million and the Florida mansion for US$36 million, albeit that it had been valued the previous year at $17.5 million. The reason, it appeared, was his need for cash to repay the $7.2 million, but another calculation would have been more accurate. American shareholders had become prolific litigators for malfeasance. Aware that he was vulnerable to endless litigation, the 'billionaire' began selling and mortgaging his assets to deter contingency lawsuits.

The consequences were painful. Black's telephone calls to Henry Kravis and other billionaire friends remained unanswered.

Within one week he had become an unperson, reviled as a leper. He and Amiel heard of parties to which they were not invited. Across Manhattan, the A-list was divided between those cutting the Blacks dead and the embarrassed loyalists who did not believe that their personal judgement could have been so faulty. Among the faithful were the iconic columnists William F. Buckley and George Will, both of whom wrote articles supporting Black. Neither mentioned their relationship with him. George Will would emphatically justify his silence about the undeclared conflict of interest. 'My business is my business. Got it?' he told an enquirer, precisely reflecting Black's own opinion of journalists.

The disenchantment in New York was slight compared to the anger in Toronto. Fred Eaton and Douglas Bassett, both directors of Hollinger Inc., had known Black since their childhood and student days. Their fidelity had been proven during the Argus coup. Their loyalty, rather than their intelligence or independence, had been Black's motive for appointing them to the board, but those bonds were strained by the revelations in New York. 'What's happening to my share price?' asked Eaton, who took his fees in Hollinger shares. 'I'm getting screwed here.' 'Too bad,' replied Black. In the days before the Hollinger Inc. board was due to meet on 21 November, these two old friends and their fellow director Allan Gottlieb offered help and advice, but his reactions during telephone conference calls ranged from hostile to ranting. 'He's crazy,' whispered Gottlieb. 'He's a megalomaniac. He thinks the Indians are surrounding him.' Although the directors had been advised to dismiss Black, they agreed to his plea for more time. Their ultimatum was Friday, 21 November 2003.

On that morning the directors gathered in Toronto while Black and Amiel spoke from New York. Both Torys, the company's lawyers, and KPMG, the auditors, had announced their intention of resigning. Maureen Sabia, the chairman of Hollinger Inc.'s audit committee, a lawyer reputed to be an expert on corporate governance, offered her guidance through the dilemma. Considering her public silence over the previous months, Sabia's advice might have been considered questionable, but Eaton and his colleagues were grateful that someone was holding their hands in the darkness of a personal tragedy. 'You took money that didn't belong to you,' said Eaton in a pained voice about the non-compete fees. 'All the money belongs to me,' replied Black. 'What do you know?' Amiel unexpectedly bellowed on the telephone. 'You Eatons all went bankrupt.' That was accurate – the Eaton store chain had collapsed. 'Barbara, you can't speak like that,' Black told her. Unseen by the Blacks, Eaton shrugged. 'It's one of the greatest tragedies that has happened in this country,' said Eaton. 'To blow the whole lot away is sad.'

After Black again refused to return US$15.6 million taken from Hollinger Inc. in non-compete fees and to resign, all the directors resigned. The following day, Eaton telephoned Black to commiserate. 'Lord Black is busy right now,' said the butler. 'He'll call you back.' There never was a call.[22] Most of the directors would never speak to Black again. He had lost his oldest friends and more. After twenty-seven years, he was asked to resign his directorship of the Canadian Imperial Bank of Commerce. On his lawyers' advice he also resigned as Hollinger Inc.'s chief executive, to protect himself from censure if he signed the latest financial accounts. He remained the company's chairman.[23]

The fallen tycoon can be a pitiful sight, but Black was too proud and too self-controlled to allow his enemies the pleasure of witnessing a wounded man. Ever since his days at Upper Canada College he had scorned those who vilified him. In the manner of his heroes, his response to mockery was to march through the public arena, defying his critics. Reflecting that boldness, on 24 November he stood in the centre of the Grill Room at the Four Seasons hotel in Manhattan welcoming his guests to the official launch party of his book. The party had been planned by Oscar and Annette de la Renta and Jayne Wrightsman, and Black anticipated that his three hundred A-list friends would appear. He was disappointed. Most of his new friends had vanished, fearful of being tainted by the looming scandal. In the half-empty room, Henry Kissinger, Alfred Taubman and Tina Brown shifted from foot to foot, glancing at Joan Collins, Candice Bergen and other fading stars. In a corner, Barbara Amiel hid behind a garment with a huge collar, embarrassed by an account of Annette de la Renta's exchange with Chris Browne days earlier. 'I think it's marvellous what you're doing,' de la Renta had told the fund manager. 'I thought Black was a friend of yours,' Browne replied. 'Oh yes, he was, but we didn't realise he was so greedy.'[24] A wake was not what Amiel had anticipated. Her humiliation was compounded by the noise of a riotous party in a neighbouring room. Robert Rubin, the former Treasury Secretary, was hosting a full house to launch his own book. Black concealed his emotions. He felt no guilt, only anger against 'Breeden and his fascists'. In a controlled, monotonous voice he told his guests, 'Those truly evil people are a menace to capitalism as any sane and civilised person would define it.'[25] Breeden, he continued, was spending millions of dollars from Hollinger's funds to attack the men who had created the wealth. He bade his guests farewell, mentioning to Henry Kissinger that he would be arriving three days later with Barbara for Thanksgiving at the Kissingers' Connecticut home. Kissinger would be reassured of his friend's innocence. Even though he was a director, he had not undertaken his own investigations, and during board meetings he still pontificated about world events, ignoring the scandal unfolding under his directorship.

As he brooded in his Park Avenue apartment, a new wave of anger overwhelmed Black. He was not only socially shunned, but commercially dead. In his favourite restaurants and salons they were joking that *Schadenfreude* had a new face: Conradfreude. Those who had suffered his arrogance, threats, writs and monologues were heartened by Black's humbling. The managers of Tweedy Browne, Cardinal Capital, Herbert Denton and other funds were still searching for material with which to topple Black. 'The greatest fun in the world with your clothes on,' said Denton about the campaign. 'Normally when I pay $1, I get a single newspaper, not the whole company,' he said of Black's purchase of two papers from Hollinger which were worth $1 million. Black's preoccupation was endless meetings with expensive lawyers to plan his defence. His isolation fed his sense of persecution as he blamed jealous miscreants for ruining his destiny. 'I'm the target,' he repeated to the few who took his calls, 'of truly wicked people executing a smear job.'

To feed his sense of injustice, he needed as usual to focus his anger on one person. 'Everyone can see Breeden is sucking the blood out of the company,' he told David Barclay, 'and he and Paris are just fattening their sinecures.' Barclay had good financial reasons for pandering to Black's splenetic outbursts. Other than his lawyers and priests, Black found few other sympathisers to listen to his confession that his signed admission on 16 November had been foolish, a breach of his first commandment – never to admit mistakes or make concessions. His imminent appearance at a hearing by the SEC could be the beginning of his downfall. The legacy of the Norcen 'consent' threatened serious consequences if he again conceded culpability. During those early days of December, he made a fateful decision. Instead of abiding by the November agreement to repay $7.2 million, he decided to sell the *Telegraph* privately and keep the money for himself. He would fight Breeden. Consciously, he had outlawed himself.

Radler, Atkinson and Boultbee were asked whether they would join his crusade. Their lawyers, Black claimed, would say they had uncovered documents proving that the non-compete payments were after all properly authorised and had been submitted in official filings to the regulators. 'If the filings were wrong,' said

Black, 'we can blame the back office.' There was no proof, he insisted, that the four directors were aware that the payments were not authorised, and the onus was on the SEC to prove that they had been. His scenario did not persuade all the other members of the cabal. Radler and Atkinson had decided to repay their share of the non-compete fees in full. Boultbee remained undecided.

Conrad Black's solitary flag of resistance was raised in Chicago on 22 December 2003. Answering the SEC's subpoena in person, he pleaded the fifth amendment to protect himself from self-incrimination and refused to answer any questions. This aroused dumbfounded disbelief, as it had been agreed with the Hollinger directors that he would assist the company in every way to resolve the problem. Black then returned to Toronto. For the first time in many years, the Blacks were not hosting a Christmas party.

Black saw Ray Seitz as his potential saviour. Encouraged by Kissinger, Seitz was seeking a peaceful resolution to avoid destroying Black, whom he still respected. The former diplomat knew how to negotiate with a former bureaucrat. There was no reason, Seitz told Breeden, not to trust Black. After all, he was cooperating in the sale of the *Telegraph*, and had appeared to be candid at a board meeting on 17 December. Asked by Bruce Wasserstein of Lazards whether he was negotiating to sell the *Telegraph*, the board's minutes recorded Black replying: 'Neither Lord Black nor Hollinger Inc. have solicited any inquiries or other sources of capital ... Lord Black has been faithful to the Lazard process and has done nothing to disturb the Lazard process [i.e. the agreed sale of the *Telegraph* by the bank].' That, Seitz told Breeden, proved Black's trustworthiness. Any recrimination should be limited. Breeden agreed. If, on 31 December 2003, Black had paid $850,000, the first instalment of the $7.2 million, he would probably have escaped the worst. Instead, on 2 January 2004, he declared war.

The newspaper headlines after New Year's Day put Black on the defensive. Lawyers representing the fund managers Cardinal Capital had filed a suit in Delaware against all of Hollinger's directors based on the minutes of the board's meetings. 'A saga of greed and deliberate indifference to fiduciary duties', Cardinal alleged in lurid prose, adding that Black and his galaxy of society scions had used the company 'like their private piggy bank'. Black was unconcerned by that criticism. The ugly pygmies, he noted, were not accusing him of any crime but gluttony, and to that he would happily plead guilty. Everything, he would say, had been approved by the board of directors and the company's professional advisers. Over the next hours, other shareholders announced their intention to sue Black and his cabal for $300 million, and Hollinger in New York announced it would sue the group for the return of the $200 million fees paid to Ravelston. The louder the protests, the more contemptuous Black became. But then journalists began requesting the directors' comments on reports that he was secretly negotiating to sell control of the *Telegraph* to the Barclays.

Richard Breeden's rage was Conrad Black's undoing. By wilfully breaking the November agreement, Black had proved his lack of integrity. His conduct put an end to Ray Seitz's desire to restrain Breeden. To frustrate the plot, the company's directors, including Seitz and Graham Savage, agreed that Hollinger would issue sufficient new shares to destroy Black's control. The 'poison pill' defence enraged Black. On 3 January 2004 he telephoned Kissinger and lost his temper. Nervous of a calamity, Kissinger told Breeden that he feared another 'Saturday Night Massacre', referring to a succession of dismissals sparked by President Nixon during the Watergate crisis.[26] 'All Conrad wants is a standstill,' Breeden was told. To calm relations, a truce was agreed during Sunday, 4 January. In return for Black not selling Hollinger Inc. to the Barclays, there would be no 'poison pill'. The truce, Black agreed, would last two weeks.

That night, Black increased the speed of his negotiations

with David Barclay. 'These are treacherous people,' he wrote to Barclay, referring to the bankers employed to sell Hollinger. 'You could get the *Telegraph* at a bargain price, and private.' He proposed that after the sale, he would like to invest $100 to $150 million in the Barclays' new venture. His plan, he concluded 'would end this drama [and score] a glorious victory over truly wicked people'. Black's proposal was too complicated for the Barclays to accept, but the negotiations continued while Black sought to dampen the hostilities and find a compromise with Breeden. He agreed to meet Breeden and Gordon Paris on 7 January in the offices of Sullivan & Cornwall, Black's lawyers. Seitz was not present. His façade of gracefulness was forgotten. Oblivious to history, he still reproached those who doubted him as an honest trader.

'Why's he glaring at us?' thought Breeden as Black entered the room. 'Has he the look of arrogance or despair?' wondered another eyewitness, forgetting that Black did not do guilt. He had simply forgotten his vulnerability. The sullen air was fractured by his explosion: 'I'm not paying the $7 million.' Then he fired his favoured weapon. 'I know where Ray Seitz has property in England,' he snarled, 'and I'm going to launch a defamation action . . . and I'll have the property taken away.' Breeden's bewildered silence encouraged Black's belief that, as usual, his pugnacious message intimidated his adversaries. The chance of brokering a permanent settlement disappeared. Ten years earlier, Black had written about Lord Hartwell's forlorn defiance: 'It had become surrealistic as tenacious resistance to the inevitable eventually always does, the surest sign that the endgame was finally afoot.'[27] Black was deaf to the echo of vengeful laughter.

After walking out of the room, Black ordered his lawyers to file a claim for $646 million against the members of the special committee alleging that in pursuit of personal enrichment they were seeking to destroy the company and himself. By the time he returned to Park Avenue, he had also triggered his next step. He would openly offer the 'deal of the decade' to the Barclays. His Hollinger Inc. shares with the 78 per cent voting rights could be bought for $500 million. David Barclay instantly accepted the offer. This was a bargain – Barclay called it 'a once-in-a-lifetime opportunity' – he could not refuse. Chortling about his coup, Black urged the Barclays to complete the deal hastily. America was tasting Black's adaptation of the military theories of Basil Liddell Hart, the British strategist. The 'expanding torrent offence' was an attack in so many directions that the enemy could not guess the next move. He cared little that he had lied to Hollinger's directors in what a judge would later damn as a 'cunning and calculated' manner. Nor did he care about being abandoned by Ray Seitz. He stood alone against Breeden, a master of America's perverted regulatory system. In his conversations with God, he was reassured that many retained their belief in his genius, and the disbelievers would ultimately be bound to answer for their lack of faith. Wilfully, Black was playing out of his league. Instead of dancing on the edge, he had jumped into the abyss.

Without warning, on Friday, 16 January 2004, Black was told that the SEC had formally charged Hollinger International with filing false reports, and that Hollinger International had filed a suit for the return of $200 million from him and Radler. Two days later, Gordon Paris announced a conference call for the directors of Hollinger International. Black was in his Park Avenue apartment. Soon after the connections were confirmed, Ray Seitz announced that the motion was to remove Black as chairman. Amiel loudly voiced objections. Quietly, Seitz explained that by taking the fifth amendment, Black had disqualified himself as chairman of a public company. 'That's all extraneous,' protested Amiel. Her husband remained silent. The vote was carried. As the conference call ended, television news programmes reported that Black had been dismissed because of allegations of dishonesty and looting. In retaliation, he sent a fax to Paris's office announcing the sale of his shares and control of the *Telegraph* to the Barclays for US$466 million. Until that moment, maintaining his dignity in public had been Black's safety net, restraining many former friends from uttering any public criticism. By openly breaking the November agreement and refusing to maintain a stoic, uncomplaining stance, Black sacrificed their goodwill. 'Why doesn't he just write out a cheque and settle this?' Richard Perle asked Paul Healy. 'I'm dumbfounded. Doesn't he have the money?'

Conrad Black had forgotten about the disputed payments. He thought only about his persecution by those who lacked faith in himself. Bereft of anyone on his payroll he trusted to listen to his confessionals, Black latched onto David Barclay. In his golden era, Black would have dismissed Barclay as an uneducated property spiv. In his new predicament, during his lonely hours, Barclay was a lifeline. 'Our prospects are good,' Black confided on 18 January about his future defeat of the SEC and the independent directors. In self-interest, Barclay played the game. 'It is a conspiracy to defraud you of your rights to sell and get maximum value for your shares,' he agreed, to sustain Black's illusions. 'It is vindictive and malicious.'[28] To his friends Barclay was more realistic: 'He's not that clever, is he?'

Cooped up in his home in Toronto, Black floundered, indecisive about his tactics when the enemy counter-attacked. Two days later, he knew the worst. On 20 January 2004, he and Barbara were asked to participate in another board meeting by telephone. Every director including Kissinger was connected to the conference call. All had read that month's *Vanity Fair* feature describing the super-rich in Palm Beach. One stunning photo showed the Blacks portrayed among the resort's billionaires. Since the day the photograph was taken, Amiel had realised her errors. Her 'extravagance' comment to *Vogue* was, she conceded, 'certainly the most ill-timed throwaway comment I could have made'.[29] Her continued confusion was reflected by her musing during the board meeting. The motion was to exclude Conrad and Barbara Black as shareholders from any negotiations about Hollinger's future. 'It was an interesting legal theory,' Amiel reflected later, 'that by virtue of marriage one could be deemed to have a conflicting interest.'[30] Amiel's naïvety was in failing to understand that the conflict of interest as Conrad Black's wife offered her some protection from legal sanctions for her own conduct as a Hollinger director. A second motion at the board meeting was the approval of a lawsuit against Black to recover the management fees paid to Ravelston. 'Frivolous and factious,' quipped Black. The votes were called. Black heard Kissinger say, after hesitating, 'Yes.' Surely, Black asked incredulously, Kissinger was not voting against his friend? 'Yes,' confirmed Kissinger. '*Et tu, Brute*,' sighed Black. 'I'm the target of a series of Pearl Harbor attacks,' he railed. 'They have hijacked the company.' The board meeting was over.

Focused on the next battle and not the outcome of the war, Black plotted his next coup to frustrate Breeden. He would change the company's rules. 'We caught [the enemy] with their pants down,' he faxed David Barclay, 'preparing more skulduggery . . . We think we can hold the fort and will be suing them in three countries next week.' Black had entered the realm of fantasy.[31] Breeden's reaction was cataclysmic. Black was sued in Delaware to prevent the sale of the company to the Barclays. In his statement to the court, Breeden explained his fear that unless he was halted by a judge's order, Black would dispose of the company and deposit the proceeds either 'in Beirut or the Outer Hebrides', depriving the shareholders of their money.

Lawsuits were Black's oxygen. He had never, he convinced himself, lost in the courts. He issued another writ for defamation against Ray Seitz, Richard Breeden and three other directors for being presented as a 'loathsome laughing stock' and 'social leper' by their dissemination of 'vicious vaporings and a vile tissue of lies'. The writ, claiming $850 million, was served on Seitz in South Carolina. Black added an additional threat that Seitz would be forced to fund his defence costs personally. 'Conrad reaches too early for the nuclear option,' lamented Seitz. 'And when Conrad reaches for the nuclear option, you react.'[32] Black was confident. 'I am looking forward to finally getting my story out,' he told David Barclay. 'If they go to trial, they are making a serious mistake.' Black was convinced that he could out-think and out-argue everyone. By the time he arrived at the courthouse in Wilmington, Delaware on 17 February 2004, he was convinced of victory.

Delaware's specialist commercial courts are efficient, reliable and staffed by expert judges. Black's added misfortune was the assignment of the forty-year-old Judge Leo Strine to his case. Reading the voluminous pleadings on the night before the trial, Strine was impressed by the repetition of certain phrases: 'inaccurate disclosure', 'unauthorised' and 'fictitious' non-compete payments. Most pertinent was Black's undisputed breach of the 16 November 2003 agreement. Looking down the witness list, Strine may have noticed that while Hollinger relied on former bankers, diplomats and a chairman of the SEC, Black's witnesses were old cronies.

While Black's fate was being considered, he himself was dining with his lawyers in the Hotel du Pont, Wilmington's only hotel. His opponents were eating in the same restaurant. Breeden could not resist the opportunity for mischief. Keen to destabilise Black, he nodded towards a lawyer. Rising from the table and walking towards Black, the lawyer paused only to alert a table of journalists. With a flourish, he theatrically served a writ on Black claiming $200 million. To Black's applause, his own lawyer contemptuously threw the papers on the floor. The murmurs around the restaurant encouraged Black's self-confidence. True Believers, he told himself, always succeeded. Helped by his remarkable memory and imperious manner, he would flatten Breeden's advocate, Martin Flumenbaum. His illusion was dashed by the end of the following day. During their cross-examination, Black's lawyers failed to destabilise Breeden, Seitz and other witnesses. His own arrival in the courthouse on 20 February was not accompanied by the fanfare he had anticipated. He was pale and unsure, and his lifeless eyes and hesitant movements no longer sustained the mystique of wealth, power and certainty. As he stood in the lavatory before giving evidence, he was served another writ. He had never anticipated such humiliation.

In the witness box, Black argued that each payment by Hollinger had been legitimate and sanctioned by his professional advisers, and that he had been alternately duped and coerced into signing the agreement on 16 November. Unable to break his habits, he had not adequately revised the company's history so as to present himself as master of the facts. Oblivious to his peril, Black appeared to be less concerned by the breach of the November agreement than by the destruction of his character in the media. 'I have been horribly defamed, characterised and stigmatised as an embezzler,' he gasped. 'I am trying to retrieve my reputation.' Conrad Black had come to the wrong court. Judge Strine was not judging defamation, but commercial honesty. In his struggle to justify the sale of the newspapers, including non-compete agreements with his own company, Black delivered what he thought was his ace. 'But the share price went up,' he told Flumenbaum with satisfaction. 'And does that give you the right to steal from shareholders?' shot back the lawyer. 'Objection!' shouted a defence voice. 'Overruled,' ordered the judge. Black's face drained. His credibility seeped away. The photograph in the morning newspapers showed him on the street next to a red 'Wrong Way' sign, encapsulating his apocalypse. Not far away, the noose was dangling. In 1978 Black had preached that there should be 'no safety net for the rich'. His only hope was the public's acceptance that he was the victim of deception and coercion.

Strine pledged to deliver a judgement within one week of the hearing. The 130-page judgement arrived on 26 February, one day before his deadline. Black's fate was sealed. In colourful language, Strine ruled that Black had breached his fiduciary duties. 'At worst the International board was purposely duped and there was fraud,' he declared. Thereafter, Black's reputation was mercilessly shredded. Strine characterised him as 'evasive and unreliable', and accused him of being a liar: 'His explanations of key events and of his own motivations do not have the ring of truth.' Black's behaviour as chief executive, Strine declared, was in 'a manner inconsistent with the duty of loyalty he owed to the company', while his attempted sale to the Barclays was 'cunning and calculated'. Among the most blatant deceits, said Strine, were the non-compete payments made in February 2001 and backdated to December 'in what, in the old days,' said Strine, 'might have been called constructive fraud'. Even the Barclays were criticised by the judge, for providing information to the court 'of questionable accuracy' and for negotiating with Black in a 'course of action that they knew was less than fully candid'.[33]

Black read the judgement in Toronto. He was paralysed. Neither he nor his lawyers had anticipated such a damnation. He was no longer castigated as a bombastic social mountaineer, but as a tycoon who systematically deceived his shareholders. 'Pilloried and mocked mercilessly' in his own words, another person might have felt the nails piercing their flesh and rooting into the wood. Even his closest allies, the members of the Manhattan Institute, a centre for self-proclaimed libertarian conservatives, turned against him. At a book signing at author Roger Herzog's house, the journalist and former speechwriter to Ronald Reagan, John Podhoretz, took Chris Browne by the hand and pulled him through the party, shouting, 'This is the guy who got Conrad!' Hands slapped Browne's back, including that of Russell Carson, a renowned venture capitalist. 'Barbara's spending habits are outrageous,' Carson said loudly. Everyone shouted agreement that Black had not been accepted, but only tolerated, after inserting himself so brutally into their midst. Not a single voice defended the Blacks; rather many nodded agreement when he was compared to Tyco's Dennis Kozlowski: 'He's a thug who never listened.' On the same day, across town, at a party hosted by the Cuban sugar magnate Jose 'Pepe' Fanjul, the former Canadian Prime Minister Brian Mulroney was laughing. 'Conrad's problem,' he roared, 'is that he's never had his arse sucked by a woman.' There was, however, some sympathy. At a dinner party hosted by Tom Wolfe, William F. Buckley declared, 'I just hope Conrad gets out of it.' He was contradicted only by Pat, his wife: 'I like Conrad, but I think he's guilty.'

Black made no attempt to conceal the damage, but he refused to lie down. In a telephone conversation with the *Sunday Times* he admitted, 'I understand the endless fascination with my downfall . . . Do what you want. I don't really care. I want to get to the relaunch of my life and will have nothing more to say to the press. I assume the sadistic fascination with my life will eventually come to an end.' This was a testing time within the Black household. Apart from the criticism and ostracism, their vision of themselves was imperilled. Ever since their twenties, Black and Amiel had successfully sought public attention on their own terms. For years they had cultivated their own image. The media spotlight they had desired now endangered their own creation. History, Conrad and Barbara Black knew, was always written by the victors. Both sought to maintain their version of their own biographies. Defending the high ground required single-minded insensitivity, the same qualities which had originally propelled both of them onto pedestals. Still majestic, but also driven by her instinct for survival, Amiel, with Black's encouragement, began disseminating a heartfelt belief. Her innocent husband, she told everyone, was the victim of envious persecutors. The villains were the corporate terrorists and the media, motivated by socialism, spite and sickness.

The attitude of Black and Amiel towards journalism was peculiar. The profession had provided their income, but both disliked what they saw as the grubbiness, ethics and low intelligence of journalists. While lauding her own writing as high-minded, Amiel had since the 1970s attacked the media's credibility. Despite their righteous aspirations, she wrote, 'Being guided by one's conscience is . . . no guarantee of being right. One should also think.' Objectivity, she suggested, was praiseworthy, yet her own career was built upon the opposite. Investigative journalism was abhorrent to Amiel – and to Conrad Black – because the truth caused embarrassment. The Blacks' sympathies were always with the top dog. 'What is unforgivable,' Amiel concluded about their would-be executioners, 'is cleansing the media of its own illusions.'[34] In 1979 she had written about the Canadian media's disillusion with Margaret Trudeau, the hippie wife of Pierre Trudeau, the then Prime Minister. Margaret Trudeau, she wrote, after 'washing her dirty linen' in a series of confessional newspaper interviews, 'became a pariah to the media that adored her'. Instead of criticising Margaret Trudeau herself, Amiel blamed the media for lampooning her hypocrisy.[35] Twenty-five years later, Lady Black's intolerance of anyone contradicting her opinions had hardened. In 2003 she had been scathing about the BBC's use of information provided by Dr David Kelly, a weapons expert employed by the Ministry of Defence who had exposed Tony Blair's deception about the existence of weapons of mass destruction in Iraq. Subsequently, Kelly had been driven to commit suicide. As a supporter of the Iraq war, Amiel deplored Kelly's conduct. Those who professed the counter-truth were, in Amiel's opinion, the Blacks' enemies. In their self-interested philosophy, the rich and famous could never receive a fair trial.

Justice administered in the spotlight, Amiel believed, meant automatic victimisation, and therefore the alleged crimes committed by those like Conrad Black deserved to be considered as having taken place in extenuating circumstances. Her theme was that the rich and famous deserve special justice. Two parallels to the discrimination being suffered by her husband were, she felt, the trials of the American footballer and actor O.J. Simpson and the singer Michael Jackson. 'The sight of a rich, vulnerable person brings out the jackal in a lot of people,' she would write during the Jackson trial. She urged leniency in that case because in her judgement the evidence was flawed, the prosecutor malignly motivated and the witnesses unreliable: 'Genius doesn't justify evil, never has, but in the face of brilliance, shouldn't society show a little more tolerance of Jackson's peculiarity?' Although she was not arguing that Conrad Black was 'peculiar', she saw a fundamental similarity to Jackson's 'miserable little morality play': 'I suppose this case filled a feeding frenzy of our times.'[36]

On 8 March 2004, one week after Judge Strine's judgement in Delaware, Amiel wrote in the *Daily Telegraph* about the conviction and imprisonment of Martha Stewart. Stewart's proven dishonesty appeared irrelevant to Amiel. In her opinion, Stewart 'fell victim to the tall poppy syndrome sweeping the business world of the United States . . . Any hint of wrongdoing gets the elders out, solemn and judgemental.' She espoused her husband's antagonism to Eliot Spitzer's brand of corporate honesty. Wealth-creators, she suggested, should not be judged by normal criteria. The famous could not rely on getting a fair trial. 'Revolution has been sweeping the boardrooms of corporate America,' she wrote, 'and the Terror is well under way . . . In checking greed in the managerial class, America seems to be instituting a system that legitimises the greed of minority shareholders. This New Revolution validates short-term profit and penalises vision.' She conveniently forgot that her husband was a minority shareholder of Hollinger, and she also failed to grasp that her status was compromised by her directorship of Hollinger and her denial of the company chairman's fraud. She preferred to present herself as a celebrity scapegoat, sharing the fate of Martha Stewart. 'When you're on a crusade,' she complained, 'when you're a zealot, it's really terrific to put a good-looking head on a pike – more people will look at it.'[37] Comparing herself to Stewart, she failed to understand, could have been seen by some as a confession of similar dishonesty. Her special pleading in the *Daily Telegraph*, she had believed, would win respect and influence. Instead, it aroused ridicule. Her column was dropped by the editor Martin Newland, and Boris Johnson also withdrew an offer of a column in the *Spectator*. 'It's too painful,' said Johnson. 'I love Barbara. I venerate her. It's higher powers, you know.'[38] She admitted to have been 'devastated' by the dismissal. 'Influence,' she later admitted, 'is an illusion. You think you're having an effect but you're not.'

Like New York, London was divided about the Blacks' predicament. There was sympathy, bemusement, shock and open hostility. Former directors including Lord Carrington were challenged to explain their association with a businessman found by an American judge to be dishonest, and their failure to check Hollinger's accounts. Embarrassed by his appearance in ermine as Black's proposer to the House of Lords, Carrington confessed to friends, 'I did it for fun and the money.' Like others, he felt foolish for having failed to spot a flawed personality. Among those visiting Black in New York to offer help was a well-known Conservative Party adviser. 'Why is everyone turning on me?' asked Black. 'Why does no one call me?' 'Because you're that sort of person,' replied the visitor. 'You don't engender sympathy.' One who did want to offer compassion was Tony Fell, a childhood neighbour who ranked among Toronto's biggest dealmakers, and who flew specially to New York to offer Black advice. Arriving at the agreed hour, Fell grew angry as he was kept waiting. On his return to Toronto he announced, 'Conrad hasn't got a hope in hell as far as I'm concerned.' Black had lost another ally. The widespread antipathy towards Black did provoke some sympathy. 'What I found truly disgusting,' wrote Dominic Lawson, the editor of the *Sunday Telegraph*, 'is the way in which in recent weeks many of those who enjoyed the Blacks' extraordinary hospitality have been cackling with glee and scorn at the revelations of corporate excess which have brought about their downfall.' He apparently judged his former employer by different criteria from those affecting other dishonest businessmen who featured in his newspaper, and delayed the publication of a commissioned article by Richard Siklos explaining the charges against Black, saying, 'I think it's a bit harsh.'

Barbara Amiel received less open hostility, but she irritated friends who called from London with offers of help. 'I don't know what you're talking about,' she replied to well-wishers. 'Everything is fine.' Ostracised in New York and suffocated by Toronto, she contemplated the legacy of her forty-year struggle for fame and fortune: ridicule, hostile newspaper clippings, broken relationships, no children, and the guarantee of future humiliation. 'Reversal of fortune,' she had written in 1993, 'is this rich bitch's reality.' To turn the wheel again, she flew alone to London for a lunch hosted by the Hong Kong businessman David Tang in honour of George Bush Senior, the former President of the United States. Her appearance aroused curiosity. Many speculated about whether the Blacks' marriage could survive; others were delighted by the couple's deflated egos and the scandal that was now attached to their names. Some remained puzzled, shocked and saddened. 'We live on the edge, with dramas all the time,' Amiel told a guest at the party. 'I never thought I would end up the laughing stock in three continents.'[39] Looking around, she suspected that those who had previously 'licked my boots will be the first to throw stones'. Paranoia gripped her. 'The minute Conrad came under attack,' she would say, 'the things for which I was once idolised or admired or praised became ammunition to attack me. If you live by the press, you die by the press.' A close friend came up to greet her while she was speaking with Tang. 'Am I interrupting?' asked the woman kindly. 'Yes,' snapped Amiel, turning her back and ending another relationship.[40] Tense and fearful, she was consoled by the comfort of some considerable cash deposits. On 12 April 2004 she sold options on Hollinger shares, earning about US$2.25 million. In addition, there was about $3 million paid by Hollinger into a deposit account in Barbados, and the remains of about $150 million personally drawn by Black from Hollinger and Ravelston since 1995. The increasing legal bills, she was assured, would not be a drain on the family's fortune. Conrad Black's lawyers would be paid by Hollinger's insurers. Financial security was the only relief from the unremitting pressure of Richard Breeden's hunt for a scalp.

On 7 May 2004, Hollinger issued a claim against the Blacks for $1.25 billion. Conrad Black and his directors, including Amiel, were accused of carrying out a 'pattern of racketeering' to 'freely plunder the company's coffers to subsidise their own lifestyles' by 'unlawfully' taking US$380 million. The fourfold multiplication of the claim was based on the Racketeer Influenced and Corrupt Organisations Act, commonly known as RICO, introduced in the 1960s as part of the American government's war on the Mafia. The claim's language, which Black, as a frequent litigator, would appreciate, was deliberately colourful in order to attract headlines. 'The Black group,' Breeden had dictated, 'used Hollinger as a cash cow to be milked of every drop of cash . . . Hollinger was a company where abusive practices were inextricably linked to every major development or action,' and 'ethical corruption was a defining characteristic of the leadership team . . . Hollinger had been wilfully and deliberately looted . . . by a persistent and repeated course of illegal conduct . . . The process for approval was cursory and riddled with deception, manipulation and outright fraud.'[41]

'Tabloid journalism masquerading as law,' fumed Black's lawyer in a weak response, conscious that the legal process had become unstoppable. On 28 June 2004, a Delaware court ordered Black and Hollinger Inc. to repay $32 million of the non-compete fees to Hollinger International. Three directors, including Black, complied. Jack Boultbee refused. One month later, on 30 July, the *Telegraph* was sold by an auction organised by Lazards to the Barclay brothers for $1.21 billion. Neither of the Blacks benefited from the $500 million dividend paid from the sale. Instead the money was paid to Hollinger Inc. and used to reduce the company's debts. The empire was in ruins, and Breeden added to the humiliation. In a special report published on 1 September, he described Black and Radler's 'corporate kleptocracy' against Hollinger in hyperbolic language. The defining characteristic of the leaders, declared Breeden, was 'ethical corruption', as shown by an 'overwhelming record of abuse, overreaching, and violations of fiduciary duties by Black and Radler'. Fraud, he said, was at the heart of Hollinger's operations, the company being 'wilfully and deliberately looted by its controlling shareholders'. The non-compete fees were a 'simply bizarre' method to 'take a cut . . . from every deal'. In Hollinger's world, he added, 'everything belonged to the Blacks'. Barbara Amiel's $1.1 million income as an editorial director was derided as the 'generous' consequence of being Black's wife. She was described as a 'ghost employee' whose duties amounted to 'nothing more than euphemisms for ordinary activities such as reading the newspaper, having lunch and chatting with her husband about current events'.[42] Black could only splutter that his foe was recycling 'exaggerated claims laced with outright lies that have been peddled in leaks to the media'. Few cared that some of his alleged excesses were common among large public corporations. The Blacks had been flattened by Breeden's knockout blow. Only their closest friends believed that they could bounce back. Neither, they knew, was prepared to surrender.

The struggle to recover started on 25 August 2004, Conrad Black's sixtieth birthday. Amiel had arranged dinner at the house in Toronto for his three children, old friend Brian Stewart, Amiel's second husband George Jonas, and former employee Ken Whyte. Even two years earlier, few could have imagined such a sombre affair. The Canadian government had placed a lien on the unsold house in Palm Beach in order to recover $11 million in unpaid taxes. Selling the New York apartment was an admission of defeat, although a tolerable one. Black found the area too noisy, and Amiel could stay at the Carlyle Hotel when visiting the city. There was, he knew, little chance of a welcome if he returned to Manhattan.

Whatever he said in public, Black understood the consequence of his miscalculations. Over the previous thirty years he had never experienced such remorseless pursuit by seasoned huntsmen. Assailed from many sides, he was outraged by the unfairness of his plight. 'I hold myself primarily responsible . . . for underestimating the force of the corporate governance movement,' he admitted in self-pity. His defence was familiar. The blame for any wrongdoing was levelled at his in-house lawyers for maintaining 'incomplete documentation'.[43] A similar defence had saved others in his predicament, including Robert Maxwell's sons Kevin and Ian in 1996.

Over the next difficult months, Conrad Black and Barbara Amiel became unseen recluses, both writing books. His was a biography of Richard Nixon, while her ambition was to write a major non-fiction book akin to the work of George Orwell. 'I want to write something,' she explained, 'genuinely original. I want to write in a way that I've never been able to write. This book is my last chance. I shall make something good from this awful time.'[44]

14

Resurrection

An invitation to the wedding of Donald Trump and Melania Knauss on 25 January 2005 at Mar-A-Lago, an exotic club in Palm Beach owned by Trump, was a good excuse for the Blacks to break out of their purdah. They stayed for two weeks in their oceanside house, served by three full-time staff. Curiously, Black was about to pay $460,279 to the Palm Beach tax collector despite his pleas of poverty; and he was paying his gardeners $9,000 a month. The Trump extravaganza, transforming Palm Beach into a party town, was the highlight of the season. Sitting at the reception with a group of New Yorkers, Black made a pitch about his innocence. 'Don't write me off,' he said. 'I'm going to become a corporate-governance counter-terrorist.' Among his audience, Leonard and Evelyn Lauder were definite sympathisers; Tina Brown, the former *New Yorker* editor, classified herself as a friend; while Rudolph Giuliani, the former Mayor of New York who as US Attorney for the Southern District of the city had won fame prosecuting Michael Milliken, was an outright antagonist. All listened politely as Black expressed his passion about combating the shareholders and regulators, drawing strength from his convinced self-righteousness. Within his own universe, he was isolated from retribution. 'All his life,' Black had written of the newspaper tycoon William Randolph Hearst, 'he had a conviction, often outrageous but sometimes magnificent, that the rules that applied to others didn't apply to him.' Similarly, Black felt that his innocent deeds had been deliberately distorted by disbelievers. Some would deride his self-delusional denial of reality; others even perceived the cold mind of a criminal. There was a third group from whom Black drew comfort: the hard core of supporters convinced of his cause. All knew that he would inevitably be judged. To secure his survival, Black demanded to be found innocent.

At the same party, sitting near Bill Clinton, Barbara Amiel, dressed in a sultry black Carolina Herrera gown and a huge emerald necklace, nodded her approval. Nearly thirty years earlier she had castigated the 'moral myopia' of John Dean, President Nixon's lawyer, for refusing to accept responsibility for his actions. Neither she nor Conrad Black appeared to recognise the parallel with their own lives. For her part, Amiel had decided to dispel the myths and assert her self-esteem in an interview with the *Toronto Sun*.

In the empty reception area of a Toronto hotel, Lady Black sought compassion. 'It's been an awful time,' she admitted. 'I'm Jewish. I do believe in suffering but there is a limit. It's not pleasant to be the object of derision on three continents.' During those months of solitude, her anger had festered and her insecurity exploded. 'I hoped I was shocking,' she explained, in a candid admission of her past self-promotion. 'I hoped I wasn't boring. I hoped I was attractive and sexy. It's a combination of money, power and glamour that is irresistible. You play for all it's worth if you can.' She had succeeded in all her ambitions. But having played hard, she found herself loathed, and contrary to modern truisms, she had not become stronger as a result. 'I don't think it has given me the character I lack,' she said with some self-awareness. Self-pityingly, she blamed her good looks and love of clothes for having distracted attention from the quality of her writing, although she admitted: 'Perhaps it's an excuse because I just never had enough talent to be what I wanted to be.' Divorce, she said, was not on the agenda. On the contrary, the problems had strengthened the Blacks' relationship. In a final quest for sympathy, she added, 'He'll be back. I'm not so sure about me.'

If Amiel had said no more, she might have regained some sympathy, but instead she offered snapshot judgements which belied reality. Even in the good times, she said, her marriage to Conrad Black had 'wrecked my life'. By dividing her time between being a socialite and a writer, 'I lost all my friends, all my work because of him. I've had to be a schizophrenic with Conrad and that's been a tremendous strain.' She seemed to forget that insulting friends had been a trademark of hers throughout her marriage, and that she had used her relationship with Black to promote her profile and increase her personal income. Her perception of capitalism remained warped. The *Telegraph*, she insisted, had 'never made any money'; she justified the £103 million pay package taken by Dick Grasso, the retiring chief executive of the New York Stock Exchange, and attacked his critics for pursuing 'corporate McCarthyism'; and she attacked envious Americans for championing 'egalitarianism' rather than capitalism. Like her husband, she believed she could persuade the world about the plight of Conrad Black as an honest man victimised by those with evil intentions.

The day of judgement was certainly approaching. David Radler, the Blacks knew, was discussing a plea bargain with prosecution lawyers representing the US Attorney in Chicago. The attorney himself, Patrick Fitzgerald, the forty-five-year-old son of an Irish-immigrant doorman, epitomised the type of crusading prosecutor whom the Blacks despised. Renowned as a workaholic and a zealous champion of morality, and with a remarkable memory for intricate details, Fitzgerald represented an additional challenge. He had successfully prosecuted al-Qaeda terrorists in New York and corrupt politicians in Chicago. Shortly, he would be chosen to investigate an alleged leak of information from the White House intended to embarrass critics of the Iraq war. Independently-minded avenging angels, in Conrad Black's opinion, were prone to grab a miscreant's jugular. Richard Breeden's headline-chasing conclusion of 'corporate kleptocracy' had not been ignored by Chicago's attorney.

Black was not entirely surprised by Radler's negotiations with the prosecution. Since the sale to CanWest, their relations had deteriorated. While Black had pursued his social ambitions, Radler and his daughter had nurtured Horizon, his new business based in Marion, Illinois, expanding to own thirty-seven newspapers. The fissures became a permanent fracture after Black reneged on the November agreement with Hollinger's directors. In Radler's opinion there was no point in fighting a political war for a lost cause. Crimes, he knew, had been committed.

Fearing that his demons were gathering for the kill, Black panicked. On 20 May 2005 he entered his former headquarters at 10 Toronto Street by a rear door without permission. He carried thirteen boxes of Hollinger papers to his waiting car, assuming that his entry would remain unnoticed because the security video machinery had broken down more than two years earlier. Unknown to him, the company's new managers had arranged the equipment's repair earlier that very week. As Black left the building, a camera turned and focused on him. Surprised, Black looked up and smiled wanly, reinforcing the impression of his dishonesty. On the court's order the boxes were eventually returned, but what Black retained was unknown.

In those messy circumstances, Conrad Black looked for a stage from which to mount a revival. There was no better venue than London, where no one had lost money on his account, and many recalled his good company. Although he had barely attended the House of Lords – making only eight appearances out of a possible 174 debates in 2002–03, and just one the following year – he contemplated a star performance in front of the peers to prove his respectability. There were other reasons for the journey. The American patron of the arts Drue Heinz, Black was pleased to note, had sent an invitation for her annual summer party. 'It's in my honour,' he told his friends. 'I'm thinking of coming to Britain. What will happen?' he asked Tim Bell. 'You'll be greeted by some, shunned by others and ignored by the rest. And if there's any publicity, the media will come for you.' 'Why?' asked Black. 'Because they think you're guilty.' Others were more reassuring. Taki exclaimed: 'Of course you've got a future in London. Just go to the House of Lords and speak.' 'At least I know now who my friends are,' replied Black. Only one decision remained: where to stay in London. The house in Cottesmore Gardens had been sold in May to a former Mexican beauty queen for £11.5 million. Her builders were ripping out the Blacks' expensive designs, while most of his furniture was in storage. The entire proceeds of the sale repaid debts. His new home would be a room at the Berkeley Hotel in Knightsbridge. 'I'm Lady Black of no fixed address,' Amiel announced.[1] Her black humour was tinged with brittleness, about both her health and her status.

Lord Black's entrance at Drue Heinz's party shocked many guests. His manner was unaltered from his behaviour two years earlier as proprietor of the *Telegraph*. He behaved as if nothing had changed. The former diplomat Sir Nicholas Henderson left the room in apparent disgust. Others were paralysed. Black moved towards Max Hastings, who was standing in a group. Seven years earlier, long after Hastings had resigned as the *Daily Telegraph*'s editor, Black had been a guest for dinner at his country home. Holding a glass of champagne, he had stood in the living room of the comfortable stone house. 'You know, Max,' he had said, 'if you'd stayed with us, you could have had a house twice the size.' In Heinz's home, Black continued the conversation as if nothing had intervened. He spoke of opportunities, and invited Hastings to consider joining an internet company, before moving to another guest to enquire whether he should make a speech in the House of Lords. 'I don't think that would be wise,' he was told.

Over the next few days, accompanied by Barbara Amiel, Black attended lunches and dinners with Princess Michael of Kent, Rupert Hambro, Maurice Saatchi and Jacob Rothschild. Twelve years earlier the Blacks had flown to Jerusalem to watch Rothschild, surrounded by twenty-two members of his family, hand over the new supreme court building, constructed with finance provided by the family's trusts, to the Israeli government. Black knew it would be hard to secure a similar public embrace from the banking family. 'Do you think I should give a speech in the House of Lords?' he asked at every party. 'You must be mad,' was one response. Black hid his disappointment, trying to give the impression that he was unaffected by his problems.

'Conrad thinks he can't do wrong because he's Conrad,' said Charles Powell. One guest at Maurice Saatchi's lunch party in the country declared that Black was like a child who just did not understand. Echoing that observation, the writer Josephine Hart, Saatchi's wife, announced, 'Conrad is the victim of his own innocence.' David Metcalfe, one of Black's original friends in London, tried to arrange a dinner party on 27 July, but found that nearly everyone was unable to accept his invitation. In the end Black arrived late, having lost his way, and stayed until nearly dawn reminiscing about the good times with Metcalfe and Algy Cluff. He misjudged his English friends' polite reticence. Their silence about his plight as the victim of the corporate-governance activists, he assumed, indicated their sympathy. In reality, they were bewildered. No one but him could imagine the custodians of the National Portrait Gallery again agreeing to exhibit the portrait of the Blacks by India-Jane Birley, the stepdaughter of James Goldsmith. Nor could he expect in the future to be invited to grand dinners at Windsor Castle or Buckingham Palace. His affiliate membership of the English establishment, and his dream of a permanent legacy inscribed in granite had been terminated.

Towards the end of their stay, the Blacks went to Annabel's. Conrad Black spotted Andrew Neil, who had published criticism of his conduct. 'You should be ashamed of yourself,' Black reprimanded Neil. 'You're the one who should be ashamed,' Neil shot back, fully understanding the sources of Black's self-enrichment. Amiel held back. Throughout their visit she had repeatedly confessed her anguish, expressing fear to her hosts about the future. At the same time, she hated those girlfriends mentioning the 'tragedy' and 'horror'. Confused and distraught, she would no longer be able to greet the Canadian wife of Tate & Lyle's chairman with a disdainful 'Do I know you?' Although Black was angry, before leaving Annabel's Amiel thanked Neil for giving her a column in the *Sunday Times*. Peace of a kind was restored. If everything went wrong, she decided, she would resume her life in a small house in London. Soon after, the Blacks returned to Canada. Behind them they left talk of hubris and retribution.

During the remainder of the summer, Conrad Black assessed his plight. In New York a handful of friends remained, including Alfred Taubman. In London there were more friends, but their unenthusiastic response to his complaints was disappointing, even if visitors like the comedian Barry Humphries restored his self-assurance. Toronto, the historic centre of antagonism towards himself, had become by default his permanent home. Four years after insulting the country and renouncing his Canadian citizenship, he had no choice but to rebuild his self-confidence in an alienated environment. Canada would be the battleground on which he would rebuke the unfaithful. Even if the Churchill Society found difficulty in filling Black's table at their annual dinner, he decided to ignore the ostracism. He would not, he resolved, be excluded from any public gathering. On the contrary, he would attend every party in order to pronounce his innocence and denounce the smears. Initially his appearances aroused excitement, but gradually this was replaced by mere curiosity.

Only occasionally was Barbara by his side. Unlike Black, she found the ceaseless stab wounds painful. Spotted sitting with her husband in the corner of a Toronto restaurant by Allan Fotheringham, she appeared 'angry, like a whipped little puppy'. She admired Black's bid for resurrection despite the sound of the gallows being erected, but she despaired about his adversaries. The American regulators, she knew, took no prisoners, and on 15 August 2005 the news was bad. David Radler and Mark Kipnis were formally charged with defrauding Hollinger's shareholders of $32 million in non-compete fees. Radler, it was revealed, would be pleading guilty, although any hopes that the prosecutors might have harboured that Kipnis would also plead guilty were dashed.

On 20 September Radler concluded his negotiations with the prosecution. He formally pleaded guilty, and agreed to testify against Black and any other directors. His punishment, if he fulfilled his promise at the trial, would be twenty-nine months' imprisonment in a Canadian 'country club' jail, and a $250,000 fine. With so many millions of dollars concealed offshore, Radler calculated that a short punishment followed by a quiet life with his family was infinitely preferable to the prospect of lengthy incarceration in a maximum-security American prison. 'Radler's a germophobe and a racist,' representatives of Black told enquirers. 'He's terrified of prison. So he copped a plea.' The habit of American prosecutors of terrifying alleged culprits with the threat of what they would undergo in prison was, Black's spokesman claimed, a practised perversion of American justice. In the forthcoming trial, Black decided that Radler would be portrayed as both the victim of extortion by business-haters like Patrick Fitzgerald, and as the Hollinger executive entirely responsible for managing the corporation's accounts. The defence was taking shape. Conrad Black would pose as a martyr for entrepreneurs fighting for justice. He saw himself as resembling Alfred Dreyfus, the Jewish French military officer who was jailed in 1895 for a crime he did not commit and was eventually pardoned after Emile Zola's famous open letter 'J'Accuse'. To his supporters he portrayed himself as the Restorer of the Faith.

The weeks before Black's appearance in court were strewn with incidents which he interpretated as demonstrating the state's vendetta against him. Hours after the completion of the sale of his Park Avenue apartment for $10.5 million, $7.5 million more than Black said was the 'fair market value' in 2001, the FBI seized $8.9 million of the proceeds as suspected loot. 'I'm going to sue the US government,' Black announced loudly at a party in Toronto celebrating the publication of George Jonas's autobiography. Standing in the centre of an uncrowded room with Amiel, he described himself as the victim of state terrorism. Seizing an unconvicted man's property, he said, was precisely the kind of arbitrary abuse of power banned by the Bill of Rights, which US prosecutors were ignoring.

There were murmurs of approval from his audience. 'You've been treated viciously,' agreed Black's Canadian lawyer Eddie Greenspan, mentioning a 'witch-hunt'. The Americans, he continued, were hungry to ridicule 'a non-American and a lord'. Hollinger had not been a bankruptcy like Enron and WorldCom. On the contrary, shareholders had seen the original £40 million investment in the *Telegraph* grow to be worth £650 million. Warming to his theme, Black denounced Fitzgerald. 'It's one massive smear job from A to Z. I accept he's a competent prosecutor, but he doesn't know anything about this case. He just swoops in for the press conference and fluffs his lines.' Not everyone was impressed. Fitzgerald had just charged US Vice President Dick Cheney's chief of staff with leaking information in order to harm a critic of the Iraq war. He was not someone to be easily dismissed. One guest told Black, 'You're like Don Quixote. You always think you can deliver a fatal blow to the enemy. Don't you realise that everyone's your enemy and you're fighting too many battles?' Black looked perplexed. Did the man not understand, he replied, that the world's greatest military strategists had long advocated attacks on every front? Exhaustion would destroy his enemies, he predicted confidently. The disbelievers would eventually be converted. Over the previous forty years he had lived his own invention. He would now survive the endgame.

The inevitable news was delivered just before 15 November 2005. Fitzgerald, Black heard, had completed the indictment against him, Atkinson, Boultbee and Kipnis. The same night, the centenary birthday party of *Maclean's* magazine was held. Ken Whyte, the editor, wanted 'a party to remember'. At Black's suggestion he asked the theatrical impresario Garth Dabrinsky, a fugitive from American justice, to arrange the entertainment. Like members of the royal family, a smiling Black and Amiel arrived at the event in the Ford Centre for the Performing Arts. 'She's just come from plastic surgery in California,' whispered one observer, amazed by Amiel's appearance. 'No, she goes to Houston,' said another, similarly impressed. Moving through the crowd, Black nodded greetings. He was on stage, performing for the cameras to prove he was not a beaten man. To capture the headlines on the eve of his indictment, he had arranged for his lawyers to spring a surprise. Toronto's journalists were to be reminded of the 'Black Terror'. His target was Peter Newman, the former editor of *Maclean's* and Black's first biographer, who was flying specially from London for the party. Black savoured the moment as Newman entered the theatre and a lawyer jumped from the crowd to serve a writ alleging defamation of Black in his recent autobiography. Shocked, Newman handed the papers claiming $2.1 million damages to Michael Levine, his lawyer. 'Suing is like sex for Conrad,' John Fraser grinned knowingly. As he sat under the hot stage lights, Black's smile broadened. The orchestra began playing 'Somewhere Over the Rainbow'. Bored and irritated, Canada's famous singer-songwriter Gordon Lightfoot walked out. Conrad Black stayed to the bitter end. The awful party was preferable to returning home.

Two days later, Fitzgerald struck. His press conference in Chicago left nothing to the imagination. 'All in all,' said Fitzgerald as he announced eight charges, 'what has happened here is a gross abuse by officers and directors and insiders who decided to line their pockets.' Robert Grant, an FBI agent, described the frauds as 'blatant and pervasive', and expressed his surprise that the rich should 'choose to steal with both hands with a greed almost unfathomable to your average American citizen'. Two weeks later, Black faced a total of twelve charges for defrauding shareholders of $84 million, with a maximum sentence of ninety-five years in prison. The charges included racketeering, obstruction of justice and mail-and-wire fraud, embracing the crime of 'depriving another of the intangible right of honest services'. Specific charges included the non-compete payments in the sales of newspapers to CanWest and Community Newspaper Holdings; the 'fraudulent misuse' of corporate funds on Barbara Amiel's birthday party at La Grenouille; the cost of the flight to Bora Bora; and the apartment swap in New York.

The indictment was short and simple. To set the scene, the prosecution would expose Conrad Black's excessive spending at the shareholders' expense, and would then describe the more complicated phoney non-compete fees. They would need a unanimous verdict from the jury. The star witness would be Radler, supported by the emails and documents. Fitzgerald knew that Radler was an unappealing witness, vulnerable to demolition by a competent defence lawyer. To help his case, Fitzgerald had decided not to pursue the three members of the audit committee. In exchange for cooperating as witnesses in the trial, at which they would be expected to denounce Black for his deceit, Governor Thompson, Marie-Josée Kravis and Richard Burt would only suffer a 'Wells' letter from the SEC, allowing them to negotiate a settlement without incurring a serious penalty, although their reputations would be sullied. Kravis was about to resign from the board of Ford Motors. Similarly, Beth DeMarchant and Hollinger's other lawyers at Torys were vulnerable to criticism after the partnership paid $30 million in an agreement to settle 'without liability' the claim that it had failed to fulfil its professional duties. Because of that, Black consoled himself that his conviction was not, as some seemed to think, a foregone conclusion. He ignored recent judgements which undermined his defence of placing all the blame on David Radler and his professional advisers.

To avoid becoming immersed in the detail of the non-compete fees, the prosecution would concentrate on Black's honesty towards his directors and professional advisers. If Black were to be convicted, the prosecution would need to prove that he knew about the crimes which Radler had admitted. The prosecution's burden was to portray Black as a greedy liar who deliberately ignored the signs of fraud by consciously turning a blind eye to wrongdoing. The chances of conviction, Fitzgerald believed, would be immeasurably improved if Conrad Black testified and subjected himself to cross-examination. A Chicago jury, he reasoned, were 'meat and potatoes folk', and would not warm towards an arrogant businessman, aggressively self-promoting and accustomed to getting his own way. Fitzgerald's hope that Black would be irresistibly drawn to grandstand in the witness box was not dampened by Black's old friend Eddie Greenspan, appointed as one of Black's defenders. 'I'm going to the trial to win,' said Greenspan, 'and the jury is our ultimate weapon.' Greenspan would work with Ed Genson, a Chicago criminal advocate who suffers from a neuromuscular condition and arrives in court on a special buggy, in which he either sits close to witnesses or shouts across the courtroom.

So much, Black knew, would depend upon image. He was

horrified by the prospect of arriving at the Chicago courthouse on 1 December 2005 handcuffed and surrounded by law officers. The photographs, he knew, would be devastating. After negotiations, that theatricality was abandoned, and Black was allowed to walk freely into the courthouse designed by Mies van der Rohe, the German architect renowned for saying 'God is in the details' and, appropriately in the circumstances, 'Less is more.' Black was photographed and fingerprinted before standing before Judge Amy St Eve, a sassy, good-looking and experienced fraud expert who had successfully prosecuted the politicians involved in the Whitewater scandal, a deception in Arkansas which some believed incriminated President and Hillary Clinton. St Eve's pleasant courtroom demeanour did not disguise the forty-one-year-old mother of three's steely ambition. Black's prosecution would guarantee her the spotlight and, if successfully managed, a chance for promotion.

Bail was agreed at $20 million, secured against the house in Palm Beach and the proceeds of the sale of the apartment in Manhattan. Black pleaded that he was impoverished, without any income. He appeared to omit to explain how he paid taxes for his homes in Toronto and Palm Beach, the source of the monthly $9,000 payment to his gardeners, and his investment in Horizon Publications. Nor did he disclose that he expected to receive $5.8 million from the sale of Horizon debentures, and that Amiel owned shares worth $10 million in Horizon Operations. The trial date was set for 5 March 2007. Eight months later, in August 2006, Fitzgerald would accuse Black of concealing his true assets. Contrary to his plea of having no income, scrutiny of Black's lifestyle by the American prosecutors showed that he was spending over $200,000 every month, including $114,000 on his Toronto home's mortgage. Embarrassingly for Black, a bank would disclose a deposit of $272,000 in his account, which he would explain was part of the $2 million he borrowed from Amiel.

Fitzgerald would mockingly tell the judge that Black possessed the 'Midas touch': 'Black's assets mysteriously increase in value without his knowledge, his debts diminish overnight, his business partners want to give him millions of dollars he never even realised he was owed, and he is able to take all the accolades for charitable distributions from a $3.1 million foundation, despite claiming no direct or indirect control over the foundation's assets.' The prosecutor would accuse Black of feeding the court 'lies, half truths, mistakes, misunderstandings and legal loopholes' about his personal finances. He would persuade Judge St Eve to increase the bail by $1 million in cash. To increase the pressure, he would also charge Black with evading payment of $29 million in taxes by Hollinger International Inc. in 1999 and 2000; and, adding spice to the case, he would ask the court to order Black to forfeit a twenty-six-carat diamond ring allegedly worth $2.6 million, accusing the former chairman of further misusing corporate funds. A Canadian court would subsequently order a freeze on all the Blacks' assets across the world, including their offshore accounts, and allow them to draw only C$50,000 (US$46,000) every month for their living expenses plus legal fees until they had properly accounted for all their assets.

The following day, Black's fate was front-page news across the world. The comparisons with other tycoons were unsettling. Bernie Ebbers of WorldCom and Dennis Kozlowski of Tyco had been sentenced to twenty-five years' imprisonment, John Rigas of Adelphia to fifteen years and his son Timothy to twenty years. Yet Ebbers' bail had been set at $10 million, while Ken Lay of Enron's had been fixed at a mere $500,000. Black appeared to be victimised by the Chicago prosecutors and judge.

Under siege, Black's public image was one of robust defiance despite the emergence of one particular statistic during the legal battles between Hollinger International, Hollinger Inc., Ravelston, Horizon, Bradford, Hollinger's shareholders and Black himself.

Between 1997 and 2003 the Black group had taken $391 million out of Hollinger in income and expenses, which amounted to 73 per cent of the company's entire net income. That amount was surpassed in Hollinger International's claim against the Black group for $425.2 million plus interest, a total of $541.9 million. The enormous claims cast uncertainty over Black's finances, especially his ability to pay his defence lawyers. About $200 million, paid by Hollinger to Black, remained to be accounted for.

Having sold or mortgaged his homes to deter potential litigants, Black felt under no obligation to reveal whether the money transferred to Barbados and the Cayman Islands was still in the original accounts. Nor did he reveal the value of his shares in Horizon Publications and Horizon Operations, worth about $22 million. In his statement to the court in Chicago, he estimated that he had just $300,000 at his disposal. Eventually he expected Hollinger's insurance policies to pay for his defence. Pending that payment, he called several friends in New York. 'Do you think you can get a group of people who might get together if the need arises,' he asked one billionaire, 'and get me some funds secured against my property?' 'How much do you want from everyone, Conrad?' asked the businessman. 'About one million each,' said Black. There was a pause. 'You're my best friend,' continued Black. 'Surely you can lend me $1 million?' 'Well, Conrad,' said the man, 'what's my private telephone number?' 'I don't know. Why?' replied Black. 'Well, if I were your best friend, you'd have it.' The first to refuse any contribution outright was Alfred Taubman. The rest followed suit. They were disdainful of a man famous for his excesses and the collapse of his empire rather than his achievements. Several months later, Hollinger International's insurers agreed to contribute towards Black's legal bills, including $4.4 million towards the costs of the Delaware trial, 50 per cent of his costs in any civil proceedings, and 75 per cent of his lawyers' fees in the criminal trial.

Ostracised in New York and an object of curiosity in London, Black was reassured by a group of sympathisers in Toronto. George Jonas, Anna Porter, John Fraser and other old admirers seemed to accept his patiently pleaded arguments that greed was not criminal, and that unlike Enron, the Hollinger débâcle had not resulted in anyone losing their jobs, pensions or money. On the contrary, Hollinger, Black insisted, was in perfect health until the intervention of Richard Breeden and Gordon Paris. Surely capitalists were entitled to cut corners in order to create wealth. Such comforting arguments ignored Black's successive concealment of his self-enriching deals from his fellow directors, and the fantasies he offered to the public. The alternative was too awful to contemplate. There was sympathy towards his complaints of persecution after courts had approved the sale of his beloved possessions owned by Hollinger, including his lake cruiser, Bud McDougald's Rolls-Royce in London and the furniture at 10 Toronto Street.

But even Conrad Black's admirers could not quite explain his abrupt demise. Just why was the self-styled billionaire so brutally humbled? The sight of his relaxed performances at Toronto's social functions, whether engaged in conversation with Bill Clinton at a $1,600-a-plate fundraiser, or among Canada's arts benefactors at the opening of Toronto's new opera house, to which the charitable Black Family Foundation had contributed $500,000, jarred with the mundane allegation that he was no more than a common white-collar criminal, lacking a conscience, deceiving legions of honest and intelligent professionals. There was comfort in wrongly blaming Lady Black's extravagance for provoking her husband's plunder; or in mentioning Conrad Black's congenital self-delusion since childhood; or in simply murmuring 'tragedy' and requoting his assurance of a sensational contest against the 'corporate terrorists', followed by acquittal. Black's performances disarmed the believers during the weeks before the trial. To those people, Conrad Black represented a question. The answer was best provided by Black himself.

'The only person who will take me way,' he once boasted, 'will be the undertaker, and when they open the coffin it will be empty. I'll be gone.' On 5 March 2007, this modern-day Houdini expects the curtain to rise for his greatest performance. Fate determined that Lord Black's life would be judged by a jury of common men and women, rather than by his peers.

Conrad Black never imagined that he would be at the mercy of people he despised. Nor did he expect ever to stand trial accused of fraud. Convinced of his abilities and his fluent performance, he was certain of permanently outwitting those he deemed his inferiors. His self-confidence was fuelled by his admirers. Dozens of educated and intelligent professionals in America and Europe were impressed by the self-styled billionaire whom they saw as an engaging romantic, endearingly energised by history's heroes, his single identifiable flaw being verbosity. His calm, courteous manner and solid conservative politics eliminated even the possibility that he could be a charlatan flouting the rules. Pertinently, while London had drawn lessons about media tycoons from the Maxwell saga, and Toronto had been permanently scarred by Black's threats, New York's financial and political community trusted the man who thrived on secrecy and menace. Unlike in Toronto and London, the praise in New York for his talents suffocated any doubts about his probity.

Those famous courtiers, eagerly accepting payment to sit quietly over lunch while their host prattled about world politics, should be ashamed of themselves. Without demur, they uncritically accepted Conrad Black on his own terms. Never once did they adequately query the absence of any vision, or the justification for the empire's dismantlement. Never did they debate Black's purpose in society. Even after the alarm was raised by shareholders at the annual general meeting in May 2002, the famous directors remained silent and disengaged. Black's talent was to pander to the vanities of those self-important noblemen, exposing their judgement as worthless. Their self-importance reflected their selfishness. As much as Conrad Black, those personalities will also be on trial in Chicago.

The consequence of their inactivity was the ease with which Black and David Radler were able to pocket over $400 million in seven years – money that belonged to the other 81 per cent of Hollinger's shareholders. Conrad Black will assert that the payments were authorised. By contrast, Radler has confessed that the diversions were, so far as he was concerned, criminal.

Barbara Amiel shares Lord Black's conviction that both are the innocent victims of the 'tall poppy syndrome' – giants attacked by envious, spiteful midgets. Mirroring the plight of Sherman McCoy in Tom Wolfe's *The Bonfire of the Vanities*, Lady Black is convinced that her husband is the target of a plot by prosecutors and the media to devour an outstanding capitalist.

Amiel's own conduct has arguably contributed to their predicament. Opinionated, ostentatious and undisguisedly extravagant, she never judged her own and her husband's obligations towards Hollinger's shareholders by the same criteria she applied to other mortals. Despite a journalistic legacy of self-revelation and self-criticism, she appears never to have questioned the source of the money which enabled her to maintain four homes, a small army of staff and a private jet. While casting moral judgements upon the Palestinians, Harold Macmillan and politically-correct politicians, she never turned the mirror upon her own commercial conduct. Had she been more self-aware, even as late as November 2003, she might well have saved her husband from the risk of life imprisonment by persuading him to honour the agreement with Hollinger's directors and repay $7.2 million. By paying that comparative trifle, Conrad Black would probably have been spared the torrid events which now await him. Self-obsession, undiluted by sufficient social conscience, has immunised Barbara Amiel from understanding the outrage provoked by her husband's conduct, even if it is found not to be criminal.

In his last email to me, on 1 April 2006, Black promised 'a spectacular trial'. His misfortune will be to forget that the production is controlled by a judge, not by himself. Individuals seeking the limelight in the cause of justice are frequently crushed by the institutionalised atmosphere and procedures of a courtroom. Conrad Black expects to be the exception – a common thread throughout his life.

To use one of his favoured expressions, there is a symmetry in Conrad Black's progress from stealing examination papers at school to standing in a courtroom accused of stealing shareholders' funds. The aberration of his life is that none of his heroes – Roosevelt, Lincoln, de Gaulle and Thatcher – would have been caught up in such sordid events. Unsurprisingly, Conrad Black was simply too lazy to learn the real lessons of history.

NOTES

Introduction:
The Wedding, 26 January 1985

1 'Nothing Succeeds Like Excess', *Chatelaine*
2 'Why Women Marry Up', *Chatelaine*, May 1986
3 *Maclean's*, 8 May 1989
4 *Maclean's*, 29 December 1980
5 'Why Women Marry Up', *Chatelaine*, May 1986
6 Ibid.

Chapter 1: A Timely Death

1 Siklos, *Shades of Black*, p.6
2 Black, *A Life in Progress*, p.154
3 Ibid., p.169
4 Ibid., p.156
5 Ibid., pp.190–1
6 Ibid., pp.154, 186
7 Ibid., p.175
8 Newman, *The Establishment Man*, p.34
9 Ibid., p.11
10 Ibid., p.15
11 Ibid., p.16
12 Ibid., p.17
13 Ibid., p.15
14 Ibid., p.17
15 Ibid., p.33
16 Ibid., p.49
17 Debbie Melnyk, *Citizen Black*, CBC TV documentary, 21 October 1996
18 Black, *A Life in Progress*, pp.71–2
19 Ibid., pp.190–1
20 Ibid., p.58
21 Ibid., p.106
22 Ibid., pp.123–4
23 Ibid., p.113
24 Ibid., p.60
25 Ibid., p.124
26 Ibid., p.181
27 Ibid., pp.134, 132
28 Ibid., p.141
29 Ibid., p.57
30 Siklos, *Shades of Black*, p.48
31 Newman, *The Establishment Man*, p.98
32 Ibid., p.91
33 Ibid., p.125
34 Black, *A Life in Progress*, p.188
35 Newman, *The Establishment Man*, p.101
36 Siklos, *Shades of Black*, p.53
37 Black, *A Life in Progress*, p.201
38 Newman, *The Establishment Man*, p.102
39 Siklos, *Shades of Black*, p.55
40 Black, *A Life in Progress*, p.205
41 Ibid., p.203
42 Ibid., p.201
43 Newman, *The Establishment Man*, p.134
44 Black, *A Life in Progress*, p.207
45 Ibid., p.214
46 Siklos, *Shades of Black*, p.57
47 Ibid., p.59
48 Black, *A Life in Progress*, p.226
49 Ibid., p.217
50 'The Argus Grab', *Maclean's*, 26 June 1978

Chapter 2: The Stain

1 Black, *A Life in Progress*, p.207
2 Ibid., p.255
3 Siklos, *Shades of Black*, p.66
4 Black, *A Life in Progress*, pp.269ff
5 Ibid., pp.269, 317–18
6 Ibid., pp.224, 256–7
7 Siklos, *Shades of Black*, p.66
8 Newman, *The Establishment Man*, p.166
9 Newman, *Here be Dragons*, p.445
10 McNish and Stewart, *Wrong Way*, p.31
11 Newman, *The Establishment Man*, p.223
12 Black, *A Life in Progress*, p.233
13 Newman, *The Establishment Man*, pp.235–6
14 Newman, *Here be Dragons*, p.416
15 Ibid., p.446
16 Black, *A Life in Progress*, p.247
17 Siklos, *Shades of Black*, p.69
18 Black, *A Life in Progress*, p.253
19 Ibid., p.251
20 Ibid., p.281
21 *Maclean's*, 21 February 1983; and court documents
22 Black, *A Life in Progress*, p.282
23 *Maclean's*, 21 February 1983; and court documents
24 Black, *A Life in Progress*, p.284
25 Ibid., p.286
26 Ibid., pp.274–5
27 Ibid., p.328
28 Ibid., p.282; Newman, *The Establishment Man*, pp.248–9
29 Black, *A Life in Progress*, p.287; Siklos, *Shades of Black*, p.90
30 *Maclean's*, 21 February 1983
31 Black, *A Life in Progress*, p.293
32 Ibid., p.299
33 Newman, *The Establishment Man*, p.449
34 Black, *A Life in Progress*, p.277
35 US SEC Form 8-K, 'Hollinger International', 30 August 2004, p.4
36 Black, *A Life in Progress*, p.290
37 Ibid., p.297
38 Newman, *The Establishment Man*, p.239
39 Black, *A Life in Progress*, p.315
40 Ibid., pp.298–306
41 Debbie Melnyk, *Citizen Black*, CBC TV
42 Newman, *The Establishment Man*, p.257
43 Black, *A Life in Progress*, p.308
44 Siklos, *Shades of Black*, p.180
45 Newman, *The Establishment Man*, p.246
46 Ibid., p.175
47 Ibid., p.174
48 Ibid., p.176
49 Ibid., p.175
50 Ibid., p.274

Chapter 3: The Survivor

1 Siklos, *Shades of Black*, p.211
2 Amiel, *Confessions*, p.39
3 Ibid., p.18
4 Ibid., p.32
5 Ibid., p.20
6 Ibid., p.32
7 Ibid., p.59
8 Ibid., p.42
9 *Tatler*, July–August 1988
10 *Daily Telegraph*, 17 April 1997
11 Amiel, *Confessions*, p.64
12 Ibid., p.45
13 Ibid., p.60
14 *Maclean's*, 18 September 1978
15 Jonas, *Beethoven's Mask*, p.224

16 *Tatler*, July–August 1988
17 Ibid.
18 *Sunday Times*, 10 July 1994
19 Amiel, *Confessions*, pp.144–5
20 Ibid., p.75
21 McNish and Stewart, *Wrong Way*, p.6
22 *Vogue*, July 2002; *Saturday Night*, November 2004
23 Zolf, *A Personal Memoir*, p.192
24 Amiel, *Confessions*, p.81
25 Ibid., p.86
26 Ibid., pp.64, 67
27 *Maclean's*, 20 August 1966
28 Newman, *Here be Dragons*, p.420
29 Ibid., p.422
30 *Maclean's*, 28 September 1981
31 *Maclean's*, 8 May 1989
32 Amiel, *Confessions*, p.129
33 Newman, *Here be Dragons*, p.419
34 Amiel, *Confessions*, p.130
35 *Vanity Fair*, November 1992
36 *Tatler*, July–August 1988
37 Amiel, *Confessions*, p.130
38 Ibid., p.128
39 Ibid., p.88
40 Ibid., p.93
41 Ibid., p.98
42 Ibid., pp.102, 103, 111
43 Ibid., p.46
44 Ibid., p.100
45 *Maclean's*, 29 December 1980
46 Amiel, *Confessions*, pp.141, 144
47 Ibid., p.108
48 *Maclean's* review of John Dean's *Blind Ambition*, 1976
49 *Maclean's*, 3 October 1994
50 'Nothing Succeeds Like Excess', *Chatelaine*

Chapter 4: Salvation

1 Debbie Melnyk, *Citizen Black*, CBC TV
2 Black, *A Life in Progress*, p.357
3 Ibid., p.352
4 Ibid., p.387; and writ
5 Black, *A Life in Progress*, p.359
6 Ibid., p.388
7 Siklos, *Shades of Black*, p.119
8 Black, *A Life in Progress*, p.346
9 Ibid., p.347
10 Newman, *Here be Dragons*, p.457
11 *Spectator*, 30 November 1985
12 *Spectator*, 23 November 1985
13 Debbie Melnyk, *Citizen Black*, CBC TV

Chapter 5: The Visit

1 Siklos, *Shades of Black*, p.x
2 Ibid., p.182
3 Hastings, *Editor*, p.82
4 Ibid., p.167
5 Ibid., p.235
6 Black, *A Life in Progress*, p.53
7 Ibid., p.102
8 *Financial Times*, 17 August 1987
9 Siklos, *Shades of Black*, p.154
10 *Canadian Business*, November 1991
11 Debbie Melnyk, *Citizen Black*, CBC TV
12 *Globe and Mail*, 25 July 1987
13 Coleridge, *Paper Tigers*, p.309
14 Boultbee letter to *Esquire*, 2 September 1992
15 Newman, *The Establishment Man*, p.403
16 Black, *A Life in Progress*, p.410
17 Ibid., p.404
18 Ibid., p.407

19 Ibid., p.396
20 Newman, *The Establishment Man*, p.109
21 *Financial Times*, 18 November 1989
22 Siklos, *Shades of Black*, p.160
23 Black, *A Life in Progress*, p.426
24 Ibid., p.427; Hastings, *Editor*, pp.188, 191
25 Debbie Melnyk, *Citizen Black*, CBC TV
26 Black, *A Life in Progress*, p.460
27 Ibid., p.446
28 Siklos, *Shades of Black*, p.208

Chapter 6: Inevitable Union

1 Amiel, *Confessions*, p.144–5
2 Hastings, *Editor*, p.236
3 *Vanity Fair*, November 1992
4 *Chatelaine*, May 1986
5 Wyatt, *Diaries, Vol. 1*, p.392; 21 July 1987
6 Ibid., pp.508, 603
7 *Tatler*, July–August 1988
8 Wyatt, *Diaries*, p.696
9 *Sunday Times*, 26 June 1994; *Maclean's*, 13 February 1989; Amiel, *Confessions*, pp.65, 80, 114; *Sunday Times*, 1 May 1994, 17 April 1994; Amiel, *Confessions*, p.157
10 *Maclean's*, 9 November 1987
11 *Sunday Times*, 29 September 1989
12 Ibid.
13 *Sunday Times*, 19 April 1992
14 *Maclean's*, 20 July 1987
15 Ibid.
16 *Maclean's*, 15 September 1986
17 Horne, *Macmillan, Vol. 2*, pp.261ff
18 *Maclean's*, 11 August 1987
19 Bower, *Blood Money*, p.20
20 *Maclean's*, 8 December 1980
21 *Maclean's*, 11 August 2003
22 Black, *A Life in Progress*, p.463
23 *Chatelaine*, 1990
24 *Daily Telegraph*, 24 December 1986
25 Debbie Melnyk, *Citizen Black*, CBC TV
26 Black, *A Life in Progress*, p.464
27 *Evening Standard*, 10 January 1992
28 *Maclean's*, 27 January 1992

Chapter 7: Demons

1 Hastings, *Editor*, p.249
2 Black, *A Life in Progress*, pp.473–4
3 *Globe and Mail*, 6 July 1991
4 *Globe and Mail*, 10 July 1991
5 Siklos, *Shades of Black*, p.250
6 *Spectator*, 12 October 1991
7 *Daily Telegraph*, 28 November 1992
8 Black, *A Life in Progress*, p.448
9 Ibid., p.450
10 Siklos, *Shades of Black*, p.203
11 Ibid.
12 Black, *A Life in Progress*, p.467
13 *Sunday Telegraph*, 28 June 1992
14 Black, *A Life in Progress*, p.476
15 Ibid., p.139
16 Siklos, *Shades of Black*, p.215
17 Black, *A Life in Progress*, p.138
18 *Canadian Business*, November 1991
19 Black, *A Life in Progress*, p.465
20 Siklos, *Shades of Black*, p.236

Chapter 8: Bliss

1 *Vanity Fair*, November 1992
2 Siklos, *Shades of Black*, p.219
3 *Vanity Fair*, November 1992
4 *Architectural Digest*, 2000
5 *Sunday Times*, 31 January 1993

6 Hastings, *Editor*, p.255
7 Ibid., pp.235, 287
8 *Maclean's*, 1 August 1994
9 *Sunday Telegraph*, 7 November 1993
10 *Wall Street Journal*, 11 September 1994
11 Rosie DiManno, *Toronto Star*, 1989
12 *Evening Standard*, 10 January 1992
13 Hastings, *Editor*, p.246
14 US SEC Form 8-K, 'Hollinger International', 30 August 2004, p.401

Chapter 9: The Torpedo

1 Hastings, *Editor*, p.356
2 Black, *A Life in Progress*, p.503
3 Siklos, *Shades of Black*, p.240
4 Debbie Melnyk, *Citizen Black*, CBC TV
5 Ibid.
6 Ibid.
7 Ibid.
8 Siklos, *Shades of Black*, p.280
9 Black, *A Life in Progress*, pp.278, 281, 347
10 Debbie Melnyk, *Citizen Black*, CBC TV
11 Siklos, *Shades of Black*, p.246
12 Black, *A Life in Progress*, p.436
13 US SEC Form 8-K, 'Hollinger International', 30 August 2004, p.388
14 Siklos, *Shades of Black*, p.269
15 Ibid., p.268
16 Hastings, *Editor*, p.362
17 Siklos, *Shades of Black*, p.268
18 *Wall Street Journal*, 11 September 1994
19 Siklos, *Shades of Black*, p.281
20 *The Times*, 8 October 1994
21 *The Times*, 8 November 2003
22 *Spectator*, 12 January 1990

Chapter 10: The A-List

1 Hollinger International writ, 29 October 2004, para. 34; US SEC Form 8-K, 'Hollinger International', August 30 2004, pp.66, 348ff, 361, 492
2 Hollinger International writ, 29 October 2004, para. 173; US SEC Form 8-K, 'Hollinger International', 30 August 2004, p.143
3 US SEC Form 8-K, 'Hollinger International', 30 August 2004, p.145
4 Ibid., p.127
5 Ibid., pp.129ff; Hollinger International writ, 29 October 2004, para. 152
6 US SEC Form 8-K, 'Hollinger International', 30 August 2004, p.482
7 Ibid., pp.449ff
8 Ibid., p.483; Hollinger International writ, 29 October 2004, paras 37, 193
9 Debbie Melnyk, *Citizen Black*, CBC TV
10 *Sunday Times*, 29 May 1994
11 *Fashion Quarterly*, winter 2003
12 *The Times*, 24 December 1986
13 *Fashion Quarterly*, winter 2003
14 Debbie Melnyk, *Citizen Black*, CBC TV
15 Ibid.
16 Cobb, *Ego and Ink*, p.93
17 Ibid., p.15
18 Ibid., pp.78, 88
19 'Let Me Declare a Conflict of

Interest', *Maclean's*, 19 October 1998

20 Cobb, *Ego and Ink*, p.117

Chapter 11: Sliding Towards the Edge

1 US SEC Form 8-K, 'Hollinger International', 30 August 2004, pp.111ff
2 Ibid., pp.126, 204, 233ff
3 Ibid., p.159
4 Hollinger International writ, 29 October 2004, paras 85–8; US SEC Form 8-K, 'Hollinger International', 30 August 2004, p.159; or repaid $42.5 million using $14 million in non-compete fees: Hollinger International writ, 29 October 2004, para. 37
5 US SEC Form 8-K, 'Hollinger International', 30 August 2004, p.16
6 Hollinger International writ, 29 October 2004, Horizon 1, paras 246ff; US SEC Form 8-K, 'Hollinger International', 30 August 2004, p.265
7 US SEC Form 8-K, 'Hollinger International', 30 August 2004, p.262
8 Ibid., p.330
9 Hollinger International writ, 29 October 2004, paras 260–1; US SEC Form 8-K, 'Hollinger International', 30 August 2004, pp.271ff
10 Hollinger International writ, 29 October 2004, para. 89
11 US SEC Form 8-K, 'Hollinger International', 30 August 2004
12 Ibid., p.279
13 Ibid., p.158
14 *British Journalism Review*, December 1998
15 US SEC Form 8-K, 'Hollinger International', 30 August 2004, p.190
16 Ibid., p.330
17 Ibid., pp.291ff
18 Hollinger International writ, 29 October 2004, para. 346
19 Siklos, *Shades of Black*, p.310
20 Cobb, *Ego and Ink*, pp.253–4
21 Debbie Melnyk, *Citizen Black*, CBC TV
22 Cobb, *Ego and Ink*, pp.238–9
23 Debbie Melnyk, *Citizen Black*, CBC TV
24 Siklos, *Shades of Black*, p.315
25 US SEC Form 8-K, 'Hollinger International', 30 August 2004, p.122
26 Ibid., pp.296ff; Hollinger International writ, 29 October 2004, para. 301
27 US SEC Form 8-K, 'Hollinger International', 30 August 2004, p.483
28 Ibid., pp.291ff; Hollinger International writ, 29 October 2004, para. 292
29 Hollinger International writ, 29 October 2004, paras 297–9
30 US SEC Form 8-K, 'Hollinger International', 30 August 2004, p.18
31 *Tatler*, January 1999
32 Cobb, *Ego and Ink*, p.238
33 *Independent*, 4 September 2001
34 Siklos, *Shades of Black*, p.323
35 Hollinger International writ, 29 October 2004, para. 110; US SEC Form 8-K, 'Hollinger International', 30 August 2004, p.33

36 US SEC Form 8-K, 'Hollinger International', 30 August 2004, pp.194–5, 211, 215
37 Hollinger International writ, 29 October 2004, para. 110; US SEC Form 8-K, 'Hollinger International', 30 August 2004, p.33
38 Hollinger International writ, 29 October 2004, paras 82, 113–14; US SEC Form 8-K, 'Hollinger International', 30 August 2004, pp.27, 33, 200, 222, 225, 499ff
39 *Sunday Times*, 20 April 2003
40 US SEC Form 8-K, 'Hollinger International', 30 August 2004, p.403
41 Debbie Melnyk, *Citizen Black*, CBC TV
42 *Sunday Times*
43 Hollinger International writ, 29 October 2004, paras 89–95; US SEC Form 8-K, 'Hollinger International', 30 August 2004, pp.21, 171ff, 180
44 US SEC Form 8-K, 'Hollinger International', 30 August 2004, pp.389ff; Hollinger International writ, 29 October 2004, paras 219, 224
45 'Being Bold', *Vogue*, August 2002
46 US SEC Form 8-K, 'Hollinger International', 30 August 2004, pp.412ff
47 Hollinger International writ, 29 October 2004, para. 95; US SEC Form 8-K, 'Hollinger International', 30 August 2004, pp.21, 27, 182
48 US SEC Form 8-K, 'Hollinger International', 30 August 2004, pp.165–7
49 Ibid., p.30; Breeden Special Report, pp.106–7
50 US SEC Form 8-K, 'Hollinger International', 30 August 2004, pp.134, 139, 141
51 Ibid., pp.230ff
52 Ibid., pp.232–9
53 Debbie Melnyk, *Citizen Black*, CBC TV
54 McNish and Stewart, *Wrong Way*, p.67
55 Newman, *The Establishment Man*, p.197
56 Debbie Melnyk, *Citizen Black*, CBC TV
57 Speech to Fraser Institute, 15 November 2001
58 *American Vogue*, August 2002
59 Hollinger International writ, 29 October 2004, paras 250, 345–51
60 Ibid., para. 330; US SEC Form 8-K, 'Hollinger International', 30 August 2004, p.318
61 US SEC Form 8-K, 'Hollinger International', 30 August 2004, pp.378, 384
62 Siklos, *Shades of Black*, p.349
63 *Daily Telegraph*, 10 July 1991
64 'Being Bold', *Vogue*, August 2002
65 Hastings, *Editor*, p.251
66 *Daily Telegraph*, 22 December 2001
67 *Sunday Times*, 17 October 1993
68 *Daily Telegraph*, 17 April 1997
69 *Evening Standard*, 27 April 1990

Chapter 12: 'Thief!'

1 Debbie Melnyk, *Citizen Black*, CBC TV

2 Siklos, *Shades of Black*, p.333
3 Breeden Special Report, p.368
4 US SEC Form 8-K, 'Hollinger International', 30 August 2004, p.484
5 Ibid., p.98; Hollinger International writ, 29 October 2004, para. 72
6 McNish and Stewart, *Wrong Way*, p.6
7 US SEC Form 8-K, 'Hollinger International', 30 August 2004, p.33; Newman, *The Establishment Man*, p.98
8 US SEC Form 8-K, 'Hollinger International', 30 August 2004, pp.283, 313; Hollinger International writ, 29 October 2004, para 254
9 Hollinger International writ, 29 October 2004, para. 254; US SEC Form 8-K, 'Hollinger International', 30 August 2004, pp.10, 19
10 *Fortune*, 13 October 2003
11 McNish and Stewart, *Wrong Way*, p.80
12 Debbie Melnyk, *Citizen Black*, CBC TV
13 US SEC Form 8-K, 'Hollinger International', 30 August 2004, pp.33, 104, 121
14 Hollinger International writ, 29 October 2004, para. 118
15 Siklos, *Shades of Black*, p.354
16 McNish and Stewart, *Wrong Way*, p.82
17 Ibid., pp.13, 85; email to Healy
18 Hollinger International writ, 29 October 2004, para. 72
19 Ibid., email dated 3 August 2002.
20 US SEC Form 8-K, 'Hollinger International', 30 August 2004, p.402
21 *Vanity Fair*, April 2004
22 4 September 2002; US SEC Form 8-K, 'Hollinger International', 30 August 2004, p.99
23 Judgement, 13 August 2002
24 *Daily Express*, 3 November 2002
25 US SEC Form 8-K, 'Hollinger International', 30 August 2004, p.107; Hollinger International writ, 29 October 2004, para. 16
26 US SEC Form 8-K, 'Hollinger International', 30 August 2004, p.405
27 *Sunday Times*, 20 April 2003
28 *Globe and Mail*; McNish and Stewart, *Wrong Way*, p.107
29 US SEC Form 8-K, 'Hollinger International', 30 August 2004, p.120
30 Debbie Melnyk, *Citizen Black*, CBC TV
31 McNish and Stewart, *Wrong Way*, p.117
32 *W* magazine, December 2003
33 Debbie Melnyk, *Citizen Black*, CBC TV
34 McNish and Stewart, *Wrong Way*, p.122
35 Debbie Melnyk, *Citizen Black*, CBC TV
36 *Daily Telegraph*, 9 June 2003
37 Siklos, *Shades of Black*, p.342

Chapter 13: The Purist

1 McNish and Stewart, *Wrong Way*, p.140
2 US SEC Form 8-K, 'Hollinger International', 30 August 2004, pp. 206, 252, 426ff, 449ff; *Fortune*,

13 October 2003
3 *Fortune*, 13 October 2003
4 US SEC Form 8-K, 'Hollinger International', 30 August 2004, p.82
5 Ibid., p.206
6 *The Times*, 8 November 2003
7 US SEC Form 8-K, 'Hollinger International', 30 August 2004, pp.484, 492ff
8 Ibid., pp.84ff
9 *The Times*, 8 November 2003
10 Burt deposition; McNish and Stewart, *Wrong Way*, p.155
11 McNish and Stewart, *Wrong Way*, p.160
12 Ibid., p.3
13 Ibid., p.171
14 Amiel, *Confessions*, p.144
15 Hollinger International writ, 29 October 2004, para. 101
16 Debbie Melnyk, *Citizen Black*, CBC TV
17 Ibid.
18 *The Times*, 18 November 2003
19 *The Times*, 8 November 2003
20 McNish and Stewart, *Wrong Way*, p.198
21 Hollinger International writ, 29 October 2004, para. 16
22 *Sunday Times*, 23 November 2003
23 Judgement of Leo Strine, Court of Chancery, State of Delaware, 26 February 2004
24 *Vanity Fair*, April 2004
25 Strine judgement, p.52; McNish and Stewart, *Wrong Way*, p.245
26 McNish and Stewart, *Wrong Way*, p.212
27 Black, *A Life in Progress*, p.347
28 McNish and Stewart, *Wrong Way*, p.224
29 *National Post*, 9 February 2004
30 McNish and Stewart, *Wrong Way*, p.225
31 Black to Barclay, 23 January 2004; McNish and Stewart, *Wrong Way*, p.228
32 Siklos, *Shades of Black*, p.424
33 Delaware court papers, 28 January 2004
34 'A Question of Press Credibility', *Maclean's*, 20 February 1984
35 'Pierre's View of Maggie', *Maclean's*, 7 May 1979
36 *Sunday Telegraph*, 12 June 2005; *Maclean's*, 6 February 1995. She assumed O.J. was guilty.
37 *Mail on Sunday*, 6 February 2005
38 *Evening Standard*, 1 June 2004
39 *Mail on Sunday*, 6 February 2005
40 Ibid.
41 US SEC Form 8-K, 'Hollinger International', 30 August 2004, pp.4–5, 16–17, 26, 44, 103
42 Ibid., p.145
43 Ibid.; Siklos, *Shades of Black*, p.450
44 *Mail on Sunday*, 6 February 2005

Chapter 14: Resurrection

1 *Maclean's*, 29 August 2005; *Spectator*, 18 August 2005

INDEX